PASADENA PUBLIC LIBRARY

Frommer's®

S0-AAZ-658

Vienna & the Danube Valley

8th Edition

by Dardis McNamee & Maggie Childs

WITHDRAWN

WILEY

A John Wiley and Sons, Ltd, Publication

Published by:

WILEY PUBLISHING, INC.

Copyright © 2011 John Wiley & Sons Ltd, The Atrium, Southern Gate, Chichester,
West Sussex PO19 8SQ, UK
Telephone (+44) 1243 779777
Email (for orders and customer service enquiries): cs-books@wiley.co.uk. Visit our Home Page on www.
wiley.com

All Rights Reserved. No part of this publication may be reproduced, stored in a retrieval system or trans-
mitted in any form or by any means, electronic, mechanical, photocopying, recording, scanning or otherwise, except under the terms of the Copyright, Designs and Patents Act 1988 or under the terms of a
licence issued by the Copyright Licensing Agency Ltd, Saffron House, 6-10 Kirby Street, London EC1N
8TS, UK, without the permission in writing of the Publisher. Requests to the Publisher should be
addressed to the Permissions Department, John Wiley & Sons Ltd, The Atrium, Southern Gate, Chichester,
West Sussex PO19 8SQ, England, or emailed to permreq@wiley.co.uk, or faxed to (+44) 1243 770620.

Designations used by companies to distinguish their products are often claimed as trademarks. All brand
names and product names used in this book are trade names, service marks, trademarks or registered
trademarks of their respective owners. The Publisher is not associated with any product or vendor mentioned in this book.

This publication is designed to provide accurate and authoritative information in regard to the subject
matter covered. It is sold on the understanding that the Publisher is not engaged in rendering professional services. If professional advice or other expert assistance is required, the services of a competent
professional should be sought.

UK Publisher: Sally Smith
Project Manager: Daniel Mersey
Commissioning Editor: Mark Henshall
Development Editor: Nick Dalton & Deborah Stone
Project Editor: Hannah Clement
Cartography: Andy Dolan
Photo Editor: Jill Emeny
Front cover photo: Description: Statue on building, Stadt, Tuchlauben, Vienna. © Jon Arnold/awl images.
Back Cover photo: Description: Catch performances by leading opera stars at the legendary State Opera.
© Photos to go.

Wiley also publishes its books in a variety of electronic formats. Some content that appears in print may
not be available in electronic books.

For information on our other products and services or to obtain technical support, please contact our
Customer Care Department within the U.S. at 877/762-2974, outside the U.S. at 317/572-3993 or fax
317/572-4002.

British Library Cataloguing in Publication Data
A catalogue record for this book is available from the British Library
ISBN: 978-0-470-97596-1 (pbk)
ISBN: 978-1-119-99193-9 (ebk)
ISBN: 978-1-119-99448-0 (ebk)
ISBN: 978-1-119-99464-0 (ebk)
Typeset by Wiley Indianapolis Composition Services
Printed and bound in the United States of America

5   4   3   2   1

CONTENTS

10 VIENNA AFTER DARK 193

11 SIDE TRIPS FROM VIENNA 209

12 FAST FACTS 238

LIST OF MAPS

ABOUT THE AUTHORS

Dardis McNamee is Editor in Chief of the English-language monthly, The Vienna Review and on the research faculty in Media Communications at Webster University Vienna. In her long career in journalism she has been a correspondent for, among others, *The New York Times* and *Conde Nast Traveler* in New York, and for the *Wall Street Journal Europe* and *Die Zeit* in Vienna, as well as a speech writer to two US ambassadors to Austria. She has lived in Vienna for 15 years.

   Maggie Childs is a journalist and travel writer for publications such as *Condé Nast Traveller US, The Vienna Review, Gig Magazine*, and various in-flight magazines. She has lived in Vienna for 14 years and also works for the Vienna bureau of the Associated Press. She is also the author of the Austria Chapter of *Europe For Dummies* and the Co-Author of *Frommer's Austria*.

ACKNOWLEDGMENTS

The authors wish to thank the following for their contributions:
Christopher Anderson (Upper Austria, Salzburg, Salzburgland)
Austin Childs (Lower Austria, Carinthia, Styria)
Jessica Spiegel (Burgenland, Innsbruck-Tyrol, Voralberg)

HOW TO CONTACT US

In researching this book, we discovered many wonderful places—hotels, restaurants, shops, and more. We're sure you'll find others. Please tell us about them, so we can share the information with your fellow travelers in upcoming editions. If you were disappointed with a recommendation, we'd love to know that, too. Please email frommers@wiley.com or write to:

Frommer's Vienna & the Danube Valley, 8th Edition
Wiley Publishing, Inc. • 111 River St. • Hoboken, NJ 07030-5774

AN ADDITIONAL NOTE

Please be advised that travel information is subject to change at any time—and this is especially true of prices. We therefore suggest that you write or call ahead for confirmation when making your travel plans. The authors, editors, and publisher cannot be held responsible for the experiences of readers while traveling. Your safety is important to us, however, so we encourage you to stay alert and be aware of your surroundings. Keep a close eye on cameras, purses, and wallets, all favorite targets of thieves and pickpockets.

FROMMER'S STAR RATINGS, ICONS & ABBREVIATIONS

Every hotel, restaurant, and attraction listing in this guide has been ranked for quality, value, service, amenities, and special features using a star-rating system. In country, state, and regional guides, we also rate towns and regions to help you narrow down your choices and budget your time accordingly. Hotels and restaurants are rated on a scale of zero (recommended) to three stars (exceptional). Attractions, shopping, nightlife, towns, and regions are rated according to the following scale: zero stars (recommended), one star (highly recommended), two stars (very highly recommended), and three stars (must-see).

In addition to the star-rating system, we also use seven feature icons that point you to the great deals, in-the-know advice, and unique experiences that separate travelers from tourists. Throughout the book, look for:

special finds—those places only insiders know about

fun facts—details that make travelers more informed and their trips more fun

kids—best bets for kids and advice for the whole family

special moments—those experiences that memories are made of

overrated—places or experiences not worth your time or money

insider tips—great ways to save time and money

great values—where to get the best deals

The following abbreviations are used for credit cards:

AE	American Express	DISC	Discover	V	Visa
DC	Diners Club	MC	MasterCard		

TRAVEL RESOURCES AT FROMMERS.COM

Frommer's travel resources don't end with this guide. Frommer's website, www.frommers.com, has travel information on more than 4,000 destinations. We update features regularly, giving you access to the most current trip-planning information and the best airfare, lodging, and car-rental bargains. You can also listen to podcasts, connect with other Frommers.com members through our active-reader forums, share your travel photos, read blogs from guidebook editors and fellow travellers, and much more.

BEST OF VIENNA

V ienna stays Vienna," says a famous old tavern song, and despite the agonies of the last century's wars and political upheaval, this lovely city nurtures a sense of leisure and the good life that sets it apart. The Viennese work hard and then hurry home—or out—to enjoy it.

Thus Vienna is a cultivated and romantic city of music, cafes, art and ideas, parks, pastries, waltzes, and wine, and a true cosmopolitan city. Over the last 3 decades, with renewed prosperity, it has emerged from a cocoon of sorts and morphed into a vibrant modern metropolis in which the new compliments the old.

From the time the Romans chose this Celtic settlement on the Danube River as one of their most important Central European forts, Vindobona (the city we now know as Vienna) has played a vital role in European history.

The many-peopled city of the Habsburg Empire has remained a vigorous place of cultural encounter: its imperial palaces, opera houses, concert halls, and museums mingle with a very modern world of cutting-edge technology, art, and design; the rethinking of space and the re-blending of sound. And when it comes to dining, Vienna is a gourmet paradise.

So having lived through war, siege, victory, defeat, the death of an empire, and the birth of a republic, foreign occupation, independence, and the new internationalism of the European Union, the Viennese character, the *Gemütlichkeit* (civility and comfort), has endured.

THE most UNFORGETTABLE EXPERIENCES

o **Strolling on Kärntnerstrasse:** Viennese and visitors alike flock to this pedestrianized street. Along with The Graben, another famous street, it is the heart of Viennese life. From morning to night, people promenade along this stately boulevard (even on Sundays when shops are closed), where street performers are always out to amuse. Stop for a break at one of the atmospheric cafes for some of the best people-watching in Vienna. See "Walking Tour 1: Imperial Vienna," in Chapter 8.

o **Enjoying a Night at the Opera:** Nothing says Vienna more than a night at the famed Staatsoper, one of the world's greatest opera houses and home to The Vienna State Opera. Climbing the grand marble staircase in your finery is almost as exhilarating as the show. Built in the 1860s, the Staatsoper suffered severe damage during World War II. It reopened in 1955 with a production of Beethoven's *Fidelio,* which marked Austria's independence from occupation. Both Richard Strauss and Gustav Mahler directed here and the world's most renowned opera stars continue to perform with the Vienna Philharmonic Orchestra in more than 50 productions a year. See p. 140.

o **Biking Along the Danube:** A riverside bike trail between Vienna and Melk links scenic villages, including Dürnstein and Spitz. As you pedal along, you'll pass ancient castles, medieval towns, latticed vineyards, and a watering hole at every turn. Route maps are available at the Vienna Tourist Office, and you can rent bikes at the ferry or train stations. For information on bike rental see Chapter 3.

o **Attending a Concert at the Musikverein:** This legendary concert hall is said to have the best acoustics in Europe. The Main hall (Goldener Saal) is suspended over the rehearsal halls beneath and resonates like a drum. This is the Carnegie Hall of Europe. The sound explodes into the air with a vividness which is startling to the uninitiated and a continuing thrill to the connoisseur. See p. 196.

o **Riding the Emperor's Train:** One memorable outing is the journey through the Wachau wine region on the Vienna-based Majestic Imperator, the most elegant train in Europe. Period cars recreate the spirit and style of the Royal Court Train of the Kaiser Franz Josef, and there is wine and hors d'oeuvres on board. Don't miss stopping at a village *Heuriger* (wine tavern) for a romantic dinner. www. imperialtrain.com. (p. 205).

o **Riding on a Fiaker (horse-drawn carriage):** Touristy, sure, but don't let that scare you off. The horses' pace is just the right speed for noticing everything and as the coacher, in full regalia, reveals Vienna's secrets you can take a look from your perch on high. Prices vary but for around 50€ you're in business.

o **Spending a Sunday in the Vienna Woods:** In the rich foliage of this famous forest, every season is special. The sweeping hillside vineyards of the Kahlenberg have breathtaking views all the way to Hungary. Start your trip by taking the 38a bus to the top of the mountain (with eateries and gift shops) for paths along the leafy walks that have inspired painters and poets for centuries. Check out the restaurant and art installations at Am Himmel (In the Heavens). No matter which way you go the area meets you with gently rolling hills, vineyards, and perfect picnic pastures. See Chapter 11.

o **Heuriger Hopping in the Wine Districts:** The *Heuriger* are rustic wine taverns that celebrate the arrival of each year's new vintage (*heurig*) by placing a pine branch over the door. The Viennese flock to the taverns to taste the new local wines, and feast on country buffets. Some *Heuriger* have garden tables with sweeping views of the Danube Valley; others provide shaded, centuries-old courtyards where you can enjoy live folk music. See "The *Heuriger*," in Chapter 10.

o **Watching the Lipizzaner Stallions:** More than a Mecca for horse-lovers, the Spanish Riding School is an entirely unique experience. The sleek white stallions and their expert riders demonstrate the classic art of military dressage in highly choreographed leaps and bounds. The stallions, a crossbreed of Spanish thoroughbreds and Karst horses, are the finest equestrian performers on Earth. Training and performances are open to the public; make reservations at least a few weeks in advance. See Chapter 7.

○ **Chilling in a Coffee house:** The coffee house still flourishes here in its most perfect form. You can spend hours reading newspapers (supplied free), writing your memoirs, or planning the rest of your stay. And, of course, there's the coffee, prepared 20 to 30 different ways, from a *kleiner Schwarzer* (espresso), *Melange* (cappuccino), to a *Maria Theresa* (double dark roast with orange liqueur and whipped cream). A small glass of water always accompanies your coffee in Vienna, as well as a choice of tasty strudels or a slice of cake. See "Coffee houses & Cafes," in Chapter 6.

○ **Working your inner Artist at the MuseumsQuartier (MQ):** Formerly the Imperial stables, this complex has it all. Art museums classic and modern are housed next to stylish eateries and the exhibitions of artists in residence. Vienna's art and fashion crowd (or wannabes) idle on courtyard lounge chairs in summer and mingle in the many cafes and restaurants in winter. See Chapter 7.

○ **Dancing 'til Dawn:** Ball season is legendary in Vienna and this is not just about waltzing and putting on the Ritz. The Viennese get quite giddy and at midnight every ball has the traditional *Quadrille*. This involves line dances calledout by the orchestra-leader, climaxing in a madcap *Galopp*, sudden direction changes and an inevitable pile-up; a great way to make new friends. See Chapter 10.

○ **Living the Music:** Walk down the Johannesgasse and music will spill out of a window: a trumpeter dazzling through scales, a pianist tackling Beethoven, a quartet playing Schubert and breaking your heart. There are gypsy bands at the *Heuriger*, and piano jazz in the cafes. Wander into any church, stumble on an open-air concert, gatecrash an art opening, lounge in a hotel, pause for a busker on the street. See section 1, "The Performing Arts," in Chapter 10.

○ **Hearing the Vienna Boys' Choir:** In this city steeped in musical traditions, one of the most remarkable is the Vienna Boys' Choir, the *Wiener Sängerknaben*. Created by Emperor Maximilian I in 1498, the choristers are selected by audition and train daily for regular public concerts. With three full choirs, one is always on duty for masses by Mozart, Haydn or Purcell at the Hofburgkapelle on Sundays and public holidays from September to June. See p. 128.

THE best LUXURY HOTELS

○ **Hotel Sacher,** Philharmonikerstrasse 4 (✆ **01/514560**): This address drips with opulence and detailed decadence, in very good taste. It's a family-run establishment which makes anyone feel at home in utter luxury. See p. 78.

○ **Ring Hotel Vienna,** Kärntnerring 8 (✆ **01/122122**): A hotel which boasts casual luxury and delivers some definition of it at every turn. Models and rock stars choose this place above the more decadent addresses because it's chic, fun, discreet, and unpretentious. See p. 80.

○ **Palais Coburg Residenz,** Coburg Bastei 4 (✆ **01/518180**): The outrageously ostentatious private home of the Coburg dynasty has been turned into the most romantic splurge in Vienna. Some of the suites here evoke the heyday of the Rothschilds and are as elegant as anything else in Vienna. You are guaranteed absolute privacy if that's what you desire. See p. 78.

o **Hotel Imperial,** Kärntnerring 16, (✆ **01/501100**): Built in 1869, this is said to be the official guesthouse of Austria. All the famous and infamous of the world have checked in, everybody from Mick Jagger to Queen Elizabeth, including both JFK and Khrushchev. In 1938 Hitler gave an address from the balcony, and Nazi hunter Simon Wiesenthal chose it for his 90th birthday. See p. 77.

THE best MODERATELY-PRICED HOTELS

o **Hotel Pertschy,** Habsburgerstrasse 5, (✆ **01/534490**): This apartment-like building is smack in the middle of town, right off The Graben. It was recently renovated and the rooms wrap around an adorable courtyard giving the place a certain romance unattainable in bigger or more highbrow establishments. See p. 86.

o **Hollmann Beletage,** Köllnerhofgasse 6, (✆ **01/9611960**): Just a 5-minute walk from St. Stephan's, this artfully run hotel is just plain inspired. Not only are the rooms charmingly modern, the hotel spa, living room, and cinema guarantee some serious R and R. They only have 24 rooms, so make sure you book ahead. Not cheap. See p. 82.

o **Altstadt Vienna,** Kirchengasse 41 (✆ **01/5226666**): This gem among design hotels makes you feel right at home. The freestanding bathtubs in the middle of some rooms delight couples and honeymooners, and each has a unique theme. See p. 93.

THE most UNFORGETTABLE DINING EXPERIENCES

o **Having Breakfast on the Waterfront:** The recently opened **Motto am Fluss** (✆ **01/25255**) is already swamped by locals. Its cruise-ship atmosphere, delectable food and fine service delight even the weariest tourist. The place is hard to miss, right smack in front of Schwedenplatz, and wisely serves breakfast from 8am to 4pm. See p. 107.

o **Eating the Best Schnitzel in Town:** This place is no secret, but for good reason. **Figlmüller,** Wollzeile 5 (✆ **01/512-6177**) is utterly charming, and in a courtyard passage near St. Stephan's. The breaded cutlets are as large as your plate and staff will advise you on local wines or beers to accompany your meal. See p. 111.

o **Sampling Succulent Starters:** The Viennese like to nibble; not that they don't clean their plates, but the idea of variety is key. At **Zum Schwarzen Kameel,** Bognergasse 5, (✆ **01/533-8125**) you can accompany a glass (or bottle) of wine with open-faced sandwiches and small tarts. This is the ultimate after-work meet-and-greet. Classy and convenient (p. 108).

o **People-watching at the Naschmarkt:** It's a secret few Viennese will betray, but there's hardly an artist, mogul, or celeb who hasn't been spotted at one of the cafe/

restaurants in the far end of the Naschmarkt. You can linger here on a lazy afternoon deep in conversation with friends or colleagues. The market itself, in Vienna's 7th District, is unique and filled with delicious smells, tastes, and sounds. See p. 122.

o **Tasting Vienna's Most Acclaimed Cuisine:** You'll find it at **Steirereck,** Stadtpark (**©** **01/7133168**). The name means "corner of Styria" and the understated elegance is just lavish enough to suit the food. This baroque villa with a tasteful modern interior is tucked in the back of the Stadtpark and has nothing to hide. It has been known for offering Vienna's best cuisine for many years. The cheese selection impresses, as does the wine list. See p. 117.

THE best THINGS TO DO FOR FREE

o **Taking your Time:** It's said that, on average, the Viennese walk at least one third slower than the inhabitants of other European capitals. Maybe it's the love of food and wine or just the appreciation of "the good life" that lies deep in the Viennese soul. You'll see business people working in a coffee house rather than at the office while enjoying a cigarette and *mélange.* Parks and benches are strategically placed at every turn to break up the business of living. This Viennese style is called *Gemütlichkeit* in German, warm and laid-back; in any case it's quite contagious. See "Parks and Gardens," Chapter 7.

o **Taking in a Free Concert or Film:** Whether you visit in winter or in summer there is always something going on outside and for free in Vienna. In winter the Christmas Markets (p. 41) and *Glühwein* (mulled wine) stands draw people out onto the city's public spaces. Although the drinks are not free, the atmosphere is priceless. In summer Vienna hosts *Donauinselfest,* the largest free music festival in Europe. But there are city-wide events, such as the *Stadtfest,* and the open air opera film festival in front of the Rathaus (for information: p. 41 or www.wien. info/en).

o **Breaking the Ice with a Native:** There is no entry in this book to guide you through this utterly rewarding experience. The Viennese are notoriously cautious when making contact with the unknown, however, when approached, they are most helpful, and charmed to be included in your discovery of their city. Attempt some German with a restaurant proprietor or passer-by, or at least use the Austrian name of a landmark you are looking for. Not only will this impress them, but many will want to try their English on you. **Note:** The Viennese protect their nightlife like a family secret, so try to get tips on hot spots during your stay and don't be put off by preliminary prickliness.

o **Taking in the Architectural Gems:** Just walking through the Inner City is like being in a hands-on, evolving museum. The city is full of amazing historical monuments and architectural feats. For example, there is no charge for visiting **St. Stephan's Cathedral** (p. 143), though there is a fee for the crypt and towers. On a walk around the ring you pass Beethoven, Maria Theresa, Strauss, and Goethe. (See "Walking tours," Chapter 8).

THE best STUFF TO BRING HOME

- **Crystals:** Nothing says glam Austria like the finery of Swarovski. Be it a necklace, figurine, or crystal headphones, this native brand has become a byword for fine crystal accessories. Stop by the flagship store on the Kärntnerstrasee for the most breathtaking display (p. 190).

- **Jugendstil:** This Austrian version of Art Deco recalls some fabled names such as Otto Wagner and Adolf Loos who have left a deep imprint in Viennese style and architecture. A lamp, paperweight or newspaper stand from this artistic era is a souvenir must for design buffs and can be found in the Spittelberg area of the 7th District (p. 184).

- **Porcelain:** The most popular and widely available ceramics are made by **Augarten Porzellan,** the 300-year-old manufacturer famous for delicate, graceful pieces with clean lines and exquisite detail, reflecting styles of each era of the company's history. These choice objects are still produced and painted by hand (p. 191).

- **Hats:** Vienna is a place where people still wear hats. You can go for the everyday variety or take the dive and get yourself a **Tiroler** felt job, to which one fastens pins or badges from each place you visit. For a wide selection check out Nagy Hüte, Schottengasse 3 (*©* **01/405662922**).

- **Music:** Vienna supports musicians in more ways than one. Imagine coming home from your trip with a compilation of Austrian pop music from **Musiktank** in the MuseumsQuartier (p. 191) or even a piece you composed yourself at **Haus der Musik** (p. 138).

THE best ACTIVITIES FOR FAMILIES

- **In the City:** Parks and green spaces are all over Vienna. In the Inner City there is the **Burggarten,** with its famous Butterfly House, and **Heldenplatz,** in front of the Hofburg. Both are home to picnickers and Frisbee- and soccer-players in the warm months. But the main attraction for any child or child-at-heart is the **Prater** (p. 152). The former Imperial hunting grounds in the 2nd District now house a year-round amusement park with the famous big wheel, lots of interactive attractions, pony rides, playgrounds, and miles of paths, woods, sports clubs, duck ponds, and riding stables, unequalled in any European capital. Bicycles, pedal carts, roller blades, and the like can be rented at the beginning of the Hauptallee, the tree-lined boulevard running the length of the park.

- The city is also famous for its adoption of the Italian gelato tradition. In summer there are numerous places selling homemade ice cream all over the city. **Zanoni & Zanoni, Tichy,** or **Eissalon Schwedenplatz** are good ones.

- The **ZOOM** children's museum (p. 134) in the MQ is great for 1–14 year olds, and **Haus der Musik** (p. 138) caters to all ages. The exhibits are hands-on and interactive in both. The **Hunderwasser Haus** or **Kunsthaus** (p. 150) is also loved by the younger visitors to Vienna. The gallery and restaurant has uneven floors and quirks of all kinds. Designed by Friedensreich Hunderwasser it is a unique work of art that can be touched and felt.

o **In the Outer Districts:** An all-time great is the **Tiergarten Schönbrunn** (p. 154). This vast zoo used to be the Imperial menagerie and is a popular local outing. Linked to the Imperial Schönbrunn Palace, the grounds are great for running around and games of hide-and-seek. The **Lainzer Tiergarten** is more a nature reserve than a zoo, but that also gets you closer to the animals. The Hermes Villa next door is architectural bliss inside and out, in a spun-sugar candy way. It was a wedding gift for Empress Elisabeth.

o **Further Afield:** A short distance from Vienna city on the edge of the *Weinviertel* region lies the Roman city of **Carnuntum** (30 minutes by car or 55 with S7 train to Petronell-Carnuntum). This ancient city was uncovered in a series of digs and has been rebuilt in the original fashion. The staff is clad accordingly and the entire experience is a discovery. Children can also try their hand at various tests of skill. Birthday children get free meals and a surprise gift. See www.carnuntum. co.at.

THE best MUSEUMS

o **Kunsthistorisches Museum (KHM):** Unquestionably one of the greatest art museums in the world. Between the MuseumsQuartier and the Hofburg, this splendid Renaissance building holds the bulk of the Imperial collections from ancient Egypt to the end of the 18th century. Particularly impressive are the Dutch and Flemish masters, Breugel, Reubens, Rembrandt, Van Dyk, and Albrecht Dürer, as well as ancient Egyptian and Greek art, and a bas-relief from the Parthenon (p. 139).

o **Wien Museum:** Since the arrival of director Wolfgang Kos in 2003, the Wien Museum has burst on to the scene with one fascinating exhibition after another, interpreting the city's history, character, and complexities with exhibitions on the cult of nostalgia, fashions of the Corso (boulevards), or train stations of the world. There's an excellent permanent exhibit on the history of the city in objects, art, and scale models. It is also in charge of many satellite spaces, palaces and apartments (p. 150).

o **Belvedere:** Built in the early 18th century for Prince Eugene of Savoy, this handsome palace and gardens are home to the most important collection of Austrian art from the Middle Ages to the present, including many of the most famous works of Gustav Klimt, Egon Schiele, and Oscar Kokoshka. The collection also includes prominent work of the French Impressionists and some of the most important works of the Viennese Biedermeier (p.135).

o **Museum Angewandte Kunst (MAK):** One of the leading museums of its kind in the world, whose former directors have included Otto Wagner and Josef Hoffman, its permanent collection displays examples of applied art from the Middle Ages, and the present. There are examples from the Wiener Werkstätte, a 19th-century co-operative workshop, such as chairs by Michael Thonet and Mundus Kohn, Gustav Klimt's sketches, and superb examples of porcelain, glass, embroidery, carpets, and silver.

o **Leopold Museum:** A major collection of modern Austrian art, with leading work by Egon Schiele, Gustav Klimt, Oskar Kokoschka, and Albin Egger-Lienz, as well as other less well-known artists such as Herbert Boeckl and Wilhelm Thöny. Also features leading 19th-century artists including Georg Waldmüller and Emil Jakob Schindler (p. 134).

o **Museum of Modern Art (MUMOK):** In the MuseumsQuartier the MUMOK showcases international 20th-century art, with an emphasis on classical modern art from expressionism and cubism to abstraction, pop art, photo realism, and contemporary media art. There's also a unique collection of Viennese Actionism art from the 1960s. This includes performance art, with aggressive attacks on social taboos. Also find Picasso, Kandinsky, Warhol, Liechtenstein, Beuys, and Rauschenberg in revolving exhibits (p. 135).

o **Albertina:** Named for Duke Albert of Saxen-Teschen, who married one of Empress Maria Theresa's daughters. He brought his graphics collection from Brussels and it has belonged to the Republic since 1919. The collection holds more than a million drawings, watercolors and prints, including Albrecht Dürer's *Rabbit*, as well as Leonardo da Vinci, Michelangelo, Raffael, Peter Paul Rubens, Oskar Kokoschka, Rembrandt, Gustav Klimt, and Egon Schiele (p. 127).

THE best CHURCHES & PALACES

o **Stephansdom:** Crowned by a 137m (450-ft.) steeple, Dompfarre St. Stephan, Vienna's cathedral, is one of Europe's great Gothic structures. "Sheer beauty lifts the spirit," Albert Stifter wrote of it in 1860. A vast, tiled roof is exactly twice the height of its walls. Intricate altarpieces, stone canopies, and masterful Gothic sculptures are just some of the treasures that lie within. Climb the spiral steps to the South Tower for a panoramic view of the city. See p. 143.

o **Jesuitenkirche:** Completed in 1631 and renovated in 1705 to become a splendid example of high baroque, the Jesuit "*Universitätskirche*" is home to one of the best resident church choirs and orchestras that perform regular full masses by Mozart, Haydn, Schubert, Beethoven, and others. Sundays at 10:30am from September to June (p. 146).

o **Ruprechtskirche:** The oldest church in Vienna, with parts of the structure dating from Roman times, when Emperor Marcus Aurelius was encamped nearby. In the Middle Ages the building served as the Salt Office that distributed the salt arriving on the Danube Channel, and ensured its quality. Today the church serves an international congregation and hosts concerts of early music (p. 146).

o **The Hofburg:** The Hofburg, the Habsburg's winter palace and still the seat of the Austrian government, is a living architectural textbook, parts of which date from 1279. A tour of the royal apartments gives a very good idea of how the family lived, with Franz Joseph's narrow bed and spartan furnishings, the tasteful elegance of his wife Sissi's (Empress Elisabeth's) study, and her frightening exercise equipment. It also houses Austria's Imperial Treasury, the *Schatzkammer,* where the crown jewels and collections of Imperial silver and rare musical instruments are displayed.

- **Schönbrunn Palace:** The beloved summer palace of the Empress Maria Theresa and later the Emperor Franz Josef, Schönbrunn is named for the artesian well of crystal clear water that long supplied the court. A UNESCO World Heritage Site, it has seen many seminal events. It is where Mozart performed at the age of 6, and the 1961 meeting between JFK and Nikita Khrushchev took place (p. 140).
- **Karlskirche:** Considered the most beautiful baroque church north of the Alps, this was designed by Johann Fischer von Erlach for Karl VI and named after St. Charles of Borromeo, the healer, following the plague of 1713. The elegant domed structure with its twin columns narrating tales of saint and patron in bas-relief, presides over Resselpark reflected in the fountain pool.
- **Palais Liechtenstein:** Built in farmland outside the city wall in around 1700, the palace's lovely gardens are now a green oasis in the 9th District. The princely family's vast art collection was returned to Vienna from Vaduz, where it had been stored since the Anschluss (the union of Austria and Germany) in 1938, for the reopening of the renovated palace-museum in 2004. The palace alone is worth a visit, but there are also paintings by Marcantonio Franceschini and frescoes by Johann Michael Rottmayr (p. 139).

THE best OF VIENNA ONLINE

- **www.vienna.info:** The official tourist board website which provides a thorough online travel guide for Vienna, covering sightseeing, music and stage shows, shopping, wining and dining, as well as hotels and travel information, includes a useful search engine.
- **www.wien.gv.at/english:** City of Vienna website, which provides up-to-date information on what to do in and around Vienna, as well as general information for visitors (calendar of events, hotel and sightseeing guide).
- **www.virtualvienna.net:** English-language guide to life in Vienna. Information includes a general living guide, event calendar, property and relocation section, and directory.
- **www.falter.at:** Website of the high-quality Austrian weekly *Falter*, with a list of events, movies, theater and restaurant reviews, and shopping guide.
- **www.viennareview.net:** Website of the Vienna Review, a monthly publication of the Vienna Journalism Institute of Webster University and Austria's only English-language newspaper, covering international as well as local events including an event calendar.
- **www.tupalo.com:** A social networking site that allows users to find, review, and share local businesses. Categories include food & drink, art & entertainment, nightlife, local services, and shopping.
- **www.vienna-expats.net:** The online forum on the website of the Vienna expats community provides a meeting place for people in Vienna. The site also includes a directory of bars and cafes, services, shops, restaurants, nightlife, cinemas, and property.
- **www.awavienna.com:** Website of the American Women's Association of Vienna, an international, non-profit group whose goal is to promote cultural exchange and charitable works of English-speaking women. The AWA arranges a variety of activities and publishes a resource guide.

- **www.wienerlinien.at:** All you need for trains, trams, and buses in the city, with timetables and maps.
- **www.vor.at:** Website of the Verkehrsverbund Ost Region (Transport Association, Eastern Region), includes public transport routes throughout Vienna and the surrounding towns.
- **www.wien.gv.at/english/culture/museums/:** A list of museums in Vienna as well as links to the English websites.
- **www.wien.gv.at/english/history/overview:** Website of the Vienna city government with an overview of the history of the city.

VIENNA IN DEPTH

When most people think of Vienna they imagine the city in its imperial heyday, a glittering capital of romance and gaiety, enchanting waltzes, luscious pastries, the operetta, and the Danube. No one conjures up these images of old Vienna more than Johann Strauss, Jr. (1825–99) whose Blue Danube Waltz is so lovely that Brahms wished he had written it. It rings out over the city rooftops each New Year's Eve.

As Vienna moves deeper into a new millennium, it's good to look back at its rich classical, culinary, and historical legacy to appreciate its present. The royal seat of the Habsburgs for more than 600 years, Vienna has always stood out as a home of art and music, as well as architecture, science, and ideas.

As the capital of a once great empire, and now one of Europe's most successful social democracies, Vienna lives with its complex legacy: Austria was the birthplace of Mozart, Freud, Kafka, and Hitler, as well as public education, alternating current, Porsche, and Red Bull. From the Congress of Vienna to the Cold War, and perhaps even today, its arts of diplomacy and disguise have earned Vienna the exotic distinction of spy capital of the world.

In 2004, recognition came on two fronts: Elfriede Jelinek, a controversial writer of lyric beauty, won the Nobel Prize for literature. On another front Charles I, the last Habsburg to rule as emperor, was beatified by the Pope.

Like the United States, the Austrian capital remains deeply polarized. The entrance of the far-right Freedom Party into a coalition government in 2000 brought Austria widespread condemnation. In contrast, many citizens of Vienna are among the most liberal, advanced, well-informed, and tolerant.

As one example of the more left-wing Austria, environmental awareness is on the rise. Recycling is more evident in Vienna than most other European capitals—in fact, recycling bins are commonplace on the city's streets. The Viennese are often seen sorting their paper, plastic, and aluminum and steel cans, and they scowl at passers-by who toss away a wrapping.

Visitors today will find a newer and brighter Vienna, a city with more *joie de vivre* than it's had since before World War II. Cafes, clubs, theaters, and concert halls are everywhere, open nightly and often sold out. Among its grand cityscapes and lovely old squares, each season hosts festivals and open markets that bring the streets alive. In spite of two world wars, much of the empire's glory remains, its treasures now glistening in museum galleries, its parks and palaces the daily settings of city life.

In 2010, more than 70 years after the Anschluss (the union of Austria and Germany) time has begun to heal many of Vienna's old wounds. For better and for worse, few witnesses to the horrors and denials, the tyrannies and resistance of World War II are still alive. This has allowed public acknowledgement and reconciliation in many settings, and for the cultural devastation of the city's creative class to be halted and gradually restored. Much property has gone through restitution, and émigrés now seem to feel comfortable in a city that welcomes them once again. Today they find a Vienna alive with the energy of cutting-edge art and ideas, and a city that knows in its deepest heart how to live well.

VIENNA TODAY

Vienna is again at the crossroads of an open and reunited Europe, just as it was as the Habsburg capital of the Austro-Hungarian Empire. During the Cold War, the government adopted a position of diplomatic neutrality, as Austrian leaders feared the return of the Russians, who left peacefully in 1955. But, since the collapse of the Iron Curtain, Austria has been moving toward greater co-operation and unity with the Western powers.

As it has always been, Vienna today is a city of hospitality, and tourism a mainstay of its thriving economy. In spite of the world financial crisis, visitors continue to fill Vienna's hotels, restaurants, theaters, and museums, helping to keep unemployment here among the lowest in Europe.

In 1998, continuing the effort to lay the past to rest, Austrian officials agreed to return to their rightful owners works of art confiscated by the Nazis.

The Austrian minister of culture, Elisabeth Gehrer, said she wanted to correct what she termed "immoral decisions" made at the end of World War II. This bold move sent reverberations throughout the museums of Europe and the U.S.

In one of the most famous cases, Maria Altmann won the restitution of five paintings by Gustav Klimt that had belonged to her uncle Ferdinand Bloch, including two portraits of his wife Adele Bloch-Bauer. It was the largest restitution of Nazi art ever, and when "Adele" left Austria in 2006, reproductions of the painting filled billboards around the city, with the text, "Adele is leaving." The painting was later purchased by the cosmetics heir Ronald Lauder for $135 million, at the time the highest sum ever paid for a painting. It is on display at Lauder's Neue Galerie in New York.

As a beacon of European culture, Vienna has more than 100 art museums, attracting 8 million visitors annually. In 2001 Vienna was designated a UNESCO World Heritage Site. In both 2009 and 2010 it was ranked first in the world in terms of quality of life.

Today, as it was under the empire, Vienna is again a city of immigration. In 2010, 32.8% of Vienna's residents were foreign born, most from another EU country (11.1%), followed by the former Yugoslavia (10.2%), and then Turkey (4.3%). The largest number of new residency permits now go to Germans.

But it was the U.S.–Russian spy swap in the summer of 2010 that reminded East and West that Vienna was still the world center of espionage. The third UN headquarters city after New York and Geneva, as well as home to energy and security alliances such as OPEC and the OSCE, Vienna is host to some 17,000 diplomats, "around half of whom have some connection to the intelligence agencies," according to Graz scholar Siegfried Beer, making Austria the country with the highest density of foreign intelligence agents in the world.

LOOKING BACK AT VIENNA

Vienna's history has been heavily influenced by its position astride the Danube, midway between the trade routes linking the prosperous ports of northern Germany with Italy. Its location at the crossroads of three great European cultures (Slavic, Teutonic, and Roman/Italian) transformed the settlement into a melting pot and, more often than not, a battlefield, even in prehistoric times.

EARLY TIMES   The 1906 discovery of the Venus of Willendorf, a Stone Age fertility figurine, in the Danube Valley showed that the region around Vienna was inhabited long before recorded history. It's known that around 1000 B.C., the mysterious Indo–European Illyrians established a high-level barbarian civilization around Vienna. After them came the Celts, who migrated east from Gaul around 400 B.C. They arrived in time to greet and resist the Romans, who began carving inroads into what is now known as Austria.

Around A.D. 10, the Romans chose the site of modern-day Vienna for a fortified military camp, Vindobona. This strategic outpost is well documented—its location is bordered today by Vienna's Rotenturmstrasse, St. Rupert's Church, The Graben, and Tiefer Graben. Vindobona marked the northeast border of the Roman Empire, and it functioned as a buffer zone between warring Roman, Germanic, and Slavic camps.

BABENBERGS & BOHEMIANS   In 803, the Frankish emperor Charlemagne swept through the Danube Valley, establishing a new territory called Ostmark (the

DATELINE

23,000 B.C. Venus of Willendorf, a figure of a Danubian fertility goddess, is crafted near Vienna.

1000 B.C. Illyrian tribes establish near Vienna.

400 B.C. Vendi tribes migrate from Gaul eastward to regions around Vienna.

100 B.C. Romans make military inroads into southern Austria.

A.D. 10 Vindobona (Vienna) is established as a frontier outpost of the Roman

Empire. Within 300 years, it's a thriving trading post.

400 Vindobona is burnt and rebuilt, but the event marks the gradual withdrawal of the Romans from Austria.

500 Vienna is overrun by Germanic Lombards.

630 The Avars take Vienna.

803 Charlemagne conquers the Danube Valley and the site of Vienna, labeling the region the Ostmark.

814 Death of Charlemagne dissolves his empire.

continues

Eastern March). When Charlemagne died in 814 and his once-mighty empire disintegrated, Vindobona struggled to survive. The earliest known reference to the site by the name we know today (Wenia) appeared in a proclamation of the Archbishop of Salzburg in 881.

In 976, Leopold von Babenberg established control over Austria, the beginning of a 3-century rule. Commerce thrived under the Babenbergs, and Vienna grew into one of the largest towns north of the Alps. By the end of the 10th century, Ostmark had become Ostarrichi, which later changed to Österreich (Austria).

Toward the end of the 12th century, Vienna underwent an expansion that would shape its development for centuries to come. In 1200, Vienna's ring of city walls was completed, financed by the ransom paid by the English to retrieve their king, Richard Coeur de Lion (the Lionheart), who had been seized on Austrian soil in 1192. Legend tells that he was captured in a tavern disguised as a monk when he paid with a gold sovereign. A city charter was granted to Vienna in 1221, with trading privileges that encouraged economic development.

In 1246, when the last of the Babenbergs, Friedrich II, died without an heir, the door was left open for a struggle between the Bohemian, Hungarian, and German princes over control of Austria. The Bohemian king Ottokar II stepped into the vacuum. However, Ottokar, whose empire extended from the Adriatic Sea to Slovakia, refused to swear an oath of fealty to the new emperor, Rudolf I of Habsburg, and the opposing armies joined in the pivotal Battle of Marchfeld, in 1278. Though Ottokar's administration was short, he is credited with the construction of the earliest version of Vienna's Hofburg.

THE HABSBURG DYNASTY   Under Rudolph of Habsburg, a powerful European dynasty was launched, one of the longest lived in history. The Habsburg rule of much of Central Europe would last until the end of World War I in 1918. The Habsburg Empire was a vast confederation anticipating the E.U., and during the next two centuries a series of annexations and consolidations of power brought both Carinthia (1335) and the Tyrol (1363) under Habsburg control.

881 First documented reference to Vienna (Wenia).	1147 A Romanesque predecessor of St. Stephan's Cathedral is consecrated as the religious heart of Vienna.
955 Charlemagne's heir, Otto I, reconquers Ostmark.	
962 Otto I is anointed the first official Holy Roman Emperor by the Pope.	1192 English king, Richard the Lionheart, is arrested and held hostage by the Babenburgers at Dürnstein. His ransom pays for construction of the city's walls, completed in 1200.
976 Leopold von Babenberg controls the Danube Valley.	
996 Austria is referred to for the first time with a derivation of its modern name (Ostarrichi).	
	1221 City charter is granted to Vienna, with independent trading privileges.
1030 After Cologne, Vienna is the largest town north of the Alps.	1246 Last of the Babenbergs, Friedrich the Warlike, dies in battle.

Many of these Habsburg rulers are long forgotten, but an exception is Rudolf IV (1339–65). Known as "The Founder," he laid the cornerstone of what was later consecrated as St. Stephan's Cathedral. He also founded the University of Vienna based on the one in Prague.

A turning point in the dynasty came in 1453, when Friedrich II was elected Holy Roman Emperor. He ruled from a power base in Vienna. By 1469, Vienna had been elevated to a bishopric, giving the city wide secular and religious authority.

Friedrich's power was not always steady: he lost control of both Bohemia and Hungary, each of which elected a king. In 1485, he was driven from Vienna by the Hungarian king Matthias Corvinus, who ruled for a 5-year period from Vienna's Hofburg.

In 1490, Corvinus died and civil war broke out in Hungary. Maximilian I (1459–1519), Friedrich's son, took advantage of the situation in Hungary to regain control of much of the territory his father had lost.

But the Habsburgs were not warriors. In fact, the family's motto became: "Let others wage wars but you, happy Austria, marry!" Often they succeeded through politically expedient marriages, a series of which brought Spain, Burgundy, and the Netherlands into their empire. In 1496, 4 years after the Spanish arrived in the New World, a Habsburg, Phillip the Fair, married the Spanish *infanta* (heiress), a union that produced Charles I (Carlos I), who became ruler of Spain and its New World holdings in 1516. Three years later, he was crowned Holy Roman Emperor as Charles V. Charles ceded control of Austria to his younger brother Ferdinand, in Vienna, in 1521. Ferdinand later married Anna Jagiello, heiress to Hungary and Bohemia, adding those countries to the empire.

In 1526, discontent in Vienna broke into civil war. Ferdinand responded with brutal repression and a new city charter that placed the city directly under Habsburg control.

PLAGUES & TURKISH INVASIONS In 1529, half of the city was destroyed by fire. Also during that year, Turkish armies laid siege to the city for 18 anxious days. They left Vienna's outer suburbs in smoldering ruins when they withdrew, but they

The Bohemian King Ottokar II succeeds him.

1278 Ottokar II is killed at Battle of Marchfeld. Rudolf II of Habsburg begins the longest dynastic rule in European history.

1335 & 1363 Habsburgs add Carinthia and the Tyrol to Austrian territory.

1433 Central spire of St. Stephan's is completed.

1453 Friedrich II is elected Holy Roman Emperor and rules from Vienna.

1469 Vienna is elevated to a bishopric.

1485–90 Hungarian king, Matthias Corvinus, occupies Vienna's Hofburg.

1490 Maximilian I recaptures Hungary and lost dominions.

1496 A Habsburg son marries the *infanta* of Spain, an act that places a Habsburg in control of vast territories in the New World.

1519 Charles I, Habsburg ruler of Spain, is elected Holy Roman Emperor as Charles V.

1521 Charles V cedes Vienna to his brother for more effective rule.

1526 Rebellion in Vienna leads to brutal repression by the Habsburgs.

1529 Turkish siege, a fire destroys half of Vienna.

continues

never breached the inner walls. Partly as a gesture of solidarity, Ferdinand I declared Vienna the site of his official capital in 1533.

In the 16th century, the Protestant Reformation shook Europe. In the second half of the century, under the tolerant Maximilian II, Vienna was almost 80% Protestant and even had a Lutheran mayor. However, Ferdinand II was rigorous in his suppression of Protestantism, and returned Vienna to Catholicism. By 1650, Vienna was a bastion of the Counter-Reformation.

Incursions into the Balkans by Ottoman Turks continued to upset the balance of power in Central Europe. During the same period there were outbreaks of the Black Death; in 1679, between 75,000 and 150,000 Viennese died. Leopold I commemorated the city's deliverance from the plague with the famous *Pestaule*—the Plague Column. It stands today on one of Vienna's main avenues, The Graben.

The final defeat of the Turks and the end of the Turkish menace came in September 1683. Along with a decline in plague-related deaths, the victory rejuvenated the city.

MARIA THERESA & POLITICAL REFORM   Freed from military threat, the city developed under Charles VI (1711–40) and his daughter, Maria Theresa, into a "Mecca of the arts." Architects like Johann Bernhard Fischer von Erlach and Johann Lukas von Hildebrandt designed lavish buildings, and composers and musicians flooded into the city from the imperial provinces.

In 1700, Charles II, last of the Spanish Habsburgs, died without an heir, signaling the final gasp of Habsburg control in Spain. Fearful of a similar fate, Austrian emperor Charles VI penned the Pragmatic Sanction, which ensured that his daughter, Maria Theresa, would follow him. Accordingly, Maria Theresa ascended to power in 1740 at the age of 23, then waged and won a 7-year War of the Austrian Succession (1740–48). She reigned for 40 years, launching an era of prosperity and a golden age of the baroque. During Maria Theresa's reign, the population of Vienna almost doubled, from 88,000 to 175,000. Her architectural legacies include sections of Vienna's Hofburg and her beloved Schönbrunn Palace, completed in 1769.

1533	Vienna is declared the official Habsburg capital.	1576	A reconversion to Catholicism of all Austrians as the Counter-Reformation begins.
1556	Charles V cedes his position as Holy Roman Emperor to his brother, the Austrian King Ferdinand.	1600–50	Hundreds of Catholic monks, priests, and nuns establish bases in Vienna as a means of encouraging the reconversion, and strengthening the Habsburg role in the Counter-Reformation.
1560	Vienna's city walls are strengthened against Turks.		
1571	Ferdinand grants religious freedom to all Austrians. Before long, 80% of Austrians have converted to Protestantism.	1618–48	Thirty Years' War almost paralyzes Vienna.
		1679	In the worst year of the Black Plague, 75,000 to 150,000 Viennese die.
1572	The Spanish Riding School is established.		

The Empress is credited with extensive reforms, including unifying the National Army, strengthening the economy through more effective tax collection, establishing a civil service, and founding the first national public education system, required for both sexes for ages 6 to 12. With her chief adviser, the Dutch physician Gerard van Swieten, she also founded the Vienna General Hospital and Europe's first research medical university, and had all her 13 children inoculated against smallpox. Many of her reforms have shaped Austrian social policy ever since.

Maria Theresa was succeeded by her son, Joseph II. An enlightened monarch who eschewed ritual, he introduced many reforms (especially in the church), made himself available to the people, and issued an "Edict of Tolerance."

NAPOLEON   The 19th century had a turbulent start. Napoleon's empire building wreaked havoc on Vienna's political landscape. His incursions onto Habsburg territories began in 1803 and culminated in the French occupation of Vienna in 1805 and 1809. Napoleon dissolved the Holy Roman Empire and ordered the new Austrian emperor, Franz I, to abdicate his position as Holy Roman Emperor. The Viennese treasury went bankrupt in 1811, causing a collapse of Austria's monetary system.

In one of the 19th century's more bizarre marriages, Napoleon married the Habsburg archduchess Marie-Louise by proxy in 1810. His days of success were numbered, however, and he was finally defeated at the Battle of Nations in Leipzig in 1813 and abdicated the following year.

METTERNICH & THE CONGRESS OF VIENNA   Aimed at re-ordering European boundaries after Napoleon's defeat, the pivotal Congress of Vienna (1814–15) included representatives of all Europe's major powers. The Congress was a showcase for the brilliant diplomacy and intrigue of Austria's foreign minister, Klemens von Metternich, who restored Austria's pride and influence within a redefined confederation of German-speaking states.

Metternich's dominance of Austria between 1815 and 1848 ushered in another golden age. The Biedermeier period was distinguished by the increased prosperity of

1683	Turks besiege Vienna but are routed by the armies of Lorraine and Poland.
1699	Turks evacuate strongholds in Hungary, ending the threat to Europe.
1700	The last of the Spanish Habsburgs dies, followed a year later by the War of the Spanish Succession.
1740	Maria Theresa ascends the Austrian throne despite initial tremors from the War of the Austrian Succession (1740–48).
1769	Maria Theresa's Schönbrunn Summer Palace is completed.
1770	The marriage of a Habsburg princess (Marie Antoinette) to Louis XVI of France cements relations between the two countries.
1780	Maria Theresa dies, and her liberal son, Joseph II, ascends to power.
1789	Revolution in France leads to the beheading of Marie Antoinette.
1805 & 1809	Napoleon's armies occupy Vienna. Napoleon routed on the fields of Deutsch Wagram.
1810	Napoleon marries Habsburg archduchess Marie-Louise.

continues

the bourgeoisie. Virtually excluded from politics, they concentrated on culture, building villas and the first big apartment houses and encouraging painting, music, literature, and design.

Advancing technology changed the skyline of Vienna as the 19th century progressed. The first steamship company to navigate the Danube was established in 1832, and Austria's first railway line (also one of the Continent's first) opened in 1837, between Vienna and Wagram.

In the meantime, despite his brilliance as an international diplomat, Metternich's domestic policies almost guaranteed civil unrest, eradicating many civil rights with a near police state, and creating an economic climate that leaned toward industrialization at the expense of wages and workers' rights.

In March 1848, events exploded not only in Vienna and Hungary, but also across most of Europe. Metternich was ousted and fled the city (some of his not-so-lucky colleagues were lynched). In response to the threat of revolutionary chaos, the Austrian army imposed a new version of absolute autocracy.

Emperor Franz Joseph I was the beneficiary of the restored order, and in 1848, at the age of 18, he began his autocratic 68-year reign.

THE METROPOLIS OF EUROPE Franz Joseph I's austere civility created the perfect foil for the cultural explosion of the newly rejuvenated city. A major accomplishment was the vast Ringstrasse, the boulevard that encircles Vienna's 1st District. Franz Joseph built on the site of the old city walls, and the construction of the Ringstrassenzone became a work of homogeneous civic architecture unparalleled throughout Europe.

Meanwhile, advanced technology helped launch Vienna into the Industrial Age, transforming the city into a glittering showcase. The empire's vast resources were used to keep theaters, coffee houses, concert halls, palaces, and homes well lit, cleaned, and maintained. A state-of-the-art water supply was installed, and the Danube regulated. A new town hall was built, and a new park, the Stadtpark, opened.

Year	Event	Year	Event
1811	Viennese treasury is bankrupted by the costs of defending the city.	1848	Violent revolution in Vienna ousts Metternich, threatens the collapse of Austrian society; Franz Joseph I takes power at 18.
1814–15	Congress of Vienna rearranges the map of Europe following the defeat of Napoleon.	1859	Austria loses control of its Italian provinces, including Venice and Milan.
1815–48	Vienna's Biedermeier period, supervised by Klemens von Metternich, marks the triumph of the bourgeoisie.	1862	Flooding on the Danube leads to a reconfiguration of its banks to a channel in Vienna's suburbs. A gravity-fed water supply serves the city.
1832	First steamship company is set up to navigate the Danube.		
1837	Austria's first railway line is opened from Vienna to Deutsch Wagram.	1867	Hungary and Austria merge, becoming the Austro-Hungarian Empire, headed by Franz Joseph I.

Austria's Most Famous Courtesan

Katharina Schratt (1855–1940) was a noted actress who became the most famous courtesan of the 19th-century German-speaking world. Born into a prosperous family in Baden, near Vienna, and known for her emotive roles at the Imperial Court Theater, she met the Emperor Franz Joseph at a private audience for the first time in 1883, and again 2 years later at one of his balls. It was a difficult time for the Emperor, probably depressed by the death of his only son and heir in which his own secret police may have had a hand, and burdened with the increasing withdrawal of the temperamental Empress Elisabeth ("Sissi"). Franz Joseph began a discrete dalliance with Katharina, eventually with the tacit approval of his wife. After Sissi's assassination by an anarchist in Geneva, the bond between Katharina and the Emperor became ever more public. When Franz Joseph died in 1917, Katharina abandoned her summer villa in Bad Ischl and retired to her winter home in Vienna, which is today the site of a comfortable hotel. Despite her potent enemies, she was honored with the role of godmother for the children of many of her friends. Some of Katharina's godchildren are still alive today, many leading discreetly elegant lives in Vienna and London.

The unification with Hungary was enshrined in a new constitution in 1867, which also made Jews full and equal citizens, with all civil and political rights, thus releasing a flood tide of creative energy and helping to usher in a half century of prosperity and the flowering of art and ideas that shaped the modern era.

The foundations of the Habsburg monarchy were shaken again in 1889 by the mysterious deaths of 30-year-old Crown Prince Rudolf, an outspoken liberal, and his 18-year-old mistress, at the royal hunting lodge of Mayerling. The possibility that they were murdered, and the insistence of his family that every shred of evidence

1869 Vienna's new State Opera House is completed.

1873 Vienna hosts the World's Fair.

1889 Crown Prince Rudolf dies at Mayerling, sparking rumors of a planned coup.

1890–1900 Vienna's outer suburbs are incorporated as city Districts 11 to 20.

1914 Assassination of Archduke Franz Ferdinand, heir to the Habsburg Empire, by a Serb nationalist sets off World War I.

1916 Franz Joseph dies and is succeeded by Charles I, the last of the Habsburgs.

1918 World War I ends, Austria is defeated, Charles I abdicates, and the Austro-Hungarian Empire is radically dismantled.

1919 Liberalization of Austrian voting laws enacts monumental changes in the social structure of Vienna. "Red Vienna" introduces major populist reforms; the city swings radically to the left.

continues

associated with the case be destroyed, led to lurid speculation and the possibility of a planned coup d'etat, unresolved to this day.

In 1890, many of the city's outer suburbs were incorporated into the City of Vienna, and in 1900 a final 20th District, Brigittenau, was also added. Women were first admitted to university in 1897, and the medical university in 1900. In 1906, women received the right to vote. By 1910, Vienna, with a population of 2 million, was the fourth-largest city in Europe, after London, Paris, and Berlin.

WORLD WAR I & THE VERSAILLES TREATY During the Belle Epoque, Europe sat on a powder keg of frustrated socialist platforms, national alliances, and conflicting colonial ambitions. The Austro-Hungarian Empire was linked by the Triple Alliance to both Germany and Italy. Europe leapt headfirst into armed conflict when Franz Joseph's nephew and designated heir, the Archduke Franz Ferdinand, was assassinated by a Serbian nationalist as he and his wife, Sophie, rode through Sarajevo on June 28, 1914. Within 30 days, the Austro-Hungarian Empire declared war on Serbia, signaling the outbreak of World War I. An embittered Franz Joseph died in 1916, midway through the conflict. His successor, Charles I, the last of the Habsburgs, abdicated in 1918.

The punitive peace treaty concluded at Versailles broke up the vast Austro-Hungarian territories into the nations of Hungary, Poland, Yugoslavia, and Czechoslovakia, a decision Winston Churchill described in his memoirs as "a cardinal tragedy." After all boundaries were redrawn tiny Austria, said French Prime Minister Clemenceau, "is that which is left." This overnight collapse of the empire caused the profound dislocation of populations and trade patterns. Some of the new nations refused to deliver raw materials to Vienna's factories or, in some cases, food to Vienna's markets. Coupled with the effects of the Versailles treaty and the massive loss of manpower and resources during the war when 80% of the Austrian army had died, Vienna soon found itself on the brink of starvation. Despite staggering odds, the new government (assisted by a massive loan in 1922 from the League of Nations) managed to stabilize the currency while Austrian industrialists hammered

1927	Violent discord between the socialists and fascists rocks Vienna.
1929	Worldwide economic depression occurs.
1933	Austria's authoritarian chancellor, Engelbert Dollfuss, outlaws the Austrian Nazi party.
1934	Dollfuss is assassinated by Nazis.
1938	German Nazi troops complete an amicable invasion of Austria that leads to the union of the two nations (Anschluss) through World War II.

1943–45	Massive bombings by Allied forces leave most public monuments in ruins.
1945	Allied forces defeat Germany and Austria. Vienna is "liberated" by Soviet troops on April 11. On April 27, Austria is redefined as a country separate from Germany and divided, like Germany, into four zones of occupation. Vienna also is subdivided into four zones.
1955	Allied forces evacuate Vienna; Vienna is the capital of a neutral Austria.

out new sources of raw materials. A democratic socialist "Red Vienna" also undertook pioneering experiments in public works and high-quality public housing that characterize Viennese life to this day.

THE ANSCHLUSS   In 1934, social tensions broke out into civil war, Europe's first confrontation between fascism and democracy. Austrian nationalism under the authoritarian Chancellor, Engelbert Dollfuss, put an end to progressive policies. Later that year, Austrian Nazis assassinated Dollfuss, and Nazis were included in the resultant coalition government. In 1938, Austria united with Nazi Germany (the *Anschluss*). Hitler returned triumphantly to Vienna, several decades after he had lived there as an impoverished and embittered artist. In a national referendum, 99.75% of Austrians voted their support.

WORLD WAR II & ITS AFTERMATH   The rise of Austria's Nazis devastated Vienna's academic and artistic communities. Many of their members, including Sigmund Freud, fled to safety elsewhere. About 60,000 Austrian Jews were sent to concentration camps, and only an estimated 2,000 survived; Austria's homosexual and Gypsy populations were similarly hit.

Beginning in 1943, Allied bombing raids demolished vast areas of the city, damaging virtually every public building of any stature. The roof of the city's most prominent landmark, St. Stephan's Cathedral, collapsed and there were fires in both towers. The city's death rate was one of the highest in Europe. For the Viennese, at least, the war ended abruptly on April 11, 1945, when Russian troops marched in from bases in Hungary.

During a confused interim that lasted a decade, Austria was divided into four zones of occupation, each controlled by one of the four Allies (the United States, the Soviet Union, Britain, and France). Vienna, deep within the Soviet zone, was also subdivided into four zones, each occupied by one of the victors. Control of the Inner City alternated every month between each of the four powers. It was a dark and depressing time in Vienna; rubble was slowly cleared away from bomb sites, but

1961   Summit in Vienna between John F. Kennedy and Nikita Khrushchev.

1979   Summit meeting in Vienna between Leonid Brezhnev and Jimmy Carter.

1986   Investigations into the wartime activities of Austrian chancellor Kurt Waldheim profoundly embarrass Austria.

1989   Empress Zita of Bourbon-Parma, wife of the last Habsburg emperor Charles I, dies after being in exile since 1919. She is buried in one of the most elaborate funerals in Vienna's history. Her son Otto organizes the Pan European Picnic in Hungary.

1995   Austria, Sweden, and Finland are admitted to the European Union.

1997   After 10 years, long-time chancellor Franz Vranitzky steps down, turning over leadership of Social Democratic Party.

1998   Austria decides to return art that Nazis plundered (much of it in museums).

1999   Right-wing Freedom Party stirs worldwide protests against Austria.

continues

some of the most glorious public monuments in Europe lay in ashes. Espionage, black-market profiteering, and personal betrayals proliferated, poisoning the memories of many older Viennese even today. In 1950, Allied commanders were replaced by diplomats. The Russian military occupation remained, stripping assets and hampering recovery until the State Treaty in 1955.

POSTWAR TIMES   On May 15, 1955, Austria regained its sovereignty as an independent, perennially neutral nation. As a non-aligned capital, Vienna became the obvious choice for meetings between John Kennedy and Nikita Khrushchev (in 1961) and Leonid Brezhnev and Jimmy Carter (in 1979). Many international organizations (including OPEC and the International Atomic Energy Agency) established offices.

Once again part of a republic, the Viennese actively sought to restore their self-image as cultural barons. Restoring the State Opera House and other grand monuments became a top priority.

In 1970, the election of Bruno Kreisky, the Rebublic's longest serving Chancellor, began a 12-year "golden age" in Austrian politics and culture, with full employment, a solid social state, an influential foreign policy and a "Sun-King" Chancellor who appeared with a solid socialist majority (never repeated) that allowed him to push through reforms.

However, Vienna's self-image suffered a blow when scandal surrounded Austria's president and former UN Secretary General, Kurt Waldheim, elected in 1986. Waldheim had been an officer in the Nazi army and had countenanced the deportation of Jews to extermination camps. The United States declared him persona non grata. Many Austrians stood by Waldheim; others were deeply embarrassed. Waldheim did not seek re-election, and in May 1992, Thomas Klestil, a career diplomat, was elected president, supported by the centrist Austrian People's Party.

In 1989, the last heiress to the Habsburg dynasty, Empress Zita of Bourbon-Parma, in exile since 1919, was buried in one of the most lavish and emotional funerals ever held in Vienna. At the age of 96, the last empress of Austria and queen

2000 The E.U. issues sanctions against Austria because of the Freedom Party, then rescinds them.	2007 Following the lifting of Schengen boundaries, Austria posts soldiers on the Hungarian border.
2004 Celebrations throughout Austria as its homegrown son, Arnold Schwarzenegger, is elected governor of California.	2008 Global warming poses a threat to ski resorts.
2006 Center-Left opposition wins in Austria, while a new Foreigners' Law raises barriers to immigration.	2009 After a post-Schengen spike in non-violent crime, international police co-operation brought levels back down again by the end of the year.

THE THIRD MAN & postwar VIENNA

The 1949 film *The Third Man,* starring Joseph Cotten, Orson Welles, Trevor Howard, and Alida Valli, remains one of the best records of a postwar Vienna in ruins. Graham Greene, who wrote the screenplay (later published as a novella by Penguin Books), found a "city of undignified ruins, which turned February into great glaciers of snow and ice." The Danube was a "gray, flat, muddy river" and the Russian zone, where the Prater lay, was "smashed and desolate and full of weeds."

In the closing weeks of World War II, the city suffered major aerial bombardment. In the summer of 1944, Vienna tried to save itself, closing all theaters and public areas. The working week was extended to 60 hours. A dreaded mass recruitment, the Volksturm, rounded up all males between the ages of 16 and 60 for a final attempt at defending the city. Hitler was in his Berlin bunker when he learned that the city of his youth, Vienna, had fallen to the Allies.

The victors found a wasted city on the verge of starvation. By 1945, Vienna had the highest death rate in Europe. Bombings had destroyed 20% of its buildings, and some 270,000 Viennese were left homeless.

The Third Man immortalized the "four men in a jeep"—that is, four military policemen from the quartet of occupying powers—patrolling the beleaguered city. The black market, on which the events in the film turn, became the way of life.

Even today, the Viennese have bitter memories of the occupation, especially by the Soviet Union. A reminder of those dreaded years survives at Schwarzenbergplatz (reached from Karlsplatz by walking along Friedrichstrasse/Lothringerstrasse). Under the Nazis, this square was called Hitlerplatz. Today, a patch of landscaped greenery surrounds a fountain and a Russian statue. The city has been none too happy with this "gift" from its former "liberators." Three times officials have tried to demolish the memorial, but so far Soviet engineering has proven indestructible. The Viennese have nicknamed an anonymous Soviet soldier's grave "the Tomb of the Unknown Plunderer."

In May 1955 the Austria State Treaty, signed by the four Allied powers and Austria, re-established full sovereignty. Why did it take so long? One reason is that the Soviets were seeking heavy reparations. But as the dust settles over history, another possibility arises. Stalin might have planned to stick around in Vienna, as he did in Berlin. After all, a toehold in Vienna would have given the Soviets penetration into the West at the peak of the Cold War. As it was, Vienna became a hub of Cold War espionage and spying—real James Bond country— and to this day has the highest density of foreign intelligence agents in the world.

---

of Hungary had always been held in some degree of reverence, a symbol of the glorious days of the Austrian empire.

In the spring of 1998, the Austrian government stunned the art world by agreeing to return artworks confiscated from Jews by the Nazis. Many Jewish families, including the Austrian branch of the Rothschilds, had fled into exile in 1938. Although they tried to regain their possessions after the war, they were not successful. Austrian journalist Hubertus Czernin wrote, "The art was stolen by the Nazis and stolen a second time by the Austrian government." One museum director claimed Austria had "a specific moral debt," which it was now repaying.

In 1999 elections the Freedom Party won notoriety (and 27% of the vote) by denouncing the presence of foreigners in Austria. Echoing Nazi rhetoric, the party blamed foreigners for drugs, crime, welfare abuse, and the spread of tuberculosis. The party remains racist and Nazi-admiring in spite of the resignation of its leader, Jörg Haider, its most controversial member. After first announcing punishing sanctions against Austria for its tilt to the far right, the European Union lifted those sanctions in September of 2000, while vowing to keep a special eye on Austria's song and dance into Right-wing politics. E.U. officials concluded that in spite of earlier defiance, the Austrian government in Vienna had taken "concrete steps to fight racism, xenophobia, and anti-Semitism."

News of an expat Austrian, a citizen of Graz, made the biggest headlines in both Vienna and the country itself in 2004. Their homegrown muscleman/movie star Arnold Schwarzenegger swept into the governor's office in California. Even though he's married to a Kennedy, Maria Shriver, Schwarzenegger is a Republican, and lent the prestige of his name in the campaign of George W. Bush for re-election.

In October of 2006, Austria's opposition Social Democrats won nationwide elections, swinging the country to the center-Left after more than 6 years of influence by the extreme Right. Immigration was a central theme in the campaign (sound familiar?), and the far Right hoped to reduce the number of foreigners in Austria by 30%. The Social Democrats countered with job creation and reduced salary differences between men and women. The politics of resistance have not worked: by 2010, Vienna's foreign-born population had increased to 32.8% from 23% in 2001.

Record warmth in recent years (with autumn temperatures in Austria prevailing even in winter) has brought home the profound threat of a climate change in the country's ski industry.

Climatologists in Vienna announced in 2008 that the warming trend will become drastic by 2020. In reports filed, these experts said that the Austrian Alps are warming twice as fast as the average in the rest of the world. They claimed that in 1980, 75% of alpine glaciers were advancing. By 2008, 90% were retreating.

VIENNA'S ART & ARCHITECTURE

Vienna's location at the intersection of the Germanic, Mediterranean, and eastern European worlds contributed to a rich and varied artistic heritage. Here the delicate curves of 18th-century Theresian churches are topped with oriental onion domes, while neo-classic columns support designs in Moorish mosaic under a soaring Gothic arch. In a visual metaphor for the city's complex cultural roots, Vienna embraces styles from Romanesque through rococo, baroque to Biedermeier, from medieval to modern, blending together into a consciously unified urban landscape.

Art

EARLY ECCLESIASTICAL ART

Most art in the early medieval period was church art. From the Carolingian period, the only survivors are a handful of **illuminated manuscripts,** now in Vienna's National Library. The most famous is the *Cutbercht Evangeliar* from around 800, a richly illuminated copy of the four gospels.

The Romanesque period reached its peak between 1000 and 1190. Notable from this time is the Admont Great Bible, crafted around 1140, one of the prized treasures of Vienna's National Library. In 1181 the famous goldsmith Nicolas de Verdun produced one of the finest **enamel works** in Europe for the pulpit at Klosterneuburg Abbey. Verdun's 51 small panels, crafted from enamel and gold, depict scenes from the religious tracts of the Augustinians. After a fire in the 1300s, the panels were repositioned onto an altarpiece known as the Verdun Altar at Klosterneuburg, where they can be seen today.

THE GOTHIC AGE

The Gothic Age in Austria is better remembered for its architecture than its painting and sculpture. Early Gothic sculpture was influenced by the *Zachbruchiger Stil* (zigzag style), identified by vivid angular outlines of forms against contrasting backgrounds. The era's greatest surviving sculptures date from around 1320 and include *The Enthroned Madonna of Klosterneuburg* and *The Servant's Madonna,* showcased in Vienna's St. Stephan's Cathedral.

By the late 1300s, Austrian sculpture was strongly influenced by Bohemia. The human form became elongated, exaggerated, and idealized, often set in graceful but unnatural S curves. Wood became increasingly popular as an artistic medium and was often painted in vivid colors. A superb example of **Gothic sculpture** is *The Servant's Madonna* in St. Stephan's Cathedral. Carved around 1320, it depicts Mary enthroned and holding a standing Christ child.

FROM THE RENAISSANCE TO THE 18TH CENTURY

During most of the Renaissance, Vienna was too preoccupied with fending off invasions, sieges, and plagues to produce the kind of painting and sculpture that flowered in other parts of Europe. As a result, in the 17th and 18th centuries, Vienna struggled to keep up with cities like Salzburg, Munich, and Innsbruck.

Most painting and sculpture during the baroque period was for the enhancement of the grandiose churches and spectacular palaces that sprang up across Vienna. Artists were imported from Italy; one, **Andrea Pozzo** (1642–1709), produced the masterpiece *The Apotheosis of Hercules* that appears on the ceilings of Vienna's Liechtenstein Palace. Baroque painting emphasized symmetry and unity, and *trompe l'oeil* was used to give extra dimension to a building's sculptural and architectural motifs.

The first noteworthy Austrian-born baroque painter was **Johann Rottmayr** (1654–1730), the preferred decorator of the two most influential architects of the age, von Hildebrandt and Fischer von Erlach. Rottmayr's works adorn some of the ceilings of Vienna's Schönbrunn Palace and Peterskirche. Countless other artists contributed to the Viennese baroque style. Notable are the frescoes of **Daniel Gran** (1694–1754), who decorated the Hofbibliothek. He also has an altarpiece in the Karlskirche.

Vienna, as it emerged from a base of muddy fields into a majestic fantasy of baroque architecture, was captured on the canvas in the landscapes of **Bernardo Bellotto** (1720–80), nephew and pupil of the famous Venetian painter Canaletto. Brought to Vienna at the request of Maria Theresa, Bellotto managed to bathe the city in a flat but clear light of arresting detail and pinpoint accuracy. His paintings today are valued as social and historical as well as artistic documents.

Dutch-born, Swedish-trained **Martin van Meytens** (1695–1770), court painter to Maria Theresa, captured the lavish balls and assemblies of Vienna's aristocracy. His canvases, though awkwardly composed and overburdened with detail, are the best visual record of the Austrian court's balls and receptions. In 1730, van Meytens was appointed director of Vienna's Fine Arts Academy.

Sculptors also made their contribution to the baroque style. **Georg Raphael Donner** (1693–1741) is best known for the remarkable life-size bronzes of the Fountain of Providence in the Neuer Markt. **Balthasar Permoser** (1651–1732) is responsible for the equestrian statues of Prince Eugene of Savoy in the courtyard of the Belvedere Palace. The famous double sarcophagus in the Kapuzinerkirche designed for Maria Theresa and her husband, Francis Stephen, is the masterpiece of **Balthasar Moll** (1717–85).

Equally influential was **Franz Xaver Messerschmidt** (1737–83), the German-trained resident of Vienna who became famous for his portrait busts. His legacy is accurate and evocative representations of Maria Theresa, her son Joseph II, and other luminaries.

REVOLT FROM "OFFICIAL ART"

In rebellion against "official art" a school of **Romantic Realist** painters emerged, drawing on biblical themes and Austrian folklore. Scenes from popular operas were painted lovingly on the walls of the Vienna State Opera. The 17th-century Dutch masters influenced their landscape paintings.

Georg Waldmüller (1793–1865), a self-proclaimed enemy of "academic art" and an advocate of realism, created one of the best pictorial descriptions of Viennese Biedermeier society in his *Wiener Zimmer* (1837). More than 120 of his paintings are on display at the Upper Belvedere museum.

The second most influential portraitist of this era was renowned court painter **Friedrich von Amerling** (1803–1887), several of whose extraordinarily vivid portraits of actors at the Burgtheater are on view at the Liechtenstein Museum.

Another realist was **Carl Moll** (1861–1945), whose graceful and evocative portrayals of everyday scenes are prized today. **Joseph Engelhart** (1864–1941) was known for his voluptuous renderings of Belle Epoque coquettes flirting with Viennese gentlemen.

THE VIENNA SECESSION

Young painters, decorators, and architects from Vienna's Academy of Fine Arts founded the Secessionist Movement (Sezessionstil) in 1897. The name captures their retreat (secession) from the Künstlerhaus (Vienna Artists' Association), which they considered pompous, sanctimonious, artificial, mediocre, and mired in the historicism favored by Emperor Franz Joseph. Their artistic statement was similar to that of the Art Nouveau movement in Paris and the Jugendstil movement in Munich.

The Secessionist headquarters, on the Friedrichstrasse at the corner of the Opernring, was inaugurated in 1898 as an exhibition space for avant-garde artists. Foremost among the group was **Gustav Klimt** (1862–1918), whose work developed rapidly into a highly personal and radically innovative form of decorative painting based on the sinuous curved line of Art Nouveau. His masterpieces include a mammoth frieze, 33m (110-ft.) long, encrusted with gemstones, and dedicated to Beethoven. Executed in 1902, it's one of the artistic focal points of the Secessionist Pavilion. Other pivotal works include *Portrait of Adele Bloch-Bauer* (1907), an abstract depiction of a prominent Jewish Viennese socialite. Its gilded geometric form is reminiscent of ancient Byzantine art.

Vienna's Art & Architecture

VIENNA IN DEPTH

THE MODERN AGE

Klimt's talented disciple was **Egon Schiele** (1890–1918). Tormented, overly sensitive, and virtually unknown during his brief lifetime, he is now considered a modernist master whose work can stand alongside that of van Gogh and Modigliani. His works seem to dissolve the boundaries between humankind and the natural world, granting a kind of anthropomorphic humanity to landscape painting. One of his most disturbing paintings is the tormented *The Family* (1917), originally conceived as decoration for a mausoleum.

Modern sculpture in Vienna is inseparable from the international art trends that dominated the 20th century. **Fritz Wotruba** (1907–75) introduced a neo-cubist style of sculpture. Many of his sculptural theories were manifested in his Wotruba Church (Church of the Most Holy Trinity), erected toward the end of his life in Vienna's outlying 23rd District. Adorned with his sculptures and representative of his architectural theories in general, the building is an important sightseeing and spiritual attraction.

Oskar Kokoschka (1886–1980) was one of Vienna's most important contemporary painters. Kokoschka expressed the frenzied psychological confusion of the years before and after World War II. His portraits of such personalities as the artist Carl Moll are bathed in psychological realism and violent emotion.

Architecture

GOTHIC

Although Vienna holds few remains of early medieval buildings, a number of Gothic buildings rest on older foundations. During the 1300s, ecclesiastical architecture was based on the Hallenkirche (hall church), a model that originated in Germany. These buildings featured interiors that resembled enormous hallways, with nave and aisles of the same height. The earliest example of this was the choir added in 1295 to an older Romanesque building, the abbey church of Heiligenkreuz, 24km (15 miles) west of Vienna.

The most famous building in the Hallenkirche style was the first incarnation of St. Stephan's Cathedral. Later modifications greatly altered the details of its original construction, and today only the foundations, the main portal, and the modestly proportioned western towers remain. Much more dramatic is the cathedral's needle-shaped central spire, completed in 1433, which still soars high above Vienna's skyline. St. Stephan's' triple naves, each the same height, are a distinctive feature of Austrian Gothic. Other examples of this construction can be seen in the Minorite Church and the Church of St. Augustine.

During the late 1400s, Gothic architecture retreated from the soaring proportions of the Hallenkirche style, and focus turned to more modest buildings with richly decorated interiors. Stonemasons added tracery (geometric patterns) and full-rounded or low-relief sculpture to ceilings and walls. Gothic churches continued to be built in Austria until the mid-1500s.

FROM GOTHIC TO BAROQUE

One of the unusual aspects of Vienna is its lack of Renaissance buildings. The Turks besieged Vienna periodically from 1529 until the 1680s, forcing planners to use most of their resources to strengthen the city's fortifications.

Although Vienna itself has no Renaissance examples, Italian influences were evident for more than a century before baroque gained a true foothold. Late in the 16th century many Italian builders settled in the regions of Tyrol, Carinthia, and Styria. In these less-threatened regions of Austria, Italian influence produced a number of country churches and civic buildings in the Renaissance style, with open porticoes, balconies, and loggias.

THE FLOWERING OF THE BAROQUE

The 47-year rule of Leopold I (1658–1705) witnessed the beginning of the golden age of Austrian baroque architecture. Italian-born Dominico Martinelli (1650–1718) designed the **Liechtenstein Palace,** built between 1694 and 1706 and inspired by the Renaissance Palazzo Farnese in Rome.

Austria soon began to produce its own architects. **Johann Bernhard Fischer von Erlach** (1656–1723) trained with both Bernini and Borromini in Rome. His style was restrained but monumental, drawing richly from the great buildings of antiquity. Fischer von Erlach knew how to transform the Italianate baroque of the south into a style that suited the Viennese. His most notable work is the **Karlskirche,** built in 1713. He also created the original design for Maria Theresa's **Schönbrunn Palace.** He had planned a sort of super-Versailles, but the project turned out to be too costly. Only the entrance facade remains of Fischer von Erlach's design. The **Hofbibliothek (National Library)** on Josephsplatz and the **Hofstalungen** are other notable buildings he designed.

Fischer von Erlach was succeeded by another great name in the history of architecture: **Johann Lukas von Hildebrandt** (1668–1745). Von Hildebrandt's design for Prince Eugene's **Belvedere Palace** (a series of interlocking cubes with sloping mansard-style roofs) is the culmination of the architectural theories initiated by Fischer von Erlach. Other von Hildebrandt designs in Vienna include the **Schwarzenberg Palace** (divided between the private residence of Prince Karl Schwarzenberg, foreign minister of the Czech Republic, and a hotel, under renovation, to reopen in 2012) and **St. Peter's Church.**

The **rococo style** developed as a more ornate, somewhat fussier progression of the baroque. Gilt stucco, brightly colored frescoes, and interiors that drip with embellishments are its hallmarks. Excellent examples include the **Abbey of Dürnstein** (1731–35) and **Melk Abbey,** both in Lower Austria. One of the most powerful proponents of rococo was Maria Theresa, who used its motifs so extensively within Schönbrunn Palace during its 1744 renovation that the school of Austrian rococo is sometimes referred to as "late-baroque Theresian style."

In response to the excesses of rococo, architects eventually turned to classical Greece and Rome for inspiration. The result was a restrained neoclassicism that transformed the skyline of Vienna and lasted well into the 19th century. The dignified austerity of Vienna's **Technical University** is a good example.

ECLECTICISM & VIENNA'S RING

As Austria's wealthy bourgeoisie began to impose their tastes on public architecture, 19th-century building grew more solid and monumental. The neoclassical style remained the preferred choice for government buildings, as evidenced by Vienna's **Mint** and the **Palace of the Provincial Government.**

The 19th century's most impressive Viennese architectural achievement was the construction of the **Ringstrasse** (1857–91). The medieval walls were demolished, and the Ring was lined with showcase buildings. This was Emperor Franz Joseph's personal project and his greatest achievement. Architects from all over Europe answered the Emperor's call, eager to seize the unprecedented opportunity to design a whole city district. Between 1850 and the official opening ceremony in 1879, the Ring's architecture became increasingly eclectic: French neo-Gothic (the Votivkirche), Flemish neo-Gothic (the Rathaus), Greek Revival (Parliament), French Renaissance (Staatsoper), and Tuscan Renaissance (Museum of Applied Arts). While the volume of traffic circling Old Vienna diminishes some of the Ring's charm, a circumnavigation of the Ring provides a panorama of eclectic yet harmonious building styles.

SECESSIONIST & POLITICAL ARCHITECTURE

By the late 19th century, younger architects were in rebellion against the pomp and formality of older architectural styles. In 1896 young **Otto Wagner** (1841–1918) published a tract called *Moderne Architektur,* which argued for a return to more natural and functional architectural forms. The result was the establishment of **Art Nouveau (Jugendstil,** or, as it applies specifically to Vienna, **Sezessionstil).** The Vienna Secession architects reaped the benefits of the technological advances and the new building materials available after the Industrial Revolution. Wagner, designer of Vienna's **Kirche am Steinhof** and the city's **Postsparkasse** (Post Office Savings Bank), became a founding member of the movement.

Joseph Hoffman (1870–1955) and **Adolf Loos** (1870–1933) promoted the use of glass, newly developed steel alloys, and aluminum. In the process, they discarded nearly all ornamentation, a rejection that contemporary Vienna found profoundly distasteful and almost shocking. Loos was particularly critical of the buildings adorning the Ringstrasse. His most controversial design is the **Michaelerplatz Building.** Sometimes referred to as "the Loos House," it was erected on Michaelerplatz in 1908. The streamlined structure was bitterly criticized for its lack of ornamentation and its resemblance to the "gridwork of a sewer." There were claims that the Emperor found it so offensive he kept the curtains closed on that side of the palace and ordered his drivers to avoid the Hofburg entrance on Michaelerplatz altogether.

Architectural philosophies were also affected during the "Red Vienna" period by the socialist reformers' desire to alleviate public housing shortages, a grinding social problem of the years between world wars. The Social Democratic Party began erecting "palaces for the people." The most obvious example is the **Karl-Marx-Hof** (Heiligenstadterstrasse 82–92, A-1190), which includes 1,600 apartments and stretches for more than a kilometer (half a mile).

TO THE PRESENT DAY

After World War II, much of Vienna's resources went toward restoring older historic buildings to their prewar grandeur. New buildings were streamlined and functional; much of Vienna today features the same kind of neutral modernism you're likely to find in postwar Berlin or Frankfurt.

Postmodern masters, however, have broken away from the 1950s and 1960s. They include the iconoclastic mogul Hans Hollein, designer of the silvery, curved-sided **Haas Haus** (1990) adjacent to St. Stephan's Cathedral. The self-consciously avant-garde **Friedensreich Hundertwasser** is a multihued, ecologically inspired apartment building at the corner of Löwengasse and Kegelgasse that appears to be randomly stacked.

Lately, **Hermann Czech** has been stirring architectural excitement, not so much by building new structures as developing daring interiors for boutiques and bistros; examples are the **Kleines Café** (Franziskanerplatz 3) and **Restaurant Salzamt** (Ruprechtsplatz 1).

2 VIENNA IN POPULAR CULTURE: BOOKS, FILM, & MUSIC

Books

HISTORY

The Austrians: A Thousand-Year Odyssey, Gordon Brook-Shepherd: Historian Brook-Shepherd looks at Austria's long history to explain its people—who they are, how they got there, and where they're going.

The Viennese: Splendor, Twilight and Exile, Paul Hofmann: A masterful social history of the city by a Vienna-born political journalist and Rome bureau chief for the *New York Times,* illuminating the city's genius and its contradictions with affection and insight.

Fin-de-Siècle Vienna: Politics and Culture, Carl E. Schorske: This landmark book takes you into the political and social world of Vienna during the late 19th and early 20th centuries.

A Nervous Splendor: Vienna 1888–1889, Frederic Morton: Morton uses the mysterious deaths of Archduke Rudolf and Baroness Marie Vetsera at Mayerling as a point of departure to capture in detail the life of Imperial Vienna at its glorious height. In a second book, *Thunder at Twilight,* Morton recreates the intense confluence of events in Vienna on the eve of World War I, when Stalin, Trotsky, Lenin, Freud and Jung, Klimt, Kafka, and Karl Kraus, were all haunting the coffee houses of Vienna conceiving the ideas that became the 20th century.

ART, ARCHITECTURE & MUSIC

J. B. Fischer von Erlach, Hans Aurenhammer: This entertaining volume illuminates the life, times, and aesthetic vision of the court-appointed architect who transformed the face of 18th-century Vienna and Salzburg.

Vienna 1900: Art, Architecture, and Design, Kirk Varnedoe: During the late 19th century, Vienna's artistic genius reached dazzling heights of modernity. These movements are explored in this appealing primer.

On Mozart, Anthony Burgess: Set in heaven, amid a reunion of the greatest composers of all time, this controversial book creates debates about music that never occurred but should have. Condemned by some critics as gibberish and praised by others as brilliant and poetic, Burgess's work is highly recommended for musical sophisticates with a sense of humor.

BIOGRAPHY

Freud: A Life for Our Times, Peter Gay: Gay's biography is a good introduction to the life of one of the seminal figures of the 20th century. Freud, of course, was Viennese until he fled from the Nazis in 1938, settling with his sofa in London.

Haydn: A Creative Life in Music, Karl and Irene Geiringer: This is the best biography of composer Franz Josef Haydn, friend of Mozart, teacher of Beethoven, and court composer of the Esterházys.

Mozart: A Cultural Biography, Robert W. Gutman: Music historian Gutman places Mozart squarely in the cultural world of 18th-century Europe.

Empress Maria Theresa, Robert Pic: The life and times of the greatest, most flamboyant Habsburg monarch is richly treated in this engrossing biography.

Wittgenstein: The Duty of Genius, Ray Monk: This is a brilliant personal and intellectual portrait of the 20th century's most influential philosopher, and explores his life in the Jewish haute bourgeoisie in pre-World War I Vienna.

Film

Though Austrians have played a major role in world cinema, most have made their movies in Berlin or Hollywood. Austrians who went on to international film fame have included Erich von Stroheim, Josef von Sternberg (who masterminded the career of Marlene Dietrich), G. W. Pabst, legendary director Max Reinhardt, Curd Jurgens, Hedy Lamar, Oscar Werner (*Jules et Jim*), Romy Schneider (*The Trial*), Maximilian Schell (*Judgment at Nuremburg*), and Klaus Maria Brandauer. The World War II Oscar-winning classic *Casablanca* was awash with Austrians, from director **Michael Curtiz** and composer Max Steiner (also *Gone with the Wind*) to co-star Paul Henreid who played resistance leader Victor Lazlo, and Peter Lorre who was the black marketeer Ugarte, while S. Z. Sakall was the waiter Carl.

Among the other distinguished émigré directors, **Billy Wilder** made some of the best Hollywood classics of all time, such as *Sunset Boulevard* (1950) with Gloria Swanson and *Some Like It Hot* (1959) with Marilyn Monroe. **Fred Zinnemann** directed some 21 feature films, including *The Men* (1949), *High Noon* (1951), and *Julia* (1976).

A first-rate film that hauntingly evokes life in postwar Vienna is *The Third Man* (1949), starring Joseph Cotten and Orson Welles. And who could visit Austria without renting a copy of *The Sound of Music* (1965)? The film won several Academy Awards, including Best Picture. Starring Julie Andrews, it was filmed in the lovely city of Salzburg.

Fritz Lang (1890–1976) was an Austrian-born director whose success was proven in Europe before emigrating to the U.S.. Often developing themes of fatalism and terror, his films were hailed for intellectualism and visual opulence. His European films included *Metropolis* (1924), a stark and revolutionary portrayal of automated urban life and, on the eve of the Nazi rise to power, the eerily clairvoyant *Das Testament des Dr. Mabuse* (1933). Welcomed into Hollywood, his credits included *Fury* (1936) and *Western Union* (1941).

Erich von Stroheim (1886–1957) was the pseudonym of Oswald von Nordenwald. He was one of the most innovative and exacting film directors in the history of cinema. Born in Vienna, he served in the Habsburg cavalry before rising within the ranks of Berlin's golden age of silent films. After emigrating to Hollywood in 1914, he worked for legendary director D. W. Griffith, becoming noted for his minute realism and his almost-impossible demands on the actors and resources of Hollywood. His directing credits included *Blind Husbands* (1919), *Foolish Wives* (1922), the epic masterpiece *Greed* (1928), and the spectacularly expensive flop that almost ended Gloria Swanson's film career, *Queen Kelly* (1928). As an actor, his most famous roles were as stiff-necked but highly principled Prussian military officers (often wearing monocles) in such films as Jean Renoir's *Grand Illusion* (1937). Most know him today for what he called "the dumb butler part" in Billy Wilder's 1950 classic, *Sunset Boulevard*.

Hedy Lamarr (1915–2000), born in Vienna into the Jewish haute bourgeoisie, Lamarr studied with Max Reinhart, who described her as "the most beautiful woman in Europe," and became one of the shining lights in MGM mogul Louis B. Mayer's cavalcade of stars. Achieving world notoriety by her nude scenes in *Ecstasy,* she later played opposite Clark Gable in *Comrade X* and made such films as *White Cargo* and the Cecil B. DeMille epic *Samson and Delilah.* She was also a gifted mathematician, and together with avant garde composer George Antheil, a neighbor, Lamarr developed a frequency-hopping technology for the animated control of musical instruments, patented in the U.S. in June 1941. Later this idea was revived as a basis for modern spread-spectrum communication, like COFDM used in Wi-Fi networks, for which she received an award in 1997 from the Electronic Frontier Foundation.

A more recent Austrian actor to achieve world fame is **Klaus Maria Brandauer,** who appeared in *Russia House* and *White Fang.* Born in 1944 in Austria, Brandauer attracted the attention of Hollywood as protagonist Hendrik Hofgen in the 1982 film version of Klaus Mann's novel *Mephisto,* directed by famed Hungarian Iztvan Szabo (*Being Julia*). Winning the Oscar for best foreign film, this stocky, balding, and short actor—not your typical leading man—is however best remembered in America as the villain in the James Bond thriller *Never Say Never Again* and as the husband of Meryl Streep in *Out of Africa,* for which he was nominated for a second Oscar as best supporting actor in 1985.

Some film critics have hailed Austria today as "the world capital of feel-bad cinema." Its most recent high-profile director is **Michael Haneke,** who came to prominence with *The Seventh Continent* in 1989, followed by *The Piano Teacher* in 2001, based on a novel by Austrian Nobel laureate Elfriede Jelenek. He also made *Caché,* in 2005, with Juliette Binoche and *The White Ribbon,* in 2009, winning the Palm d'Or at Cannes.

Austria has won further Oscars: Best Foreign Film in 2007 for Stefan Ruzowitzky's *The Counterfeiters,* and Best Supporting Actor in 2009 for Christoph Waltz playing the creepy Nazi general (in three languages) in Quentin Tarantino's *Inglourious Basterds.*

The best-known Austrian actor is, of course, Arnold Schwarzenegger. This son of a policeman from Graz became a multimillionaire superstar in America, turning a bodybuilding career into that of a world-class action star, going from *The Terminator* to political life as the California "Governator." However, the Austrian émigré with the biggest footprint in Hollywood history is probably Eric Pleskow, former president of United Artists and Orion Pictures, and producer of a long list of greats including *One Flew Over the Cuckoo's Nest, Rocky, Annie Hall, Amadeus, Dances with Wolves,* and *Silence of the Lambs.* Since 1998, Pleskow has spent time here again as president of the Vienna International Film Festival, the Viennale.

Music

Music is central to Viennese life. From the concertos of Mozart and Johann Strauss's waltzes, to opera and folk tunes, the Viennese are surrounded by music—and not only in the concert hall and opera house, but at smaller places as well. The works of the musicians mentioned below are available on classical CDs.

THE CLASSICAL PERIOD

The classical period was a golden age in Viennese musical life. Two of the greatest composers of all time, Mozart and Haydn, lived and worked in Vienna. Maria Theresa herself trilled arias on the stage of the Schlosstheater at Schönbrunn, and with her children and friends, performed operas and dances.

Classicism's first great manifestation was the development of *Singspiele,* a reform of opera by **Christoph Willibald Ritter von Gluck** (1714–87). Baroque opera had become overburdened with ornamentation, and Gluck introduced a more natural musical form. In 1762, Maria Theresa presented Vienna with the first performance of Gluck's innovative opera *Orpheus and Eurydice.* It and *Alceste* (1767) are his best-known operas, regularly performed today.

Franz Joseph Haydn (1732–1809) is the creator of the classical sonata, which is the basis of classical chamber music. Haydn's patrons were the rich and powerful Esterházy family, whom he served as musical director. His output was prodigious. He wrote chamber music, sonatas, operas, and symphonies. His strong faith is in evidence in his oratorios; among the greatest are *The Creation* (1798) and *The Seasons* (1801). He also composed the Austrian national anthem (1797), which he later elaborated in his quartet, *Opus 76, no. 3.*

The most famous composer of the period was **Wolfgang Amadeus Mozart** (1756–91). The prodigy from Salzburg charmed Maria Theresa and her court with his playing when he was only 6 years old. His father, Leopold, exploited his son's talent—"Wolferl" spent his childhood touring all over Europe. Later, he went with his father to Italy, where he absorbed that country's fertile musical traditions. Leaving Salzburg, he settled in Vienna, at first with great success. Eccentric and extravagant, he was unable to keep a patronage or land any lucrative post; he finally received an appointment as chamber composer to the Emperor Joseph II at a minimal salary. Despite hard times, Mozart refused the posts offered him elsewhere, possibly because in Vienna he found the best of all musical worlds: the best instrumentalists, the finest opera, the most talented singers. He composed more than 600 works in practically every musical form known to the time and his greatest are unmatched in beauty and profundity. He died in poverty, and was buried in a pauper's grave, the whereabouts of which is uncertain.

THE ROMANTIC AGE

Franz Schubert (1797–1828), the only one of the great composers born in Vienna, was also one of the most Viennese of musicians. He turned *lieder,* popular folk songs often used with dances, into an art form. He was a master of melodic line, and he created hundreds of songs, chamber music works, and symphonies. At 18, he set the words of German poet Goethe to music in *Margaret at the Spinning Wheel* and *The Elf King.* While his *Unfinished Symphony* remains best-known to many concert-goers, connoisseurs consider his greatest achievement in chamber music to be pieces like the *C Major Strings Quintet* (with 2 cellos) and the song cycles, performed at home soirees called *Schubertiades.* None of his music was ever performed in public in his lifetime.

THE 19TH CENTURY

After 1850, Vienna became the world's capital of light music, exporting it to every corner of the globe. The **waltz,** originally developed as a rustic Austrian country dance, was enthusiastically adopted by Viennese society.

Johann Strauss (1804–49), composer of more than 150 waltzes, and his talented and entrepreneurial son, **Johann Strauss Jr.** (1825–99), who developed the art form further, helped spread the stately and graceful rhythms of the waltz across

Europe. The younger Strauss also made popular the operetta, the genesis of the Broadway musical.

The tradition of Viennese light opera continued to thrive, thanks to the efforts of **Franz von Suppé** (1819–95) and Hungarian-born **Franz Lehár** (1870–1948). Lehár's witty and mildly scandalous *The Merry Widow* (1905) is the most popular light opera ever written.

Vienna did not lack for important serious music in the late-19th century. **Anton Bruckner** (1824–96) composed nine symphonies and a handful of powerful masses. **Hugo Wolf** (1860–1903), following in Schubert's footsteps, reinvented key elements of the German *lieder* with his five great song cycles. Most innovative of all was **Gustav Mahler** (1860–1911). A pupil of Bruckner, he expanded the size of the orchestra, often added a chorus or vocal soloists, and composed evocative music, much of it set to poetry.

THE NEW VIENNA SCHOOL

Mahler's musical heirs forever altered the world's concepts of harmony and tonality, and introduced what were then shocking concepts of rhythm. **Arnold Schoenberg** (1874–1951) expanded Mahler's style in such atonal works as *Das Buch der Hangenden Garten* (1908) and developed a 12-tone musical technique referred to as "dodecaphony" (*Suite for Piano*, 1924). Later, he pioneered "serial music," series of notes with no key center, shifting from one tonal group to another. **Anton von Webern** (1883–1945) and **Alban Berg** (1885–1935), composer of the brilliant but esoteric opera *Wozzeck,* were pupils of Schoenberg's. They adapted his system to their own musical personalities.

Finally, this discussion of Viennese music would not be complete without mention of the vast repertoire of folk and tavern songs (*Wienerlieder*), Christmas carols, and country dances that have inspired both professional musicians and ordinary folk for generations. The most famous Christmas carol in the world, "**Stille Nacht, Heilige Nacht**" ("Silent Night, Holy Night"), was composed and performed for the first time in Oberndorf, near Salzburg in 1818 and heard in Vienna for the first time that year.

EATING & DRINKING IN VIENNA

It's pointless to argue whether a Viennese dish is of Hungarian, Czech, Austrian, Slovenian, or even Serbian origin. All were part of the empire, and in Vienna all count as local cuisine. Our palates respond well to *Wienerküche* (Viennese cooking), a centuries-old blend of foreign recipes and homespun concoctions.

From Wiener Schnitzel to Sachertorte

Of course everyone knows Wiener schnitzel, the breaded veal cutlet that has achieved popularity worldwide. The most authentic local recipes call for the schnitzel to be lightly fried in lard, and when done properly it is light and tender. These days, though, you're likelier to find healthier versions, and pork used instead.

Another renowned meat dish is boiled beef, or *Tafelspitz,* said to reflect "the soul of the empire." This was Emperor Franz Joseph's preferred dish. For the best, try it at Hotel Sacher; if you're on a budget, then order *Tafelspitz* at a *Beisl*, a cousin of the French bistro.

Roast goose is served on festive occasions such as Christmas, but at any time of the year you can order *eine gute Fettgans* (a good fat goose). After such a rich dinner you might want to relax over some strong coffee, followed by schnapps.

For a taste of Hungary, order a goulash. Goulashes (stews of beef or pork with paprika) can be prepared in many different ways. The local version, *Wiener Gulasch*, is lighter on the paprika than most Hungarian versions. And don't forget *Gulyassuppe* (a Hungarian goulash soup), which can be a meal in itself.

Viennese pastry is probably the best in the world, both rich and varied. The familiar strudel comes in many forms; *Apfelstrudel* (apple) is the most popular, but you can also order cherry and other varieties. Viennese cakes defy description: look for *Gugelhupf, Wuchteln,* and *Mohnbeugerl*. Many tarts (*Torten*) are made with ground hazelnuts or almonds in place of flour. You can put whipped cream on everything. Don't miss *Rehruken*, a chocolate "saddle of venison" cake that's studded with almonds.

Even if you're not addicted to sweets, there's a gustatory experience you mustn't miss: the Viennese Sachertorte. Many gourmets claim to have the authentic, original recipe for this "king of tortes," a rich chocolate cake with a layer of apricot jam. Master pastry baker Franz Sacher created the Sachertorte for Prince von Metternich in 1832, and it is still available in the Hotel Sacher. Outstanding imitations can be found throughout Vienna.

Coffee

Although it might sound heretical, Turkey is credited with establishing the famous Viennese coffee house. Legend holds that Turks retreating from the siege of Vienna abandoned several sacks of coffee which, when brewed by the victorious Viennese, established the Austrian passion for coffee for all time. The first *Kaffeehaus* was established in Vienna in 1683.

In Vienna, *Jause* is a daily 4pm coffee-and-pastry ritual in the city's coffee houses. You can order your coffee a number of different ways—everything from the ubiquitous *Melange* (cappuccino), to *Verkehrt* (cafe latte), to *Mocca* (ebony black). Note that in Vienna, only strangers ask for *einen Kaffee* (a coffee). If you do, you'll be asked what kind. Your safest choice is a *grosser* (large) or *kleiner* (small) *Brauner* — coffee with milk. There's *Kaffee mit Schlagobers* (with whipped cream) for a sweet tooth. You can even order *eine doppelte Portion Schlagobers* (double whipped cream).

Beer, Wine, & Liqueurs

Vienna imposes few restrictions on the sale of alcohol, so you should be able to order beer or wine with your meal, even if it's 9am. Many Viennese have a first drink in the morning, preferring beer over coffee to get them going.

More than 99% of all **Austrian wine** is produced in vineyards in eastern Austria, principally Vienna, Lower Austria, Styria, and Burgenland. Traditionally, Austrian wines were served when new, and consumed where they're produced. This has changed in recent years, however, with some of the best widely available abroad. Following the 1985 revelation that some vintners had been adulterating their wine with diethylene glycol (antifreeze), the industry went through a wrenching overhaul of methods and standards, resulting in a rebirth, and Austrian wines now regularly win in blind competitions against leading wines world wide.

The most popular Austrian white wine varieties are the Grüner Veltliner and the Welchriesling, the best of which grow primarily in the Wachau region west of

THE legendary SACHERTORTE

In a city fabled for its desserts, the Sachertorte has emerged as the most famous. At a party thrown for Prince Klemens von Metternich in 1832, Franz Sacher first concocted and served the dessert. It was an instant success, and news of the torte spread throughout the Austro-Hungarian Empire. Back then, everyone wanted the recipe but it was a closely-guarded secret.

Like all celebrities, the Sachertorte has been the subject of a lawsuit. A 25-year legal battle over the exclusive right to the name "Original Sachertorte" was waged between the Hotel Sacher and the patisserie Demel. In 1965, an Austrian court ruled for the Hotel Sacher.

Even after endless samplings of the torte from both the Demel and the Hotel Sacher, though, only the most exacting connoisseur can tell the difference—if there is any. Here, with permission of the Hotel Sacher, is its recipe for Sachertorte:

Cake:
o ½ cup butter, softened
o ½ cup confectioners' sugar

o 1 tsp. vanilla
o 6 eggs (separated)
o 5 oz. dark chocolate (melted)
o ½ cup granulated sugar
o 1 cup flour
o Apricot jam (as desired)

Combine butter, confectioners' sugar, and vanilla, and mix well. Add egg yolks and beat. Mix in chocolate. Whip the egg whites until stiff, and add to the mixture along with the granulated sugar. Stir with a wooden spoon. Add flour, then place in a dish. Bake at 350°F (170°C) for 15 minutes with the oven door ajar, then for 1 hour more with the door shut. Turn out of the mold and allow to cool for 20 minutes. Coat with warm apricot jam.

Icing:
o ⅔ cup confectioners' sugar
o ½ cup water
o 6 oz. chocolate

Heat sugar and water for 5 to 6 minutes, add melted chocolate, and stir with a wooden spoon until the mixture is moderately thick. Layer the cake with the icing (¼ in.) and allow to cool.

Vienna. The leading reds, the Blauer Zweigelt and Blaufränkisch, come from Burgenland and Styria to the south. Most astonishing to a visitor, 700 of the country's 49,000 hectares of vineyards are within the city limits.

Austrian beers are relatively inexpensive and quite good, and they're sold throughout Vienna. Vienna is home to the excellent Schwechater as well as Ottakringer brewed locally in the 16th District and widely sold in Vienna's bars and taverns. Gösser, from Styria, is also popular and comes in both light and dark, as does the more robust Stiegl from Salzburg. And then there is Null Komma Josef, a local alcohol-free beer.

Two of the most famous **liqueurs** are any of a long list of different sorts of Schnapps, Obstbrand, or fruit brandies, primarily, apple, pear, or apricot. Slivovitz (a plum brandy that originated in Croatia) is also popular, as is the Slovak Borovicka.

The most festive drink is *Bowle* (pronounced *bole*), which is often served at parties, prepared by soaking berries and sliced peaches or apricots overnight in brandy, adding three bottles of dry white wine, and letting it stand for another 2 to 3 hours. Before serving, pour over a bottle of champagne. Prost!

The Heuriger

In 1784, Joseph II decreed that each vintner in the suburbs of Vienna could sell his own wine along with a cold menu right on his own premises without a restaurant license, launching a tradition that continues today. *Der heurige Wein* refers to the "new wine" or, more literally, "of this year."

The *Heuriger,* or wine taverns, lie on the outskirts of Vienna, mainly in Grinzing, Nussdorf, Neustift am Walde, and Stammersdorf. In summer, in fair weather, much of the drinking takes place in vine-covered gardens. In some, on a nippy night, you'll find a crackling fire in a flower-bordered ceramic stove. There's likely to be a gypsy violinist, an accordionist, or perhaps a zither player entertaining with Viennese songs. Most *Heuriger* are rustic, with wooden benches and tables, and it's perfectly acceptable to bring your own snacks. Today most serve warm buffets as well, of meats, cheeses, breads, and vegetables. Because many Viennese visiting the *Heuriger* outside the city didn't want to get too drunk, they started diluting the new wine with club soda or mineral water. Thus the *Spritzer* was born. The mix is best with a very dry white wine.

For more information, see Chapter 10.

PLANNING YOUR TRIP TO VIENNA

3

Vienna has so much to offer year round and much more than you could possibly cover in one visit. Many of the world famous events are seasonal activities and a public festival (stage, cinema, jazz, dance, etc.) takes place every month, so it pays to read up ahead of time. The Opera, Mozart, the Habsburgs, and the Prater alone could keep you busy for weeks, but Vienna has a lot more under the surface.

Over the last decade, Vienna, like much of Austria, has changed from somewhere heavy on tradition to a place with a cutting edge. While it still reverberates with the stately elegance of the Habsburg Dynasty, its imperial palaces and art collections mingle with very modern installations. Gourmets will find themselves overwhelmed by the quality and variety of good food. Take a look at some suggestions in Chapter 6.

Vienna has all the charm of any leading European city, coupled with much less grime and a laid-back attitude all its own. Even the rest of Austria and the German-speaking world see Vienna as very laissez faire. A few things do take getting used to however. For one, the waiters in coffee houses pride themselves on a distinct lack of interest. This is especially hard for Americans to get used to, but it grows on you and you can stay and sit as long as you want. The reason why the likes of Mozart, Haydn, Beethoven, Schubert, the Strauss family, Brahms, and Mahler wrote some of their best music here has, astonishingly, not changed. It is without question a romantic city. Plan for at least two to three days in Vienna— or longer to take in all the sights, with time just to walk, sample delectable pastries, and people-watch in a fantastic city at the crossroads of Europe.

TOURIST OFFICES   Before you book your tickets to go, we recommend you contact a local Austrian tourism office.

In the United States: Austrian National Tourist Office, P.O. Box 1142, New York, NY 10108-1142 (© **212/944-6880**).

In Canada: Austrian National Tourist Office, 2 Bloor Street E., Suite 3330, Toronto, ON M4W 1A8 (© **416/967-3381**).

In Great Britain: Austrian National Tourist Office, 14 Cork Street, W1X 1PF (© **0845/101-1818**).

WEBSITES   The impressive Austrian National Tourist Office website www. austria.info has the same address around the globe but with local information and language. The **Vienna Tourist Board** (www.vienna.info) is also very good (and you can also contact them on © **0810/101818**). On both websites you will find help with hotel bookings as well as deals on private home rentals, or rooms in farm houses for trips to the countryside.

When in Vienna and Austria, you'll see signs with a fat "i" symbol which means that a tourist office, or at least some tourist information, is nearby. You should be able to get maps of the area, help in finding a hotel, or getting tickets for events.

MAPS   When exploring Vienna you will do a lot of footwork, therefore you'll need a very good and detailed map. The city has some 2,400km (1,488 miles) of streets and alleys (many of them narrow) and many restaurants and hotels lie in these alleyways, so routine overview maps that are given away at hotels or the tourist office won't do. You'll need the best city map in Vienna. It's called *Streetwise Vienna* and it's laminated, pocket size, and contains an easy accordion fold. This map and the Freytag and Berndt Buchplan Wien map booklet are sold at all major newsstands in Vienna, at bookstores, and in many hotels. If you do get lost don't be afraid to ask. Most Viennese are glad to help.

WHEN TO GO

Vienna experiences its high season from April until October, with July and August being the less crowded times. Bookings around Christmas are also heavy because many Austrians visit during this festive time. Always arrive with reservations during these peak seasons. During the off-seasons, hotel rooms are plentiful and less expensive, and there's less demand for tables in the top restaurants.

Climate

Vienna has a moderate sub-alpine climate; the January average is 30°F (-1°C) and in July it's 68°F (20°C). Spring and fall are quite short in the surrounding mountain regions, but longer and milder in the city, where good weather generally lasts from Easter until mid-October. It is not usually humid as the city sits in the Danube Valley where a steady breeze keeps the heat bearable. Opera and stage seasons run from September until June, but in general Vienna is fun year-round and Christmas and summer are the most popular for visitors.

Average Daytime Temperature & Monthly Rainfall in Vienna

	JAN	FEB	MAR	APR	MAY	JUNE	JULY	AUG	SEPT	OCT	NOV	DEC
Temp. (°F)	30	32	38	50	58	64	68	70	60	50	41	33
Temp. (°C)	-1	0	3	10	14	18	20	21	16	10	5	1
Rainfall (in.)	1.2	1.9	3.9	1.3	2.9	1.9	.8	1.8	2.8	2.8	2.5	1.6

Calendar of Events

For an exhaustive list of events beyond those here, check http://events.frommers.com, where you'll find a searchable, up-to-the-minute roster of what's happening in cities all over the world, including Vienna.

JANUARY

New Year's Eve/New Year's Day. The famed concert of the Vienna Philharmonic Orchestra launches Vienna's biggest night. For tickets and information, contact the Wiener Philharmoniker, Bösendorferstrasse 12, A-1010 Vienna (© **01/505-6525;** www.wienerphilharmoniker.at). The **Imperial Ball** in the Hofburg follows the concert. For information and tickets, contact the Hofburg Kongresszentrum, Hofburg, Heldenplatz, A-1014 Vienna (© **01/587-3666;** www.hofburg.com). December 31/January 1.

FEBRUARY

Eistraum (Dream on Ice). During the coldest months of the Austrian winter, the monumental plaza between the Town Hall and the Burgtheater is flooded and frozen. Lights, loudspeakers, and a stage are hauled in, and the entire civic core is transformed into a gigantic ice-skating rink. Sedate waltz tunes accompany the skaters during the day, and DJs spin rock, funk, and reggae after the sun goes down. Around the rink, dozens of kiosks sell everything from hot chocolate and snacks to wine and beer. For information, call © **01/409-0040;** www.wienereistraum.com. Last week of January to mid-March.

Fasching. Shrove Tuesday marks the beginning of Lent and the Austrians celebrate *Fasching,* the famous Carnival day, (Mardi Gras). The date of the festivities and craziness is 6 weeks before Easter and therefore can also fall in March. If you are in Vienna during this time you'll have to partake of the delicious traditional jelly doughnut the *Krapfen.* The Viennese dress up and flock to parties all over town, before the beginning of Lent.

Opera Ball. Vienna's high society gathers at the Staatsoper for the grandest ball of the season, on the last Thursday before *Fasching* in either February or March. The evening opens with a performance by the Opera House Ballet. You don't need an invitation, but you do need a ticket, which, as you might guess, isn't cheap. For information, call the Opera House (© **01/514-44-2250;** www.staatsoper.at).

MARCH

Osterklang. At this Sound of Easter festival you can always count on music by the world's greatest composers, including Mozart and Brahms, and also lesser-known greats from the period (© **01/58885;** www.osterklang.at). Late March or early April.

MAY

International Music Festival. This traditional highlight of Vienna's concert calendar features top-class international orchestras, distinguished conductors, and classical greats. You can hear Beethoven's *Eroica* in its purest form, Mozart's *Jupiter Symphony,* and perhaps Bruckner's *Romantic.* The list of conductors and orchestras reads like a "who's who" of the international world of music. Konzerthaus, Lothringerstrasse 20, 1030 (© **01/242002;** www.konzerthaus.at). Early May until late June.

Vienna Festival (Wiener Festwochen). An exciting array of operas, operettas, musicals, drama, and dances, this festival presents new productions of classics alongside avant-garde premieres, all staged by leading international directors, along with celebrated productions from renowned European companies. Expect such productions as Mozart's *Così Fan Tutte,* Alban Berg's *Wozzek* or *Lulu* alongside ruthless avant-garde shows. For bookings, contact Wiener Festwochen, Lehárgasse 11, A-1060 Vienna (℡ **01/589-2222;** www.festwochen.at). Second week of May until mid-June.

JUNE

Vienna Jazz Festival. This is one of the world's top jazz events, based at various locations like the Staatsoper, the Konzerthaus, Jazzland, and Porgy & Bess. The line-up features more than 50 international and local stars. For information and bookings, contact the Verein Jazz Fest Wien, Lammgasse 12 (℡ **01/712-4224;** www.viennajazz.org). Late June to early July.

Donauinselfest. The largest free open-air music festival in Europe takes place on Vienna's Danube Island every year with around 3 million visitors. The festival is not as orderly as the rest of the city but if you're in Vienna it's definitely worth checking who's playing on more than 30 stages. (www.donauinselfest.at)

JULY–AUGUST

Music Film Festival. Opera, operetta, and masterly concert performances captured on celluloid play free under a starry sky in front of the neo-Gothic City Hall on the Ringstrasse. Selections focus on Franz Schubert, Gustav Mahler, or Johannes Brahms. You might view Rudolf Nureyev in *Swan Lake* or see Leonard Bernstein wielding the baton for Brahms. Vienna performances by names such as Stephane Grappelli or Oscar Peterson are also common. For more information, contact Ideenagentur Austria, Opernring 1R, A-1010 Vienna (℡ **01/4000-8100;** www.wien-event.at). Mid-July to mid-September.

Life Ball. Since 1993 the city of Vienna has hosted this colossal AIDS gala, the largest of its kind. The motto is "Fighting AIDS and celebrating Life." The dress code: no tie at all, since the guests are meant to look crazy and flamboyant. Amazing dancers, performers, and international celebrities flock to this celebration in Vienna's City Hall (℡ **01/595-5600,** www.Lifeball.org).

OCTOBER

Wien Modern. Celebrating its 24th year in 2011, the Wien Modern was founded by Italian conductor Claudio Abbado and is devoted to the performance of contemporary music. You might catch works from Iceland, Romania, or Portugal, in addition to Austria. Performances are at Verein Wien Modern, Lothringerstrasse 20; the booking address is Wiener Konzerthaus, Lothringerstrasse 20 (℡ **01/242-002;** www.konzerthaus.at). Late October until late November.

DECEMBER

Christmas Markets. Between late November and New Year, look for pockets of folk charm (and, in some cases, kitsch) associated with the Christmas holidays. The so-called *Weihnachtsmärkte* consist of small outdoor booths usually adorned with evergreen boughs, red ribbons, and, in some cases, religious symbols, which sprout up in clusters around the city. They sell old-fashioned toys, *Tannenbaum* (Christmas tree) decorations, and gift items. Food vendors offer sausages, cookies and pastries, candied fruit, roasted chestnuts, *Kartoffelpuffer* (charcoal-roasted potato slices), and, of course, hot mulled wine (*glühwein*). The greatest concentration of open-air markets is in front of the Rathaus, the famous ***Christkindlmarkt***. Other good ones are in the Spittelberg Quarter (7th District), at Freyung, the historic square in the northwest corner of the Inner City, or on the University campus grounds called *Altes AKH* (Old General Hospital).

ENTRY REQUIREMENTS

Passports

Citizens of the United States, Canada, the United Kingdom, Australia, Ireland, and New Zealand need only a valid passport to enter Austria. No visa is required.

Customs

Visitors who live outside Austria in general are not liable for duty on personal articles brought into the country temporarily for their own use, depending on the purpose and circumstances of each trip. Customs officials have great leeway. Travelers 17 years of age and older may carry up to 200 cigarettes, 50 cigars, or 250 grams of tobacco; 1 liter of distilled liquor and 2 liters of wine or 3 liters of beer duty-free. However, cash amounts above 10,000 € must be declared at customs.

U.S. CITIZENS   Returning U.S. citizens who have been away for 48 hours or more are allowed to bring back, once every 30 days, $800 worth of merchandise duty-free. You'll pay a flat rate of 10% duty on the next $1,000 worth of purchases. Be sure to have your receipts handy. On gifts, the duty-free limit is $200. For more specific guidance, write to the **Customs & Border Protection (CBP)** (*©* 877/287-8667; www.cbp.gov), and request the free pamphlet *Know Before You Go*. You can also download the pamphlet from the Internet at **www.cbp.gov**.

BRITISH CITIZENS   United Kingdom citizens can buy wine, spirits, or cigarettes in an ordinary shop in Austria and bring home almost as much as they like. But if you buy goods in a duty-free shop, the old rules still apply: the allowance is 200 cigarettes and 2 liters of table wine, plus 1 liter of spirits or 2 liters of fortified wine. If you're returning home from a non-European Union country, the same allowances apply, and you must declare any goods in excess of these allowances. British Customs tends to be strict and complicated. For details, get in touch with **H.M. Revenue Customs** (*©* 0845/010-9000; www.hmrc.gov.uk).

CANADIAN CITIZENS   For a clear summary of Canadian rules, write for the booklet *I Declare*, issued by **Canada Border Services Agency** (*©* 800/461-9999 in Canada, or 204/983-3500; www.cbsa-asfc.gc.ca). Canada allows its citizens a C$750 exemption, and you're allowed to bring back, duty-free, 200 cigarettes, 200 grams of tobacco, 1.5 liters of liquor, and 50 cigars. In addition, you may mail gifts to Canada from abroad at the rate of C$60 a day, provided they are unsolicited and aren't alcohol or tobacco (write on the package: "Unsolicited gift, under $60 value"). Before departure from Canada, declare all valuables on the Y-38 Form, including serial numbers of, for example, expensive foreign cameras that you already own. *Note:* The C$750 exemption can be used only once a year and only after an absence of 7 days.

AUSTRALIAN CITIZENS   The duty-free allowance in Australia is A$900 or, for those under 18, A$450. Personal property mailed back from Austria should be marked "Australian goods returned" to avoid duties. Upon returning to Australia, citizens can bring in 250 cigarettes or 250 grams of loose tobacco, and 2.25 liters of alcohol. If you're returning with valuable goods you already own, such as foreign-made cameras, you should file Form B263. A brochure, available from Australian consulates or Customs offices, is called *Know Before You Go*. For more information, contact **Australian Customs Services,** GPO Box 8, Sydney NSW 2001 (✆ **1300/363-263** in Australia; www.customs.gov.au).

NEW ZEALAND CITIZENS The duty-free allowance for New Zealand is NZ$700. Citizens over 17 can bring in 200 cigarettes, 50 cigars, or 250 grams of tobacco (or a mixture of all three if their combined weight doesn't exceed 250 grams), plus 4.5 liters of wine and beer or 1.125 liters of liquor. New Zealand currency does not carry import or export restrictions. Fill out a certificate of export, listing the valuables you are taking out of the country; that way, you can bring them back without paying duty. Most questions are answered in a free pamphlet available at New Zealand consulates and Customs offices, called *New Zealand Customs Guide for Travellers*, Notice No. 4. For more information, contact **New Zealand Customs Services** (✆ **0800/428-786** or 04/473-786; www.customs.govt.nz).

GETTING THERE & GETTING AROUND

Getting There

BY PLANE

As a gateway between Western and Eastern Europe, Vienna International Airport (VIE) has seen an increase in air traffic. Although a number of well-respected European airlines serve Vienna, many flights from America require a transfer in another European city, such as Paris, London, Zurich, or Frankfurt.

The Major Airlines

FROM THE UNITED STATES You can fly directly to Vienna on **Austrian Airlines** (✆ **800/843-0002** in the U.S. and Canada; www.austrianair.com), the national carrier of Austria. There's a non-stop service from New York (approximately 9 hrs.), Washington, and Toronto. Austrian's partner, United Airlines, also serves this route. (✆ **800/UNITED 1;** www.united.com).

British Airways (✆ **800/AIRWAYS** in the U.S. and Canada; www.britishairways.com) provides excellent service to Vienna. Passengers fly first to London—usually non-stop—from 23 gateways in the United States, 5 in Canada, 2 in Brazil, or from Bermuda, Mexico City, or Buenos Aires. From London, British Airways has 2 to 5 daily non-stop flights to Vienna from either Gatwick or Heathrow airport.

Flights on **Lufthansa** (✆ **800/645-3880** in the U.S. and Canada; www.lufthansa.com), the German national carrier, depart from North America frequently for Frankfurt and Düsseldorf, with connections to Vienna.

American Airlines (✆ **800/433-7300** in the U.S. and Canada; www.aa.com) funnels Vienna-bound passengers through Zurich or London.

FROM CANADA You can usually connect from your hometown to **British Airways** (✆ **800/AIRWAYS** in Canada; www.britishairways.com) gateways in Toronto, Montréal, and Vancouver. Non-stop flights from both Toronto's Pearson Airport and Montréal's Mirabelle Airport depart every day for London; flights from Vancouver depart for London 3 times a week. In London, you can stay for a few days (arranging discounted hotels through the British Airways tour desk) or head directly to Vienna on any of the 2 to 5 daily non-stop flights from either Heathrow or Gatwick.

| New Security Measures |

Check the **Transportation Security Administration** site, www.tsa.gov, for the latest information before you travel. At the time of writing, all liquids and gels including shampoo, toothpaste, perfume, hair gel, suntan lotion, and all other items with similar consistency **are limited to 100ml containers packed in a separate clear bag** within your carry-on baggage at the security checkpoint.

FROM LONDON There are frequent flights to Vienna, the majority of which depart from London's Heathrow Airport. Flight time is 2 hours and 20 minutes.

Austrian Airlines (℃ **0870/124-2625** from the U.K.; www.austrianair.com) has 2–5 daily non-stop flights into Vienna from Heathrow.

British Airways (℃ **0870/850-9850** in London; www.britishairways.com) has 2–5 daily flights from Heathrow, with easy connections through London from virtually every other part of Britain.

BMI (℃ **0844/8484 888**, www.flybmi.com), which can be a cheaper option, also flies daily from Heathrow. Budget online airline easyJet (www.easyjet.com) generally flies daily from Gatwick although services are more likely to seasonally change.

Getting into Town from the Airport

Vienna International Airport (**VIE**; ℃ **01/70070**; www.viennaairport.com) is 19km (12 miles) southeast of the city. The airport has connections with a number of Austrian cities via an excellent budget airline, Fly Niki, owned by Niki Lauda, the former Formula 1 driver.

The official **Vienna Tourist Information Office** in the arrival hall of the airport is open daily 7am to 10pm and there is free Wi-Fi throughout the airport.

There's a regular speed-train service (the City Airport Train or CAT) between the airport and the **Wien Mitte** station, next to the Vienna Hilton, where you can easily connect with subway and tramlines. Trains run every 30 minutes from 6:05am to 11:35pm. The trip takes 16 minutes and costs 9€ per person. There's also a bus service between the airport and other destinations: Schwedenplatz, Westbahnhof, the UN Complex, and Südtirolerplatz, leaving every 30 minutes to an hour. Fares are 6€.

The local train service, Schnellbahn (S-Bahn), runs from the airport to Wien Nord and Wien Mitte rail stations. Trains go every half hour from 5am to 11:40pm and leave from the station below the airport. Trip time is 25 to 30 minutes, and the fare is 3.60€. This ticket can also be used for further travel by public transportation within Vienna. In general ticket prices vary for children, students, and seniors.

Flying for Less: Tips for Getting the Best Airfare

Passengers sharing the same airplane cabin rarely pay the same fare. Those who need to buy tickets at the last minute, change their itinerary at a moment's notice, or fly one-way often get stuck paying the premium rate. Here are some ways to keep your airfare costs down.

o Passengers who can book their ticket **long in advance,** who can **stay over Saturday night,** or who **fly midweek** or **at less-busy hours** may pay a fraction of the full fare. If your schedule is flexible, say so and ask if you can secure a cheaper fare by changing your flight plans.

- You can also save on airfares by keeping an eye out in local newspapers for **promotional specials** or **fare wars,** when airlines lower prices on their most popular routes. You rarely see fare wars offered for peak travel times, but if you can travel in the off-months, you may get a bargain.

- Search **the Internet** for cheap fares. Besides the well-known www.expedia.com, there are also flight search engines like www.checkfelix.com, www.momondo.com and www.orbiz.com.

- **Consolidators,** also known as bucket shops, are great sources for international tickets, although they usually can't beat the Internet on fares within North America. Start by looking in Sunday newspaper travel sections; U.S. tourists should focus on the *New York Times, Los Angeles Times,* and *Miami Herald.* For less-developed destinations, small travel agents who cater to immigrant communities in large cities often have the best deals. *Beware:* Bucket shop tickets are usually non-refundable or rigged with stiff cancellation penalties, often as high as 50% to 75% of the ticket price, and some put you on charter airlines which may leave at inconvenient times and experience delays.

- Several reliable consolidators are worldwide and available online. **STA Travel** (℃ **800/781-4040;** www.statravel.com) has been the world's lead consolidator for students since purchasing Council Travel, but their fares are competitive for travelers of all ages. **Flights.com** (℃ **800/TRAV-800;** www.Flights.com) has excellent fares worldwide, particularly to Europe. They also have "local" websites in 12 countries. **FlyCheap** (℃ **800/FLY-CHEAP;** www.1800flycheap.com) has especially good fares to sunny destinations. **Air Tickets Direct** (℃ **888/858-8884;** www.airticketsdirect.com) is based in Montréal and is usually good for low fares.

- Join **frequent-flier clubs.** Accrue enough miles, and you'll be rewarded with free flights and elite status. It's free, and you'll get the best choice of seats, faster response to phone inquiries, and prompter service if your luggage is stolen, your flight is canceled or delayed, or you want to change your seat. You don't need to fly to build frequent-flier miles—**frequent-flier credit cards** can provide thousands of miles for doing your everyday shopping.

BY TRAIN

If you plan to travel a lot on the European or British rail systems on your way to or from Vienna, you'd do well to secure the latest copy of the *Thomas Cook European Timetable.* It's available exclusively online at **www.thomascooktimetables.com**.

Vienna has rail links to all the major cities of Europe. From Paris (Gare de l'Est) a train at around 8am gets in around 9pm; from Munich, a train at around 9am gets in around 2pm; from Zurich, a train at around 9pm gets in around 7am.

Rail travel in Austria is superb, with fast, clean trains taking you just about anywhere in the country and through some incredibly scenic regions.

Train passengers using the **tunnel** under the English Channel can go from London to Paris in just 3 hours on Eurostar, then on to Vienna (see above). The Eurotunnel Shuttle accommodates passenger cars, charter buses, taxis, and motorcycles and covers the 50km (31-mile) journey in just 35 minutes. This train runs from Folkestone, England, to Calais, France. Service is year-round, 24 hours a day.

Rail Passes for North American Visitors

EURAILPASS   If you plan to travel extensively in Europe, the **Eurail Global Pass** might be a good bet. It's valid for first-class rail travel in 20 European countries. With one ticket, you travel whenever and wherever you please; more than 100,000 rail miles are at your disposal. Here's how it works: the pass is sold only in North America. A Eurailpass good for 15 days costs $669, a pass for 21 days is $869, a 1-month pass costs $1,085, a 2-month pass is $1,529, and a 3-month pass goes for $1,889. Children under 4 travel free if they don't occupy a seat; all children under 12 who take up a seat are charged half-price. If you're under 26, you can buy a **Eurail Global Pass Youth,** which entitles you to unlimited second-class travel for 15 days ($435), 21 days ($565), 1 month ($705), 2 months ($995), or 3 months ($1,229). Those considering buying a 15-day or 1-month pass should estimate rail distance before deciding whether a pass is worthwhile. To take full advantage of the tickets for 15 days or a month, you'd have to spend a great deal of time on the train. Eurailpass holders are entitled to substantial discounts on certain buses and ferries. Travel agents in all towns and railway agents in such major cities as New York, Montréal, and Los Angeles sell all of these tickets. For information on Eurailpasses and other European train data, call **RailEurope** at ℰ **877/272-RAIL,** or visit it on the Web at **www.eurail.com.**

Eurail Global Pass Saver offers a 15% discount to each person in a group of three or more people who travel together between April and September, or two people who travel together between October and March. The price of a Saverpass, valid all over Europe for first class only, is $569 for 15 days, $739 for 21 days, $919 for 1 month, $1,299 for 2 months, and $1,609 for 3 months. Even more freedom is offered by the **Saver Flexipass,** which is similar to the Eurail Saverpass, except that you are not confined to consecutive-day travel. For travel over any 10 days within 2 months, the fare is $675; for any 15 days over 2 months, the fare is $889.

The **Eurail Select Pass** offers unlimited travel on the national rail networks of any 3, 4, or 5 bordering countries out of the 23 Eurail nations linked by train or ship. Two or more passengers can travel together for big discounts, getting 5, 6, 8, 10, or 15 days of rail travel within any 2-month period on the national rail networks of any 3, 4, or 5 adjoining Eurail countries linked by train or ship. A sample fare: for 5 days in 2 months you pay US$425 for 3 countries. **Eurail Select Pass Youth** for travelers under 26 allows second-class travel within the same guidelines as Eurail Select-pass, with fees starting at US$275. **Eurail Select Pass Saver** offers discounts for 2 or more people traveling together, first-class travel within the same guidelines as Eurail Selectpass, with fees starting at US$359.

Rail Passes for European Travelers

If you plan to do a lot of exploring, you might prefer one of the three rail passes designed for unlimited train travel within a designated region during a predetermined number of days. These passes are sold in most European countries and can be used only by European residents.

An **InterRail Global Pass** (www.interrail.net) allows unlimited travel through Europe, except Albania.

Adults purchasing an InterRail Global Pass can travel first or second class. First class prices are 374€ for 5 days in 10 days; 539€ for 10 days in 22 days; 704€ for 22 days continuous, or 899€ for 1 month. In second class, the cost is 249€ for 5 days in 10 days; 359€ for 10 days in 22 days; 469€ for 22 days continuous; and 599€ for 1 month continuous.

An **InterRail Global Youth Pass** is also sold and is available only in second class. A youth is defined as those from age 12 up to and including 25. The cost is

159€ for 5 days in 10 days; 239€ for 10 days in 22 days; 309€ for 22 days continuous, and $399 for 1 month continuous.

For information on buying individual rail tickets or any of the just-mentioned passes, contact any larger train station in Europe or simply the Austria ÖBB. Tickets and passes are also available at any of the larger railway stations as well as selected travel agencies throughout Europe.

BY CAR

If you're already on the Continent, you might want to drive to Vienna. That is especially true if you're in a nearby country, such as Italy or Germany; however, arrangements should be made in advance with your car rental company.

The Eurotunnel running under the English Channel means you can get your car between England and France in 35 minutes. Passengers drive their cars aboard the train, *the Eurotunnel Shuttle,* at Folkestone in England, and vehicles are transported to Calais, France. Your continuing journey to Vienna can also be partly covered by train. Prices are reasonable (but vary) and the system is easy to use.

Vienna can be reached from all directions on major highways called *autobahnen* or by secondary highways. The main artery from the west is Autobahn A-1, coming in from Munich (466km/291 miles), Salzburg (334km/207 miles), and Linz (186km/115 miles). Autobahn A-2 runs from the south from Graz and Klagenfurt (both in Austria). Autobahn A-4 comes in from the east, connecting with route E-58, which runs to Bratislava and Prague. Autobahn A-22 takes traffic from the northwest, and Route E-10 brings you to the cities and towns of southeastern Austria and Hungary.

Unless otherwise marked, the speed limit on *autobahnen* is 130km/h (81 mph); however, when estimating driving times, figure on 80 to 100km/h (50–62 mph) because of traffic, weather, and road conditions.

When you arrive in Vienna, park your car or find a garage, because in Vienna driving and parking is no fun at all. (See "Getting around By Car" and "Parking" below.)

BY BUS

Because of the excellence of rail service funneling from all parts of the Continent into Vienna, bus transit is limited and not especially popular. **Eurolines,** part of National Express Coach Lines (✆ **0871/781-8181;** www.nationalexpress.com), operates two express buses per week between London's Victoria Coach Station and Vienna. The trip takes about 29 hours and makes 45-minute rest stops en route about every 4 hours. Buses depart from London at 8:15am every Friday and Sunday, traverse the Channel between Dover and Calais, and are equipped with reclining seats, toilets, and reading lights. The one-way fare is 52€ to 72€; a round-trip ticket costs 80€ to 104€. You won't need to declare your intended date of return until you actually use your ticket (although advance reservations are advisable), and the return half of your ticket will be valid for 6 months. The return to London departs from Vienna every Sunday and Friday at 7:45pm, arriving at Victoria Coach Station about 29 hours later.

BY BOAT

To arrive in Vienna with flair befitting the city's historical opulence, take advantage of the many cruise lines that navigate the Danube. One of the most accessible carriers is **DDSG The *Donaudampfschifffartsgesellschaft,*** one of the longest words in the German language, **or Blue Danube Shipping Company,** Donaureisen, Fredrick Strasse 7, Vienna (✆ **01/588-80;** fax 01/5888-0440; www.ddsg-blue-danube.at).

They offer mostly 1-day trips to Vienna from as far away as Passau, Germany. It also serves Vienna from Bratislava, Budapest, and beyond, depending on the season and itinerary. Extended trips can be arranged, and cruises are priced to meet every budget. See "Cruising the Danube" in Chapter 6.

Getting Around
BY PUBLIC TRANSPORTATION

Whether you want to visit the Inner City's historic buildings or the outlying Vienna Woods, the *Wiener Linien* (Vienna Transit Authority) can take you there. This vast network of U-Bahns (subway), streetcars, and buses is safe, clean, and easy to use. Pick up a map that outlines their routes and those of the local trains (Schnellbahn, or S-Bahn). For information on tickets and passes or for directions visit one of the five **Vienna Public Transport Information Centers (Informationdienst der Wiener Verkehrsbetriebe)** at Opernpassage (an underground passageway next to the Wiener Staatsoper), Karlsplatz, Stephansplatz (near Vienna's cathedral), Westbahnhof, and Praterstern. These offices are open Monday to Friday 6:30am to 6:30pm. For information about any of these outlets, call ✆ **01/790-9100.**

Vienna maintains a uniform fare that applies to all forms of public transport. A ticket for the bus, subway, or tram costs 1.80€ if you buy it in advance at one of the automated machines in U-Bahn stations, or at a *Tabac-Trafik* (a store or kiosk selling tobacco products and newspapers) or 2.20€ if you buy it onboard. Smart Viennese buy their tickets in advance, usually in blocks of at least five at a time, from any of the city's thousands of *Tabac-Trafiken* or at any vending machine. No matter what vehicle you decide to ride within Vienna, remember that once a ticket has been stamped (validated) by either a machine or a railway attendant, it's valid for one trip in one direction, anywhere in the city, including transfers. For other options see the "Transportation for Less" box below.

By U-Bahn (Subway)

The U-Bahn is a fast way to get across town or reach the suburbs. It consists of five lines labeled **U1, U2, U3, U4,** and **U6** (there is no U5). Karlsplatz, in the heart of the Inner City, is the most important underground station for visitors: the U4, U2, and U1 converge there. The U2 traces part of the Ring and then continues across the Danube, the U4 goes to Schönbrunn, and the U1 can take you from Stephansplatz to the Prater. The U3 also stops in Stephansplatz and connects to Westbahnhof. During the week the underground runs from 5am to shortly after midnight and on Friday and Saturday it runs all day and night.

By Tram (Streetcar)

Riding the trams (*Strassenbahnen*) is not only a practical way to get around but also a great way to see the city. Tram stops are well marked. Each line bears a number or letter. Lines include the 18 (Südbahnhof to Westbahnhof), D (from Nussdorf hedging around part of the Ring before veering off to Südbahnhof), and 1 and 2 (each do a half circle of the Ring and continue into outer districts: 1 to the west, 2 to the east). The 1 takes you past the University and Rathaus on the north side of the Ring and the 2 takes you past the Stadtpark. Both leave the Ring at the opera and at Schwedenplatz. There is also a yellow Ring Tram that circles the Ring and costs 6€ for adults and 4€ for children. The 38 tram also takes you from Schottentor to the vineyards in Grinzing.

TRANSPORTATION for LESS

The **Vienna Card** is the best ticket when using public transportation within the city limits. It's extremely flexible and functional for tourists because it allows unlimited travel, plus various discounts at city museums, restaurants, and shops. You can buy a Vienna Card for 18.50€ at tourist information or public transport offices, and some hotels, or order one over the phone with a credit card (✆ **01/7984400148**).

You can also buy tickets that will save you money if you plan to ride a lot on the city's transport system. A ticket valid for unlimited rides during any 24-hour period costs 5.70€; an equivalent ticket valid for any 72-hour period goes for 13.60€.

These tickets are also available at *Tabac-Trafiken,* vending machines in underground stations, the airport's arrival hall (next to baggage claim), the *Reichsbrücke* (DDSG landing pier), and the *Österreichisches Verkehrsbüro* (travel agencies) of the two main train stations.

By Bus

Buses with hybrid engines traverse Vienna in all directions, operating daily, including at night. Night buses leave every 10 to 30 minutes from Schwedenplatz, fanning out across the city. It's usually not necessary to change lines more than once. Normal tickets are valid aboard these late night buses (no extra charge). On buses you can buy tickets from the driver.

BY TAXI

Taxis are easy to find within the city, but be warned that fares can quickly add up. Taxi stands are marked by signs, or you can call ✆ **01/31300,** 01/60160, 01/713-7196, or 01/40100. The basic fare is 2.50€, plus 1.20€ per kilometer. There are extra charges of 1€ for luggage. For night rides after 11pm, and for trips on Sunday and holidays, there is a surcharge of 2.50€. There is an additional charge of 2€ if ordered by phone. The fare for trips to or from the airport is 33 € to or from anywhere in Vienna. Otherwise the fare for trips outside the city should be agreed upon with the driver in advance, and a 10% tip is the norm.

BY BICYCLE

Vienna has more than 1,000km (620 miles) of marked bicycle paths within the city limits. In the summer, many Viennese leave their cars in the garage and ride bikes. You can take bicycles on specially marked U-Bahn cars for free, but only from Monday to Friday, 9am to 3pm and 6:30pm to midnight, during which time you'll pay half the full-ticket price to transport a bike. At weekends in July and August, bicycles are carried free from 9am to midnight.

There is a virtually free way to wheel it in Vienna, which is to use a **Citybike** (www.citybikewien.at). The kiosks are all over the city and the bikes can be rented with a Visa or Maestro card from which 1 euro is taken. After registering you can ride your city bike for free for the first hour of every rental and then simply return it to any other kiosk. The second hour costs 1€, the 3rd 2€, and every further hour 4€. For a more comfortable or high-tech bike try rental stores around the Prater (see Chapter 6) and along the banks of the Danube Canal, which is the much-loved bike route for most Viennese. One of the best of the many places for bike rentals is **Pedal Power,** Ausstellungsstrasse 3 (℡ **01/729-7234;** www.pedalpower.at), which is open from March to October from 8am to 7pm. The Vienna Tourist Board can also supply a list of rental shops and more information about bike paths. Bike rentals begin at about 27€ ($43) per day.

BY CAR

When in Austria use a car only for excursions outside Vienna's city limits; don't try to drive around the city. Parking is a problem; the city is a maze of one-way streets; and the public transportation is too good to endure the hassle of driving.

If you do venture out by car, information on road conditions is available in English (and French) on the radio station FM4 (103.8) and also 7 days a week from 6am to 8pm from the **Österreichischer Automobil-, Motorrad- und Touringclub (ÖAMTC),** Schubertring 1–3, A-1010 Vienna (℡ **01/711-990**). This auto club also maintains a 24-hour emergency road service number (℡ **120** or 0810/120-120).

CAR RENTALS   It's best to reserve rental cars in advance, but you can rent a car once you're in Vienna. You'll need a passport and a driver's license that's at least 1 year old. Some minimum age restrictions may apply, so ask about these if you are under age 25. Avoid renting a car at the airport, where there's an extra 6% tax in addition to the 21% value-added tax on all rentals. Major car-rental companies include **Avis,** Laaer Berg Strasse 43 (℡ **01/587-62-41**); **Budget Rent-a-Car,** Laaer Berg Strasse 43 (℡ **01/ 601870**); and **Hertz,** Kärntner Ring 17 (℡ **01/5128677**).

PARKING   Curbside parking in Vienna's 1st District, site of most of the city's major monuments, is virtually non-existent. When curbside parking is available at all, it's within one of the city's "blue zones" and is usually restricted to 90 minutes or less from 8am to 6pm. If you find an available spot within a blue zone, you'll need to display a *Parkschein* (parking voucher) on the dashboard of your car. Valid for only 30, 60, or 90 minutes, they're sold at branch offices of Vienna Public Transport Information Center (see above) and, more conveniently, within *Tabac-Trafiken.* You'll have to fill in the date and the time of your arrival before displaying the voucher on the right side of your car's dashboard. Be warned that towing of illegally parked cars is not an uncommon sight here. Frankly, it's much easier to simply pay the price that's charged by any of the city's dozens of underground parking garages and avoid the stress of looking for one of the few curbside parking spots.

Underground **parking garages** are widely available throughout the city, and most of them charge between 3.60€ and 6€ per hour. Every hotel in Vienna is acutely aware of the location of the nearest parking garage so if you're confused, ask. Some convenient 24-hour garages within the 1st District include **Garage Am Hof** (℡ **01/533-5571;** www.garageamhof.at); **Parkgarage Freyung,** Freyung (℡ **01/535-0450**); and **Tiefgarage Kärntnerstrasse,** Mahlerstrasse 8 (℡ **01/512-5206**).

DRIVING & TRAFFIC REGULATIONS   In general, Austria's traffic regulations do not differ much from those of other countries where you *drive on the right.* In Vienna, the speed limit is 50km/h (31 mph). Out of town, in areas like the Wienerwald, the limit is 130km/h (81 mph) on motorways and 100km/h (62 mph) on all other roads. Honking car horns is forbidden everywhere in the city.

MONEY & COSTS

Foreign currency and euros can be brought in and out of Vienna as long as it's less than 10,000€. Although there are many ways to change currency, it can be simplest and cheapest to get euros from an ATM using your debit or credit card from home.

Currency

The **euro,** the single European currency, is the official currency of Austria and 15 other participating countries. The symbol of the euro is a stylized E: €. Exchange rates of participating countries are locked into a common currency. For more details on the euro, check out **www.europa.eu.int**.

The relative value of the euro fluctuates against the world's other currencies, therefore its value might not be the same by the time you travel to Vienna. We advise a last-minute check before your trip.

THE EURO, THE U.S. & CANADIAN DOLLAR, & THE BRITISH POUND

The U.S. Dollar and the Euro: At the time of writing, US$1 was worth approximately .764 eurocents. Inversely stated, 1€ was worth approximately US$1.35.

The British Pound, the U.S. Dollar, and the Euro: At press time, £1 was approximately US$1.56, and approximately 1.19€.

The Canadian Dollar, the U.S. Dollar, and the Euro: At press time, C$1 was approximately US$1 and approximately .714€.

The chart below reflects the figures in the paragraphs above, but because international currency ratios can and almost certainly will change prior to your arrival in Europe, you should confirm up-to-date currency rates before you go.

Euro	US$	Can$	UK£	Aus$	NZ$
1	1.35	1.38	0.85	1.40	1.80
2	2.60	2.75	1.70	2.80	3.60
3	4.00	4.10	2.60	4.20	5.50
4	5.40	5.50	3.40	5.60	7.30
5	6.70	6.90	4.30	7.00	9.20
6	8.00	8.30	5.10	8.40	11.00
7	9.40	9.70	6.00	9.80	12.85
8	10.70	11.00	6.80	11.20	14.70
9	12.00	12.40	7.70	12.60	16.50
10	13.00	14.00	9.00	14.00	18.00
15	20.00	21.00	13.00	21.00	28.00
20	27.00	28.00	17.00	28.00	37.00
25	34.00	35.00	21.00	35.00	46.00
50	67.00	69.00	43.00	70.00	92.00

Exchange rates are generally better at the point of arrival than at the departure point. Nevertheless, it's often helpful to exchange at least some money before going abroad (standing in line at the exchange bureau in Vienna airport isn't fun after a long overseas flight). Check with any of your local American Express or Thomas Cook offices or major banks. Or order in advance from **American Express** (✆ **800/221-7282,** cardholders only; www.americanexpress.com) or **Thomas Cook** (✆ **800/223-7373;** www.thomascook.com).

It's best to exchange currency or traveler's checks at a bank, not at a currency service, hotel, or shop. Currency and traveler's checks (for which you'll receive a better rate than cash) can be changed at all principal airports and at some travel agencies, such as American Express and Thomas Cook.

ATMs

ATMs are prevalent in all Austrian cities and even smaller towns. ATMs are linked to a national network that most likely includes your bank at home. Though there will be small fees for extracting money in a foreign country the fees will not be as high as when changing cash anywhere but an Austrian bank. Both the **Cirrus** (✆ **800/424-7787;** www.mastercard.com) and the **PLUS** (✆ **800/843-7587;** www.visa.com) networks have automated ATM locators listing the banks in Austria that will accept your card. Or, just search out any machine with your network's symbol emblazoned on it.

Traveler's Checks

You can buy traveler's checks at most banks. They are offered in denominations of $20, $50, $100, $500, and sometimes $1,000. Generally, you'll pay a service charge ranging from 1% to 4%.

The most popular traveler's checks are offered by **American Express** (✆ **800/528-4800** or **800/221-7282** for cardholders. This number accepts collect calls, offers service in several foreign languages, and exempts Amex gold and platinum cardholders from the 1% fee). **Visa** (✆ **800/732-1322**): AAA members can obtain Visa checks for a $9.95 fee (for checks up to $1,500) at most AAA offices or by calling ✆ **866/339-3378;** and **MasterCard** (✆ **800/223-9920**): Thomas Cook issues MasterCard checks in the UK ✆ **0800/622101,** or in the US call citicorp ✆ **1 800 223 7373.**

American Express, Thomas Cook, Visa, and **MasterCard** offer **foreign currency traveler's checks,** which are useful if you're traveling to one country, or to the euro zone; they're accepted at locations where dollar checks may not be.

If you carry traveler's checks, keep a record of their serial numbers separate from your checks in the event that they are stolen or lost. You'll get a refund faster if you know the numbers.

Credit Cards

Credit cards are invaluable when on your travels. They're a safe way to carry money and a convenient record of all your expenses. You can also withdraw cash advances from your cards at any bank (although this should be reserved for dire emergencies only, because you'll start paying hefty interest the moment you receive the cash).

Note, however, that many banks, including Chase and Citibank, charge a 2% to 3% service fee for transactions in a foreign currency.

WHAT THINGS COST IN VIENNA	EURO€	US$/C$	UK£
Bus from the airport to the city	6.00	7.85	5.00
U-Bahn (subway) from St. Stephan's to Schönbrunn Palace	1.80	2.35	1.50
Double room at das Triest (expensive)	289.00	377.80	241.45
Double room at the Am Parkring (moderate)	133.00	174.00	111.00
Double room at the Pension Dr. Geissler (inexpensive)	65.00	104.00	52.00
Lunch for one, without wine, at König von Ungarn (expensive)	40.00	52.00	33.50
Lunch for one, without wine, at Griechenbeisl (moderate)	30.00	39.20	25.00
Dinner for one, without wine, at Plachutta (expensive)	40.00	52.00	33.50
Dinner for one, without wine, at Firenze Enoteca (moderate)	28.00	36.60	23.40
Dinner for one, without wine, at Café Leopold (inexpensive)	12.00	15.60	10.00
Glass of wine	2.50	3.25	2.00
Half-liter of beer in a *beisl*	3.50	7.00	3.50
Coca-Cola in cafe	3.00	3.90	2.50
Cup of coffee (*ein kleiner Brauner*)	3.00	3.90	2.50
Movie ticket	10.00	13.00	8.30
Admission to Schönbrunn Palace	12.90	17.00	10.80

STAYING HEALTHY

You'll encounter few health problems while in Austria. The tap water is not only safe to drink, but tastes fine, the milk is pasteurized, and health services are good.

There's no need to get any shots before visiting Austria, but you might pack some anti-diarrhea medications. It's not that the food or water in Austria is unhealthy; it's just that it's different and might at first cause digestive problems for those unfamiliar with it.

It's easy to get over-the-counter medicine. Fortunately, generic equivalents of common prescription drugs are available at most destinations in which you'll be traveling. It's also easy to find English-speaking doctors and to get prescriptions filled at all cities, towns, and resorts. You might experience some inconvenience, of course, if you travel in the remote hinterlands.

What to Do If You Get Sick Away from Home

Nearly all doctors in Vienna speak English. If you get sick, consider asking your hotel concierge to recommend a local doctor, even his or her own. You can also try the emergency room at a local hospital. Many hospitals also have walk-in clinics for

The following government websites offer up-to-date health-related travel advice.
  ○ **Australia:** www.dfat.gov/au/travel/
  ○ **Canada:** www.hc-sc.gc.ca/index_e.html

  ○ **U.K.:** www.dh.gov/uk/PolicyAnd Guidance/HealthAdviceForTravellers/ fs/en
  ○ **U.S.:** www.cdc.gov/travel/

emergency cases that are not life-threatening; you may not get immediate attention, but you won't pay the high price of an emergency room visit. We list hospitals and emergency numbers for Vienna under "Fast Facts" in Chapter 12.

If you worry about getting sick away from home, consider purchasing **medical travel insurance** and carry your ID card in your purse or wallet. In most cases, your existing health plan will provide the coverage you need. See the section on insurance, under "Fast Facts" in chapter 12, for more information.

If you suffer from a chronic illness, consult your doctor before you depart. For conditions such as epilepsy, diabetes, or heart problems, wear a **Medic Alert Identification Tag** (© 888/633-4298; www.medicalert.org), which will immediately alert doctors to your condition and give them access to your records through Medic Alert's 24-hour hot line.

Pack **prescription medications** in your carry-on luggage and carry prescription medications in their original containers with pharmacy labels, otherwise they won't make it through airport security. Also, bring along copies of your prescriptions in case you lose your pills or run out. Don't forget an extra pair of contact lenses or prescription glasses. Carry the generic name of prescription medicines, in case a local pharmacist is unfamiliar with the brand name.

Contact the **International Association for Medical Assistance to Travelers** (**IAMAT;** © 716/754-4883 or 416/652-0137; www.iamat.org) for tips on travel and health concerns in the countries you're visiting and lists of local, English-speaking doctors. The U.S. **Centers for Disease Control and Prevention** (© 800/311-3435 or 404/498-1515; www.cdc.gov) provides up-to-date information on necessary vaccines and health hazards by region or country. In Canada, contact **Health Canada** (© 613/957-2991; www.hc-sc.gc.ca). The website **www.tripprep.com**, sponsored by a consortium of travel medicine practitioners, may also offer helpful advice on traveling abroad. You can find listings of reliable clinics overseas at the **International Society of Travel Medicine** (www.istm.org). Any foreign consulate can provide a list of area doctors who speak English.

U.K. nationals will need a **European Health Insurance Card** (**EHIC;** © 0845/606-2030; www.ehic.org.uk) to receive free or reduced-costs health benefits during a visit to a European Economic Area (EEA) country (European Union countries plus Iceland, Liechtenstein, and Norway) or Switzerland.

We list **hospitals** and **emergency numbers** under "Fast Facts: Vienna," p. 238.

CRIME & SAFETY

Austria has a low crime rate, and violent crime is rare. However, visitors can become targets of pickpockets and purse-snatchers who operate where tourists tend to gather. Some of the most frequently reported spots include Vienna's Westbahnhof and Südbahnhof, the plaza around St. Stephan's Cathedral, and the nearby pedestrian shopping areas (in Vienna's 1st District). Just pay attention, keep your bag zipped or closed and the thieves won't have much of a chance.

Mostly, however, Vienna is a very safe city and even at night there is little to worry about in the middle of town, or where most of tourist life takes place.

If your passport is lost or stolen, report it immediately to the local police and the nearest embassy or consulate. The same is true when you have been a victim of crime oversees. The embassy/consulate staff, for example, can assist you in finding appropriate medical care, contacting family members or friends, and explaining how funds could be transferred. Although the investigation and prosecution of the crime is solely the responsibility of local authorities, consular officers can help you understand the local criminal justice process and find an attorney, if needed.

SPECIALIZED TRAVEL RESOURCES
Travelers with Disabilities

Laws in Austria compel rail stations, airports, hotels, and most restaurants to follow strict regulations about **wheelchair accessibility** for restrooms, ticket counters, and the like. Museums and other attractions conform to the regulations, however, old buildings with historic preservation laws may not be equipped. Call ahead to check on accessibility in hotels, restaurants, and sights you want to visit.

Organizations that offer assistance to travelers with disabilities include **MossRehab** (℃ 800/CALL-MOSS; www.mossresourcenet.org), which provides a library of accessible-travel resources online; **SATH** (**Society for Accessible Travel and Hospitality; ℃ 212/447-7284;** www.sath.org), which offers a wealth of travel resources for all types of disabilities and informed recommendations on destinations, access guides, travel agents, tour operators, vehicle rentals, and companion services; and the **American Foundation for the Blind** (AFB; ℃ 800/232-5463 or 212/502-7600; www.afb.org), a referral resource for the blind or visually impaired that provides information on traveling with Seeing Eye dogs.

AirAmbulanceCard.com (℃ 877/424-7633) is now partnered with SATH and allows you to preselect top-notch hospitals in case of an emergency.

Access-Able Travel Source (℃ 303/232-2979; www.access-able.com) offers a comprehensive database on travel agents from around the world with experience in accessible travel; destination-specific access information; and links to such resources as service animals, equipment rentals, and access guides.

Many travel agencies offer customized tours and itineraries for those with disabilities. Among them are **Flying Wheels Travel** (℃ 507/451-5005; www.flying wheelstravel.com) and **Accessible Journeys** (℃ 800/846-4537 or 610/521-0339; www.disabilitytravel.com).

Flying with Disability (www.flying-with-disability.org) is a comprehensive information source on airplane travel.

Also check out the quarterly magazine *Emerging Horizons* (www.emerging horizons.com), available by subscription (US$17 year in the U.S.; US$22 outside the U.S.).

The "Accessible Travel" link at **Mobility-Advisor.com** (www.mobility-advisor. com) offers a variety of travel resources to persons with disabilities.

British visitors should contact **Holiday Care** (© 0845-124-9971 in the U.K. only; www.holidaycare.org.uk) to access a wide range of travel information and resources for disabled and elderly people.

For more on organizations that offer resources to travelers with disabilities, go to frommers.com.

Gay & Lesbian Travelers

Vienna has a slogan *"Wien ist Anders"* (Vienna is different) and in recent years this has become more and more true. The gay scene is constantly growing in the form of bars, clubs, and restaurants.

For information about gay-related activities in Vienna, go to **Rainbow Online** (www.gay.or.at).

Most of the famous gay bars are in the 6th District close to the MuseumsQuartier and Karlsplatz. For more information see Gay and Lesbian Bars in Chapter 10.

In Austria, the minimum age for consensual homosexual activity is 18.

The International Gay and Lesbian Travel Association (**IGLTA;** © 800/448-8550 or 954/776-2626; www.iglta.org) is the trade association for the gay and lesbian travel industry, and offers a directory of gay and lesbian-friendly travel businesses; go to its website and click on Members.

In Canada, contact **Travel Gay Canada** (© 416/761-5151; www.travelgay canada.com).

Many agencies offer tours and travel itineraries specifically for gay and lesbian travelers, such as **Above and Beyond Tours** (© 800/397-2681; www.above beyondtours.com). **Now, Voyager** (© 800/255-6951; www.nowvoyager.com) is a well-known San Francisco-based gay travel service. **Olivia Cruises & Resorts** (© 800/631-6277; www.olivia.com) charters entire resorts and ships for exclusive lesbian vacations and offers smaller group experiences for both gay and lesbian travelers. **Gay.com Travel** (© 800/929-2268 or 415/834-6500; www.gay.com/ travel or www.outandabout.com) is an excellent online successor to the popular *Out & About* print magazine. It provides regularly updated information about gay-owned, gay-oriented, and gay-friendly lodging, dining, sightseeing, nightlife, and shopping establishments in every important destination worldwide. It also offers trip-planning information for gay and lesbian travelers for more than 50 destinations, along various themes, ranging from Sex & Travel to Vacations for Couples.

The following travel guides are available at many bookstores, or you can order them from any online bookseller: *Spartacus International Gay Guide* (Bruno Gmünder Verlag; www.spartacusworld.com/gayguide) and *Odysseus: The International Gay Travel Planner* (www.odyusa.com), both good, annual, English-language guidebooks focused on gay men; and the *Damron* guides (www.damron. com), with separate, annual books for gay men and lesbians. For more gay and lesbian travel resources, visit frommers.com.

Senior Travel

Many Austrian hotels offer discounts for seniors. Mention the fact that you're a senior citizen when you make your travel reservations.

Members of **AARP**, 601 E St. NW, Washington, DC 20049 (© 888/687-2277; www.aarp.org), get discounts on hotels, airfares, and car rentals. AARP offers members a wide range of benefits, including *AARP: The Magazine* and a monthly newsletter. Anyone over 50 can join.

Many reliable agencies and groups target the 50-plus market. **Elderhostel** (*©* **800/454-5768;** www.elderhostel.org) arranges study programs for those aged 55 and over (and a spouse or companion of any age) in the U.S. and in more than 80 countries around the world, including Austria. Most courses last 2 to 4 weeks abroad, and many include airfare, beds in university dormitories or modest inns, meals, and tuition.

Recommended publications offering travel resources and discounts for seniors include: the quarterly magazine *Travel 50 & Beyond* (www.travel50andbeyond. com); *Travel Unlimited: Uncommon Adventures for the Mature Traveler* (Avalon); and *Unbelievably Good Deals and Great Adventures That You Absolutely Can't Get Unless You're Over 50* (McGraw-Hill), by Joann Rattner Heilman.

Frommers.com offers more information and resources on travel for seniors.

Family Travel

If you have enough trouble getting your kids out of the house in the morning, dragging them thousands of miles away may seem like an insurmountable challenge. But family travel can be immensely rewarding, and Vienna is a great place to take your kids. The pleasures available for children (which most adults enjoy just as much) range from watching the magnificent Lipizzaner stallions at the Spanish Riding School to exploring the city's many castles and dungeons.

Another outstanding attraction is the Prater amusement park, with its giant ferris wheel, roller coasters, merry-go-rounds, arcades, and Lilliputbahn (tiny railroad). Even if your children aren't very interested in touring palaces, take them to Schönbrunn where the zoo and coach collection will thrill, and the museum made especially for children will introduce them to imperial history in a child-friendly manner. In summer, beaches along the Alte Donau (the Old Danube) are suitable for swimming. Try the *Gänsehäufel* for grassy beaches, pools, and beachside sports. And don't forget the lure of the *Konditorei*, little bakeries that sell scrumptious Viennese cakes and pastries.

Babysitting services are available through most hotel desks or by applying at the tourist information office in the town where you're staying. Many hotels have children's game rooms and playgrounds.

Throughout this guide, look for the Kids icon, which highlights child-friendly destinations.

Recommended family travel Internet sites include **Family Travel Forum** (www. familytravelforum.com), a comprehensive site that offers customized trip planning; **Family Travel Network** (www.familytravelnetwork.com), an award-winning site that offers travel features, deals, and tips; **Traveling Internationally with Your Kids** (www.travelwithyourkids.com), a comprehensive site offering sound advice for long-distance and international travel with children; and **Family Travel Files** (www.thefamilytravelfiles.com), which offers an online magazine and a directory of off-the-beaten-path tours and tour operators for families.

For a list of more family-friendly travel resources, turn to the experts at frommers.com.

Student Travel

If you're planning to travel outside the U.S., you'd be wise to arm yourself with an **International Student Identity Card (ISIC),** which offers substantial savings on rail passes, plane tickets, and entrance fees. It also provides you with basic health and life insurance and a 24-hour help line. The card is available for $22 from **STA Travel** (© **800/781-4040** in North America; www.sta.com; www.statravel.co.uk in the U.K.), the biggest student travel agency in the world. If you're no longer a student but are still under 26, you can get an **International Youth Travel Card**

IT'S easy BEING GREEN

Here are a few simple ways you can help conserve fuel and energy when you travel:

○ Each time you take a flight or drive a car greenhouse gases release into the atmosphere. You can help neutralize this danger to the planet through carbon offsetting: paying someone to invest your money in schemes that reduce your greenhouse gas emissions by the same amount you've added. Before buying carbon offset credits, just make sure that you're using a reputable company, one with a proven record that invests in renewable energy. Reliable carbon offset companies include **Carbonfund** (www.carbonfund.org), **TerraPass** (www.terrapass.org), and **Carbon Neutral** (www.carbonneutral.org).

○ Whenever possible, choose non-stop flights; they generally require less fuel than indirect flights that stop and take off again. Try to fly during the day. Some scientists estimate that night-time flights are twice as harmful to the environment. And pack light, each 15 pounds of luggage on an 8,047km (5,000-mile) flight adds up to 50 pounds of carbon dioxide emitted.

○ Where you stay during your travels can have a major environmental impact. To determine the green credentials of a property, ask about trash disposal and recycling, water conservation,

and energy use; also question if sustainable materials were used in the construction of the property. The website **www.green hotels.com** recommends green-rated member hotels around the world that fulfill the company's stringent environmental requirements. Also consult **www. environmentallyfriendlyhotels. com** for more green accommodation ratings.

○ At hotels, do not request that your sheets and towels are changed daily. (Many hotels already have schemes like this in place.) Turn off the lights and air-conditioning (or heater) when you leave your room.

○ Use public transport where possible: trains, buses, and even taxis are more energy-efficient forms of transport than driving. Even better is to walk or cycle; you'll produce zero emissions and stay fit and healthy on your travels.

○ If renting a car is necessary, ask the rental agent for a hybrid, or rent the most fuel-efficient car available. You'll use less fuel and save money at the tank.

○ Eat at locally-owned and operated restaurants that use produce grown in the area. This contributes to the local economy and cuts down on greenhouse gas emissions by supporting restaurants where the food is not flown or trucked in across long distances.

(IYTC) for the same price from the same people, which entitles you to some discounts (but not on museum admissions). **Travel CUTS** (☎ **800/592-CUTS;** www.travelcuts.com) offers similar services for both Canadians and U.S. residents. Irish students may prefer to turn to **USIT** (☎ **01/602-1906;** www.usitnow.ie), an Ireland-based specialist in student, youth, and independent travel.

For general travel resources for students, go to frommers.com.

RESPONSIBLE TOURISM

If you're arriving from elsewhere in Europe, the best way to be a responsible tourist when visiting Vienna is to consider catching the **train** rather than flying. High-speed trains now criss-cross much of the continent making travel by rail a serious alternative to flying. See "Getting There & Around" above.

Since so much of Austria's tourism is due to the natural beauty of the Alps and the sustainability of ski resorts, the country takes the environment very seriously. Although it has no coastline, Austria is full of lakes and rivers. This gift is not taken for granted, however. Water power has become a vital energy source. In Austria there is no longer a monopoly for energy providers and various companies offer green electricity from water, wind, and solar power.

Austria is number five on the Reader's Digest Green list of countries, after Finland, Iceland, Norway, and Sweden. Sustainability, respect for nature preservation and organic food are all very important to Austrians. You won't find off-season fruits and vegetables in a normal supermarket as Austria adheres to strict transportation laws.

There is a deposit on some glass and plastic bottles of around .25 €, so with four bottles you'd get a euro back from the machines in supermarkets. Otherwise the Austrians recycle at every open market in the city. You'll also find recycling containers in groups in every small neighborhood too, mostly on street corners.

When in Austria and Vienna, waste is frowned on in general, as is littering. Besides the occasional cigarette butt and dog dropping, the streets are virtually spotless. Also look in to bike-rentals and bike-tours for fun outings that are pollution-free and easy to access thanks to the multitude of bike paths throughout the city. (See "Getting around by Bike," above.)

Below are a few tips on how to be a green tourist and respect Austria's natural beauty.

PACKAGES FOR THE INDEPENDENT TRAVELER

Tour Operators

A sampling of some well-recommended tour operators follows, but you should always consult a good travel agent for the latest offerings.

British Airways Holidays (☎ **800/AIRWAYS;** www.britishairways.com) offers a far-flung and reliable touring experience. Trips usually combine Vienna and other Austrian attractions with major sights in Germany and Switzerland. BA can arrange a stopover in London en route for an additional fee, and allow extra time in Vienna before or after the beginning of any tour for no additional charge.

Other attractive options are North America's tour-industry giants. They include **Delta Vacations** (℃ 800/221-6666; www.deltavacations.com), **American Express Travel** (℃ 800/297-2977; www.americanexpress.com), and an unusual, upscale (and very expensive) tour operator, **Abercrombie and Kent** (℃ 800/554-7016; www.abercrombiekent.com), long known for its carriage-trade rail excursions through Eastern Europe and the Swiss and Austrian Alps.

Watersports

In addition to short trips to Vienna a number of British package companies offer week-long trips to Lakes nearby the city, perfect for a side trip. A good option is **Crystal Lakes & Mountains** (℃ 0871/231 4716, www.crystallakes.co.uk). Austria has no coastline, but from Bodensee (Lake Constance) in the west to Neusiedl See (Lake Neusiedl) in the east, the country is rich in lakes and boasts some 150 rivers and streams.

Swimming is, of course, possible year-round if you want to use an indoor pool or swim at one of the many health clubs in winter. Swimming facilities have been developed at summer resorts, especially those on the warm waters of Carinthia, where you can swim from May to October, and in the Salzkammergut between Upper Austria and Land Salzburg.

The beauty of Austria underwater is confirmed by those who have tried diving in the lakes. Most outstanding are the diving and underwater exploration possibilities in the Salzkammergut and in Weissensee in Carinthia. You can book lessons and equipment at both places.

If you prefer to remain on the surface, you can go sailing, windsurfing, or canoeing on the lakes and rivers.

The sailing (yachting) season lasts from May to October, with activity centered on the Attersee in the Salzkammergut , on Lake Constance out of Bregenz, and on Lake Neusiedl, a large shallow lake in the east. Winds on the Austrian lakes can be treacherous, but there is a warning system and rescue services are alert. For information on sailing, contact **Österreichischer Segel-Verband,** Seestrasse 17b, A-7100 Neusiedl am See (℃ 02/167402430; www.segelverband.at).

Most resorts on lakes or rivers where windsurfing can be safely enjoyed have equipment and instruction available. This sport is increasingly popular and has been added to the curriculum of several sailing schools, especially in the area of the Wörthersee in Carinthia, the warmest of the Alpine lakes. If you're interested in riding the rapids of a swift mountain stream, or just paddling around on a placid lake, don't miss the chance to go canoeing in Austria.

You can canoe down slow-flowing lowland rivers such as the Inn or Mur, or tackle the wild waters of glacier-fed mountain streams suitable only for experts. Special schools for fast-water paddling operate from May to September in the village of Klaus on the Steyr River in Upper Austria; in Opponitz in Lower Austria on the Ybbs River, and in Abtenau in the Salzburg province.

STAYING CONNECTED

Telephone

The country code for Austria is 43. To call Austria from the United States, dial the international access code 011, then 43, then the city code, then the regular phone number. To call from inside Europe just replace the 011 with 00 or +. **Note:** The phone numbers listed in this book are to be used within Austria; when calling from abroad, omit the initial 0 in the city code.

For directory assistance: Dial ✆ **118877** if you're looking for a number inside Austria, and dial ✆ **1613** for numbers to all other countries.

For operator assistance: If you need operator assistance in making a call, dial ✆ **0180/200-1033.**

Local and long-distance calls may be placed from all post offices and from most public telephone booths. About half of these operate with phone cards, the others with coins. Phone cards are sold at post offices and news stands in denominations of 6€ to 25€. Rates are measured in units rather than minutes. The farther the distance, the more units are consumed. Telephone calls made through hotel switchboards (rare these days) can double, triple, or even quadruple the base charges at the post office, so be alert to this before you dial. In some instances, post offices can send faxes for you, and many hotels offer Internet access for free or for a small charge to their guests.

Austrian phone numbers are not standard. In some places, numbers have as few as three digits. In cities, one number may have five digits, whereas the phone next door might have nine. Austrians also often hyphenate their numbers differently. But since all the area codes are the same, these various configurations should pose no problems once you get used to the fact that numbers vary from place to place.

Toll-free numbers: Numbers beginning with 08 and followed by 00 are toll-free. But be careful. Numbers that begin with 08 followed by 36 carry a .35€ surcharge per minute.

Similarly, many companies maintain a service line beginning with 0180. These lines might appear to be free but really are costing .12€ per minute. Other numbers that begin with 0190 carry a surcharge of 1.85€ per minute or even more. Don't be misled by calling a 1-800 number in the United States from Austria. This is not a toll-free call but costs about the same as an overseas call.

To call the U.S. or Canada from Austria, dial 001, followed by the country code (1), then the area code, and then the number. Alternatively, you can dial the various telecommunication companies in the States for cheaper rates.

If you're calling from a public pay phone in Austria, you must first deposit the basic local rate.

Cellphones/mobiles

The Austrian cellphone network is quite state of the art. Although there are holes in reception (that's mountains for you), the service is mostly constant. You even have reception in the U-Bahn. In order to have a local number, you'll need a SIM Card (Scriber identity Module Card). This is a small chip that gives you a local phone number and plugs you into a regional network. If your cellphone is locked to your home provider, you can use an Austrian card from that provider, or get it unlocked at certain stores. In the U.S., T-Mobile, AT&T Wireless, and Cingular use this quasi-universal system; in Canada, Microcell and some Rogers customers are GSM, and all Europeans and most Australians use GSM. Unfortunately, per-minute charges can be high in western Europe. Make sure you find out before your trip.

For many, **renting** a phone is a good idea. While you can rent a phone from any number of overseas sites, including kiosks at airports and at car-rental agencies. You can also rent the phone before you leave home, however, depending on how much you use it and how long you stay it may make more sense to buy.

Buying a phone can be economically attractive, as many nations have cheap pre-paid phone systems. Once you arrive at your destination, stop by a local cell-phone shop and get the cheapest package; you'll probably pay less than 60 € for a phone and a starter calling card. Local calls may be as low as .10€ per minute, and in many countries incoming calls are free.

Internet & Email

WITH YOUR OWN COMPUTER

More and more hotels, cafes, and retailers have Wi-Fi (wireless fidelity) hot spots or free wireless. **T-Mobile Hotspot** (www.t-mobile.com/hotspot) serves up wireless connections at coffee shops nationwide. **Boingo** (www.boingo.com) and **Wayport** (www.wayport.com) have set up networks in airports and high-class hotel lobbies. iPass providers (see below) also give you access to a few hundred wireless hotel lobby setups. To locate other hot spots that provide **free wireless networks** in cities in Austria, go to **www.jiwire.com**.

For dial-up access, most business-class hotels offer dataports for laptop modems, and a few thousand hotels in Austria now offer free high-speed Internet access. In addition, major Internet service providers (ISPs) have **local access numbers** around the world, allowing you to go online by placing a local call. The **iPass** network also has dial-up numbers around the world. You'll have to sign up with an iPass provider, who will then tell you how to set up your computer for your destination(s). For a list of iPass providers, go to www.ipass.com and click on Individuals Buy Now. One solid provider is **i2roam** (℗ **866/811-6209** or 920/233-5863; www.i2roam.com).

Wherever you go, bring a **connection kit** of the right power and phone adapters, a spare phone cord, and a spare Ethernet network cable, or find out whether your hotel supplies them to guests.

WITHOUT YOUR OWN COMPUTER

Cybercafes are found in all large Austrian cities, but they do not tend to cluster in any particular neighborhoods because of competition. They are spread out, but can be found on almost every business street in large cities. For locations check www.bignet.at.

Aside from formal cybercafes, most **youth hostels** and **public libraries** have Internet access. Most **hotel business centers** don't charge for guest usage anymore, but it's good to check before you log on.

Vienna International airport now has free **Internet kiosks** scattered throughout. These give you basic web access for a per-minute fee that's usually higher than cybercafe prices.

Newspapers & Magazines

You can buy some English language fashion magazines, but only in select shops in the middle of town. Most useful for English speakers are the *International Herald Tribune,* and the locally-printed versions of British newspapers such as *The Times.* For an inside view on Vienna in English, ask for *The Vienna Review* at any *Tabac-Trafik* or news stand.

SUGGESTED VIENNA ITINERARIES

I n truth, the city of Vienna merits a week stay or longer, especially if you want to appreciate the old world art of Viennese *Gemütlichkeit,* the "good life."

However, many trips don't allow for more than a few days. If your time is limited, make the most of it with these ready-made itineraries that help you to have a rounded, unforgettable visit.

Part of the joy of any great city of Europe is making your own special discoveries—ducking down that little cobblestone lane to some antique curio shop or dropping in for a glass of new wine or a pint of beer at a local tavern.

Vienna doesn't wear its heart on its sleeve, as do some cities; she is a lady who takes some courting, some patience and appreciation; she wants you to take the time to notice and absorb. Vienna is a city where a visitor never comes empty- handed, always bringing wine or flowers, a local brandy, or hand-made preserves. So you do the same; little courtesies will be returned to you many times over.

But begin at the beginning: to fortify yourself for the day, try a *Wiener Frühstuck,* a Viennese breakfast, of a fresh Kaiser roll (*Semmel*), butter and preserves, and perhaps slices of ham and cheese, with your espresso and steamed milk, a *melange*. Although there will often be a generous buffet at your hotel, you will eventually want to venture out for an *Eierspeise* (a rustic omelette filled with ham), a Balkan breakfast of dark bread, goat's cheese, tomatoes, and olives or any of the splendid pastries in a *Kaffeehaus*.

And then you are off, for a museum, a palace, an afternoon concert, or a walk in the Wienerwald. But never fear. In Vienna, there is always a *Gasthaus* or a *Beisl* (a traditional cafe), or a buffet, with sausages, goulash, and a beer just around the next bend. It's fine to plan a full day. But the best part will always be the recollections, when the adventure becomes a story to be shared with friends over that glass of wine in a *Heuriger* as the light fades.

Areas in Brief

Visitors spend most of their time in the heart of the city, and many of Vienna's best hotels and restaurants are conveniently located in or just outside the 1st District. In this section, we profile the Inner City, or Innere Stadt, and the districts that immediately surround it.

Innere Stadt (1st District) This compact area is the oldest part of Vienna, bordered on all sides by the legendary Ring, the street tracing the former city walls. This district remains at the heart of Viennese life. The Inner City has dozens of streets dedicated to pedestrian traffic, including the **Kärntnerstrasse,** which leads from the Vienna State Opera House, to The **Graben,** joining at Stephansplatz and the site of the famous cathedral. Competing with Vienna's twin gods of the church (Stephansdom) and music (Staatsoper) is the **Hofburg,** the Habsburg palace that houses a showcase of attractions, including the magnificent National Library, the Spanish Riding School, and six museums. Other landmarks include the City Hall (Rathaus), the Parliament, the University of Vienna, the Museum of Natural History (Naturhistorisches Museum) and the Museum of Fine Arts (Kunsthistorisches Museum), and the elegant Stadtpark.

Leopoldstadt (2nd District) Once inhabited by Balkan traders and later by Vienna's Jewish community, this district borders the canal side of Ringstrasse, to the north, across from Schwedenplatz or Schottenring. The district is rich in greenery as well as the fascinating old Jewish quarter, Karmeliterviertel. In addition to the tree-lined gravel paths of the baroque **Augarten,** you'll find the massive **Prater Park,** with a famous old amusement park, miles of tree-lined walking paths, and many sports facilities, including tennis courts, race tracks, a golf course, a public swimming pool, and a stadium. At the western edge is Vienna's renowned trade-fair exhibition site. After a spree of development along the canal, the Leopoldstadt has become one of the hottest spots of Bohemian Vienna.

Landstrasse (3rd District) The stately **Stadtpark** spreads into this district, where you'll see block after block of streets dotted with churches, monuments, and palaces. One is the grand **Palais Schwarzenberg,** divided between a hotel and the private residence of Prince Karl Schwarzenberg,

who in true Austrian fashion also happens also to be the foreign minister of the Czech Republic; another is the looming **Konzerthaus** that is home to the Vienna Symphony. However, the top attraction remains Prince Eugene of Savoy's **Belvedere Palace,** an exquisite example of baroque architecture, with gardens patterned after Versailles. Several embassies are in a small section of Landstrasse that's known as Vienna's diplomatic quarter. The **Wien Mitte Rail Station** and the **City Air Terminal for the CAT (City Airport Train)** are also here.

Wieden (4th District) This small area extends south from Opernring and Kärntnering, and is nearly as fashionable as the 1st District. Most activity focuses on **Karlsplatz,** an historic square with its domed namesake, **Karlskirche.** Also nearby are Vienna's **Technical University** and the **Historical Museum of the City of Vienna.** Kärntnerstrasse, the main boulevard of the city, turns into **Wiedner-Hauptstrasse** as it enters this district, and the **Südbahnhof,** one of the two main train stations, lies at its southern tip.

Margareten (5th District) Southwest of the 4th District, Wieden, this area does not border the Ring and thus lies a bit farther from the Inner City. Here you'll start to see more residential areas, representing the continual growth of Vienna's middle class. The historic homes of composers Franz Schubert and Christoph Gluck still stand here among modern apartment complexes, industry, and warehouse performance spaces.

Mariahilf (6th District) One of Vienna's busiest shopping streets, the **Mariahilferstrasse,** runs through this bustling area. The sprawling, lively **Naschmarkt** (produce market), selling fresh fruits, vegetables, breads, cheeses, and more, is ideal for people-watching. On Saturdays, the adjacent **Flohmarkt** (flea market) adds to the lively but sometimes seedy atmosphere as vendors sell antiques and junk. Right across the Wienzeile is the famed **Theater an der Wien,** Vienna's oldest opera house, that premiered Johann Strauss's legendary operetta *Die Fledermaus.* In the surrounding streets you'll find the occasional *beisl* (small pub), cabaret theater, cafe, and tavern. Farther out, Vienna turns into villages.

Neubau (7th District) Bordering the expansive MuseumsQuartier on one end and Westbahnhof on the other, this is a good base of operations. The picturesque **Spittelberg quarter** lies atop a hill just beyond Vienna's most famous museums and is a hub of crafts and antiquing, a vibrant cultural community popular with all ages. The old Spittelberg houses have been renovated into appealing crafts boutiques, restaurants, cafes, a brew pub, several theaters, and art galleries—a perfect backdrop for an afternoon stroll.

Josefstadt (8th District) The smallest of Vienna's 23 districts is named after Habsburg Emperor Joseph II and was once home to Vienna's civil servants. Like Neubau, this quiet, friendly spot sits behind the City Hall and the adjacent grand museums of the Ringstrasse. Here you'll find secluded

parks, charming cafes, and elaborate monuments and churches. Vienna's oldest and most intimate theater, **Theater in der Josefstadt,** has stood here since 1788. **Vienna's** charming **English Theater** is right around the corner on Josefsgasse. Shops and restaurants in the 8th have a varied clientele, from City Hall lawmakers to university students.

Alsergrund (9th District) This area is often referred to as the Academic Quarter, not just because it houses most of the University of Vienna, but also because of its many research hospitals and medical clinics. This is Freud territory, and you can visit his home, now the **Freud Museum,** on Berggasse. Here you'll also stumble upon the **Liechtenstein Palace,** one of Vienna's biggest and brightest, which today houses the family's collection from over 4 centuries. At the northern end of Alsergrund is the **Franz-Josef Bahnhof,** an excellent depot for excursions to Lower Austria, Krems, Dürnstein, and the wine country of the Wachau.

THE BEST OF VIENNA IN 1 DAY

Touring Vienna in 1 day—a city filled with some of the world's greatest art and baroque palaces—can be done if you get an early start and have a certain stamina and good walking shoes. This "greatest hits" itinerary focuses on the Altstadt, or Old Town, the inner core of ancient Vienna. Start: U-Bahn to Stephansplatz.

1 Stephansdom ★★★

This Gothic gem dates from the 12th century, and is the grandest such edifice in Austria (p. 143). The basilica is filled with such treasures as the carved wooden Wiener Neustadt altarpiece and the tomb of Emperor Frederick III. Here there are free concerts almost every day, of resident musicians and visiting choirs and orchestras from around the world. To cap your visit, climb the south tower with its 343 spiral steps for a workout and a splendid panoramic view right from the heart of Vienna. There is also an elevator to the top of the north tower, which was never completed. The view isn't quite as spectacular, but you'll live to tell the tale!

After a tour of the cathedral, you can stroll up the pedestrian-only:

2 Kärntnerstrasse

This is the main shopping street of Vienna, comparable to Fifth Avenue in New York City, or Bond Street in London. Its shops display some of the world's most

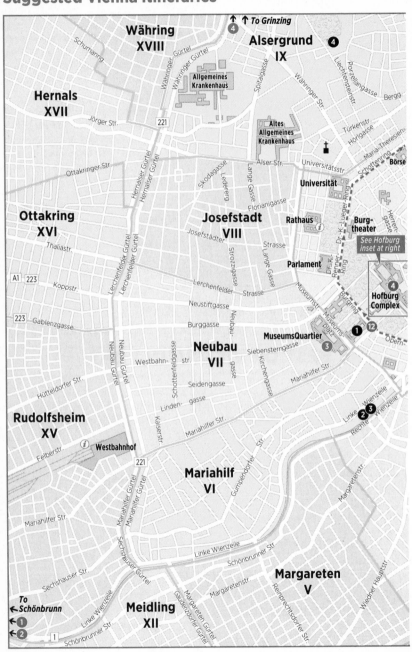

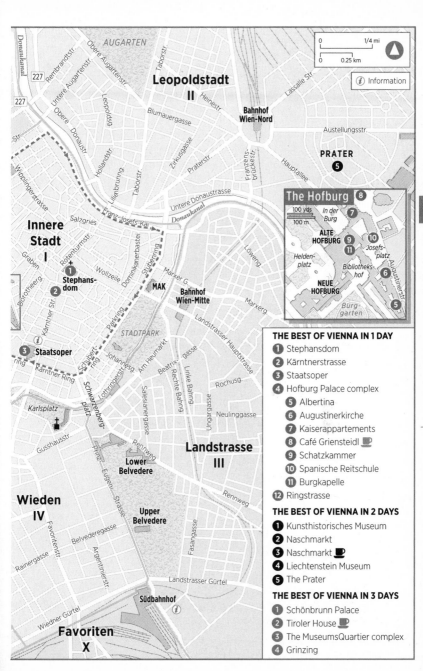

THE BEST OF VIENNA IN 1 DAY

1. Stephansdom
2. Kärntnerstrasse
3. Staatsoper
4. Hofburg Palace complex
   5. Albertina
   6. Augustinerkirche
   7. Kaiserappartements
   8. Café Griensteidl ☕
   9. Schatzkammer
   10. Spanische Reitschule
   11. Burgkapelle
12. Ringstrasse

THE BEST OF VIENNA IN 2 DAYS

1. Kunsthistorisches Museum
2. Naschmarkt
3. Naschmarkt ☕
4. Liechtenstein Museum
5. The Prater

THE BEST OF VIENNA IN 3 DAYS

1. Schönbrunn Palace
2. Tiroler House ☕
3. The MuseumsQuartier complex
4. Grinzing

glittering merchandise, and house some of Austria's most venerable retailers. This is a place to do very chic window-shopping and not every shop is pricy.

Kärntnerstrasse will lead you to the regal:

3 Staatsoper ★★★

With its elegant arcades and renowned acoustics, this is among Europe's leading opera houses. The Staatsoper mounts over 60 operas and ballets a season, 3 times any other house and at remarkably affordable prices (p. 195). Some of the world's greatest music—often from fabled Austrian composers—is presented here in this Neo-Renaissance building, one of the first to be erected along the Emperor's Ringstrasse (see below). The main facade and front salons were all that was left after Allied bombing in 1945. Handsomely restored in the early 1950s, it is a beloved haunt of the Viennese from all walks of life, and all will happily dress to the nines for a gala night at the opera.

With the time remaining in your day, you can head for the:

4 Hofburg Palace Complex ★★★

Depending on where you are in the city, the U1 or U3 to Stephansplatz (see above) can take you here, as well as the U3 or U2 to Herrengasse or Volkstheater.

This was the winter palace of the Habsburgs, who ruled over much of Europe from this sprawling complex. There is much to see. But the main attractions are the Albertina Museum, the Augustinerkirche, the Kaiserappartments (Imperial Apartments), and the glittering Schatzkammer (Imperial Treasury).

It's a matter of timing (and needs careful planning), but the lucky hundreds can see a performance at the Spanische Hofreitschule (Spanish Riding School) and perhaps a concert at the Burgkapelle, home of the Vienna Boys' Choir.

Within the complex, try to visit the:

5 Albertina ★

Originally part of an Augustinian monastery, this 18th-century palace houses Austria's celebrated Collection of Graphic Art. More than a million sheets (old masters' drawings, engravings, and architectural designs) illustrate the development of graphic arts since the 1300s. The highlight of the collection is a series of drawings and engravings by Dürer. See p. 127.

6 Augustinerkirche ★

The 14th-century Church of the Augustinians, built within the Hofburg complex, was the parish church of the imperial Habsburgs. While easy to overlook from the street, the interior is dramatic, a long nave of soaring Gothic arches in the glow of polished brass chandeliers, with a regal dignity of line rather than ornament, after the baroque detail was stripped in a re-dedication in 1748. The resident choir and orchestra are first rate, and perform full masses of Mozart, Haydn, Schubert, or Massenet weekly. One highlight is the marble tomb of the Archduchess Maria Christina, favorite daughter of Maria Theresa, by Italian sculptor, Canova. See p. 128.

7 Kaiserappartements

The Imperial Apartments (p. 129) are on the first floor of the Chancellery Wing. Of the 2,600 rooms in the Hofburg, only 20 are on the well-narrated tours, and worth a visit. The monarchs and their families lived in these richly decorated but remarkably livable suites; tours include bedrooms, sitting rooms, studies, and dressing rooms as well as more public spaces. A highlight: the Imperial Silver and Porcelain collections.

8 Café Griensteidl

Since the Hofburg complex is so vast, you may want to head for the Café Griensteidl on Michaelerplatz for coffee and snacks or a good meal. This classic kaffeehaus is one of the most famous turn-of-the-century literary cafes restored in the 1990s, popular with government types from the ministries around the corner. It's a great place to study your guidebooks and write postcards.

The grandest attraction at the Hofburg is the:

9 Schatzkammer ★★★

The Imperial Treasury contains the glittering Habsburg jewels. Look for the royal portrait of the Emperor Francis I in imperial mantel and regalia, and in the next case the jewels themselves. The greatest treasure is the Imperial crown, dating from 962. See p. 132.

10 Spanische Reitschule ★

The Spanish Riding School is where the famed Lipizzaner stallions strut their stuff, as they have for 4 centuries. Performing routines developed to overpower the enemy in warfare, the dressage horses are considered the finest in the world, their feats, with perfect balance and impulsion, unequaled. The tails and manes of the stallions are plaited with gold ribbons, and along with the half pass and *levade*, they dance the polka, the gavotte, the quadrille, and the slow waltz (we kid you not).

11 Burgkapelle

The home of the Vienna Boys' Choir is in the Hofmusikkapelle, part of the Burgkapelle, a Gothic chapel dating from 1447. Seeing a performance can be a bit tricky (p. 129), but it is easier than it used to be as there are now three full choirs and one is always in Vienna. The voices of the *Wiener Sängerknaben* have been called "heavenly," but they are simply a group of talented boys from many countries who have won their sponsored studies by open audition.

12 Ringstrasse ★★★

As night falls over Vienna, take a ride in a yellow streetcar around the entire Ringstrasse, beginning at Schwedenplatz at 15 and 45 minutes after the hour, past the extraordinary buildings of *Grunderzeit*, built between 1860 and 1910. If it is already after six, the 1 and 2 trams take you halfway around in each direction—just make sure you hop off at the right spot. The trams follow the route of the medieval fortifications. For more information on how to do this, refer to p. 131.

THE BEST OF VIENNA IN 2 DAYS

For Day 1, see above. On Day 2, tackle two of the finest art museums of Austria with an afternoon to sidle through the stands of the Naschmarkt, a great imperial palace, and top it off by a night at Vienna's legendary amusement park.

Take the U-Bahn to Volkstheater to see:

1 Kunsthistorisches Museum ★★★

Across from the Hofburg Palace (see above) stands one of Europe's greatest art museums, which owes its existence largely to the Habsburgs. They assembled their collection from all corners of Europe, even from Egypt. The famous Venus von Willendorf statue is on exhibit here, as are several bas-reliefs from the north side of the Parthenon. The unmatched collection of master paintings includes the Seasons of Pieter Bruegel, along with Dürer, Rubens, and Rembrandt. See p. 139 for more details.

Before your feet grow museum tired, head for the:

2 Naschmarkt

At Wienzeile (p. 189) in the 6th District (U-Bahn: Karlsplatz), just south of the Ring, you can explore the most famous open-air market of Vienna. Viennese merchants have operated here since the Middle Ages, selling their produce grown on the fertile farms of Lower Austria. Naschmarkt is one of Europe's greatest open-air markets. Little shops sell Austrian cheeses, preserves, and wines. You'll find stall after stall of stacked fruits and vegetables, most of which were recently harvested. The spice fragrances assailing your nostrils (in a pleasant way) evoke the souks of the Middle East. It's a fun place to try out your half-remembered languages or just watch the people.

3 Noshing at the Market

The Naschmarkt offers dozens of eateries or snack stands where you can sample treats from Austrian, Balkan, and Mediterranean traditions. There are wonderful Polish sausages, Greek olives and cheeses, North African fruit, nuts, and spices. When tired, numerous cafes and restaurants will help refuel your engines.

After lunch, take the U4 to Roßauerlände or the D tram to Seegasse to get to the:

4 Liechtenstein Museum ★★★

Since its opening in 2004, this museum housing the princely collection of the Liechtenstein family has become a mandatory stopover for first-time visitors to Vienna. Housed in a spectacular 18th-century baroque palace with a fine private library and gardens, the collection includes several 18th-century portrait landscapes by Bernardo Bellotto, showing family life, the terraces, and the gardens. See major works from Renaissance to baroque, masterpieces by Van Dyck, Raphael, and Rembrandt, as well as one of the world's greatest collections of Rubens. Also decorative arts, porcelain, and even the most stunning exhibit of ceremonial carriages in Austria. See p. 139.

For a night of fun and revelry, head for Praterstern on the U1 and to:

5 The Prater ★

This is *the* great European amusement park packed with history. See p. 152. Joseph II opened it in 1766 on the former Imperial hunting grounds. Its most celebrated attraction is its gigantic ferris wheel, originally built in 1896 but reconstructed after Allied bombings in 1945. Come here for a panoramic view of Vienna at night from a height of 200 feet (60m). The wheel was featured in the film *The Third Man*. From the top you can see over the whole city and get an idea of just how huge the Prater is. See p. 152.

THE BEST OF VIENNA IN 3 DAYS

Spend Days 1 and 2 as outlined above. On Day 3, take in the Belvedere, spend the afternoon at MuseumsQuartier before hitting one of the famous *heuriger* or wine taverns. Nothing is more typically Viennese than spending a night drinking and eating at one of these taverns on the edge of the Vienna Woods.

In the morning of Day 3, take U-Bahn 4 to:

1 Schönbrunn Palace

This was the baroque summer palace of the Habsburgs. Built between 1696 and 1730, it contains a staggering 1,441 rooms. Empress Maria Theresa and her 16 children left the greatest impact on the palace. Franz Josef I, who was born in the palace and reigned for 68 years, was the last emperor to live here. The tours of the State Apartments are engaging and well worth the time, with insider tales of Marie Theresa's children, and of the Empress Sissi's starvation diets and her frustrations with her mother-in-law. Take a walk up to the Gloriette, a marble summerhouse, and around the palace's glorious rose gardens. See p. 142. The Tiergarten Schönbrunn (Imperial Zoo), dating from 1752, is the oldest zoo in the world and is fun in all types of weather. Also charming are the exotic butterflies and wild baby quail amid the tropical plantings in the Schmetterlinghaus and the Imperial Palm Gardens (Palmenhaus). (See p. 154).

2 Tiroler House

To the west of Gloriette lies Tiroler House, Schönbrunner Schlosspark (no phone). This was a retreat of the Empress Elisabeth, but today is a small restaurant and cafe. It's open in good weather but may close in heavy rains.

In early afternoon, take the U-Bahn 2 or 3 to Volkstheater or MuseumsQuartier to visit:

3 The MuseumsQuartier Complex ★★★

This giant complex is host to many attractions, notably three great museums, including Kunsthalle Wien, a showcase for cutting-edge modern and classic modern art. An even more impressive showcase, Leopold Museum, has a vast collection of Austrian art, including the world's largest collection of the works of Egon Schiele (1890–1918). A final museum, MUMOK, is devoted to some of the best collections of modern art in Central Europe, even American pop art. You can spend the better part of an afternoon—at least—wandering through this Bohemian feast of art and ideas. If time remains, there is a vast array of other attractions as well, including installations by the artists in residence, in the arched rooms at the front of the complex, and a children's museum. See p. 134 for complete details.

For your final night in Vienna, head for:

4 Grinzing

On the edge of the Vienna Woods, take tram 1 or U2 to Schottentor, then change to tram no. 38 for Grinzing. This is the most popular area for a night at a *heuriger* or wine tavern. The sound of the zither or the accordion lasts long into a summer night. This is fun in groups or as a couple. For recommendations of *heuriger* in the area, refer to p. 205.

WHERE TO STAY

Vienna has some of the greatest hotels in Europe and a long-standing tradition of service that has set a standard worldwide. But finding a room can be a problem if you arrive without a reservation, especially in August and September. During these peak months, you might have to stay on the outskirts, in the Grinzing or the Schönbrunn districts, for example, and come in to the Inner City by streetcar, bus, or U-Bahn. Not that this is difficult, as Vienna's public transport is the envy of other cities even in Europe. And the outlying areas are nice, and the ride is fun. Plus, staying outside the city's bustling heart makes sense, as you can pay 20% to 25% less for a hotel outside the Ringstrasse.

High season in Vienna encompasses most of the year: from May to October or early November, and during some weeks in midwinter, when the city hosts major trade fairs, conventions, and other cultural events. If you're planning a trip around Christmas and New Year's Day, room reservations should be made *at least* a month in advance. Some reductions (usually 15%–20%) are available during slower midwinter weeks—it always pays to ask.

Note: A smoking ban came into effect throughout Austria on January 1, 2009, transforming almost all hotel rooms to nonsmoking. The ban also covers all public spaces, so most lobbies are now off limits to smokers as well.

Finding a Hotel

Any branch of the **Austrian National Tourist Office** (© 01/588660, **www.austria.info**), as well as the Vienna Tourist Board (www.vienna. info), will help you book a room. The Vienna Tourist Board has branch offices in the airport, train stations, and near major highways that access Vienna (see Chapter 10).

The city's travel agencies can also help. Three of the largest are **Austropa,** Friedrichsgasse 7, A-1010 (© **01/588-00510**); **Austrobus,**

Dr.-Karl-Lueger-Ring 8, 1010 (✆ **01/534-110**); and **Blaguss Reisen,** Wiedner Hauptstrasse 15 1040 (✆ **01/50180**). All can reserve hotel space as well as sell airline tickets, and procure hard-to-get tickets for music festivals. Most of the employees speak English fluently.

Seasonal Hotels

From July to September, a number of student dormitories in Vienna are transformed into fully operational hotels. Three of the most viable and popular are the **Academia Hotel,** Pfeilgasse 3A; the **Avis Hotel,** Pfeilgasse 4; and the **Atlas Hotel,** at Lerchenfelderstrasse 1. All are within a block of one another, and each is an angular, 1960s-style building. They're comfortable and reasonably priced, and only a 20-minute walk west of St. Stephan's. They will definitely take you back to your dorm days, though each room has a phone and a private bath. Many groups book well in advance, but individual tourists are welcome if space is available. Depending on the hotel, doubles cost from 80€ to 108€ a night, and triples run from 105€ to 130€ each. Breakfast is included. Bookings at all three are arranged through the Academia Hotel, which functions as the headquarters for the Academia chain. For reservations and information, call ✆ **01/401-76-55,** or fax 01/401-76-20; reservation@academia hotel.at; www.academiahotels.at. To get to the Academia and Avis hotels, take the U-Bahn to Thaliastrasse, and then transfer to tram no. 46 and get off at Strozzigasse. For access to the Atlas Hotel, take the U-Bahn to Volkstheater or Rathaus. These hotels accept American Express, Diners Club, MasterCard, and Visa for payment.

Private Homes & Furnished Apartments

For those who like to have more space than an average hotel room, or are staying for a longer period of time, apartments are available. These can be money-saving options, depending on the season and the size of the place. There is an online booking portal for rentals in Vienna at **www.apartment.at**, or **http://viennas apartments.com**. Both have a wide range of places on offer. For real luxury and serviced options try **www.my-place.at** (Rossauer Lände 23, 1090 Vienna, ✆ **01/5131717**).

INNERE STADT (INNER CITY)

Very Expensive

Do & Co. Hotel ★★   A quirky but relentlessly upscale and obsessively design-conscious venue created when Do & Co., one of the city's most high-profile restaurants, took over four floors of the Haas Haus. Some find it pretentious and others love it. You take an elevator from an impersonal ground-floor entry up to the check-in on level six, somewhat awkwardly positioned within a busy area that otherwise functions as a vestibule for the stylish **Onyx Bar.** The rooms are artfully minimalist and very comfortable, with yummy but hard-to-define tones of toffee and putty. Sybaritic details include see-through showers. Bedrooms have mahogany, louvered doors, lots of polished travertine, dark-grained hardwoods, and floor plans that follow the curved walls and tucked-away balconies of the Haas Haus. Views encompass the crowds scurrying around the all-pedestrian Graben and the Stephansplatz.

Where to Stay in Vienna's Inner City

Do & Co. Hotel **12**
Graben Hotel **11**
Grand Hotel Wien **25**
Hollman Beletage **34**
Hotel Amadeus **7**
Hotel Ambassador **16**
Hotel Am Parkring **31**
Hotel Am Schubertring **27**
Hotel Astoria **17**
Hotel Austria **35**
Hotel Bristol **23**
Hotel Capricorno **37**
Hotel de France **2**
Hotel Imperial **26**
Hotel Kaiserin Elisabeth **15**
Hotel Kärntnerhof **33**
Hotel König
    Von Ungarn **32**
Hotel Opernring **5**
Hotel-Pension Arenberg **39**
Hotel-Pension Suzanne **22**
Hotel Pertschy **10**
Hotel Post **36**
Hotel Römischer Kaiser **20**
Hotel Royal **13**
Hotel Sacher Wien **18**
Hotel Wandl **8**
K + K Palais Hotel **6**
Le Meridien Vienna **4**
Mailberger Hof **21**
Palais Coburg Hotel
    Residenz **30**
Pension Dr. Geissler **38**
Pension Neuer Markt **14**
Pension Nossek **9**
Radisson/SAS Palais Hotel
    Vienna **28**
Radisson/SAS Style Hotel **3**
Rathauspark Hotel **1**
Ring Hotel Vienna **24**
Vienna Marriott **29**
Zur Wiener Staatsoper **19**

WHERE TO STAY | Innere Stadt (Inner City)

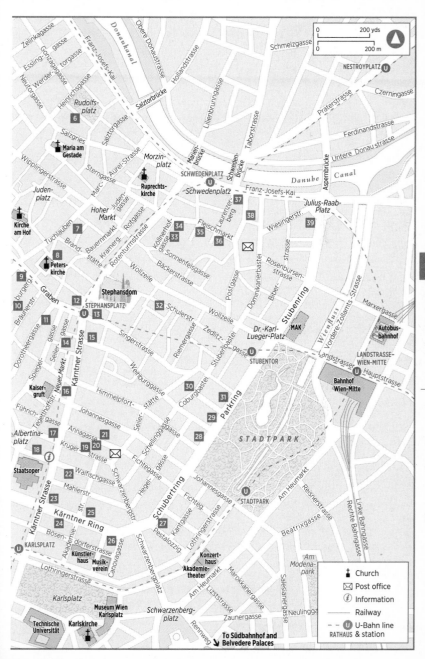

In the Haas Haus, Stephansplatz 12, 1010 Vienna. ℭ **01/24188.** Fax 01/24188444. www.doco.com. 43 units. 165€–350€ double; from 740€–1,550€ suite. AE, DC, MC, V. U-Bahn: Stephansplatz. **Amenities:** Restaurant; bar; room service. *In room:* A/C, TV, minibar, hair dryer, safe, free Wi-Fi.

Grand Hotel Wien ★★ Some of the most discerning hotel guests in Europe, from visiting soloists to diplomats, prefer this deluxe hotel to the more traditional and famous Imperial or Bristol. Just along from the Staatsoper, the spacious sound-proof rooms and suites are posh, with all the modern luxuries, such as heated floors, coffeemakers, and phones in marble bathrooms. Silk wallpaper, marble and mahogany woodwork envelop bed, bath and minibar. The more expensive rooms have more elaborate furnishings and decoration, including ornamental plaster features. The main dining room has Austrian and international dishes, and there's also a Japanese restaurant that serves the town's best sushi brunch on Sunday. High standards and taste are satisfied at every turn—excepting for the tiny fitness room and absent pool and sauna.

Kärntner Ring 9, 1010 Vienna. ℭ **01/515800.** Fax 01/5151310. www.grandhotelwien.com. 205 units. 211€–299€ double; from 1,000€ suite. AE, DC, MC, V. Parking 28€. U-Bahn: Karlsplatz. **Amenities:** 3 restaurants; 2 bars; fitness room; boutiques; room service; babysitting; rooms for those w/limited mobility. *In room:* A/C, TV, minibar, hair dryer, free Wi-Fi.

Hotel Ambassador ★ Until it became a hotel in 1866, the Ambassador was a wheat and flour warehouse, a far cry from its status today as one of Vienna's most refined contemporary hotels. Much more modern than the Bristol or Imperial, it also has the advantage of a great location, between the Vienna State Opera and St. Stephan's Cathedral, on the Neuer Markt square facing the Donner Fountain. Shop-lined Kärntnerstrasse is on the other side. Mark Twain stayed here, as has a host of diplomats and celebrities, including Theodore Roosevelt. Bedrooms are furnished with Biedermeier and Art Nouveau period pieces. The quieter rooms overlook Neuer Markt, although you'll miss the view of lively Kärntnerstrasse. Comfortable beds, marble bathrooms, nice toiletries, and ample storage space add to the allure. The restaurant, Léhar, serves high-quality Austrian and international cuisine.

Kärntnerstrasse 22, A-1010 Vienna. ℭ **01/961610.** Fax 01/5132999. www.ambassador.at. 86 units. 220€–404€ double; 700€ junior suite. AE, DC, MC, V. Parking 30€. U-Bahn: Stephansplatz. **Amenities:** Restaurant; bar; room service. *In room:* A/C, TV, minibar, hair dryer, Wi-Fi: 1hr 8€, 3hrs 15€, 24hrs 18€.

Hotel Astoria A first-class hotel, the Astoria has an eminently desirable location on the shopping mall near St. Stephan's Cathedral and the Vienna State Opera. Decorated with a tasteful, understated elegance that honors turn-of-the-20th-century Vienna, the hotel offers well-appointed traditional bedrooms where comfort is not just on the surface. The interior rooms tend to be too dark, and singles are a little too cramped. Rooms contain built-in armoires, well-chosen linens and duvets on good beds, and bathrooms that, for the most part, are spacious and have extras such as dual basins, heated racks, and bidets. A recent renovation has left the old style unharmed; and the management seems genuinely concerned about offering high-quality service.

Kärntnerstrasse 32–34, 1010 Vienna. ℭ **01/515770.** Fax 01/5157782. www.austria-trend.at. 118 units. 103€–118€ single;158€–450€ double; 650€ suite. Rates include breakfast. AE, DC, MC, V. Parking 22€–32€. U-Bahn: Stephansplatz. **Amenities:** Restaurant; bar; room service; babysitting. *In room:* TV, minibar, hair dryer.

Hotel Bristol Connoisseurs maintain that for service, comfort, and convenience, this is a superb choice. Constructed in 1894 next to the Vienna State Opera, it has been updated to provide guests with black-tile bathrooms and other modern conveniences. Each bedroom includes a living-room area, and many have a small balcony providing a rooftop view of the Vienna State Opera and Ringstrasse.

Many of the hotel's architectural embellishments rank as objets d'art in their own right, including the black carved-marble fireplaces and the oil paintings in the salons. The Bristol Club Rooms in the tower offer comfortable chairs, an open fireplace, a self-service bar, library, stereo, deck, and sauna. Corkscrew columns of rare marble grace the Korso, Bristol's restaurant, which is one of the best in Vienna.

Kärntner Ring 1, 1015 Vienna. ⓒ **888/625-5144** in the U.S., or 01/515160. Fax 01/51516550. www.westin. com/bristol. 146 units. 271€–439€ double; from 526€ suite. Rates include breakfast. AE, DC, MC, V. Parking 30€. U-Bahn: Karlsplatz. Tram: 1 or 2. **Amenities:** 2 restaurants; bar; free access to nearby fitness center; sauna; room service; babysitting; dry cleaning; laundry service; rooms for those w/limited mobility. *In room:* A/C, TV, minibar, hair dryer, Wi-Fi: 1hr 9€, 24hrs 19€.

Hotel de France Right on the Ring, the Hotel de France has long been a popular choice with international visitors. It has central location and is next to the university and the Votivkirche. Its chiseled gray facade is little changed from when it was first erected in 1872. Converted into a hotel after World War II, it now boasts modern elements alongside unobtrusively conservative decor. In such a subdued undemanding atmosphere, you encounter businesspeople from all over the world who appreciate the dignity of the high-ceilinged public rooms and oriental carpets, the generously-padded armchairs, yet without the trappings of a celebrity hotel. The bedrooms are among the finest for their price range in Vienna. The best units are on the fifth floor, although too high to offer the view unless you're very tall!

Schottenring 3, 1010 Vienna. ⓒ **01/31368.** Fax 01/3195969. www.hoteldefrance.at. 212 units. 185€– 330€ double; from 495€ suite. Rates include buffet breakfast. AE, DC, MC, V. Parking 20€. U-Bahn: U2 or Schottentor. Tram: 1, 2, 37, or D. Bus: 1A. **Amenities:** 2 restaurants; 3 bars; sauna; room service. *In room:* A/C, TV, minibar, hair dryer, free Wi-Fi.

Hotel Imperial ★★★ Listed by Relais et Chateaux as among the world's most beautiful hostelries, this hotel of princes has been the host of Austria's visitors of state since it was reclaimed from Russian forces in1955. Here in the former home of the Prince of Württemberg you are afforded the essence of royalty in every velvet brocade curtain and cherry-wood cabinet, and your butler serves a hand-ironed newspaper with morning coffee. It also has perhaps the sweetest period cocktail bar in town, where Thomas at the Bösendorfer plays everything from Hungarian polkas to Cole Porter. Some of the most desirable rooms are on the 4th and 5th floor, on a more human scale than the overwhelming "state" suites. As you go higher, life becomes more "bourgeois;" appointments diminish, as do bathroom sizes. If this superb 5-star hotel has a weakness, it is the fitness rooms and (despite the lovely sauna) the lack of a spa.

Kärntner Ring 16, 1015 Vienna. ⓒ **800/325-3589** in the U.S., or 01/501100. Fax 01/50110410. www.luxurycollection.com/imperial. 138 units. 700€ double; from 1,000€ suite. AE, DC, MC, V. Parking 32€. U-Bahn: Karlsplatz. **Amenities:** 2 restaurants; bar; health club; sauna; room service; babysitting; rooms for those w/limited mobility. *In room:* A/C, TV, minibar, hair dryer, Wi-Fi: 1hr 9€ 24hrs 19€.

What, No Palace Fit for a Queen?

The 1969 visit of England's Queen Elizabeth II to Vienna was one of the Hotel Imperial's high points. She was not initially pleased at the idea of lodging in a hotel. Wasn't there a spare palace in this former imperial city? Sure. But none of them offered the luxurious splendor of the Imperial. As it turned out, Queen Elizabeth enjoyed her stay very much. According to the hotel manager, the Queen left with warm words of gratitude and a little present for every single employee.

Hotel Sacher Wien ★★★ The fame of this 152-room, privately-owned hotel could just as well be due to the luscious brocade drapes and attentive service, but for most people, it's all about chocolate cake. The Café Sacher Wien, where the world-famous delicacy with its apricot middle and shiny near-black chocolate top was invented, is still going strong (and still guarding its recipe jealously), but there's also an enchanting hotel attached, at the heart of Viennese life since 1876. Recently renovated, this hotel opposite the Staatsoper couldn't be more central, with all the silk wallpaper, 19th-century oils, and Biedermeier furniture you could wish for. Nine suites have adjoining 23 sq. m (250 sq. ft.) terraces with stunning views. The Spa offers "hot chocolate treatments" following the Sachers' sweet tradition. Along with the Confiserie and Café, there's the Anna Sacher Restaurant, post-opera haunt, the Blaue Bar, and the sexy Rote Bar, with its charming winter garden.

Philharmonikerstrasse 4, 1010 Vienna. ✆ **01/514560.** Fax 01/51256810. www.sacher.com. 152 units. 299€–464€ double; from 650€ junior suite; from 720€ executive suite. AE, DC, MC, V. Parking 32€. U-Bahn: Karlsplatz. Tram: 1, 2, 62, 65, D, or J. Bus: 4A. **Amenities:** 2 restaurants; cafe; confiserie; 2 bars; spa; room service; babysitting. *In room:* A/C, TV, minibar, hair dryer, Wi-Fi: 1hr 6€, 24hrs 36€.

Le Meridien Vienna Right on the famous Ringstrasse, this is a true glam hotel, a 5-star, high-shine hostelry next to the Academy of Fine Arts and a short stroll from the Vienna State Opera. Extensive renovations converted an apartment block of turn-of-the-20th-century Viennese architecture into this city landmark, the first here for this popular French chain. Luscious maple wood and satin-chrome steel and glass create an aura of understated elegance in public rooms, and special lighting effects are used dramatically. The midsize-to-spacious bedrooms feature designer beds, parquet floors, warm carpeting, and "sink-in" armchairs. Windows were designed to capture the most light possible, and decorators created drama using pinks and blues accented by earth tones.

Opernring 13-A, 1010 Vienna. ✆ **01/588900.** Fax 01/588909090. http://vienna.lemeridien.com. 294 units. 170€–385€ double; from 655€ suite. AE, DC, MC, V. U-Bahn: Karlsplatz. **Amenities:** Restaurant; 2 bars; indoor heated pool; gym; sauna; room service; babysitting; rooms for those w/limited mobility. *In room:* A/C, TV, minibar, hair dryer, free Wi-Fi.

Palais Coburg Hotel Residenz ★★ Built in 1846 by August von Sachsen-Coburg-Saalfeld (who's family managed to sire the House of Windsor and most of the monarchs of western Europe) as the dynasty's Vienna residence, this magnificent, sprawling palace, wrecked by the occupying Russian army, was recently rebuilt over 6 years, and all traces of the mundane have been banished. The smaller and less expensive suites are contemporary, intensely design-conscious, and very comfortable. The more expensive are high-end posh, with pale satin upholstery and valuable antiques. All this grandeur is the personal property of an (individual) Austrian investor, whose stated ambition involves the on-site compilation of the largest and most comprehensive wine collection in Europe. A full-service spa is reserved for residents.

Coburgbastei 4, 1010 Vienna. ✆ **01/518-180.** Fax 01/518-181. www.palais-coburg.com. 35 suites. 560€–1,900€ suites. Rates include breakfast. Parking 40€. AE, DC, MC, V. **Amenities:** 2 restaurants; indoor pool; health club; spa; room service. *In room:* A/C, TV, full kitchen w/bar, free Wi-Fi.

Radisson/SAS Palais Hotel Vienna ★ This is one of Vienna's grandest renovations, converted to a hotel in 1985; in 1994, another palace next door was added, doubling its size. Near Vienna's gracious Stadtpark, the hotel boasts facades accented with cast-iron railings, reclining nymphs, and elaborate cornices. The interior is lushly outfitted with 19th-century architectural motifs, all impeccably restored and dramatically illuminated. The lobby contains arching palms, a soaring ceiling, and a bar with evening piano music. The result is an uncluttered, tastefully conservative, and well-maintained hotel that is managed in a breezy, highly efficient manner. Bedrooms feature either soothing pastels or, in the new wing, summery shades of green and white. The hotel also offers several duplex suites, or maisonettes; conventional suites; and rooms in the Royal Club, which has upgraded luxuries and services.

Parkring 16, 1010 Vienna. ✆ **800/333-3333** in the U.S., or **01/515170.** Fax 01/5122216. www.radisson. com. 247 units. 169€–284€ double; from 334€ junior suite. AE, DC, MC, V. Parking 30€. U-Bahn: Stadtpark. Tram: 2. **Amenities:** Restaurant; 2 bars; fitness center; spa; room service; babysitting; 1 room for those w/limited mobility. *In room:* A/C, TV, minibar, hair dryer, free Wi-Fi.

Radisson/SAS Style Hotel ★ In the early 1900s, this building was the headquarters of an Austrian bank, but in 2005 it was converted into an elegant, neo-Jugendstil hotel. The result is a quirky and somewhat eccentric design with an enviable facade that's embellished with gilded, Secessionist-era bas-reliefs. There is virtually no signage in front, while a style-conscious, avant-garde interior takes the era's design elements and adapts them with just enough swagger to pull it off. Right across the street from the famed Café Central, the hotel offers bedrooms that are comfortable, and angular-minimalist, with warm earth tones. The dramatic lounge

 Dream Dates in Vienna

Imagine waking one morning to the sound of church bells from St. Stephan's Cathedral, having champagne with your sumptuous breakfast at an elegant hotel, then strolling the cobblestone streets of the city center or visiting famed museums and marveling at old masters. Not a bad way to spend a honeymoon or anniversary. Some of Vienna's most elegant hotels, such as the **Grand Hotel Wien** (p. 76) and the **Mecure Hotel Biedermeier** (p. 90), offer excellent wedding packages as well as honeymoon and anniversary arrangements. For more information on wedding and honeymoon packages, contact the Vienna Tourist Board, Obere Augartenstrasse 40, 1020 Vienna (special hotels line ✆ **01/24555;** fax 01/24555-666; www.vienna.info).

has oversized, high-backed chairs that define the space and the most appealing public area is perhaps the H-12 wine bar, a long, narrow space with hard metallic surfaces, and an alabaster bar surface that's illuminated from within.

Herrengasse 12, 1010 Vienna. © **01/22780-0.** Fax 01/22780-77. www.style.vienna.radissonsas.com. 78 units. 199€–310€ double, 555€–585€ suite. AE, DC, MC, V. U-Bahn: Herrengasse. **Amenities:** Restaurant; wine bar; health club; sauna; room service. *In room:* A/C, TV, minibar, free Wi-Fi.

Ring Hotel Vienna ★★   Vienna's self-dubbed "Casual Luxury Hotel" opened in 2006 and is frequented by touring musicians and fashion icons. It is warm and inviting, simple prints adorn the walls, and the designer decor is stylish but cozy. Visit the delicious spa for a massage, and the seductive glimpse of the Karlskirche from the sauna. The restaurant "at eight" has little to boast for atmosphere but the food is great. Best of all, the impeccable service adds the finishing touch of personal luxury and the casual theme does not diminish the 5-star quality. It is a welcome and less expensive alternative to the usual imperial or Art Deco stylings.

Kärntnerring 8, 1010 Vienna. © **01/122-122.** Fax 01/221-22-900. 68 units. 200€–420€ double; from 500€ suite. Rates include buffet breakfast. AE, DC, MC, V. Valet parking 26€. U-Bahn: Karlsplatz. **Amenities:** Restaurant; bar; fitness room; spa; room service; massage; babysitting; laundry service; rooms for those w/limited mobility. *In room:* A/C, TV, minibar, hair dryer, nespresso machine, free Wi-Fi.

Vienna Marriott   This Marriott is popular because of the service and convenience rather than the decor, which is one grade above an airport. Opposite the Stadtpark, the location is great and the American consulate is in the same building. The lobby culminates in a stairway whose curved sides frame a splashing waterfall surrounded with plants. Many of the comfortably modern bedrooms are larger than those in the city's other contemporary hotels, although furnishings are a bit commercial. The British Bookshop is around the corner on Weihburggasse.

Parkring 12A, 1010 Vienna. © **888/236-2427** in the U.S., or 01/515180. Fax 01/515186736. www.marriott. com. 313 units. 229€–294€ double; 429€–690€ suite. AE, DC, MC, V. Parking 32€. Tram: 1 or 2. **Amenities:** 3 restaurants; 3 bars; indoor heated pool; fitness center; Jacuzzi; sauna; room service; babysitting; solarium; rooms for those w/limited mobility. *In room:* A/C, TV, minibar, hair dryer, free Wi-Fi for executive lounge guests, Internet: 1 hr 6€.

Expensive

Hotel Das Triest ★★ 🎒   Sir Terence Conran, the famous English restaurant owner and designer, created the interior for this contemporary hotel which is loved by artists and musicians. It is in the heart of Vienna, a 5-minute walk from St. Stephan's Cathedral. The building was originally a stable for horses pulling stagecoaches between Vienna and Trieste—hence its name, "City of Trieste." Its old cross-vaulted rooms, which give the structure a distinctive flair, have been transformed into lounges and suites. Bedrooms are midsize to spacious, tastefully furnished, and comfortable.

Wiedner Hauptstrasse 12, 1040 Vienna. © **01/589180.** Fax 01/5891818. www.dastriest.at. 73 units. 273€ double; 338€–556€ suite. Rates include buffet breakfast. AE, DC, MC, V. Parking 25€. U-Bahn: Stephansplatz. **Amenities:** Restaurant; bar; fitness center; sauna; room service; babysitting; solarium. *In room:* A/C, TV, minibar, hair dryer, free Wi-Fi.

Hotel Kaiserin Elisabeth   This yellow-stone hotel is near the cathedral. The interior is decorated with oriental rugs on well-maintained marble and wood floors. The main salon has a pale-blue skylight suspended above it, with mirrors and half-columns in natural wood. The small, quiet rooms have been considerably updated since Wolfgang Mozart, Richard Wagner, Franz Liszt, and Edvard Grieg stayed here, but their musical descendants continue to frequent the place. Polished wood, luxury linen, and perhaps another oriental rug grace the rooms. Bathrooms are a bit cramped.

Weihburggasse 3, 1010 Vienna. ℂ **01/515260.** Fax 01/515267. www.kaiserinelisabeth.at. 63 units. 216€–245€ double. Rates include buffet breakfast. AE, DC, MC, V. Parking 30€. U-Bahn: Stephansplatz. **Amenities:** Restaurant; bar; room service. *In room:* A/C (in most units), TV, minibar, hair dryer, free Wi-Fi.

Hotel König Von Ungarn ★   On a narrow street near St. Stephan's, this hotel occupies a dormered building dating back to the early-17th century and is Vienna's oldest continuously operated hotel. In all, this is an evocative, intimate retreat. It was once a pied-à-terre for Hungarian noble families during their stays in the Austrian capital. In 1791, Mozart reportedly resided and wrote some of his immortal music in the upstairs apartment that's now a Mozart museum. A mirrored solarium/bar area has a glass-roofed atrium with a tree growing in it. Tall windows overlook the Old Town, and Venetian mirrors adorn the walls. Everywhere you look, you'll find low-key luxury, tradition, and modern convenience. Guest rooms have been newly remodeled with Biedermeier accents and traditional furnishings. Try for the two rooms with balconies. Some rooms lack an outside window.

Schulerstrasse 10, 1010 Vienna. ℂ **01/515840.** Fax 01/515848. www.kvu.at. 33 units. 215€ double; 295€–345€ apt. Rates include breakfast. AE, DC, MC, V. U-Bahn: Stephansplatz. **Amenities:** Restaurant; bar; room service; babysitting. *In room:* A/C, TV, minibar, hair dryer, free Wi-Fi.

Hotel Römischer Kaiser ★ ☺   A Best Western, housed in a National Trust building. It's in a traffic-free zone between St. Stephan's Cathedral and the Vienna State Opera, on a side street off Kärntnerstrasse. It was constructed in 1684 as the private palace of the Imperial chamberlain; it later housed the Imperial School of Engineering before becoming a hostelry at the turn of the 20th century. The rooms are romantically decorated; the one we love has a red satin upholstered chaise lounge. Double-glazed windows keep down the noise, and baroque paneling is a nice touch. Some rooms—notably nos. 12, 22, 30, and 38—can accommodate three or four beds, making this a family-friendly place. The red-carpeted sidewalk cafe has a bar and tables shaded with flowers and umbrellas.

Annagasse 16, 1010 Vienna. ℂ **800/528-1234** in the U.S., or 01/51277510. Fax 01/512775113. www.bestwestern.com. 23 units. 132€–229€ double; 195€ suite. Rates include buffet breakfast. AE, DC, MC, V. Parking 21€. U-Bahn: Stephansplatz. **Amenities:** Restaurant; bar; room service. *In room:* A/C, TV, minibar, hair dryer, free Wi-Fi.

K + K Palais Hotel ★   This hotel, with its severely dignified facade, sheltered the affair of Emperor Franz Josef and his celebrated mistress, Katherina Schratt, in 1890. Occupying a desirable position near the river and a 5-minute walk from the Ring, it remained unused for 2 decades until it was renovated in 1981. Vestiges of its imperial past remain, in spite of the contemporary but airy lobby and the lattice-covered bar. The public rooms are painted a shade of imperial Austrian yellow, and one of Ms. Schratt's antique secretaries occupies a niche near a white-sided tile stove. The bedrooms are comfortably outfitted and stylish. Rooms have a certain Far East motif, with light wood, wicker, and rattan.

Rudolfsplatz 11, 1010 Vienna. ℂ **01/5331353.** Fax 01/533135370. www.kkhotels.com. 66 units. 185€–255€ double. Rates include buffet breakfast. AE, DC, MC, V. U-Bahn: Schottenring. **Amenities:** Bistro; bar; room service; babysitting. *In room:* A/C, TV, minibar, hair dryer, Wi-Fi.

Moderate

Graben Hotel   Back in the 18th century, this was called Zum Goldenen Jäger-horn; over the years, it has attracted an array of Bohemian writers and artists. The poet Franz Grillparzer was a regular guest; and during the dark days of World War II, it was a gathering place for writers like Franz Kafka, Max Brod, and Peter Altenberg. The hotel stands on a narrow street off the Kärntnerstrasse, in the very heart of the city. Guests gather around the stone fireplace in winter and look at fascinating memorabilia, including original postcards left by Altenberg. Rooms are high-ceil-inged but a bit cramped. Although there are some Art Nouveau touches, much of the furniture is simple and will feel spartan to someone looking for luxury. Sunlight streams into the front rooms, but not the darker havens in the rear.

Dorotheergasse 3, 1010 Vienna. ✆ **01/51215310.** Fax 01/512153120. www.kremslehnerhotels.at. 41 units. 160€–195€ double. Rates include buffet breakfast. AE, DC, MC, V. Parking 27€. U-Bahn: Karlsplatz. **Amenities:** Restaurant; lounge; room service; babysitting. *In room:* TV, minibar, hair dryer, Wi-Fi: 30mins 3€, 24hrs 12€.

Hollman Beletage ★★ 🎁   This discovery, smack in the heart of town, has beau-tifully designed rooms in a typically modern Austrian style. The waterfall showers and beautiful baths, plus the spa area, will pamper after long, eventful days. The breakfast is rich and the staff prides itself on being hosts rather than just employees. The in-house cinema shows three films a day all relating somehow to Vienna, for instance Orson Welles' *The Third Man*. This establishment is small, sophisticated, and simple, while aiming to be the best and perhaps only place of its kind. Make sure you book ahead as it only has 24 rooms.

Köhlnerhofgasse 6.✆ **01/9611960.** Fax: 01-513-9698. www.hollmann-beletage.at. 24 units. 140€–250€ double. Rates include breakfast. AE, DC, MC, V. U-Bahn: Stephansplatz. **Amenities**: Restaurant; break-fast room; fitness center; spa; garden; cinema. *In room*: TV, minibar, hair dryer, free Wi-Fi.

Hotel Amadeus   Cozy and convenient, this boxlike hotel is only 2 minutes from Stephansdom and within walking distance of practically everything of musical or historical note in Vienna. It is on the site of a once-legendary tavern (Zum roten Igel), a haunt of Johannes Brahms and Franz Schubert. Behind a dull 1960s facade, the bedrooms and public rooms are pleasant, furnished in a comfortable, modern style, many with views of the cathedral. Ceilings are uncomfortably low, and the double-glazing on the windows fails to obliterate street noise. Tiled bathrooms are midsize. Eight rooms have showers but no tubs. It's good value for money, but the staff is somewhat reserved.

Wildpretmarkt 5, 1010 Vienna. ✆ **01/5338738.** Fax 01/533-87383838. www.hotel-amadeus.at. 30 units. 178€–203€ double. Rates include buffet breakfast. AE, DC, MC, V. U-Bahn: Stephansplatz. **Amenities:** Breakfast room; lounge; babysitting; rooms for those w/limited mobility. *In room:* A/C, TV, minibar, hair dryer, free Wi-Fi.

Hotel Am Parkring   This well-maintained hotel occupies the top 3 floors of a 13-story office building near the edge of Vienna's Stadtpark. A semiprivate elevator whisks you from street level. There are sweeping views of the city from all of its bed-rooms, which are furnished in a conservative but comfortable style. Business guests and tourists alike use this hotel, although the atmosphere is a bit sterile if you're seek-ing nostalgic Vienna. Rooms are a standard, reliable choice. This hotel is not the kind-est to the lone tourist, as single rooms tend to be small, often using sofa beds.

WHERE TO STAY | Innere Stadt (Inner City)

Parkring 12, 1015 Vienna. ✆ **01/514800.** Fax 01/5148040. www.bestwestern.com. 64 units. 149€–230€ double; 360€ suite. Rates include buffet breakfast. AE, DC, MC, V. Parking 19€. U-Bahn: Stadtpark or Stubentor. Tram: 1 or 2. **Amenities:** Restaurant; bar; room service; babysitting. *In room:* A/C, TV, minibar, hair dryer, Wi-Fi.

Hotel Capricorno   In the heart of Vienna, a short stroll from St. Stephan's and next to the Danube Canal. Outside it's a dull, cube-shape building; but inside it's warm and inviting, with modern Art Nouveau accents, tiles, and brass trim in the reception area. Rooms are compact—even cramped, in many cases—but are well furnished and maintained. Singles are particularly small, mainly because the beds are more spacious than most. Some, especially those on the lower levels, suffer from noise pollution.

Schwedenplatz 3–4, 1010 Vienna. ✆ **01/53331040.** Fax 01/53376714. www.schick-hotels.com. 46 units. 131€–186€ double. AE, DC, MC, V. Rates include buffet breakfast. U-Bahn: Stephansplatz. **Amenities:** Breakfast room; lounge; room service. *In room:* A/C, TV, minibar, hair dryer, free Wi-Fi.

Hotel-Pension Arenberg ★   This genteel but unpretentious hotel-pension, a Best Western, occupies the second and third floors of a six-floor apartment house from the turn of the 20th century. On the Stubenring across from the Stadtpark and the Museum of Applied Arts, it offers small, soundproof bedrooms outfitted in old-world style with Oriental carpets, conservative furniture, and intriguing artwork. The hotel appeals to those with a sense of history, and has a helpful English-speaking staff.

Stubenring 2, 1010 Vienna. ✆ **800/528-7234** in the U.S., or 01/5125291. Fax 01/5139356. www.best western.com. 23 units. 158€–208€ double; 293€ triple. Rates include breakfast. AE, DC, MC, V. Parking 15€. U-Bahn: Schwedenplatz. **Amenities:** Lounge; breakfast-only room service; babysitting; rooms for those w/limited mobility. *In room:* A/C, TV, minibar, hair dryer, free Wi-Fi.

Hotel Royal ★   This dignified hotel on Singerstrasse is less than a block from St. Stephan's Cathedral, with a piano in the lobby on which Wagner composed *Die Meistersinger von Nürnberg*. Each of the ample rooms is furnished differently, with some good reproduction antiques and even an occasional original. Opened in 1931, the hotel was rebuilt in 1982. Try for a room with a balcony and a view of the cathedral. Corner rooms have spacious foyers, although those facing the street tend to be noisy.

Singerstrasse 3, 1010 Vienna. ✆ **01/515680.** Fax 01/513-9698. www.kremslehnerhotels.at. 81 units. 140€–200€ double. Rates include breakfast. AE, DC, MC, V. U-Bahn: Stephansplatz. **Amenities:** 2 restaurants; bar; wine bar; room service. *In room:* TV, minibar, hair dryer, Wi-Fi: 30mins 3€, 24hrs 12€.

Hotel Viennart ★ 🛍   The decor is sock-it-to-you modern, in red, white, orange, and black. It's a good choice for lovers of modern art and convenient for the MuseumsQuartier (see p. 134). The location is at the edge of the Spittelberg, a district locals call "the Montmartre of Vienna." Rooms are outfitted in a functional style, with some nice details.

Breite Gasse 9, 1070 Vienna. ✆ **01/523-13-450.** Fax 01/523-13-45-111. www.austrotel.at. 56 units. 100€–170€ double; 246€ suite. Children under 12 stay free in parents' room. Rates include buffet breakfast. AE, DC, MC, V. U-Bahn: Volkstheater. **Amenities:** Breakfast room; babysitting. *In room:* TV, minibar, hair dryer, free Wi-Fi.

Mailberger Hof ★   This old palace was built in the 14th century as a mansion for the knights of Malta and a Maltese cross still hangs over the two large wooden entry doors. The vaulted ceiling, leather armchairs, and marble walls would all still remind the knights of their former home … possibly the cobblestone courtyard, too. Otherwise the friendly, family-run establishment is new and modern. The moderate-size bedrooms are often brightened with pastels. In general, though, the public rooms are nicer.

Annagasse 7, 1010 Vienna. ℂ **01/5120641.** Fax 01/512064110. www.mailbergerhof.at. 40 units. 180€–260€ double; 210€–280€ suite. Rates include buffet breakfast. AE, DC, MC, V. Parking 29€. U-Bahn: Karlsplatz. **Amenities:** Bar; room service (7am–10pm); babysitting. *In room:* A/C, TV, minibar, hair dryer, free Wi-Fi.

Inexpensive

Drei Kronen ✐ The "3 crowns" in the German name (Austria, Hungary, and Bohemia from the old Austro-Hungarian Empire) are displayed on top of the building. The hotel enjoys one of Vienna's best locations, right next to the Naschmarkt. Built in 1894, the five-floor hotel has comfortable rooms although they are small, some not big enough for full-size beds.

Schleifmuehlgasse 25, 1040 Vienna. ℂ **01/5873289.** Fax 01/587328911. www.hotel3kronen.at. 41 units. 75€ double; 85€ triple. AE, DC, MC, V. Parking 15€. U-Bahn: Karlsplatz. **Amenities:** Breakfast room; lounge; babysitting. *In room:* TV, free Wi-Fi.

Hotel Austria This unpretentious, family-owned hotel is a corner building on a small, quiet cul-de-sac. The comfortable furnishings in the lobby and in the chandeliered breakfast room are beautifully cared for, guest rooms have reproduction period furniture accenting a stylish modern decor, and every detail of service is carried out with style. The staff is knowledgeable about goings on locally for a good meal or a glass of wine, and offer printouts explaining the area's medieval origins.

Am Fleischmarkt 20, 1011 Vienna. ℂ **01/51523.** Fax 01/51523506. www.hotelaustria-wien.at. 46 units. 42 w/bathroom. 69€–90€ double w/no bathroom; 115€–178€ double w/bathroom. Rates include buffet breakfast. AE, DC, MC, V. Parking 19€. U-Bahn: Schwedenplatz. Tram: 1 or 2. **Amenities:** Breakfast room; lounge; breakfast-only room service; babysitting. *In room:* TV, minibar, hair dryer, free Wi-Fi.

Hotel Kärntnerhof ★ ☺ Only a 4-minute walk from the cathedral, the Kärntnerhof has been refurbished and renovated, and is now more comfortable and just as friendly. The decor of the public rooms is tastefully arranged around Oriental rugs, well-upholstered chairs and couches with cabriole legs, and an occasional 19th-century portrait. The midsize to spacious rooms are up-to-date, usually with the original parquet floors and striped or patterned wallpaper set off by curtains. Many of the guest rooms are large enough to handle an extra bed, making this good for families. The owner is also helpful, directing guests to nearby services and Vienna landmarks.

Grashofgasse 4, 1011 Vienna. ℂ **01/5121923.** Fax 01/513222833. www.karntnerhof.com. 44 units. 110€–175€ double; 180€–280€ suite. Rates include buffet breakfast. AE, DC, MC, V. Parking 17€. U-Bahn: Stephansplatz. **Amenities:** Breakfast room; lounge; room service; laundry service; dry cleaning. *In room:* TV, free Wi-Fi.

Hotel-Pension Shermin ✐ This small, inviting, family-run boarding house in the heart of the city is much nicer than its price would suggest. Bedrooms are big and comfortable, the details are chosen with taste and the owners do a lot with less. The location is central, with most attractions a 5-minute walk away. Furnishings are modern albeit lacking flair, but are exceedingly comfortable, attracting many repeat guests.

Rilkeplatz 7, 1040 Vienna. ℂ **01/58661830.** Fax 01/586618310. www.hotel-pension-shermin.at. 11 units. 72€–114€ double. Rates include buffet breakfast. AE, DC, MC, V. Parking 7€ Mon–Fri, free Sat–Sun.

U-Bahn: Karlsplatz. **Amenities:** Breakfast room; lounge; breakfast-only room service. *In room:* TV, hair dryer, free Wi-Fi.

Hotel-Pension Suzanne ★ ☺

Just along from the opera house, this is a real discovery. Once you get past its post-war facade, the interior warms considerably; it is brightly decorated in comfortable, Viennese turn-of-the-20th-century style with antique beds, plush chairs, and the original molded ceilings. Rooms are a reasonable size and well maintained, facing either the busy street or a courtyard. Some contain three beds, making the hotel suitable for families. Some bedrooms are like small apartments, with kitchenettes.

Walfischgasse 4. ℂ **01/5132507.** Fax 01/5132500. www.pension-suzanne.at. 26 units. 100€–112€ double; 135€–145€ triple. Rates include buffet breakfast. AE, DC, MC, V. U-Bahn: Karlsplatz. **Amenities:** Breakfast room; lounge; breakfast-only room service; babysitting; free Wi-Fi at reception. *In room:* TV, hair dryer.

Hotel Post ⚓

The Post lies in the medieval slaughterhouse district, just above Schwedenplatz and backing on to the Vienna Chamber Opera and the tiny theater, Drachengasse, that hosts English language Improv every other Friday night (see p. 198). A major renovation has given the hotel a bright, airy feel to the modest to midsize rooms that makes this an even better value for the money. The manager is quick to tell you that both Mozart and Haydn frequently stayed in a former inn at this address, and their music is still played in the coffeehouse, Le Café, just renovated, below the hotel.

Fleischmarkt 24, 1010 Vienna. ℂ **01/515830.** Fax 01/51583808. www.hotel-post-wien.at. 107 units, 77 w/bathroom. 76€ double w/no bathroom; 125€ double w/bathroom; 100€ triple w/no bathroom; 152€ triple w/bathroom. Rates include buffet breakfast. AE, DC, MC, V. Parking 18€. Tram: 1 or 2. **Amenities:** Restaurant; lounge; 1 room for those w/limited mobility; free Wi-Fi in Lobby. *In room:* TV, hair dryer, free Internet.

Hotel Wandl ★

Under the same ownership for generations, the Wandl lies in the Inner City behind the Peterskirche and around the corner from the famed literary Café Korb, haunt of journalists and actors. Many of the rooms offer views of the steeple of St. Stephan's Cathedral (often from small balconies). The breakfast room is a high-ceilinged, two-toned room with chandeliers. The bedrooms are spacious, and comfortable, many with sitting-room space. Beds are frequently renewed. All in all, a comfortable choice.

Petersplatz 9, 1010 Vienna. ℂ **01/534550.** Fax 01/5345577. www.hotel-wandl.com. 138 units. 158€–205€ double; 220€ suite. Rates include breakfast. AE, DC, MC, V. U-Bahn: Stephansplatz. **Amenities:** Breakfast room; lounge; room service. *In room:* TV, hair dryer, Internet: 24hrs 5€.

Pension Dr. Geissler ⚓

Unpretentious lodgings at extremely reasonable prices are offered here at the edge of the Danube Canal. The bedrooms in this attractive, informal guesthouse are furnished with simple pale wood headboards and a few utilitarian pieces. Most rooms have their own small bathrooms.

Postgasse 14, 1010 Vienna. ℂ **01/5332803.** Fax 01/5332635. www.hotelpension.at. 35 units, 21 w/bathroom. 65€ double w/no bathroom; 95€ double w/bathroom. Rates include buffet breakfast. AE, DC, MC, V. U-Bahn: Schwedenplatz. **Amenities:** Breakfast room; bar; breakfast-only room service; babysitting. *In room:* TV, Wi-Fi on top 2 floors: 1hr 1 €.

Pension Neuer Markt ⚑

Near the cathedral, in the heart of Vienna, this pension is housed in a white baroque building that faces a square with an ornate fountain. The small, carpeted rooms, with white walls accented with strong tones, are well maintained. Some have large windows. Bathrooms with tub/shower combinations are small, seemingly added as an afterthought; but for Vienna the price is delicious. We recommend reserving 30 days in advance.

Seilergasse 9, 1010 Vienna. © 01/5122316. Fax 01/5139105. www.hotelpension.at. 37 units. 80€–135€ double. Rates include buffet breakfast. AE, DC, MC, V. Parking 4.60€. U-Bahn: Stephansplatz. **Amenities:** Breakfast room; bar; breakfast-only room service; babysitting. *In room:* TV, free Wi-Fi.

Pension Nossek Mozart lived here from 1781 to 1782, and wrote the *Haffner* symphony and *The Abduction from the Seraglio*. Walk out of the front door and you are in the heart of Vienna. The pension lies on one of Vienna's best shopping streets, just blocks away from all the major sights. In 1909, the building was converted into a guesthouse and has always been a good bet for clean, comfortable rooms with decent (mostly comfortable) beds. Most have been renovated, and all but a few singles contain small private bathrooms.

Graben 17, 1010 Vienna. © 01/53370410. Fax 01/5353646. www.pension-nossek.at. 30 units. 110€–115€ double; 143€ suite. Rates include breakfast. No credit cards. Free parking. U-Bahn: Stephansplatz. **Amenities:** Breakfast room; lounge. *In room:* TV, minibar, hair dryer (some), Wi-Fi: 24hrs 5€.

Hotel Pertschy ★ These apartment-like digs are a more affordable Inner City alternative to the classic hotel experience. Several rooms overlook a central courtyard and are scattered among six or seven private apartments, whose residents are used to foreign visitors roaming through the building. The recent renovations have left the quarters elegant and simple, without losing the Old Vienna touch. This family run establishment exudes comfort and it's right off the Graben.

Habsburgergasse 5, 1010 Vienna. © 01/534490. Fax 01/5344949. www.pertschy.com. 50 units, 2 w/ kitchen. 119€–151€ double. AE, DC, MC, V. Parking 16€. U-Bahn: Stephansplatz. **Amenities:** Breakfast room; lounge. *In room:* TV, minibar, hair dryer, free Wi-Fi.

Zur Wiener Staatsoper 📷 This simple but well-run family hotel has a facade that's more evocative of Vienna's late-19th-century golden age than any equivalently rated hotel in town. Built in 1896 as a private home, it retains some of the charms (and the drawbacks) of its origins. Rooms are high-ceilinged, functional, relatively comfortable, and, other than small bathrooms (with showers only), adequate for most needs. Literary fans appreciate that this hotel provided the inspiration to John Irving for one of the settings (a run-down hotel that had evolved into a whorehouse) in his novel *Hotel New Hampshire*.

Krugerstrasse 11, A-1010 Wien. © 01/513-12-74. www.zurwienerstaatsoper.at. 22 units. 113€–150€ double; 135€–175€ triple. Rates include buffet breakfast. DC, MC, V. U-Bahn: Karlsplatz. **Amenities:** Breakfast room; lounge. *In room:* TV, free Wi-Fi.

LEOPOLDSTADT (2ND DISTRICT)

Expensive

Austria Trend Hotel Messe Wien ★ Located across from the Messezentrum Wien, Vienna's trade fair and convention hall, the Trend is new and shiny and (if you need to be here), unbeatably convenient. The convex shape and inclining facade leaves all the rooms flooded with light, and some of the architectural features continue through the hotel's corridors and rooms. The well-appointed guest rooms feature French windows with a view of the fair grounds. The top two levels house business rooms and suites with panoramic views of the city.

Messestrasse 2, 1020 Vienna. ☎ **01/727270.** Fax 01/72727-100. www.austriatrend.at. 243 units. 250€– 270€ double; 400€ suite. AE, DC, MC, V. U-Bahn: Praterstern. **Amenities:** Restaurant; bar; sauna; room service. *In room:* A/C, TV, minibar, hair dryer, free Wi-Fi on 6th and 7th floors.

Hilton Vienna Danube ★★   Vienna has a larger, but less central Hilton hotel, this one lying on the Danube River next to Messezentrum Wien, a 10-minute ride from the city (there's a free shuttle), and a short walk from Prater Park. Business people like its proximity to international companies, although it's equally suitable for holidaymakers, with a stunning setting on the river and a bike path to Klosterneuburg and the Wachau in one direction and Hungary in the other. The hotel has the largest guest rooms of any hotel in Vienna. Dining is a special feature here; the Symphony Donau Restaurant serves international and Austrian cuisine on a beautiful terrace overlooking the river. The chef is famous for his Sunday (noon to 3pm) Royal Swedish Smörgasbord, a buffet of Swedish specialties. There is also an attractive traditional coffee shop with excellent coffee, pastries, and international newspapers.

Handelskai 269, 1020 Vienna. ☎ 800-HILTONS or **01/727770.** Fax 01/7277782200. www.vienna-danube.hilton.com. 367 units. 125€–205€ double; 250€–295€ suite. AE, DC, MC, V. U-Bahn: U1 to Prat-erstern and then tram 21 to Meiereistrasse. **Amenities:** Restaurant; bar; outdoor pool; tennis court; gym; sauna; room service; rooms for those w/limited mobility. *In room:* A/C, TV, minibar, hair dryer, Wi-Fi: 1hr 10€, 24hrs (limited download) 17€, 24hrs (unlimited) 22€, free for gold and diamond customers.

Moderate

Hotel Stefanie   This well-regarded traditional hotel is just across the Danube Canal from Schwedenplatz, a short walk to the rest of the city. A hotel since the 1700s, it was renamed in 1870 by the Schick family after the marriage of the Crown Prince Rudolf to the Princess Stefanie. Guest rooms are today furnished in sleek Viennese styling, with reproduction antiques, although some are a bit small. The bar is more modern, with black leather armchairs on chrome swivel bases, and the concealed lighting throws an azure glow over the artfully displayed bottles.

Taborstrasse 12, 1020 Vienna. ☎ **800/528-1234** in the U.S., or 01/211500. Fax 01/21150160. www.schick hotels.com. 131 units. 149€–211€ double. Rates include buffet breakfast. AE, DC, MC, V. Parking 19€. U-Bahn: Schwedenplatz. Tram: 21. **Amenities:** Restaurant; bar; room service. *In room:* A/C, TV, minibar, hair dryer, free Wi-Fi.

LANDSTRASSE (3RD DISTRICT)

Very Expensive

Hilton Vienna ★★   This 15-story box overlooks the Wienfluss and offers plush rooms and elegant public areas. Despite the hotel's slick modernity, it manages to provide plenty of Viennese appeal, with bedrooms in a range of styles, including Biedermeier, contemporary, baroque, and Art Nouveau. Its attractive cafe-lounge and bar areas are popular meeting places for business people, by day, the local after-work crowd, and more business partying late in the evening. Towering over the city skyline (with a soaring atrium), it also affords great views from the upper floors. The lovely Stadtpark is across the street and connected by a footbridge, which strollers and joggers use during excursions into the landscaped and bird-filled park.

Where to Stay in Leopoldstadt

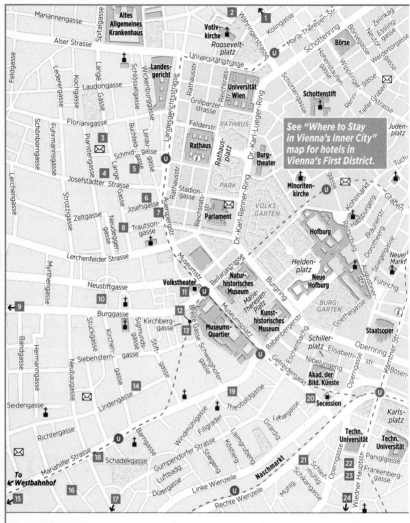

See "Where to Stay in Vienna's Inner City" map for hotels in Vienna's First District.

Altstadt Vienna **10**

Altwienerhof **17**

Austria Trend Hotel Albatros **1**

Austria Trend Hotel Messe Wien **26**

Cordial Theaterhotel Wien **4**

Drei Kronen **21**

Falkensteiner Hotel Am
  Schottenfeld **9**

Fürst Metternich Hotel **16**

Golden Tulip Wien City **15**

Hilton Vienna **28**

Hilton Vienna Danube **27**

Hotel Bellevue **1**

Hotel Das Triest **23**

Hotel Das Tyrol **19**

Hotel Erzherzog Rainer **24**

Hotel Graf Stadion **5**

Hotel Ibis Wien **15**

Hotel Kummer **18**

Hotel Mercure Josefshof **6**

Hotel Mercure Secession **20**

Hotel Parliament Levante **7**

Hotel-Pension Museum **11**

Hotel-Pension Shermin **22**

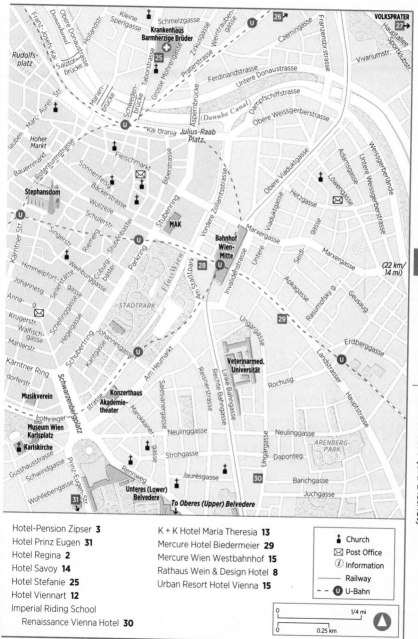

Hotel-Pension Zipser **3**
Hotel Prinz Eugen **31**
Hotel Regina **2**
Hotel Savoy **14**
Hotel Stefanie **25**
Hotel Viennart **12**
Imperial Riding School
　　Renaissance Vienna Hotel **30**

K + K Hotel Maria Theresia **13**
Mercure Hotel Biedermeier **29**
Mercure Wien Westbahnhof **15**
Rathaus Wein & Design Hotel **8**
Urban Resort Hotel Vienna **15**

† Church
✉ Post Office
ⓘ Information
—— Railway
- - Ⓤ U-Bahn

0 ————— 1/4 mi
0 ————— 0.25 km

5

WHERE TO STAY | Landstrasse (3rd District)

Am Stadtpark, 1030 Vienna. © **800/445-8667** in the U.S., or 01/717000. Fax 01/7130691. www.hilton.com. 579 units. 205€–310€ double; from 355€ suite. AE, DC, MC, V. Parking 27€. The Hilton is at the City Air Terminal and the City Airport Train 17 minutes to Schwechat. U-Bahn: Landstrasse. **Amenities:** Restaurant; cafe; bar; indoor heated pool; fitness center; Jacuzzi; sauna; children's playground; babysitting; laundry service; rooms for those w/limited mobility. *In room:* A/C, TV, minibar, hair dryer, Wi-Fi: 1hr 10€, 24hrs(limited download) 22€, 24hrs(unlimited) 27€, free for gold and diamond customers.

Expensive

Imperial Riding School Renaissance Vienna Hotel
In the city's diplomatic quarter, close to the baroque Belvedere Palace, this was a military riding school before its conversion in the 1990s. South of Stadtpark, it's an impressive mid-19th-century Tudor-style castle to which a modern glass structure has been added. The elegant lobby has vaulted ceilings, contemporary sculpture, and marble pillars leading off to many charming side rooms, including a library. The stylish guest rooms in the hotel's newer building hold such luxuries as oversize tubs.

Ungargasse 60, 1030 Vienna. © **01/711-750.** Fax 01/711-758143. www.renaissancehotels.com/viese. 342 units. 146€–227€ double; 195€–295€ suite. AE, DC, MC, V. Parking 21€. Tram: U3 or U4 to Landstrasse Wien Mitte. **Amenities:** Restaurant; bar; indoor pool; fitness center; sauna; room service; babysitting; rooms for those w/limited mobility; Wi-Fi in lobby: 24hrs 16.90€. *In room:* A/C, TV, minibar, hair dryer, Internet: 16.90€.

Mercure Hotel Biedermeier ★★ ☺
This hotel, established in 1983, is in a very attractively renovated late-18th-century Biedermeier apartment house enclosing a charming narrow cobblestone walk, or "Zinnhofpassage." Although the hotel is near the Wien Mitte train and subway station, most bedrooms overlook the pedestrian-only walkway lined with shops and cafes that is another world altogether. Duvets cover the firm beds, and double glazing keeps noise to a minimum. On the premises are the formal restaurant Zu den Deutschmeistern and the very appealing Weissgerberstube, used by locals. One child stays free with parents.

Landstrasser Hauptstrasse 28, 1030 Vienna. © **800/780-5734** in the U.S., or 01/716710. Fax 01/71671503. www.dorint.de. 203 units. 180€–233€ double; 315€–350€ suite. Rates include breakfast. AE, DC, MC, V. Parking 15€. U-Bahn: Rochusgasse. **Amenities:** 2 restaurants; 2 bars; room service; babysitting; rooms for those w/limited mobility. *In room:* A/C, TV, minibar, hair dryer, free Internet.

WIEDEN & MARGARETEN (4TH & 5TH DISTRICTS)

Moderate

Hotel Erzherzog Rainer
Popular with groups and business guests, this very appealing family-run hotel was built just before World War I. A short subway or tram ride takes you to the Vienna State Opera, the Musikverein or Kärntnerstrasse, with a U-Bahn stop just steps away. The bedrooms are well decorated and come in a variety of sizes; you'll find good beds, but not always soundproofing. The singles are small; and like many traditional hotels in Austria, there is no air-conditioning, although it's fair to say that in Vienna's temperate climate, this is rarely an issue. An informal brasserie serves Austrian dishes, and the bar is modishly decorated with black and brass.

Wiedner Hauptstrasse 27–29, 1040 Vienna. © **01/22111.** Fax 01/22111-350. www.schick-hotels.com. 84 units. 135€–203€ double. Rates include breakfast. AE, MC, V. Parking 18€. U-Bahn: Taubstummengasse;

Tram 61, 62, on the Wiedner Hauptstrasse. **Amenities:** Restaurant; bar; room service; babysitting; rooms for those w/limited mobility. *In room:* TV, minibar, hair dryer, free Wi-Fi.

Hotel Prinz Eugen ★   In the embassy quarter, this handsome hotel is opposite the Belvedere Palace and just down from the Südbahnhof rail station. Subways and trams will carry you quickly to the city, and there are good highway connections both east and south. The decor is a mixture of antiques, Oriental rugs, and such stylishly glitzy touches as glass walls with brass trim. Rooms have soundproof windows opening on to balconies and come in a wide range of sizes, all comfortable. Singles are decidedly small, but suitable if you don't have too much luggage.

Wiedner Gürtel 14, 1040 Vienna. ℂ **01/5051741.** Fax 01/505174119. www.hotelprinzeugen.at. 110 units. 135€–220€ double; 245€ suite. Rates include buffet breakfast. AE, DC, DISC, MC, V. Parking 19€. U-Bahn: Südtiroler Platz; D Tram Südbahnhof. **Amenities:** Restaurant; bar; room service; babysitting. *In room:* TV, minibar, hair dryer, Wi-Fi: 1hr 10€, 24hrs 17€.

MARIAHILF (6TH DISTRICT)
Expensive

Hotel Das Tyrol ★★ 🎒   It's friendly, fairly priced, loaded with charm, and lies within a short walk of one of the densest concentrations of museums in Europe. The only drawback is that it's so good that it's often booked weeks in advance. The Das Tyrol occupies what, 175 years ago, was built as a convent, and which later functioned as a simple hotel. In 1999, it was bought by an Austrian member of Parliament, Helena von Ramsbacher, one of the youngest women ever to become an MP. After pouring money into restoration, she justifiably defines it as a boutique-style luxury hotel. What you get are high ceilings, contemporary furnishings, a fascinating collection of art, a sense of uncluttered spaciousness, a lovely glassed, period elevator, and a winding central staircase, that all preserve the building's timeless feel. Rooms are just as lovely.

Mariahilferstrasse 15, 1060 Vienna. ℂ **01/587-54-15.** Fax 01/587-54-15-49. www.das-tyrol.at. 30 units. 185€–239€ double; 259€ junior suite. Rates include breakfast. Parking 18€. U-Bahn: U2 Museums-Quartier, Volkstheater, or U3 Neubaugasse. **Amenities:** Sauna and wellness center; room service. *In room:* A/C, TV, minibar, nespresso machine, free Wi-Fi.

Hotel Kummer   Established by the Kummer family in the 19th century, this hotel was built in response to the growing power of the railways as they forged new paths of commerce and tourism through Central Europe, but has all the dignity of a palace in the 1st District. A short walk from Vienna's Westbahnhof, the hotel lies at a busy intersection, but the rooms have soundproof windows. Many have stone balconies with a fine view over the comings and goings below. There are a variety of rooms—some feature superior appointments and deluxe furnishings. Try for a corner room—they have better light and are bigger.

Mariahilferstrasse 71A, 1060 Vienna. ℂ **01/588950.** Fax 01/5878133. www.hotelkummer.at. 100 units. 95€–255€ double. Rates include buffet breakfast. AE, DC, MC, V. Parking 15€. U-Bahn: Neubaugasse. Bus: 13A or 14A. **Amenities:** Restaurant; bar; room service. *In room:* TV, minibar, hair dryer, Wi-Fi: 1 hr 12€, 24hrs 27€.

Moderate

Fürst Metternich Hotel ★ 🎒   Pink-and-gray walls and ornate stone window trim identify this handsome, solidly-built 19th-century hotel, formally an opulent private

FAMILY-FRIENDLY hotels

- **Falkensteiner Hotel Am Schottenfeld** (p. 94)   Spacious rooms, bright decor, and a children's club makes this hotel a chic destination for families.

- **Hotel Am Schubertring** Children under 6 stay free with a parent, and several rooms in this historic hotel easily accommodate three or more.

- **Hotel Graf Stadion** (p. 95) Many of the rooms at this hotel (a longtime haunt of families on a tight budget) contain two double beds, suitable for parties of three or four.

- **Hotel Kärntnerhof** (p. 84)   A family-oriented *gutbürgerlich* (old middle-class) hotel, this establishment lies right in the heart of Vienna; and its helpful management welcomes children with open arms.

- **Hotel Mercure Josefshof** (p. 95)   A central location and a number of rooms with kitchenettes make this a great choice for families.

- **Hotel Mercure Biedermeier** (p. 90)   A charming, protected location along the pedestrian Zinnhofpassage in the 3rd District. One child stays free with parents.

- **Hotel Opernring** Ample rooms overlooking central Vienna; many sleep three or four.

- **Hotel-Pension Suzanne** (p. 85)   Inexpensive and centrally located, many rooms here sleep three or more, and several feature small kitchens.

- **Hotel Römischer Kaiser** (p. 81)   The former palace of the imperial chamberlain, this Best Western affiliate offers a glimpse of imperial Vienna from around 1684. Its staff is extremely hospitable and gracious to visiting families.

home. It's located between the Ring and the Westbahnhof near Mariahilferstrasse, about a 20-minute walk to the city. Many of the grander details have been retained, including a pair of red stone columns in the entranceway and an old-fashioned staircase guarded with griffins. The high-ceilinged bedrooms are relatively neutral and not all that roomy, although do have lovely feather pillows. Windows at the front are only partially soundproof, so if you are a light sleeper, ask for a room in the rear. The Barflys Club, a popular hangout open daily, offers 120 different exotic drinks.

Esterházygasse 33, 1060 Vienna. ✆ **01/58870.** Fax 01/5875268. www.austrotel.at. 55 units. 100€–170€ double. Rates include buffet breakfast. AE, DC, MC, V. Parking 17€. U-Bahn: Zieglergasse. **Amenities:** Breakfast room; bar; babysitting. *In room:* TV, minibar, free Wi-Fi.

Golden Tulip Wien City   This concrete-and-glass hotel was designed in 1975 with enough angles in its facade to give each bedroom an irregular shape. Usually the rooms have two windows that face different skylines. Aside from the views, bedrooms are a good size with comfortable furnishings. Opt for a studio with a terrace on the seventh floor. The hotel also has a public rooftop terrace where guests sip drinks in summer.

Wallgasse 23, A-1060 Vienna. ✆ **01/599900.** Fax 01/5967646. www.goldentulipwiencity.com. 77 units. 150€–230€ double; from 270€ suite. Rates include buffet breakfast. AE, DC, MC, V. Parking 15€. U-Bahn:

Gumpendorfer. Bus: 57A. **Amenities:** Breakfast room; bar; breakfast-only room service; babysitting. *In room:* A/C, TV, minibar, hair dryer, free Wi-Fi.

Hotel Mercure Secession ★   Sitting at the corner of Lehárgasse and the Getreidemarkt just behind Olbrich's stunning gold-domed Secession, this central hotel is a modern building with panoramic windows on the ground floor, warmly decorated with some 19th-century antiques and comfortably upholstered chairs. And while not the cheapest, the friendly service added to the location near theaters, concert halls, and galleries makes it much-used by musicians, singers, actors, and other artists; families are especially fond of the place as many rooms contain kitchenettes.

Getreidemarkt 5, 1060 Vienna. ⓒ **01/588380.** Fax 01/58838212. www.mercure.com. 68 units. 150€–175€ double. Rates include buffet breakfast. AE, DC, MC, V. Parking 18€. U-Bahn: Karlsplatz. **Amenities:** Breakfast room; bar; room service; babysitting. *In room:* A/C, TV, minibar, hair dryer, safe, free Wi-Fi.

Inexpensive

Hotel Ibis Wien   The graceless facade looks like a small town department store but is a good find, just a few minutes' walk from the Westbahnhof. Although this is a chain and its units are purely functional, there are modern comforts and the rates are good for Vienna. Be warned: the sturdy furnishings might not always be tasteful (one guest called the upholstery "psychedelic"). Still, the roof terrace provides a panoramic city view. Groups are booked here, and you'll meet all of them in the impersonal restaurant, which serves reasonably priced meals and wine.

Mariahilfer Gurtel 22, 1060 Vienna. ⓒ **01/59998.** Fax 01/5979090. www.accorhotels.com. 341 units. 59€–93€ double. Rates include buffet breakfast. AE, DC, MC, V. Parking 11€. U-Bahn: Westbahnhof, Gumpendorferstrasse. **Amenities:** Restaurant; bar; rooms for those w/limited mobility. *In room:* A/C, TV, free Wi-Fi.

NEUBAU (7TH DISTRICT)

Expensive

K + K Hotel Maria Theresia ★   The hotel's initials are a reminder of the empire's dual monarchy (*Kaiserlich und Königlich*—Imperial and royal, i.e. "by appointment to the Emperor of Austria and King of Hungary"). Even the surrounding streets, home to some major museums and many buildings from the late 19th-century *Grunderzeit*, (the time before the 1873 economic crash) is reminiscent of the days of the monarchy. It is now a sleek example of contemporary Vienna design and offers ample, well-appointed rooms. The hotel is in the artists' colony of Spittelberg, within an easy walk of the Art History and Natural History Museums, the Volkstheater, and the shopping street Mariahilferstrasse.

Kirchberggasse 6–8, 1070 Vienna. ⓒ **800/537-8483** in the U.S., or 01/52123. Fax 01/5212370. www.kkhotels.com. 123 units. 230€ double; from 280€ suite. Rates include buffet breakfast. AE, DC, MC, V. Parking 16€. U-Bahn: Volkstheater. Tram: 49. **Amenities:** Restaurant; bar; fitness center; sauna; room service; babysitting. *In room:* A/C, TV, minibar, hair dryer, free Wi-Fi.

Moderate

Altstadt Vienna ★★ 🎒   Otto Ernst Wiesenthal knows what it means to feel at home abroad. The creator of what he calls "your personal residence in Vienna" takes pride in finding each guest the right room (all uniquely and stylishly quirky) with big windows, parquet floors, vivid walls, mismatched upholstery fabrics, and original art. Each room has books, art magazines, and CDs, and the hotel boasts the best collection of lamps in Austria. The hotel now also offers apartments for longer stays (prices on request). Not only is a hearty breakfast included but also tea and cakes in the afternoon. To complete the artistic atmosphere, guests can also use the Bösendorfer piano in the cafe. The affordability of the magnificent rooms is impressive.

Kirchengasse 41, 1070 Vienna. ☎ **01/5226666.** Fax 01/5234901. www.altstadt.at. 47 units. 119€–200€ double; 169€–369€ suite. AE, DC, MC, V. Parking 18€. U-Bahn: Volkstheater. **Amenities:** Breakfast room; bar; room service; babysitting. *In room:* TV, minibar, hair dryer, free Wi-Fi.

Falkensteiner Hotel Am Schottenfeld ★ ☺   The design of the hotel is young, modern, and chic, just like many of its guests. A skillful use of light combines the contemporary with selected Biedermeier fabrics and pieces of 1900s Jugendstil for a successful reinvention of Wien Modern. Rooms offer tasteful, contemporary comfort, and bathrooms are an image of elegance with marble floors. Outside the hotel is a wide range of small bars and restaurants, along with antique and junk shops, trendy boutiques, and antiquarian book sellers.

Schottenfeldgasse 74, 1070 Vienna. ☎ **01/5265181.** Fax 01/5265181-160. www.falkensteiner.com. 95 units. 157€–249€ double; 50€ extra for junior suite. AE, DC, MC, V. U-Bahn: Volkstheater. **Amenities:** Bistro; bar; sauna; children's club; room service; babysitting; Turkish bath; sauna; solarium. *In room:* A/C, TV, minibar, hair dryer, Wi-Fi: 15mins 2€, 1hr 4€, 3hrs 8€, 24hrs 15€.

Inexpensive

Hotel-Pension Museum 🛏️ 🍴   Originally a private home dating from the 1600s, the exterior of this gracious hotel was transformed around 1890 into the elegant Art Nouveau facade it has today. Right behind the Volkstheater and across from the Imperial Museums, there is little you will want to do that is more than a pleasant walk away. Bedrooms vary, with some spacious, and others are a bit cramped. However, the rates are very modest, particularly for the quality.

Museumstrasse 3, 1070 Vienna. ☎ **01/52344260.** Fax 01/523442630. www.tiscover.com/hotel. museum. 15 units. 70€–135€ double. Rates include breakfast. AE, DC, MC, V. Parking 22€ Mon–Fri, free Sat–Sun. U-Bahn: Volkstheater. **Amenities:** Breakfast room; lounge; room service. *In room:* TV, hair dryer, free Wi-Fi.

Hotel Savoy   Built in the 1960s, this well-managed hotel rises six stories above one of Vienna's busiest shopping districts and just opposite the Neubaugasse entrance to U-Bahn line U3. The decor is tasteful and most rooms have picture-window views. The hotel serves breakfast and the surrounding streets offer the rest.

Lindengasse 12, 1070 Vienna. ☎ **01/5234646.** Fax 01/5234640. www.hotelsavoy.at. 43 units. 83€–150€ double; 121€–180€ triple. Rates include buffet breakfast. AE, DC, MC, V. Parking 16€. U-Bahn: Neubaugasse. **Amenities:** Breakfast room; babysitting. *In room:* TV, minibar, hair dryer, free Wi-Fi.

JOSEFSTADT (8TH DISTRICT)

Expensive

Cordial Theaterhotel Wien   Radically brought up to date in the late 1980s, this 19th-century hotel right by the Theater an der Josefstadt is much used by Austrian businessmen, who profit from the proximity to the city's wholesale buying outlets. Each simply furnished room contains its own small but efficient kitchenette. The on-site Theater-Restaurant is especially busy before and after performances.

Josefstadter Strasse 22, 1080 Vienna. ✆ **01/4053648.** Fax 01/4051406. www.cordial.at. 54 units. 107€–194€ double; 174€–317€ suite. Rates include buffet breakfast. AE, DC, MC, V. Parking 15€. U-Bahn: Rathaus. **Amenities:** Restaurant; bar; fitness center; sauna; room service; massage; babysitting. *In room:* TV, minibar, hair dryer, Wi-Fi: 1hr 1€.

Hotel Parliament Levante ★   This is a good example of the wave of design-conscious hotels that opened in Vienna this century. It sits behind a five-story facade of distressed concrete, which, in 1908, was chiseled into a Bauhaus-inspired design. Its design was a radical departure from the neo-Gothic facade of the nearby Rathaus (City Hall) and the cool, elegant Greek Revival style of the Austrian Parliament. After a radical reconfiguration, the hotel gives the impression that every interior angle and every interior line was meticulously plotted into a postmodern, avant-garde design. The decor includes lots of white Turkish travertine and marble, dark-grained wood. Most of the rooms face a quiet but dull inner courtyard, and each is comfortable, decoratively neutral, and postmodern.

Auerspergstrasse 15, 1080 Vienna. ✆ **01/228-280.** Fax 01/228-2828. www.thelevante.com. 70 units. 280€ double; 355€ suite. Extra bed 45€. Rates include breakfast. Parking 22€. AE, DC, MC, V. U-Bahn: Rathaus. **Amenities:** Fitness room w/sauna; room service; free Wi-Fi in lobby. *In room:* A/C, TV, minibar, Wi-Fi: 1hr 3€, 24hrs 9€.

Moderate

Hotel Mercure Josefshof ★ ☺   This very attractive Jugendstil 170-room hotel is thoroughly modern yet still captures the easy grace of its pre-World War I style. On a narrow lane right next to Vienna's English Theater, it is close to the U2 entrance for the Rathaus (City Hall), the Parliament, and the Burgtheater just across the park. The Princess Bar is open 24 hours, thus an ideal spot for an after theater drink and more. Breakfast is served from 7am to noon, perfect for revelers.

Josefsgasse 4–6, 1080 Vienna. ✆ **01/40419.** Fax 01/40419 150. http://www.josefshof.com. 170 units. 10 smoking, 89 €–159€ double; 189€ suite. AE, DC, MC, V. U-Bahn: Rathaus. **Amenities:** Bar; fitness center; sauna; room service; babysitting; rooms for those w/limited mobility; solarium. *In room:* A/C, TV, mini-bar, hair dryer, Wi-Fi: 1hr 7 €, 3hrs 8.50€, 24hrs 10€.

Rathauspark Hotel   Notable as being the former home of Stefan Zweig, the Austrian author who in the 1930s was one of the world's most widely-translated writers. It's actually an old palace, and the 4-star hotel sits behind an elaborate wedding-cakefacade. The interior doesn't quite live up to outward expectation, but does tastefully combine the old with the new. Rooms vary from average to spacious, and all have been updated with contemporary furnishings. The setting is very central.

Rathausstrasse 17, 1010 Vienna. ✆ **01/404-120.** Fax 01/404-12-761. www.austria-trend.at. 117 units. 119€–169€ double. AE, DC, MC, V. Rates include buffet breakfast. No parking. U-Bahn: Rathaus. **Amenities:** Breakfast room; bar; babysitting. *In room:* A/C (in some), TV, minibar, hair dryer, free Wi-Fi.

Inexpensive

Hotel Graf Stadion ★ ☺   This is one of the few genuine Biedermeier-style hotels left in Vienna, right behind the Rathaus, a 10-minute walk from most of the central monuments. The facade evokes early-19th-century elegance, with triangular or half-rounded ornamentation above many of the windows. The refurbished bedrooms are comfortably old-fashioned, and many are spacious enough to accommodate an extra bed for people with small children.

Buchfeldgasse 5, 1080 Vienna. ✆ **01/405-5284.** Fax 01/4050111. www.graf-stadion.com. 40 units. 105€–150€ double. Rates include buffet breakfast. AE, DC, MC, V. Parking 15€. U-Bahn: Rathaus. **Amenities:** Breakfast room; bar; babysitting. *In room:* TV, hair dryer, Wi-Fi: 1hr 1€, 6hrs 5€.

Hotel-Pension Zipser A 5-minute walk from the Rathaus, this pension features a renovated interior tastefully adorned with wood detailing. Generous-size bedrooms are furnished in a functional, modern style, with some opening on to balconies above the garden. The people who work here are very friendly.

Lange Gasse 49, 1080 Vienna. ✆ **01/404540.** Fax 01/4045413. www.zipser.at. 47 units. 85€–165€ double. Rates include buffet breakfast. AE, DC, MC, V. Parking 14€. U-Bahn: Rathaus. Bus: 13A. **Amenities:** Breakfast room; bar; lounge. *In room:* TV, hair dryer, free Wi-Fi.

ALSERGRUND (9TH DISTRICT)
Moderate

Austria Trend Hotel Albatros A 10-minute ride from the city, the Trend is dull on the outside but lively inside. Well-furnished rooms are medium in size and fitted with comfortable upholstery and small but efficient bathrooms (shower only).

Liechtensteinstrasse 89, 1090 Vienna. ✆ **01/317-35-08.** Fax 01/317-35-08-85. www.austria-trend.at. 70 units. 128€–248€ double. Rates include buffet breakfast. AE, DC, MC, V. Parking: 17€ U-Bahn: Friedensbrücke. **Amenities:** Breakfast room; bar; sauna. *In room:* A/C, TV, minibar, hair dryer, free Wi-Fi.

Hotel Bellevue This hotel was built in 1873, at about the same time as the Franz-Josefs Bahnhof, a short walk away, whose passengers it was designed to house. Its wedge shape on the acute angle of a busy street corner is reminiscent of the Flatiron Building in Manhattan. Unfortunately most of the old details have been stripped from the public rooms, although renovation has left clean lines and a handful of antiques. Some 100 guest rooms are in a wing added in 1982. All rooms are functional and well maintained, and contain comfortable low beds and utilitarian desks and chairs.

Althanstrasse 5, 1091 Vienna. ✆ **01/313-480.** Fax 01/3134-8801. www.hotelbellevue.at. 173 units. 210€–240€ double; from 250€ suite. Rates include buffet breakfast. AE, DC, MC, V. Parking 19€. U-Bahn: Friedensbrücke. Tram: 5 or D. **Amenities:** Restaurant; bar; sauna; room service; babysitting. *In room:* TV, minibar, hair dryer, Wi-Fi: 30mins free in Deluxe rooms, otherwise .35€/min, 24hrs 17€.

Hotel Regina Established in 1896 next to the Votivkirche, this hotel was built in the "Ringstrasse" style. The facade is appropriately grand, reminiscent of a French Renaissance palace, while inside it is unashamedly an old-world hotel with red salons and interminable corridors. Guest rooms are well maintained and traditionally furnished; some have canopied beds and elaborate furnishings. Room sizes vary, but it all works. The tree-lined street is usually calm.

Rooseveltplatz 15, A-1090 Vienna. ✆ **01/404-460.** Fax 01/408-8392. 128 units. 107€–250€ double; 185€–300€ deluxe double. Rates include buffet breakfast. AE, DC, MC, V. Parking 20€. U-Bahn: Schottentor. Tram: 1, D, 37, 38, 40, 41, or 42. **Amenities:** Restaurant; cafe; bar; room service. *In room:* TV, minibar, hair dryer, Wi-Fi: 30mins 3€, 1hr 6€, 24hrs 12€.

Rathaus Wein & Design Hotel ★★ 📖 From the outside, this government-rated 4-star hotel has a glowing 18th-century facade in Schönbrunner yellow. Inside, photographs record the building's radical upgrade, a minimalist and very tasteful contemporary design, a glistening white-with-touches-of-alabaster wine bar that doubles as a breakfast room, and one of the most unusual blends of hotel and wine-industry marketing in Austria. Bedrooms, scattered over five floors, are each dedicated to an Austrian vintner, each entryway has a door-size wine label identifying that room's allegiance to, say, the Triebaumer or Jamek wineries, or to any of 31 other vintners. Bedrooms are comfortable, high-ceilinged, and large, with a palette of neutral earth tones, stylish bathroom fixtures, and a sense of postmodern hip.

Lange Gasse 13, 1080 Vienna. ✆ **01/400-11-22.** Fax 01/400-11-22-88. www.hotel-rathaus-wien.at. 33 units. 148€–198€ double. Parking 15€. AE, DC, MC, V. U-Bahn: U3 or U4 to Volkstheater. **Amenities:** Wine bar; breakfast room; limited room service; babysitting. *In room:* TV, minibar, hair dryer, safe, free Wi-Fi.

WESTBAHNHOF (15TH DISTRICT)
Inexpensive

Mercure Wien Westbahnhof   Not exactly old-world Viennese charm, but you'll find comfort and convenience at an affordable price. Located next to the Westbahnhof, this is a good middle-bracket property. The corner building with a nine-floor turret offers completely rejuvenated rooms. Furnishings are durable rather than stylish. Light sleepers should ask for a room opening on to the patio in the rear. Deluxe units offer a little sitting area.

Selberstrasse 4, 1150 Vienna. ✆ **01/98111-0.** Fax 01/98111-930. www.mercure.com. 252 units. 69€–109€ double. AE, DC, MC, V. U-Bahn: Westbahnhof. **Amenities:** Restaurant; bar; sauna; babysitting; rooms for those w/limited mobility. *In room:* TV, minibar, hair dryer, Wi-Fi: 1hr 8€, 24hrs 18€.

NEAR SCHÖNBRUNN
Inexpensive

Altwienerhof 🏨 ☺   An unassuming hideaway in the heart of the city with large, individually-furnished rooms. There are also two family apartments in Old Vienna style, and family specials are on offer. A good buffet breakfast is served in a winter garden, overlooking the outside garden. Wine- and cheese-tasting is offered in the vaulted cellar *vinotek.*

Herklotzgasse 6, 1150 Vienna. ✆ **01/892-6000.** Fax 01/892-60008. www.altwienerhof.at. 23 units. 89€–130€ double. Rates include buffet breakfast. AE, DC, MC, V. Parking 10€. U-Bahn: Gumpendorferstrasse. Tram: 6, 8, or 18. **Amenities:** Restaurant; lounge. *In room:* TV, free Wi-Fi on the 1st floor.

Urban Resort Hotel Vienna ★ ✦   This is a steal! A 10-minute walk from Schönbrunn and a 15 minute U-Bahn ride to Karlsplatz and the Opera, this hotel oozes chic, savvy design and sophistication. The rooms have functional furnishings but stylish decor and beautiful bathrooms with a shower but no tub. The staff is helpful and capable and despite the lack of real luxury this place provides the basics for an unbeatable price.

Sechshauserstrasse 83, 1150 Vienna. ✆ **01/8921387.** Fax 01/8921387777. www.urbanresorthotel.at. 43 units. 65€–85€ double. AE, DC, MC, V. U-Bahn: Schönbrunn. **Amenities:** Restaurant; babysitting; rooms for those w/limited mobility. *In room:* TV, hair dryer, free Wi-Fi.

6 | WHERE TO DINE

I n Vienna, dining out is a local pastime; while there are expensive restaurants, many are not, and you can eat out very well for little more than what you might have spent for a good meal at home. And there is so much to choose from. Along with Austrian and Mediterranean cuisine, you'll find fine restaurants serving Croatian, Serbian, Slovenian, Slovak, Hungarian, and Czech food, as well as Asian, French, and Russian.

MEALS & DINING CUSTOMS Although traditional Viennese *Gasthaus* meals are simple and filling, international influences, principally from Italy, the Balkans, and Turkey, have long influenced Austrian cuisine. Today, this trend is even stronger, and innovative chefs throughout the city now turn out lighter versions of the classics along with combinations of old and new. And this pleases the health-conscious and environmentally-aware Viennese who like to eat well in both senses of the word. Breakfast usually consists of hearty bread, or a fresh *Semmel* (Kaiser roll) with butter, preserves, or cheese, along with milk and coffee. But if you missed round one, you have another chance around 10am when a *Gabelfrühstück* (snack breakfast) may be served (often at business meetings or conferences) when you might be offered little finger food pastries filled with fruit or fish, or perhaps little sausages. Lunch at midday can be a filling meal, say liver and onions or *Gulasch*, but also might be built around a soup and *Spinatstrudel*, (spinach strudel), broiled fish, or *Backhendlsalat* (fried chicken salad), and the afternoon *Jause* consists of coffee, open sandwiches, and the luscious pastries that the Viennese make so well. Dinners can also be hearty, although many locals prefer a light evening meal.

Vienna is a city of concert halls and opera houses, and with performances beginning at 7:30pm, après-théâtre is all the rage, with many restaurants and cafes staying open late, usually serving dinners until at least 11pm and often later, settling up in time to catch the last U-Bahn home.

Unlike those in other western European capitals, many of Vienna's restaurants observe Sunday closings (marked by SONNTAG RUHETAG signs). Also beware of summer holiday closings, when restaurateurs prefer to take their own long-awaited holidays to nearby lake resorts than cook for Vienna's summer visitors. Sometimes restaurants announce closings only a week or two before shutting down, so it's best to check.

RESTAURANTS BY CUISINE

ASIAN
Akakiko (Innere Stadt, $, p. 109)
DOTS ★ (Neubau, $$$, p. 121)

AUSTRIAN
Altes Jägerhaus ★ (Leopoldstadt, $, p. 114)
Altwienerhof ★★★ (Near Schönbrunn, $$$, p. 124)
Amerlingbeisl (Neubau, $, p. 121)
Augustinerkeller (Innere Stadt, $, p. 109)
Bauer ★★ (Innere Stadt, $$$, p. 104)
Die Fromme Helene ★ (Josefstadt, $$, p. 122)
Esterházykeller (Innere Stadt, $, p. 111)
Figlmüller (Innere Stadt, $, p. 111)
Finkh (Mariahilf, $$, p. 119)
Gasthaus Ubl ★ (Wieden & Margareten, $, p. 119)
Gergely's (Wieden & Margareten, $, p. 119)
Gräfin vom Naschmarkt (Mariahilf, $, p. 119)
Griechenbeisl ★ (Innere Stadt, $$, p. 106)
Gulaschmuseum ★ (Innere Stadt, $, p. 111)
Hansen ★ (Innere Stadt, $$, p. 106)
Hietzinger Bräu (Near Schönbrunn, $$, p. 125)
Kardos (Innere Stadt, $, p. 111)
Kern's Beisel (Innere Stadt, $, p. 112)
Leopold (Leopoldstadt, $$, p. 116)
Leupold's Kupferdachl ★ (Innere Stadt, $$, p. 107)
Motto (Wieden & Margareten, $$, p. 118)
Österreicher im MAK (Innere Stadt, $$, p. 107)
Palmenhaus ★ (Innere Stadt, $$, p. 112)
Piaristenkeller (Josefstadt, $$, p. 123)
Plutzer Bräu ★ (Neubau, $, p. 121)
Restaurant Salzamt ★ (Innere Stadt, $, p. 108)
Saint Charles Alimentary ★ (Mariahilf, $, p. 120)
Schnattl ★ (Josefstadt, $$, p. 123)
Schweizerhaus (Leopoldstadt, $, p. 117)
Skopik & Lohn (Leopoldstadt, $$, p. 116)
Steirereck ★★★ (Landstrasse, $$$$, p. 117)
Stiegl Ambulanz (Alsergrund, $, p. 123)
Vestibül ★ (Innere Stadt, $$, p. 108)
Vikerl's Lokal (Westbahnhof, $$, p. 124)
Weibels Wirtshaus ★ (Innere Stadt, $$$, p. 105)
Zu den 3 Hacken ★ (Innere Stadt, $, p. 112)
Zum Kuchldragoner (Innere Stadt, $, p. 112)

BALKAN
Dubrovnik (Innere Stadt, $, p. 110)

COFFEEHOUSES, TEA-ROOMS & CAFES
Café Central ★ (Innere Stadt, $, p. 114)
Café Demel ★★ (Innere Stadt, $, p. 114)
Café Diglas (Innere Stadt, $, p. 114)
Café Dommayer (Near Schönbrunn, $, p. 114)
Café Frauenhuber (Innere Stadt, $, p. 114)
Café Landtmann ★ (Innere Stadt, $, p. 115)
Café Sperl (Neubau, $, p. 115)
Café Tirolerhof (Innere Stadt, $, p. 115)
Demmers Teehaus (Innere Stadt, $, p. 115)
Motto am Fluss Café (Innere Stadt, $, p. 107)

KEY TO ABBREVIATIONS:
$$$$ = Very Expensive $$$ = Expensive $$ = Moderate $ = Inexpensive

Where to Dine in Vienna

Abend-Restaurant
  Feuervogel **2**
Akakiko **55**
Alfi's Goldener Spiegel **18**
Alte Backstube **9**
Altes Jägerhaus **44**
Altwienerhof **15**
Amerlingbeisl **12**
Augustinerkeller **23**
Bauer **42**
Blaustern **1**
Bohème **9**
Buffet Trzésniewski **54**
Café Central **27**
Café Cuadro **21**
Café Demel **24**
Café Diglas **51**
Café Dommayer **18**
Café Frauenhuber **60**
Café Landtmann **6**
Café Leopold **11**
Café Phil **16**
Café Restaurant Halle **11**
Café Sperl **17**
Café Tirolerhof **58**
Cantinetta Antinori **40**
Danieli **59**
Demmers Teehaus **5**
Die Fromme Helene **9**
Do & Co. **53**
DOTS **13**
Dubrovnik **46**
Esterházykeller **26**
Fabios **31**
Figlmüller **41**
Finkh **15**
Gasthaus Ubl **20**
Gergely's **21**
Gräfin vom Naschmarkt **19**
Griechenbeisl **36**
Gulaschmuseum **49**
Hansen **3**
Hietzinger Bräu **18**
Hollerei **13**
Julius Meinl **25**
Kardos **43**
Kent **9**
Kern's Beisel **30**
Kervansaray und
  Hummer Bar **61**
Leopold **35**
Leupold's Kupferdachl **4**
Mörwald im Ambassador **57**
Motto **21**
Motto am Fluss **37**
Motto am Fluss Café **37**
Niky's Kuchlmasterei **38**
Ofenloch **29**
Österreicher im MAK **47**
Palmenhaus **22**
Piaristenkeller **9**
Plachutta **48**
Plutzer Bräu **12**

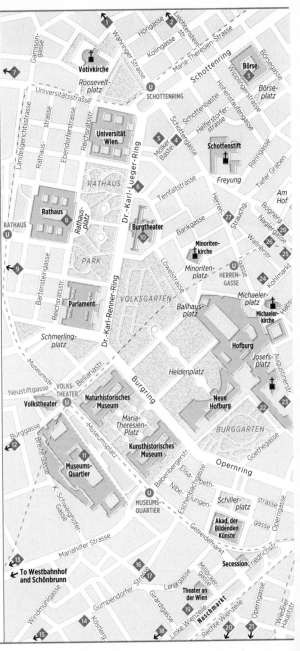

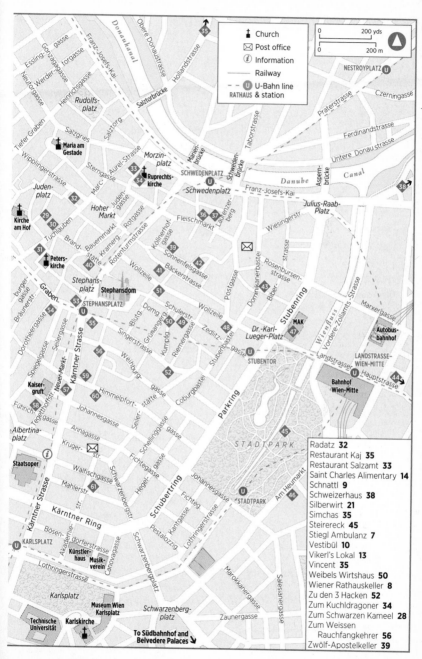

Church
Post office
Information
Railway
U-Bahn line
RATHAUS & station

NESTROYPLATZ

Radatz **32**
Restaurant Kaj **35**
Restaurant Salzamt **33**
Saint Charles Alimentary **14**
Schnattl **9**
Schweizerhaus **38**
Silberwirt **21**
Simchas **35**
Steirereck **45**
Stiegl Ambulanz **7**
Vestibül **10**
Vikerl's Lokal **13**
Vincent **35**
Weibels Wirtshaus **50**
Wiener Rathauskeller **8**
Zu den 3 Hacken **52**
Zum Kuchldragoner **34**
Zum Schwarzen Kameel **28**
Zum Weissen
    Rauchfangkehrer **56**
Zwölf-Apostelkeller **39**

CONTINENTAL

Bauer ★★ (Innere Stadt, $$$, p. 104)
Blaustern (Outer Districts, $, p. 125)
Gräfin vom Naschmarkt (Mariahilf, $, p.119)
Julius Meinl ★ (Innere Stadt, $$, p. 103)
Leopold (Leopoldstadt, $$, p. 116)
Motto am Fluss (Innere Stadt, $$, p. 107)
Vincent ★ (Leopoldstadt, $$$, p. 113)

CROATIAN

Dubrovnik (Innere Stadt, $, p. 110)
Restaurant Kaj (2nd District, $, p. 116)

FRENCH

Altwienerhof ★★★ (Near Schönbrunn, $$$, p. 124)

GAME

Altes Jägerhaus ★ (Leopoldstadt, $, p. 114)

HUNGARIAN

Alte Backstube (Josefstadt, $$, p. 121)
Gulaschmuseum ★ (Innere Stadt, $, p. 111)
Kardos (Innere Stadt, $, p. 111)

INTERNATIONAL

Bohème ★ (Neubau, $$, p. 120)
Café Cuadro (Wieden & Margareten, $, p. 118)
Café Leopold ★ (Innere Stadt, $, p. 110)
Café Restaurant Halle (Innere Stadt, $, p. 110)
Dining room ★★★ (Leopoldstadt, $$$, p. 117)
Do & Co. ★ (Innere Stadt, $$$, p. 104)
Fabios ★★ (Innere Stadt, $$$, p. 103)
Gergely's (Wieden & Margareten, $, p. 119)
Hansen ★ (Innere Stadt, $, p. 106)
Motto am Fluss (Innere Stadt, $$, p. 107)
Niky's Kuchlmasterei ★ (Landstrasse, $$$, p. 117)
Skopik & Lohn (Leopoldstadt, $$, p. 116)
Wiener Rathauskeller ★★ (Innere Stadt, $$$, p. 105)

Zum Schwarzen Kameel (Stiebitz) (Innere Stadt, $$, p. 108)

ITALIAN

Cantinetta Antinori ★ (Innere Stadt, $$, p. 106)
Motto (Wieden & Margareten, $$, p. 118)

MEDITERRANEAN

Fabios ★★ (Innere Stadt, $$$, p. 103)
Hansen ★ (Innere Stadt, $, p. 106)

RUSSIAN

Abend-Restaurant Feuervogel (Alsergrund, $$, p. 123)

SANDWICHES

Buffet Trzésniewski ★ (Innere Stadt, $, p. 109)

SEAFOOD

Kervansaray und Hummer Bar ★★ (Innere Stadt, $$$$, p. 103)

SLOVENIAN

Kardos (Innere Stadt, $, p. 111)

TURKISH

Kent (Rudolfsheim-Fünfhaus, $$, p. 124)

VEGETARIAN

Hollerei (Rudolfsheim-Fünfhaus, $$, p. 124)
Saint Charles Alimentary ★ (Mariahilf, $, p. 120)

VIENNESE

Alfi's Goldener Spiegel (Mariahilf, $, p. 120)
Alte Backstube (Josefstadt, $$, p. 121)
Bohème ★ (Neubau, $$, p. 120)
Dubrovnik (Innere Stadt, $, p. 110)
Finkh (Mariahilf, $$, p. 119)
Leupold's Kupferdachl ★ (Innere Stadt, $$, p. 107)
Mörwald im Ambassador ★★★ (Innere Stadt, $$$$, p. 104)
Niky's Kuchlmasterei ★ (Landstrasse, $$$, p. 117)
Ofenloch (Innere Stadt, $$, p. 107)
Österreicher im MAK Gasthof & Bar ★★ (Innere Stadt, $, p. 107)
Plachutta ★ (Innere Stadt, $$$, p. 105)

Silberwirt (Wieden & Margareten, $$, p. 118)

Steirereck ★★★ (Landstrasse, $$$$, p. 117)

Stiegl Ambulanz (Alsergrund, $, p. 123)

Wiener Rathauskeller ★★ (Innere Stadt, $$$, p. 105)

Zum Weissen Rauchfangkehrer (Innere Stadt, $$, p. 109)

Zwölf-Apostelkeller (Innere Stadt, $, p. 113)

INNERE STADT (INNER CITY)
Very Expensive

Fabios ★★ INTERNATIONAL/MEDITERRANEAN   This is the trendiest and most sought-after restaurant in Vienna, with considerable jockeying among the city's glitterati. The creation of the young and fun Fabio Giacobello, this space is bigger inside than you might think from the street. Most of the visual distraction in this predominantly black, but plush and artfully lit, environment comes from its fashion-conscious (and usually good-looking) clients. The menu might include warm octopus marinated with olive oil and parsley served on a bed of cold gazpacho cream sauce, and roasted rack of lamb with cold marinated tomatoes served with deep-fried polenta *gnocchetti*. The wine bar here is also a top nightlife option. Enough drama unfolds around its rectangular surface to keep a few tabloid writers busy, and someone famous within the inner workings of Vienna's media and politics always seems to be popping up for air and a drink or two.

Tuchlauben 6. ✆ **01/532-2222.** www.fabios.at. Reservations recommended. Main courses 29€–32€. AE, MC, V. Mon–Sat 10am–1am. U-Bahn: Stephansplatz.

Julius Meinl ★ CONTINENTAL   This upmarket and appealingly formal restaurant is the most sought-after of the three elements within the Julius Meinl trio, which includes, on the same premises, one of the most comprehensive delicatessens and wine shops in Austria, as well as a cellar wine bar. The restaurant is upstairs with big-windowed views that sweep out over the all-pedestrian grandeur of the Graben. There's dark wood, touches of gilt, and a voluptuous-looking bar within a few steps of the bustling and brightly illuminated delicatessen. Restaurant choices might include tuna with avocado cream and a carrot and ginger-flavored vinaigrette, or marinated gratin of lobster with fennel. For dessert consider a praline mousse with raspberries and tonka-bean ice cream, or a semolina soufflé with plums and elderberries. And then there's the cheese trolley, a work of art in its own right.

Graben 19. ✆ **01/532-3334.** www.meinl.at. Reservations recommended. Main courses 24€–35€. Mon–Sat 8am–midnight. U-Bahn: Stephansplatz.

Kervansaray und Hummer Bar ★★ SEAFOOD   Here you'll sense the historic link between the Habsburgs and the 19th-century Ottoman Empire. On the restaurant's ground floor, polite waiters announce a changing array of daily specials and serve tempting salads from an hors d'oeuvre table. Upstairs, guests enjoy the bounties of the sea at the Lobster Bar. There's also a deli. A meal often begins with a champagne cocktail, followed by, possibly, a lobster and salmon caviar cocktail. The menu has a short list of meat dishes such as filet mignon with Roquefort sauce, but it deals mostly in seafood, including grilled filet of sole with fresh asparagus,

Impressions

The people of Vienna are completely different from western and alpine Austrians, with a different set of morals and attitudes from the rest of the country. They regard their city as incomparable—as indeed it is, after a fashion. No European capital has such a stately, imperial   *air . . . the double-headed eagle still broods overhead wherever you go—and no other European capital has such delightful surroundings.*
                            —Richard Bassett, The Austrians: Strange Tales from the Vienna Woods, 1988

Norwegian salmon with a horseradish-and-champagne sauce, and, of course, lobster. There's lots of shellfish, but be prepared to pay for your indulgence.

Mahlerstrasse 9. © **01/5128843.** www.hummerbar.at. Reservations recommended. Main courses 25€–50€. AE, DC, MC, V. Restaurant Mon–Sat noon–midnight. U-Bahn: Karlsplatz. Tram: 1 or 2. Bus: 3A.

Mörwald im Ambassador ★★★ VIENNESE   Views from the greenhouse-style windows, two floors above street level, sweep out over the Neue Markt and one of Vienna's most memorable outdoor fountains. Bankers, diplomats, and what one local food critic called "Helmut Lang-clad hipsters" show up for the sophisticated twists on classic Viennese cuisine. Menu items change with the seasons, but are likely to include tartar of French-derived Limousin beef with rosemary toasts and cocktail sauce; foie gras with kumquats and a sauce made from sparkling wine; ravioli stuffed with lamb, artichoke hearts, and mint sauce; and roasted loin of veal with chanterelles and a spicy potato-based cream sauce.

On the second floor of the Hotel Ambassador, Kärntner Strasse 22. © **01/961610.** Reservations required. Main courses 24€–34€; set price lunches 29€–39€; set-price dinners 75€–110€. AE, DC, MC, V. Daily noon–3pm and 6–11pm. U-Bahn: Stephansplatz.

Expensive

Bauer ★★ AUSTRIAN/CONTINENTAL   It's upscale, it's *gemütlich* (warm and welcoming), and it's on the shortlist of restaurants that concierges at some of Vienna's best hotels recommend to guests. You'll find it on a narrow street a few blocks northeast of the cathedral, beneath 500-year-old ceiling vaults, now painted a dark shade of pink, that evoke a venue that's more folksy and rustic than this sophisticated restaurant really is. The fact that there are only 30 seats enhances a venue that was established in its present format in 1989. Expect glamorous food. The finest examples include carpaccio of beef with mustard sauce; sweetbreads with vanilla sauce and braised chicory; and stuffed squid with lemon sauce and pepper cream sauce.

Sonnenfelsgasse 17. © **01/512-9871.** Reservations recommended. Main courses 26€–32€; 4-course set-price menu 62€. AE, DC, MC, V. Mon 6–11pm, Tues–Fri noon–2pm and 6–11pm. Closed Sat and Sun, 1 week at Easter, and mid-July to mid-Aug. U-Bahn: Stephansplatz, Schwedenplatz, or Stubentor.

Do & Co. ★ INTERNATIONAL   On the 7th floor of a radically angular hyper-modern building (the also-recommended hotel), across from St. Stephan's, this restaurant is in demand. It's difficult to overstate its fame within the complicated but steely hierarchy of fine and/or stylish Viennese dining. If you didn't reserve, or your table isn't ready, consider a pre-dinner cocktail at the stylish Onyx Bar on the building's 6th floor, then climb a circular staircase to the 7th-floor dining room. Here, *if you've reserved,* you'll be presented with a slightly claustrophobic table and a confusingly diverse set of menu items. Dishes are divided into categories that include "Tastes of the World" (Tataki of Atlantic tuna, or sushi), "Catch of the Day" (potpourri of scallops), "Beef & Co." (French breast of duck with green beans and creamy kumquat polenta), "Kebab, Wok & Curries" (dishes inspired by Asia, especially Thailand), and "Austrian Classics" (deep-fried monkfish with potato salad).

In the Haas Haus, Stephansplatz 12. © **01/24188.** www.doco.com. Reservations required. Main courses 18€–26€. AE, DC, MC, V. Daily noon–3pm and 6–11:45pm. U-Bahn: Stephansplatz.

Plachutta ★ VIENNESE Few restaurants have built such a fetish around one dish as Plachutta has done with *Tafelspitz,* offering 10 variations of the boiled beef dish, which was adored by Emperor Franz Josef throughout his prolonged reign. The differences between the versions are a function of the cut of beef you request. We recommend *Schulterscherzel* (shoulder of beef) and *Beinfleisch* (shank of beef), but if you're in doubt, the waiters are knowledgeable about one of the most oft-debated subjects in Viennese cuisine. Hash brown potatoes, chives, and an appealing mixture of horseradish and chopped apples accompany each order. Other Viennese staples such as goulash soup, calf's liver, and braised pork with cabbage are also available.

Wollzeile 38. © **01/5121577.** www.plachutta.at. Reservations recommended. Main courses 18€–26€. DC, MC, V. Daily 11:30am–midnight. U-Bahn: Stubentor.

Weibels Wirtshaus ★ 🎁AUSTRIAN Don't be fooled by the unpretentious feel to this place, which at first glance might look like a simple tavern. Food is considerably better than the *Wirtshaus* (tavern) appellation implies, and the clientele is a lot more upscale than the usual wurst-with-potatoes-and-beer crowd. There are only two rooms (and about 40 seats) within this woody restaurant, each on a separate floor of a building estimated to be around 400 years old. In good weather, there are another 30 seats in the garden. The wine list, with more than 250 varieties of Austrian wine, looks like a patriotic, pro-Austrian statement in its own right. Menu items include pumpkin-seed soup, sliced breast of duck with lentils, well-prepared schnitzels of veal and chicken, and a superb saddle of lamb with polenta and spinach.

Kumpfgasse 2. © **01/5123986.** www.weibel.at. Reservations recommended. Main courses 14€–19€; fixed-price menu 36€. AE, MC, V. Daily 11:30am–midnight. U-Bahn: Stephansplatz.

Wiener Rathauskeller ★★ INTERNATIONAL/VIENNESE City halls throughout the Teutonic world have traditionally maintained restaurants in their basements, and Vienna is no exception. Although Vienna's famous Rathaus was built between 1871 and 1883, its cellar restaurant wasn't added until 1899. Today, in half a dozen richly-atmospheric dining rooms, with high vaulted ceilings and stained-glass windows, you can enjoy good and reasonably priced food. The chef's special is a *Rathauskellerplatte* for two, consisting of various cuts of meat, including a veal schnitzel, lamb cutlets, and pork medallions. One section of the cellar is devoted every evening to a Viennese musical soiree beginning at 8pm. Musicians ramble through the world of operetta, waltz, and *schrammel* (traditional Viennese music) as you dine.

Rathausplatz 1. ☎ **01/405-1210.** www.wiener-rathauskeller.at. Reservations required. Main courses 11€–39€. AE, DC, MC, V. Mon–Sat 11:30am–3pm and 6–11pm. U-Bahn: Rathaus.

Moderate

Cantinetta Antinori ★ ITALIAN   This is one of three European restaurants run by the Antinori family, who own Tuscan vineyards and whose name is synonymous with Chianti. The traditions and aesthetics of the original restaurant, in Florence, have been reproduced here to showcase Antinori wines and the culinary zest of Tuscany. Within a 140-year-old building overlooking the Stephansplatz and the cathedral, you'll find a high-ceilinged dining room, as well as a greenhouse-style "winter garden" that transports you straight to Tuscany. Start off with an order of *antipasti tipico,* a medley of marinated vegetables and seafood. This might be followed by ravioli stuffed with porcini mushrooms and summer truffles, or perfectly grilled lamb steaks with sun-dried tomatoes and Mediterranean herbs. *Panna cotta,* a creamy flan, is a simple but classic way to finish a meal. A large selection of wines is served by the glass.

Jasomirgottstrasse 3–5.☎ **01/5337722.** www.antinori.it. Reservations required. Main courses 19€–29€. AE, DC, MC, V. Daily 11:30am–11pm. U-Bahn: Stephansplatz.

Danieli ★★ ITALIAN   This is one of Vienna's premier Italian restaurants, on a side street near St. Stephan's. It has a red-brick interior with chandeliers and cushioned leather seating, and serves high-end versions of Italian classics. Start with antipasti, served on a tower of plates, and then choose from the classic pasta variations and delicious wood oven pizzas. The fish and meat dishes are inspired yet remain loyal to Italian cooking traditions. The wine list is overwhelming, but the attentive staff will help you choose a suitable accompaniment. Upstairs is great for a romantic table for two.

Himmelpfortgasse 3. ☎ **01/5137913.** www.danieli.at. Reservations recommended. Main courses 10€–26€. AE, DC, MC, V. Daily 10am–midnight. U-Bahn: Stephansplatz.

Griechenbeisl ★ AUSTRIAN   Astonishingly, Griechenbeisl was established in 1450 and is still one of the city's leading restaurants. There's a maze of dining areas on three different floors, all with low-vaulted ceilings, smoky paneling, and wrought-iron chandeliers. As you enter, look down at the grate under your feet for an illuminated view of a pirate counting his money. Inside, check out the so-called inner sanctum, with signatures of former patrons such as Mozart, Beethoven, and Mark Twain. The beer is well chilled, and the food is hearty and ample. Menu items include fried breaded chicken with cucumber-potato salad; and roast pikeperch with almonds. Extravagantly-garbed waiters scurry around with large trays of food and there's entertainment with accordion and zither music.

Fleischmarkt 11. ☎ **01/5331941.** www.griechenbeisl.at. Reservations required. Main courses 16€–23€. AE, DC, MC, V. Daily 11am–1am (last order 11:30pm). Tram: N, 1, 2, or 21.

Hansen ★ 🍴 AUSTRIAN/INTERNATIONAL/MEDITERRANEAN   One of the most intriguing and stylish restaurants in Vienna opened as a partnership between a time-tested culinary team and the downtown showrooms of one of Austria's most famous horticulturists and gardening stores (Lederleitner). You'll find them cheek-by-jowl in the vaulted cellars of Vienna's stock exchange, a Beaux Arts pile designed in the 1890s by the restaurant's namesake, Theophile Hansen. Part of the charm of this place involves trekking through masses of plants and elaborate garden ornaments on your way to your dining table. The menu may include a spicy bean salad with strips of chicken breast served in a summer broth, risotto with cheese and sour cherries, and poached *Saibling* (something akin to trout from the coldwater streams of the Austrian Alps) with a potato and celery puree and watercress.

In the cellar of the Börse (former Vienna Stock Exchange), Wipplingerstrasse 34 at the Schottenring. © **01/5320542.** www.vestibuel.at. Reservations recommended. Main courses 9€–22€. AE, DC, MC, V. Mon–Fri 9am–8pm (last order); Sat 9am–3:30pm (last order). U-Bahn: Schottenring.

Leupold's Kupferdachl ★ VIENNESE/AUSTRIAN   Run by the Leupold family since the 1950s, this choice is known for "new Austrian" cuisine, although the chef does prepare traditional dishes. Recommended items include beef tenderloin (Old Viennese style) with dumplings boiled in a napkin, lamb loin breaded and served with potatoes, and chicken breast Kiev. The interior is both rustic and elegant, decorated with Oriental rugs and cozy banquettes with intricate straight-back chairs. The restaurant operates a beer-only pub, with good music and better prices, open daily from 10am to midnight.

Schottengasse 7. © **01/5339381.** www.leupold.at. Reservations recommended. Main courses 10€–20€. AE, DC, MC, V. Mon–Fri 10am–3pm; Mon–Sat 6pm–midnight. U-Bahn: Schottentor. Tram: 2, 43, or 44.

Motto am Fluss ★★ INTERNATIONAL/CONTINENTAL   In a boat-like structure that functions as the docking station for passenger ships along the Danube and canal, this cafe/restaurant in the Schwedenplatz area is a welcome change from the present concentration of *beisl* and bars. The famous mother restaurant in the 5th District (see Motto below) has long been praised. Upstairs, at the cafe, the breakfast and burgers are spectacular, with light fare and hearty sausage-slathered inspirations (see "Cafes" below). Downstairs the menu is eclectic and somewhat confusing, with starters and main courses all in one list, however the prices make the portions clear. Marinated tuna and yellowtail on a lime-infused onion with sesame dressing and sprout salad, or goose-liver terrine with ginger plums and Bali pepper are good examples of this varied selection. Sip and nibble as you gaze at the urban waterfront.

Schwedenplatz 2. © **01/25-255-10.** www.motto.at. Reservations recommended. Main courses: 10€–26€. AE, DC,MC, V. 6pm–2am. Closed Sat–Sun. U-Bahn: Schwedenplatz.

Ofenloch VIENNESE   Viennese have frequented this spot since the 1600s, when it functioned as a tavern. The present management dates from the mid-1970s and maintains a well-deserved reputation for its nostalgic, old-fashioned eating house. Waitresses wear classic Austrian regalia and will give you a menu that looks more like a magazine, with some amusing mock-medieval illustrations inside. The hearty soup dishes are popular, as is the schnitzel. There are also salads and cheese platters, plus an entire page devoted to one-dish meals. For dessert, choose from old-style Viennese dishes.

Kurrentgasse 8. © **01/5338844.** www.ofenloch.at. Reservations required. Main courses 10€–19€. AE, DC, MC, V. Tues–Sat 11am–midnight. U-Bahn: Stephansplatz. Bus: 1A.

Österreicher im MAK ★★ VIENNESE/AUSTRIAN   The oft-decorated star chef of the Stadtpark's Steirereck restaurant, Helmut Österreicher, also runs this place at the Museum of Applied Arts. The "Österreicher" has quickly become *the* place to go for anyone who is anybody in the art, architecture, and design world. The decor mixes classical art with modern. The enormous chandelier above the bar is a collage of wine bottles, the original parquet floor and impossibly high ceilings inset with paintings are themselves a design event. The menu reflects this stylistic dissonance, offering artistic renditions of classical Austrian dishes alongside Österreicher's own creations, such as a white-wine calf stew with a dark bread omelette followed by salmon trout in a muesli crust. Sample the Austrian wine list: the Knoll Riesling or the Nittnaus Pinot Noir. For intimacy, take the back room, which is more floral and modern but less noisy.

In the MAK (Museum für Angewante Kunst), Stubenring 5. ℂ **01/714-0121.** www.oesterreicherimmak. at. Reservations recommended. Main courses 8€–22€. AE, DC, MC, V. Daily 8:30am–1am. U-Bahn: Stubentor or Schwedenplatz.

Restaurant Salzamt ★ AUSTRIAN   The Salzamt evokes a turn-of-the-20th-century Viennese bistro, replete with Wiener Werkstätte-inspired chairs and lighting fixtures, cream walls, and dark tables and banquettes where you're likely to see an artsy, sometimes surprisingly prominent, clientele of loyal repeat diners, including Karl Lagerfeld and the Prince of Monaco. Sit within its vaulted interior or—if weather permits—move out to tables on the square that overlook Vienna's oldest church, St. Ruprecht. Well-prepared items include a terrine of broccoli and artichoke hearts, light-textured pastas, filets of pork with a Gorgonzola cream sauce, several kinds of goulash, and fresh fish. One of the most noteworthy of these is fried filets of *saibling* served with lemon or tartar sauce.

Ruprechtsplatz 1. ℂ **01/5335332.** Reservations recommended. Main courses 8€–19€. V. Daily 5pm–midnight. U-Bahn: Schwedenplatz.

Vestibül ★ 🎭 AUSTRIAN   This Viennese brasserie at the Vienna Burgtheater is a real discovery. The restaurant entrance originally existed for the emperor's coach when he came to performances. Before or after shows, guests gather in the elegant bar for an aperitif, digestif, or coffee. Tapas are also served, with tables opening on to a view of the City Hall and Ringstrasse. Throughout the spring and summer there are also tables in the garden. The food is classic cuisine using market-fresh ingredients. Fresh oysters might be followed by such main dishes as traditional paprika chicken (inspired by nearby Hungary) or a traditional *beuschel* (a Viennese-style hash made of heart and lung). Styrian beef is also a local special.

Dr.-Karl-Lueger-Ring 2. ℂ **01/5324999.** www.vestibuel.at. Reservations recommended. Main courses 14€–24€. AE, DC, MC, V. Mon–Fri 11am–midnight; Sat 6pm–midnight, July–Aug closed Sat. U-Bahn: Schottentor or Herrengasse.

Zum Schwarzen Kameel ★★ INTERNATIONAL   This Jugendstil restaurant has been in the same family since 1618. A delicatessen against one wall sells wine and cured meat, although most of the action takes place among the chic clientele in the cafe. On Saturday mornings, it is packed with locals trying to recover from a late night. Uniformed waiters will bring you a drink here, and you can select open-face sandwiches from the trays on the black countertops. Try the rosy hand-carved *Beinschinken* (boiled ham with freshly grated horseradish). Beyond the cafe is a perfectly preserved Art Deco dining room, with jeweled copper chandeliers. The walls are a combination of polished panels and yellowed ceramic tiles, with a dusky plaster ceiling-frieze of grape leaves. The restaurant has just 11 tables, and it's the perfect place for a nostalgic lunch. The hearty cuisine features herring filet Oslo, potato soup, tournedos, Roman saltimbocca (veal with ham), and daily fish specials.

Bognergasse 5. ⓒ **01/5338125.** www.kameel.at. Main courses 19€–37€. AE, DC, MC, V. Mon–Sat 8am–midnight. U-Bahn: Schottentor. Bus: 2A or 3A.

Zum Weissen Rauchfangkehrer VIENNESE   Established in the 1860s, this dinner-only place is the former base for Vienna's chimney sweeps. In fact, the restaurant's name (translated as the "white chimney sweep") comes from the story of a drunken and blackened chimney sweep who fell into a kneading trough and woke up the next day covered in flour. The dining room is rustic, with deer antlers, fanciful chandeliers, and pine banquettes that vaguely resemble church pews. A piano in one of the inner rooms provides nighttime music and adds to the comfortable ambience. Big street-level windows let in lots of light. The hearty menu offers Viennese fried chicken, both Tyrolean and Wiener schnitzel, wild game, veal goulash, bratwurst, and several kinds of strudel. You'll certainly want to finish with the house special, a fabulously rich chocolate cream puff.

Weihburggasse 4. ⓒ **01/5123471.** www.weisser-rauchfangkehrer.at. Reservations required. Main courses 15€–26€. DC, MC, V. Tues–Sat 6pm–midnight. Closed July and Aug. U-Bahn: Stephansplatz.

Inexpensive

Akakiko ⬧ ASIAN   It's busy and loaded with Asians living permanently or temporarily within Vienna. And as a member of a chain with eight branches throughout Vienna, it boasts a carefully rehearsed and inexpensive formula for Asian food within an otherwise very expensive area. Pass the open kitchen and then in the brightly-lit modern dining room, outfitted in tones of white and bamboo green, you'll pick from menu items that include sushi, sashimi, teppanyaki, bento boxes, wok versions of duck, chicken, beef, fish, and vegetarian dishes inspired by the cuisines of China.

Singerstrasse 4. ⓒ **057/333-140.** www.akakiko.at. Reservations not accepted. Main courses 8.95€–14€. MC, V. Daily 10:30am–11:30pm. U-Bahn: Stephansplatz.

Augustinerkeller AUSTRIAN   Since 1857, the Augustinerkeller has served wine, beer, and food from the basement of one of the grand Hofburg palaces. It attracts a lively and diverse crowd that gets more boisterous as the *schrammel* is played late into the night. The vaulted brick room, with worn pine-board floors and wooden banquettes, is an inviting place to grab a drink and a simple meal. Be aware that this long and narrow dining room is usually as packed with people as it is with character. An upstairs room is quieter and less crowded. This place offers one of the best values for wine tasting in Vienna. The ground-floor lobby lists prices of vintage local wines by the glass. Tasters can sample from hundreds of bottles near the stand-up stainless-steel counter. Aside from the wine and beer, the kitchen serves simple food, including roast chicken, schnitzel, and *tafelspitz*.

Augustinerstrasse 1. ⓒ **01/5331026.** Main courses 9€–17€. AE, DC, MC, V. Daily 10am–midnight. U-Bahn: Stephansplatz.

Buffet Trzésniewski ★ SANDWICHES   Everyone in Vienna, from the most hurried office worker to the most elite hostess, knows about this spot. Franz Kafka lived next door and used to come here for sandwiches and beer. It's unlike any buffet you've seen, with six or seven cramped tables and a rapidly moving line of people, all jostling for space next to the glass counters. Indicate to the waitress the kind of sandwich you want (if you can't read German, just point). Most people hurriedly devour the delicious finger sandwiches, which come in 18 different combinations of cream cheese, egg, onion, salami, herring, tomatoes, lobster, and many other tasty ingredients. If you do order a drink, the cashier will give you a rubber token, which you'll present to the person at the far end of the counter.

Dorotheergasse 1. ✆ **01/5123291.** Reservations not accepted. Sandwiches .90€. No credit cards. Mon–Fri 8:30am–7:30pm; Sat 9am–5pm. U-Bahn: Stephansplatz.

Café Leopold ★ 🎁 INTERNATIONAL   Set one floor above street level in the Leopold Museum, and with a schedule that operates long after the museum is closed for the night, it's sheathed in the same pale pink sandstone as the museum's exterior. The marble walls and huge windows accent the touches of Jugendstil in the establishment rounded off by a chandelier shaped like a UFO. During the day, the place functions as a conventional cafe and restaurant, serving a postmodern blend of Central European and Asian food. Examples include roasted shoulder of veal with Mediterranean vegetables, Thai curries, Vietnamese spring rolls, and arugula-studded risottos. Several nights a week, however, from around 10pm till at least 3am, any hints of kitsch and calm are banished as soon as a DJ begins cranking out dance tunes for hard-drinking night-owls. For more on this cafe's role as a nightclub, see "Vienna After Dark," in Chapter 8.

In the Leopold Museum, Museumsplatz 1. ✆ **01/5236732.** www.cafe-leopold.at. Main courses 5.90€–11€. AE, DC, MC, V. Sun–Wed 10am–2am; Fri–Sat 10am–4pm. U-Bahn: Volkstheater or MuseumsQuartier.

Café Restaurant Halle INTERNATIONAL   Set within the Kunsthalle, this is the direct competitor of the also-recommended Café Leopold (above). Larger and with a more sophisticated menu than the Leopold, but without any of its late-night emphasis on dance music, this is a postmodern, airy, big-windowed quartet of cream, wood-trimmed rooms. The menu changes every 2 weeks, and service is efficient, conscientious, and in the old-world style. The first thing you'll see when you enter is a Spartan-looking cafe area, with a trio of more formal dining rooms at the top of a short flight of stairs. Despite the commitment of its staff to changing the *carte* very frequently, the menu always contains a half-dozen meal-size salads, many garnished with strips of steak, chicken, or shrimp; two daily homemade soups; and a rotating series of platters that might include tasty braised filets of shark and roasted lamb, prepared delectably in the Greek style, with yogurt-and-herb dressing.

In the Kunsthalle Wien, Museumsplatz 1, in the MuseumsQuartier. ✆ **01/5237001.** Main courses 8€–17€. MC, V. Daily 10am–2am. U-Bahn: MuseumsQuartier.

Dubrovnik BALKAN/CROATIAN/VIENNESE   Dubrovnik's allegiance is to the culinary (and cultural) traditions of Croatia. The restaurant, founded in 1965, consists of three dining rooms on either side of a central vestibule filled with busy waiters in Croat costume. The menu lists a lengthy choice of Balkan dishes, including gooseliver pâté; stuffed cabbage; and filet of veal with boiled potatoes, sour cream, and sauerkraut. Among the fish dishes, the most exotic is *Fogosch* (a whitefish) served with potatoes and garlic. For dessert, try baklava or an assortment of Bulgarian cheeses. The restaurant schedules live piano entertainment nightly. On site is an unconventional-looking cafe (the Kono-Bar) that serves drinks and many of the main courses available during the grander restaurant's daily mid-afternoon closing.

Am Heumarkt 5. (℗ **01/713-7102.** Reservations recommended. Main courses 8€–18€. AE, DC, MC, V. Daily 11am–3pm and 6pm–midnight; cafe Mon–Fri 11am–midnight. U-Bahn: Stadtpark.

Esterházykeller ☺ AUSTRIAN This subterranean beer hall is a locals' haunt and a very well kept secret with occasional live gypsy music. The buffet-style eatery also serves a la carte, but the real fun is choosing from the cutlets, spreads, and salads at the bar. The network of caves and long rooms give it a very personal feel despite the vastness of the cellar. No one will mind if kids want to explore the caves and they'll have fun sampling the finger food and *Almdudler* (herbal soda). This is a good Inner City alternative to the more rural *heuriger* (see "*Heurigen*" in Chapter 10).

Haarhof 1, off Naglergasse around the corner from the Graben. (℗ **01-533 34 82.** www.esterhazykeller. at. Reservations not necessary. U-Bahn: Stephansplatz. Main courses: 6.50€; buffet 15€. AE, DC, MC, V. Daily 11am–11pm. U-Bahn: Stephansplatz.

Figlmüller AUSTRIAN The latest branch of a wine tavern whose original home, established in 1905, lies only a few blocks away. This one, thanks to a location on three floors of a thick-walled 200-year-old building and lots of old-world memorabilia attached to the walls, evokes Old Vienna with style and panache. The waiters are unflappable and its schnitzels are the kind of plate-filling, golden-brown delicacies that people always associate with schmaltzy Vienna. Menu items include goulash soup, onion-flavored roast beef, Vienna-style fried chicken, and strudels. During mushroom season (autumn and early winter), expect many variations, perhaps most deliciously served in a herbed cream sauce over noodles. This restaurant's nearby twin, at Wollzeile 5 (℗ **01/5126177;** www.figlmueller.at), offers basically the same menu, prices, and richly nostalgic wine-tavern ambience.

Bäckerstrasse 6. (℗ **01/5121760.** www.figlmueller.at. Reservations recommended. Main courses 11€–15€. AE, DC, MC, V. Daily 11:30am–midnight. Closed Aug. U-Bahn: Stephansplatz.

Gulaschmuseum ★ ☺ AUSTRIAN/HUNGARIAN If you thought that goulash was available in only one form, think again. This restaurant celebrates at least 15 varieties, each an authentic survivor of the culinary traditions of Hungary, and each redolent with the taste of the national spice, paprika. The Viennese adopted goulash from their former vassal centuries ago, and have long since added it to their culinary repertoire. You can order goulash made with roast beef, veal, pork, or even fried chicken livers. Vegetarians rejoice: versions made with potatoes, beans, or mushrooms are also available. Boiled potatoes and rough-textured brown or black bread usually accompany your choice. An excellent starter is the Magyar national crepe, *hortobágy palatschinken,* stuffed with minced beef and paprika cream sauce. If you prefer an Austrian dish, there are *tafelspitz,* Wiener schnitzel, fresh fish from Austria's lakes, and such desserts as homemade *apfelstrudel* and Sachertorte.

Schulerstrasse 20. (℗ **01/5121017.** www.gulasch.at. Reservations recommended. Main courses 8€–16€. MC, V. Mon–Fri 9am–midnight; Sat–Sun 10am–midnight. U-Bahn: Wollzeile or Stephansplatz.

Kardos AUSTRIAN/HUNGARIAN/SLOVENIAN This folkloric restaurant keeps alive the strong tastes and potent traditions that developed in different parts of what used to be the Austro-Hungarian Empire. Similarly, the setting celebrates the idiosyncratic folklore of various regions of the Balkans and the Great Hungarian Plain. Newcomers are welcomed with piquant little rolls known as *Grammel,* seasoned with minced pork and spices, and a choice of grilled meats. Other specials include Hungarian *fogosch* (a form of pikeperch) that's baked with vegetables and parsley potatoes, Hungarian goulash, and braised cabbage. The cellar atmosphere is gypsy schmaltz—pine-wood accents and bright Hungarian accessories. During the winter, you're likely to find a strolling violinist. To begin, try a glass of Barack, an aperitif made from fermented apricots.

Dominikaner Bastei 8. ℂ **01/5126949.** www.restaurantkardos.com. Reservations recommended. Main courses 8€–20€. AE, DC, MC, V. Mon–Sat 11:30am–2:30pm and 6–11pm. U-Bahn: Schwedenplatz.

Kern's Beisel 🔥 AUSTRIAN   The term *beisl* implies an unpretentious tavern where food is plentiful and cheap, and the waiters have minimal attitude. That's very much the case with this locals' haunt a few steps from the city's tourist and cultural core, Stephansplatz. You'll dine in an old-fashioned, wood-paneled dining room, darkened by smoke throughout the ages. The tables at the back, near the kitchen and separated from the front with a wooden partition, are nicer than those near the front, which are more brightly lit. Here, you might discover groups of wine-drinking friends, sometimes middle-aged ladies, celebrating their after-work rituals. The dinner menu changes weekly. There are dishes of xwurst with dumplings, beefsteaks, goulash soup, and Wiener schnitzels of both veal and pork, and, in autumn, some well-prepared game dishes.

Kleeblattgasse 4. ℂ **01/533-9188.** www.kernbeisl.at. Reservations recommended. 7€–15€ at lunch, 7€–19€ at dinner. MC, V. Mon–Fri 9am–11pm. Closed Sat–Sun. U-Bahn: Stephansplatz.

Palmenhaus ★ AUSTRIAN   Many architectural critics consider the Jugendstil glass canopy of this greenhouse the most beautiful in Austria. Overlooking the formal terraces of the Burggarten, it was built between 1901 and 1904 by the Habsburgs' court architect, Friedrich Ohmann, as a graceful architectural transition between the Albertina and the National Library. Damaged during wartime bombings, it was restored in 1998. Today, it functions as a chic cafe and, despite the lavishly historic setting, an appealingly informal venue. No one will mind if you drop in for just a drink and one of the voluptuous pastries displayed near the entrance. But if you want a meal, there's a sophisticated menu that changes monthly and might include fresh Austrian goat's cheese with stewed peppers and zucchini salad; young herring with sour cream and horseradish.

In the Burggarten. ℂ **01/5331033.** www.palmenhaus.at. Reservations recommended for dinner. Main courses 15€–18€. AE, DC, MC. V. Daily 10am–2am. U-Bahn: Opera.

Zu den 3 Hacken (at the Three Axes) ★ AUSTRIAN   Small and charming, this restaurant was established 350 years ago and today bears the reputation as the oldest *Gasthaus* (guesthouse) in Vienna. In 1827, Franz Schubert had an ongoing claim to one of the establishment's tables as a site for entertaining his cronies. Today, the establishment maintains midsummer barriers of green-painted lattices and potted ivy for tables that jut on to the street. Inside are three wood-finished dining rooms, each evocative of an inn high in the Austrian Alps. Expect an old-fashioned menu replete with the kind of dishes that fueled the Austro-Hungarian Empire. Examples include *Tafelspitz*, beef goulash, mixed grills piled high with chops and sausages.

Singerstrasse 28. ℂ **01/5125895.** www.vinum-wien.at. Reservations recommended. Main courses 7.50€–18€. AE, DC, MC, V. Mon–Sat 11am–11pm. U-Bahn: Stephansplatz.

Zum Kuchldragoner AUSTRIAN   Some aspects of this place will remind you of an historic Austrian tavern, perhaps one that's perched high in the mountains, far from any congested city. The feeling is enhanced by the pine trim and the battered *gemütlichkeit* of what you'll soon discover is a bustling, irreverent, and sometimes jaded approach to

Impressions

What if the Turks had taken Vienna, as they nearly did, and advanced westward? Martial spoils apart, the great contest has left little trace. It was the beginning of coffee-drinking in the West, or so the Viennese maintain. The earliest coffee houses, they insist, were kept by some of the Sultan's Greek and Serbian subjects who had sought sanctuary in Vienna. But the rolls which the Viennese dipped in the new drink were modeled on the half-moons of the Sultan's flag. The shape caught on all over the world. They mark the end of the age-old struggle between the hot-cross-bun and the croissant.

feeding traditional cuisine to large numbers of urban clients, usually late into the night after everyone has had more than a drink or two. You can settle for a table inside, but our preferred venue is outdoors, next to the Romanesque foundation of Vienna's oldest church, St. Ruprechts. Come here for foaming steins of beer and such Viennese staples as Wiener schnitzel, schnitzel cordon bleu, and grilled lamb cutlets.

Seitenstettengasse 3 or Ruprechtsplatz 4–5. © **015338371.** www.kuchldragoner.at. Reservations recommended. Main courses 7.80€–15€. MC, V. Mon–Thurs 11am–2am; Fri–Sun 11am–4am. U-Bahn: Schwedenplatz.

Zwölf-Apostelkeller VIENNESE   For those seeking a taste of Old Vienna, this is the place. Sections of this wine tavern's walls predate 1561. Rows of wooden tables stand under vaulted ceilings, with lighting partially provided by streetlights set into the masonry floor. It's so deep that you feel you're entering a dungeon. Students love the low prices and proximity to St. Stephan's. In addition to beer and wine, you can get hearty Austrian fare, including Hungarian goulash soup, meat dumplings, and a *schlachtplatte* (a selection of hot black pudding, liverwurst, pork, and pork sausage with a hot bacon and cabbage salad).

Sonnenfelsgasse 3. © **01/5126777.** www.zwoelf-apostelkeller.at. Main courses 6.50€–12€. AE, DC, MC, V. Daily 11am–midnight. Closed July. U-Bahn: Stephansplatz. Tram: 1, 2, 21, D, or N. Bus: 1A.

LEOPOLDSTADT (2ND DISTRICT)

Expensive

Vincent ★ CONTINENTAL   The decor of this restaurant is smooth and easy-going, and there are 3 dining rooms accented with flickering candles, flowers, and crystal, any of which might remind you of a richly upholstered, carefully-decorated private home. The set menus change with the season and the whim of the chef. The food is elegant, and includes a well-prepared rack of lamb with bacon; whitefish or pikeperch in white-wine sauce; turbot with saffron sauce; filet of butterfish with tiger prawns served with a consommé of shrimp; and, in season, many different game dishes, including quail and venison.

Grosse-Pfarrgasse 7. © **01/2141516.** www.restaurant-vincent.at. Reservations required. 5-course menu 50€; 7-course menu 69€; 10-course menu 95€. AE, DC, MC, V. Mon–Sat 5:30pm–1am. U-Bahn: Schwedenplatz.

COFFEE HOUSES & cafes

Café Central ★, Herrengasse 14 (℡ 01/5333764; U-Bahn: Herrengasse), stands in the middle of Vienna across from the Hofburg and the Spanish Riding School. This grand cafe offers a glimpse into 19th-century Viennese life—it was once the haunt of Austria's literati. Even Lenin is said to have met his colleagues here. The Central offers a variety of Viennese coffees, a vast selection of pastries and desserts, and Viennese and provincial dishes. It's a delightful spot for lunch. It is open Monday to Saturday from 7:30am to 10pm, Sunday 10am to 10pm.

The windows of the venerated 1888 **Café Demel** ★★, Kohlmarkt 14 (℡ 01/5351717; U-Bahn: Herrengasse; Bus: 1A or 2A), are filled with fanciful spun-sugar creations of characters from folk legends. Inside you'll find a splendidly baroque landmark where dozens of pastries are available daily, including the *Pralinen,* Senegal, truffle, *Sand,* and *Maximilian* tortes, as well as *Gugelhupf* (cream-filled horns). Demel also serves a mammoth variety of sandwiches made with smoked salmon, egg salad, caviar, or shrimp. If you want to be traditional, ask for a Demel-Coffee, which is filtered coffee served with milk, cream, or whipped cream. It's open daily from 10am to 7pm.

Café Diglas, Wollzeile 10 (℡ 01/5125765; www.diglas.at; U-Bahn: Stubentor), evokes prewar Vienna better than many of its competitors, thanks to a decor that retains some of the accessories from 1934, when it first opened. The cafe prides itself on its long association with composer Franz Léhar. It offers everything in the way of run-of-the-mill caffeine fixes, as well as more elaborate, liqueur-enriched concoctions like the *Biedermeier* (with apricot schnapps and cream). If you're hungry, ask for a menu (foremost among the platters is an excellent Wiener schnitzel). It is open daily from 7am to 11pm.

Café Dommayer, Auhofstrasse 2 (℡ 01/8775465; U-Bahn: Schönbrunn), boasts a reputation for courtliness that goes back to 1787. In 1844, Johann Strauss, Jr., made his musical debut here; and, in 1924, the site became known as *the* place in Vienna for tea dancing. During clement weather, a garden with seats for 300 opens in back. The rest of the year, the venue is restricted to a high-ceilinged, black-and-white, old-world room. Every Saturday from 2 to 4pm, a pianist and violinist perform; and every third Saturday, an all-woman orchestra plays mostly Strauss. Most patrons come for coffee, tea, and pastries, but if you have a more substantial appetite, try the platters, including Wiener schnitzel, *Rostbraten* (roast beef), and fish. It's open daily from 7am to 10pm.

Even the Viennese debate the age of **Café Frauenhuber,** Himmelpfortgasse 6 (℡ 01/5125353; U-Bahn: Stephansplatz). But regardless of whether 1788 or 1824 is correct, it has a justifiable claim to being the oldest continuously operating coffee house in the city. The old-time decor is a bit battered and more than a bit smoke-stained. Wiener schnitzel, served with potato salad and greens, is a good bet, as are any of the ice-cream dishes and pastries. It's open daily Monday to Saturday 8am to 11pm.

Moderate

Altes Jägerhaus ★ AUSTRIAN/GAME Little about the decor here has changed since this place opened in 1899. Located 1.5km (1 mile) from the entrance

One of the Ring's great coffee houses, **Café Landtmann ★**, Dr.-Karl-Lueger-Ring 4 (✆ **01/241000;** tram: 1, 2, or D), has a history dating to the 1880s and has long drawn a mix of politicians, journalists, and actors. It was also visited regularly by Freud. The original chandeliers and the prewar chairs are still here, albeit refurbished. Take an hour or so here, perusing the newspapers, sipping coffee, or planning the day's itinerary. The cafe is open daily from 7:30am to midnight (lunch is served 11:30am to 3pm and dinner is served 5 to 11pm).

Part of the success of **Café Sperl,** Gumpendorferstrasse 11 (✆ **01/5864158;** www.cafesperl.at; U-Bahn: Karlsplatz), derives from the fact that the Gilded Age panels and accessories that were installed in 1880 are still in place. Platters include salads; toast; baked noodles with ham, mushrooms, and cream sauce; steaks; and Wiener schnitzels. The staff evoke a bemused kind of courtliness; but in a concession to modern tastes, there's a billiard table and dartboards. It's open Monday to Saturday 7am to 11pm and Sunday 11am to 8pm (closed Sun July–Aug).

Café Tirolerhof, Fürichgasse 8 (✆ **01/5127833;** U-Bahn: Stephansplatz or Karlsplatz), has been under the same management for decades. It's a convenient sightseeing break, particularly from a tour of the nearby Hofburg complex. One coffee special is the Maria Theresia, a large cup of mocha with apricot liqueur and topped with whipped cream. If coffee sounds too hot, try the tasty milkshakes. You can also order a Viennese breakfast

of coffee, tea, or hot chocolate, two Viennese rolls, butter, jam, and honey. Open Monday to Saturday 7:30am to 10pm.

Thirty kinds of tea are served at **Demmers Teehaus,** Mölker Bastei 5 (✆ **01/5335995**; www.demmer.at; U-Bahn: Schottentor), along with dozens of pastries, cakes, toasts, and delicate sandwiches. Demmer's is managed by the previously recommended restaurant, Buffet Trzésniewski; however, the tea house offers you a chance to sit down, relax, and enjoy your drink or snack. It's open Monday to Friday from 9am to 6pm.

Motto am Fluss Café, Schwedenplatz 2 (✆ **01/35355-11**; www.motto.at; U-Bahn: Schwedenplatz) is a more modern version of the Viennese sit-and-sip tradition. Above the restaurant (see above) this cafe is refined and modern, with all the great offerings of the traditional establishments. In warm weather try for outdoor seating by the left entrance, where the sun shines longest. The in-house patisserie is also a great place for a baked pick-me-up to go. It's open daily, 8am to 2am.

Café Phil, Gumpendorferstrasse 10-12, (✆ **01/581-0489;** www.phil.info; U-Bahn: MuseumsQuartier.) This cafe-bookshop has become a live-in reading room for an entire generation of university students and stage people. With a mix of easy chairs, upholstered benches, and booths in and around several rooms of bookshelves, as well as public readings, readings, and the required assortment of newspapers on hand to soak in at your leisure, the place can be habit-forming. Open Tuesday to Sunday, 9am to 1am.

to the Prater in a park, it's a welcome escape from the more crowded restaurants of the Inner City. Grab a seat in any of the 4 old-fashioned dining rooms, and order beer or wine. Seasonal game like pheasant and venison are house specials, but you'll also find an array of seafood dishes that might include freshwater and saltwater trout, zander, or salmon. The menu also features a delicious repertoire of Austrian staples such as *tafelspitz* and schnitzel.

Freudenau 255. ℂ **01/72895770.** www.altes-jaegerhaus.com. Reservations recommended. Main courses 13€–25€. AE, DC, MC, V. Daily 10am–11pm. U-Bahn: Schlachthausgasse, then bus 77A.

Leopold 🏠 ☺ AUSTRIAN/CONTINENTAL   A simplistic, modern establishment, which is home to a sophisticated kitchen whose menu will make your mouth water. Besides the usual *schnitzel* and *Eiernockerl* (dumpling noodles) the hip bohemian clientele enjoys a monthly menu of local and seasonal dishes with such temptations as ginger-lime chicken with lychees and basmati rice or a simpler local catfish served with olives, capers, and mashed potatoes. The food is always inspired, light, and delectable. This is a dinner-only restaurant except on Sundays when there is a vast brunch buffet from 10am to 3pm that is all you can eat for 13€. Dig in!

Grosse Pfargasse 11. ℂ **01/2182281.** www.restaurant-leopold.at. Main courses 7€–14€. AE, DC, MC, V. Daily 5–11pm. U-Bahn: Taborstrasse. Tram: 2.

Simchas ★ JEWISH/BULGARIAN   This is one of Vienna's few kosher restaurants, and the Natanov family prides itself in mixing Jewish cooking traditions from around the world. They were part of the Jewish Diaspora and fled to Bulgaria and Uzbekistan, making the cuisine a many-cultured product of the generation who returned to Vienna. In the tastefully modern interior, the friendly staff serves delicious dishes such as hummus starters, luscious meat and fish skewers, samosa, borscht, plus 5 small salads with your main course. The food is top-notch, but first courses are quite large so, to leave room for your main dish, it may make sense to share.

Taborstrasse 47. ℂ **01/2182833.** www.simchas.at. Main courses 12€–25€. AE, DC, MC, V. Daily 10am–11pm. U-Bahn: Taborstrasse. Tram: 2.

Skopik & Lohn ★ AUSTRIAN/INTERNATIONAL   Here, a charismatic ex-New Yorker of Viennese descent serves up his twin cultures with a nod to his in-laws from Tuscany and Provence. The interior is striking, with wild scribblings of black paint all over the white ceilings. Try Hungarian paprika chicken with *topfenspätzle* (curd cheese pasta) and chive sauce or an Italian *buratta* with pepperonatta sauce. The food is inspired and very artfully served in a place that is the first bite of the Big Apple-feeling in Vienna's Leopoldstadt.

Leopoldgasse 17. ℂ **01/2198977.** www.skopikundlohn.at. Main courses 10€–22€. AE, DC, MC, V. Daily 6pm–1am. U-Bahn: Shottenring. Tram: 2.

Inexpensive

Restaurant Kaj ★★ CROATIAN   Simple and intimate, this captivating little spot is a quick side-trip to the Dalmatian coast. Fresh fish arrives each morning by train to the South Station and finds its way to Kaj, where it will be carried out on a platter for you to examine, and make your selection. Everything is cooked fresh, and while you're waiting, order an antipasto platter, and in minutes an extravagance of delicious sea food and roasted veggies will arrive, served cold and perfectly spiced. The Balkan wines are also fun to try; let yourself be advised. This is a pauper's feast, hard to duplicate anywhere. Reserve 2 days ahead.

Fugbachgasse 9. ℂ **01/216 6495.** www.fischrestaurant-kaj.at. Main courses 6.50€–15€. AE, DC, MC, V. Daily 11am–3pm, 5:30 to 11pm. U-Bahn: Praterstern.

Schweizerhaus ★ AUSTRIAN   This place is legend. Not only does it seat what seems like millions, it has been a beer hall since 1868. The Kolarik family, who now run the place, call it Vienna's biggest beer barrel and although that may be accurate (endless numbers of *Krügerl*, or large beers, are hauled past on massive trays) the food is very good too. The *Schweinsstelzen* (leg of pork) is served on the bone with a knife and cutting board as your only aid. Other top dishes include *Schnitzel*, goulash, and *Kartoffelpuffer* (fried potato medallions) as well as homemade beer chocolate. A visit is in order after romping through the Prater. You'll find it at the far end of the amusement park.

Prater 116. ℂ **01/7280152-13.** www.schweizerhaus.at. Main courses 5€–16€. AE, DC, MC, V. Daily 11am–11pm. U-Bahn: Praterstern or Stadion.

LANDSTRASSE (3RD DISTRICT)
Very Expensive

Steirereck ★★★ AUSTRIAN/VIENNESE   *Steirereck* means "corner of Styria," which is exactly what this intimate and rustic restaurant is. Traditional Viennese dishes and "new Austrian" selections appear on the menu. Begin with a caviar-semolina dumpling or roasted turbot with fennel, or opt for the most elegant and expensive item of all, goose-liver Steirereck. Some enticing main courses include asparagus with pigeon, saddle of lamb for two, prime Styrian roast beef, and red-pepper risotto with rabbit. The menu is wisely limited and well prepared, changing daily depending on what's fresh at the market. The restaurant is popular with after-show diners, and the wine cellar holds some 35,000 bottles.

Am Heumarkt 2A. ℂ **01/7133168.** www.steirereck.at. Reservations required. Main courses 15€–25€; 5-course fixed-price dinner 100€. AE, DC, MC, V. Mon–Fri 11:30am–2:30pm and 6:30–11pm. Closed holidays. Tram: N. Bus: 4.

Expensive

Dining Room ★★★ 🏠 INTERNATIONAL   On a quiet lane outside town, this little restaurant has only four tables, seating 12 guests. It's in a private home and follows a European trend of hideaway restaurants for those who appreciate great food served in a very intimate and personal atmosphere. The owner and chef, Angelika Apfelthaler, prepares each meal herself, offering a set menu. Each night's menu is dedicated to a special theme, including, perhaps, white truffles in Piedmont, Moroccan nights, or cooking with spices from around the world. Top-quality products go into every menu, and the bread, jams, and chutneys are all homemade. You might begin with a chestnut and hazelnut soup, followed by an arugula salad with sautéed porcini mushrooms. A main course might be a juicy duck breast with a creamy saffron-laced risotto.

Maygasse 31. ℂ **01/804-8586.** Reservations required. Fixed-price menu 44€. DC, MC, V. Dinner is served most evenings at 7:00pm (but confirm exact time when you call for a reservation). U-Bahn: Hietzing, then tram 60 to Riedelgasse/Orthopädisches Krankenhaus (a 5-minute walk from here).

Niky's Kuchlmasterei ★ INTERNATIONAL/VIENNESE   The decor features old stonework with some modern architectural innovations, and the extensive menu boasts well-prepared food. The lively crowd of loyal habitués adds to the welcoming ambience, making Niky's a good choice for an evening meal, especially in summer when you can dine on its unforgettable terrace. After a long and pleasant meal, your

FAMILY-FRIENDLY dining

Gulaschmuseum ★ (p. 111) If your children think ordering hamburgers in a foreign country is adventurous eating, this is a great place to introduce them to goulash—it comes in at least 15 delicious varieties. And it really is little more than hamburger stew. Few youngsters will turn down the home-made *Apfelstrudel*.

bill will arrive in an elaborate box suitable for jewels, along with an amusing message in German that offers a tongue-in-cheek apology for cashing your check.

Obere Weissgerberstrasse 6. ✆ **01/7129000.** www.kuchlmasterei.at. Reservations recommended. Main courses 18€–20€; 3-course fixed-price lunch 19€; 7-course fixed-price dinner 51€. AE, DC, MC, V. Mon-Sat noon-midnight. U-Bahn: Schwedenplatz.

WIEDEN & MARGARETEN (4TH & 5TH DISTRICTS)

Moderate

Motto AUSTRIAN/INTERNATIONAL This is the premier gay-friendly restaurant of Austria, with a cavernous red-and-black interior, a busy bar, and a clientele that has included many of the glam figures (Thierry Mugler, John Galliano, and lots of stage types) of the international circuit. Even Helmut Lang worked here briefly as a waiter. It's set behind green doors and a sign that's so small and discreet as to be nearly invisible. In summer, it's enhanced with tables in the garden. No one will mind if you pop in just to chat, as it's a busy nightlife entity in its own right. But cuisine is about as eclectic as it gets, ranging from sushi and Thai-inspired curries to *gutbürgerlich* (home and hearth) food like grandma used to make.

Schönbrunnerstrasse 30 (entrance on Rudigergasse). ✆ **01/5870672.** www.motto.at. Reservations recommended. Main courses 7€–21€. MC, V. Daily 6pm-4am. U-Bahn: Pilgramgasse.

Silberwirt VIENNESE Despite the fact that it opened a quarter of a century ago, this restaurant oozes with Old Viennese style and resembles the traditional *beisl* (bistro) with its copious portions of conservative, timeless Viennese food. You can dine within a pair of dining rooms or move into the beer garden. Menu items include stuffed mushrooms, *tafelspitz*, schnitzels, and filets of zander, salmon, and trout.

Schlossgasse 21. ✆ **01/5444907.** www.schlossquadr.at. Reservations recommended. Main courses 9€–22€. V. Daily noon-10pm. U-Bahn: Pilgramgasse.

Inexpensive

Café Cuadro INTERNATIONAL Trendy, countercultural, and arts-oriented, this cafe and bistro is little more than a long, glassed-in corridor with vaguely Bauhaus-inspired detailing. There are clusters of industrial-looking tables, but many clients opt for a seat at the long, luncheonette-style counter above a Plexiglas floor, with four-sided geometric patterns illuminated from below. In keeping with the establishment's name (Cuadro), the menu features four of everything: salads (including a very good Caesar), juicy burgers, homemade soups, steak, and—if you're an early riser—breakfast.

Margaretenstrasse 77. ℂ **01/544-7550.** www.schlossquadr.at. Breakfast 4€–8€; main courses 5€–12€. V. Mon–Sat 8am–midnight; Sun 9am–11pm. U-Bahn: Pilgramgasse:

Gasthaus Ubl ★ 🍴 AUSTRIAN   This closely-guarded Viennese secret is where locals go when they want to enjoy some of the famous dishes enjoyed by their last great emperor, Franz Josef. There's an authentic guesthouse-like atmosphere with an old Viennese stove and friendly staff. Three sisters run it, and the whole place screams Old Vienna—nothing flashy or touristy here. Begin with one of the freshly-made salads or soups, then follow with the classics—the best *Tafelspitz* in the area or timeless dishes such as *Schweinsbraten* (a perfectly roasted pork). Desserts are old-fashioned and yummy.

Pressgasse 26. ℂ **01/5876437.** Reservations recommended. Main courses: 10€–15€. AE, DC, MC, V. Daily noon–2pm and 6–10pm. U-Bahn: Karlsplatz. Bus: 59A.

Gergely's AUSTRIAN/INTERNATIONAL   This little restaurant is in a turn-of-the-century building decorated with a pleasant mishmash of old and new furnishings, much like those you would find in someone's home. It serves classic Austrian fare as well as some interesting, palate-pleasing Asian dishes, such as Indonesian satay and Chinese stir-fry, and excellent steaks.

Schlossgasse 21. ℂ **01/544-0767.** www.schlossquadr.at. Reservations recommended. Main courses 8€–24€. V. Mon–Sat 6pm–1am. U-Bahn: Pilgramgasse.

MARIAHILF (6TH DISTRICT)
Moderate

Finkh ★ 🍴 AUSTRIAN/VIENNESE   This tiny, new restaurant, way off the beaten track, resembles a radically minimalist work of art in some Berlin gallery. The menu is equally small and consists of genuinely good and simple versions of Austrian classics and mirrors the wine list, which is also select, but sufficient. The menu changes weekly and is always fresh, seasonal, local, and organic. The owner, Fridolin Fink, and cook Elias Zenzmaier are both young, inspired souls that have already received much acclaim in local circles. The schnitzel was grandiose as was the *Blunzengröstl* (a blood sausage special).

Esterházygasse 12. ℂ **01/913-8992.** www.finkh.at. Reservations not necessary. Main courses 7€–29€. MC, V. Tues–Sat 3pm–midnight, Sun 10am–3pm. U-Bahn: Neubaugasse. Bus: 13A.

Gräfin vom Naschmarkt AUSTRIAN/CONTINENTAL   This restaurant, near the Naschmarkt, is open 24 hours a day. Early-morning truckers loading and unloading at the nearby market drop in for beer and schnitzel, perching next to soggy insomniacs from the area's many straight and gay bars. It also does a roaring business from the after-show crowd at the nearby Theater an der Wien, and by 4am the place is usually packed. Menu items include Styrian-style chicken salad with pine nuts, bacon-studded dumplings with green salad, pork cutlets with potato salad, and what a local paper (*Kurier*) defined as "Vienna's best *Gulaschsuppe.*"

Linke Wienzeile 14. ℂ **01/586-3389.** Reservations not necessary. Main courses 7€–29€. MC, V. 24 hours a day, although service and menu items are reduced as the restaurant is cleaned, every morning between 2–4am. U-Bahn: Karlsplatz or Kettenbrückengasse.

The Emperor's Nonsense

There are many theories about the origin of the name *Kaiserschmarrn* for the legendary Austrian dessert. Literally "Emperor's Nonsense," it consists of a thick pancake broken into pieces and served with powdered sugar, a treat to say the least. One legend has it that Kaiser Franz Joseph was given *holzfällerschmarrn* (lumberjack pancake) on a hunting trip in the Salzkammergut. The special version was made with fresh milk, raisins, and eggs, and therefore was not an ordinary *holzfällerschmarrn*, but a *Kaiserschmarrn*. Another story recounts that the imperial cook was trying to make the emperor *palatschinken* (crepes) and the batter was too thick. When he then presented it to Franz Joseph, the ruler sent the torn dessert back saying "This nonsense is not fit for an emperor."

Inexpensive

Alfi's Goldener Spiegel VIENNESE   Along with Motto, this is the leading gay restaurant in Vienna. The food and ambience, however, might remind you of a simple Viennese *beisl* in a working-class district. Expect large portions of traditional Viennese dishes such as Wiener schnitzel, roulade of beef, steak with pepper sauce, and *tafelspitz*. Its position near Vienna's Naschmarkt, the city's biggest food market, ensures that the food served is impeccably fresh.

Linke Wienzeile 46 (entrance on Stiegengasse). ☎ **01/5866608.** www.goldenerspiegel.com. Main courses 6.50€–15€. No credit cards. Daily 7pm–2am. U-Bahn: Kettenbrückengasse.

Saint Charles Alimentary ★ 🎁 AUSTRIAN/VEGETARIAN   Unique in Vienna, this is a pharmacy restaurant. Head chef Philipp Furtenbach takes fresh seriously, often gathering his ingredients directly from local farmers or in the forests around Vienna. He aims to bring out the natural taste and healing power of native herbs and plants. The unique restaurant is not strictly vegetarian, as the restaurant also procures wild game shot especially for them. Start perhaps with a wild root soup that is very aromatic. Your freshly-made salad might be one of green lentils with Jerusalem artichoke slices, everything bound together by pumpkin-seed oil. A meatless main course might be a robust porridge of spelt with roast pumpkin, red peppers, and walnuts, served with hard cheese from the district of Vorarlberg in the west.

Gumpendorferstrasse 33. ☎ **01/586-1365.** www.saint.info. Reservations not required. Fixed-price menu 14€. MC, V. Mon–Thurs 10am–3pm; Fri–Sat 9am–midnight. U-Bahn: Gumpendorfer.

NEUBAU (7TH DISTRICT)

Expensive

Bohème ★ INTERNATIONAL/VIENNESE   This one-time bakery was built in 1750 in the baroque style. Today its historic street is an all-pedestrian walkway loaded with shops. Bohème attracts a crowd that's knowledgeable about the nuances of wine, food, and the opera music that reverberates throughout the two dining rooms. Even the decor is theatrical; it looks like a cross between a severely dignified stage set and an artsy, turn-of-the-19th-century cafe. Menu items are listed as movements in an opera, with overtures (aperitifs), prologues (appetizers), and first and second acts (soups and main courses). As you'd guess, desserts provide the finales. Some tempting items include Andalusian gazpacho, platters of mixed fish filets with tomato risotto, and *Tafelspitz* with horseradish.

Spittelberggasse 19. ℭ **01/5233173.** www.boheme.at. Reservations recommended. Main courses 10€–23€. AE, DC, MC, V. Mon–Sat 11am–midnight. Closed Jan 7–23. U-Bahn: Volkstheater.

DOTS ★ 🍴 ASIAN   This 'experimental sushi' restaurant is a joy. Inhabiting a hidden area only reachable through a passageway off Mariahilferstrasse, the interior is all in white. The business, nightlife, and fashion community fill the clear plastic chairs and elegant waiters are skilled at coping with the pickiest of clientele. From octopus and salmon teppanyaki, to traditional sushi and maki, and inspired creations such as truffle-asparagus maki, this cuisine is beautifully tasty and fun to eat. Try one of the eclectic sushi sets. The staff will be glad to help you choose.

Mariahilferstrasse 103. ℭ **01/920-9980.** www.dots-lounge.com. Reservations recommended. Main courses 11€–23€. DC, MC, V. Mon–Sat noon–midnight; Sun 3pm–midnight. U-Bahn: Zieglergasse.

Inexpensive

Amerlingbeisl AUSTRIAN   The hip clientele, occasionally blasé staff, and minimalist, somewhat industrial-looking decor give Amerlingbeisl a modern sensibility. If you get nostalgic, you can opt for a table out on the cobblestones of the early-19th-century building's glassed-in courtyard, beneath a grape arbor, where horses used to be stabled. Come to this locals' spot for simple but good food and a glass of beer or wine. The menu ranges from simple sandwiches and salads to more elaborate fare, such as Argentinean steak with rice, turkey or pork schnitzels with potato salad, and dessert crepes stuffed with marmalade.

Stiftgasse 8. ℭ **01/526-1660.** www.amerlingbeisl.at. Main courses 7.60€–8.70€. DC, MC, V. Daily 9am–2am. U-Bahn: Volkstheater.

Plutzer Bräu ★ 🍴 AUSTRIAN   This is one of the best examples in Vienna of the explosion of hip and trendy restaurants within the city's 7th District. An offshoot of the Plutzer Brewery, it occupies the cavernous cellar of an imposing 19th-century building. Any antique references are quickly lost once you're inside, thanks to an industrial decor with exposed heating ducts, stainless steel, and accessories that might remind you of the cafeteria in a central European factory. You can stay at the long, accommodating bar and drink fresh-brewed Plutzer beer; but if you're hungry (and this very good beer will probably encourage an appetite), head for the well-scrubbed dining room, where the menu reflects Old Viennese traditions. Food is excellent and includes veal stew in beer sauce with dumplings, "brewmaster's-style" pork steak, and pasta with herbs and feta cheese. Dessert might include curd dumplings with poppy seeds and sweet breadcrumbs.

Schrankgasse 2. ℭ **01/5261215.** www.plutzerbrau.at. Reservations not necessary. Main courses 6.90€–17€. MC, V. Daily 10am–midnight. U-Bahn: Volkstheater.

JOSEFSTADT (8TH DISTRICT)
Moderate

Alte Backstube HUNGARIAN/VIENNESE   This spot is worth visiting just to admire the baroque sculptures that crown the top of the doorway. The building was

PICNICS & street FOOD

Picnickers will find that Vienna is among the best-stocked cities in Europe for food supplies. The best—and least expensive—place is the **Naschmarkt,** an open-air market that's only a 5-minute stroll from Karlsplatz (the nearest U-Bahn stop). Here you'll find hundreds of stalls selling fresh produce, breads, meats, cheeses, flowers, tea, and more. Fast-food counters and other stands peddle ready-made foods such as grilled chicken, Austrian and German sausages, sandwiches, and even beer. The market is open Monday to Friday from 6am to 6:30pm, Saturday from 6am to 1pm. You can also buy your picnic at one of Vienna's many delis, such as **Radatz,** Wipplingerstrasse 3 (ⓒ **01/535-6134;** www.radatz.at).

With your picnic basket in hand, head for Stadtpark, Burggarten, or Volksgarten, or even to the courtyard of Museums-Quartier. Even better, if the weather is right, plan an excursion into the Vienna Woods (the Bellevue Wiese is a local favorite with a beautiful vista).

On street corners throughout Vienna, you'll find one of the city's most popular snack spots, the **Würstelstand.** These small stands sell beer and soda, plus frankfurters, bratwurst, curry wurst, and other Austrian sausages, usually served on a roll *mit senf* (with mustard). Try the *käsekrainer,* a fat sausage with tasty bits of cheese. Conveniently-located stands are on Seilergasse (just off Stephansplatz), Albertinaplatz (behind the Opera), and Kupferschmiedgasse (just off Kärntnerstrasse).

designed as a private home in 1697, and 4 years later it was transformed into a bakery, complete with wood-burning stoves. For more than 2½ centuries, the establishment served the baking needs of the area. In 1963, the owners added a dining room, a dainty front room for drinking beer and tea, and a collection of baking-related artifacts. Once seated, you can order such wholesome, robust dishes as braised pork with cabbage, Viennese-style goulash, and roast venison with cranberry sauce and bread dumplings. There's an English-language menu if you need it. Try the house special dessert, cream-cheese strudel with hot vanilla sauce.

Lange Gasse 34. ⓒ **01/4061101.** www.backstube.at. Reservations required. Main courses 10€–19€. MC, V. Tues–Thurs and Sat–Sun noon–midnight; Fri 5pm–midnight. Closed mid-July to Aug 30. U-Bahn: Rathaus. Go east along Schmidgasse to Lange Gasse.

Die Fromme Helene ★ AUSTRIAN   This is the kind of upscale tavern where the food is traditional and excellent, the crowd is animated and creative, and the staff is hip enough to recall the names of the many actors, writers, and politicians who come here regularly. Part of its theatrical allure derives from a location that's close to several of the city's theaters (including the English Theater); and to prove it, there are signed and framed photographs of many of the quasi-celebrity clients who have eaten and made merry here. Expect a wide range of traditional and well-prepared Austrian dishes, including schnitzels of both veal and pork. The establishment's enduring dish is *alt Wiener Backfleisch,* a long-marinated and spicy version of steak that's breaded, fried, and served with potato salad. The restaurant's name derives from the comic-book creation of a 19th-century illustrator, Wilhelm Busch, whose hard-drinking but well-meaning heroine, "pious Helen," captivated the imagination of the German-speaking world.

15 Josefstädter Strasse. ℡ **01/4069144.** www.frommehelene.at. Reservations recommended. Main courses 11€–20€. AE, DC, MC, V. Mon–Sat 11am–1am. Tram: J to Theater in der Josefstadt.

Piaristenkeller AUSTRIAN   A vast cavern with centuries-old vaulted ceilings, this place was founded in 1697 by Piarist monks as a tavern and wine cellar. The kitchen, which once served the cloisters, still dishes out traditional Austrian dishes based on original recipes. Zither music starts at 7:30pm, and in summer the garden at the church square is open from 11am to midnight. Wine and beer are available whenever the cellar is open. Advance booking is required for a guided tour of the cloister's old wine vaults.

Piaristengasse 45. ℡ **01/4059152.** www.piaristenkeller.at. Reservations recommended. Main courses 14€–22€. AE, DC, MC, V. Mon–Sat 6pm–midnight. U-Bahn: Rathaus.

Schnattl ★ AUSTRIAN   Even the justifiably proud owner of this place, Wilhelm (Willy) Schnattl, dismisses its decor as a mere foil for the presentation of his sublime food. Schnattl is near Town Hall, a location convenient for most of the city's journalists and politicians, and features a bar area and a medium-size dining room, an inviting, intimate space of enormous comfort and charm. Dishes show intense attention to detail and—in some cases—a megalomaniacal sweep from a chef whom the press has called a "mad culinary genius." Roasted sweetbreads are served with a purée of green peas; marinated freshwater fish (a species known locally as *hochen*) comes with a parfait of cucumbers. Try the celebrated parfait of pickled tongue (a terrine of foie gras and a mousse of tongue, blended and wrapped in strips of tongue and served with a toasted corn brioche).

40 Lange Gasse. ℡ **01/405-3400.** www.schnattl.com. Reservations required. Main courses 17€–26€. AE, DC, MC, V. Mon–Fri 6–11pm. Closed weekends,for 2 weeks at Easter, and for 2 weeks late Aug. U-Bahn: Rathaus.

ALSERGRUND (9TH DISTRICT)
Moderate

Abend-Restaurant Feuervogel RUSSIAN   Since World War I, this restaurant has been a Viennese landmark, bringing Russian cuisine to a location across from the palace of the Prince of Liechtenstein. You'll eat in romantically Slavic surroundings with Gypsy violins playing Russian and Viennese music. Specialties include chicken Kiev, beef Stroganoff, veal Dolgoruki, borscht, and many other dishes that taste as if they came right off the steppes. For an hors d'oeuvre try *sakkuska*, a variety platter that's popular in Russia. You can also order a gourmet fixed-price dinner with 5 courses. Be sure to sample the Russian ice cream known as *plombier*.

Alserbachstrasse 21. ℡ **01/3175391.** www.feuervogel.at. Reservations recommended. Main courses 11€–16€. AE, DC, MC, V. Mon–Sat 6pm–midnight. Closed July 20–Aug 8. U-Bahn: Friedensbrücke. Bus: 32.

Stiegl Ambulanz AUSTRIAN/VIENNESE   Smack in the middle of the university campus at the Old General Hospital (Altes AKH) the Austrian beer brewery Stiegl has opened a modern *Gasthaus* that translates as "Stiegl emergency room." In summer the beer garden is always full of students, professors, and locals. Inside, one room has lines of long tables, while a lounge area with sofas is slightly separate. The food is simple and tasty and the establishment makes a point of always ensuring organic, free range, and local ingredients.

40 Lange Gasse. ✆ **01/402-1150.** www.stiegl.com. Main courses 7€–15€. AE, DC, MC, V. Mon–Fri 11am–midnight, Sun 11am–9pm. U-Bahn: Schottentor, Tram: 5.

WESTBAHNHOF (15TH DISTRICT)

Moderate

Hollerei ★ VEGETARIAN   This fresh, bright place features delectable vegetarian and vegan cuisine. Only 10 minutes from Schönbrunn, the stylish interior is only topped by the overgrown garden seating area, which is a great place to take a veggie date. The food has Asian and Mediterranean influences, prepared in a style all its own. Gnocchi with mushrooms over cranberries and root vegetables, or red Thai curry with sweet potatoes, ginger, and tofu over coconut rice, are just a couple of tasty options. The clientele is not even all vegetarian, but likes a chic alternative to *wurst* and *schnitzel*.

Hollergasse 9. ✆ **01/892-3356.** www.hollerei.at. Reservations recommended. Main courses 11€–15€. MC, V. Mon–Sat 11:30am–3pm and from 6pm; Sun 11:30am–afternoon. U-Bahn: Hütteldorf. Bus: 57A.

Kent ★★ TURKISH   Right near the lively Brunnenmarkt, the interior of this local landmark somewhat resembles an elegant mess hall or cafeteria, but don't let that scare you off. The scrumptious Turkish specials feature everything from a classic Kebab to stuffed zucchinis and bell peppers, sarma (stuffed cabbage leaves) and roast lamb. They also serve an array of vegetarian dishes. The service is friendly and fast, used to large groups and busy nights. The Viennese Turks praise this place for its authenticity and the natives are surprised to find more than the usual kebab and other street foods. It's always busy so do reserve, and try the *Musakka*.

Brunnengasse 67. ✆ **01/405-9173.** www.kent-restaurant.at. Reservations recommended. Main courses 6€–20€. MC, V. Mon–Sat 6pm–2am U-Bahn: Schweglerstrasse.

Vikerl's Lokal AUSTRIAN   This tavern has been a fixture since before World War II, when it got its name from the nickname of its since-departed founder, Victor. It now serves food that is a lot more sophisticated than the simple setting. In two dining rooms, covered with intricate panels, you'll find a menu that changes every 2 weeks. One particularly luscious dish is a thick-sliced calf's liver, served on a bed of crisp-fried tripe prepared with ginger. Chocolate-walnut cake makes a satisfying dessert.

Würffelgasse 4. ✆ **01/894-3430.** www.vikerls.at. Reservations recommended. Main courses 12€–20€. MC, V. Tues–Sat 5pm–midnight; Sun 11:30am–4pm. U-Bahn: Westbahnhof, then tram 52 or 58 to Würffelgasse.

NEAR SCHÖNBRUNN

Expensive

Altwienerhof ★★★ AUSTRIAN/FRENCH   A short walk from Schönbrunn Palace lies one of the premier dining spots in Vienna. The building is completely modernized, but it was originally designed as a private home in the 1870s. Mr. Günter brings sophistication and charm to the dining rooms, which retain many Biedermeier embellishments from the original construction. The chef prepares nouvelle cuisine

OFF TO wine COUNTRY

To get out of the urban hubbub, most Viennese choose to go to the outer districts of Vienna, preferably Grinzing or Nussdorf to the legendary **Heuriger**, where this year's wine is served with traditional hearty fare. See Chapter 10, *"Heuriger."*

using only the freshest and highest-quality ingredients. The menu changes frequently and the maître d' is always willing to assist with recommendations. Each night the chef prepares a tasting menu, which is a sampling of the kitchen's best nightly dishes. The wine list consists of more than 700 selections, each of which is chosen by Mr. Günter himself. The cellar below houses about 18,000 bottles.

In the Altwienerhof Hotel, Herklotzgasse 6. © **01/8926000.** www.altwienerhof.at. Reservations recommended. Main courses 12€–21€. AE, DC, MC, V. Mon–Sat 5–11pm. Closed first 3 weeks in Jan. U-Bahn: Gumpendorferstrasse.

Moderate

Hietzinger Bräu AUSTRIAN   Established in 1743, this is the most famous and best-recommended restaurant in the vicinity of Schönbrunn Palace. Everything about it evokes a sense of bourgeois stability—wood paneling, a staff wearing folkloric costume, and platters heaped high with *gutbürgerlich* cuisine. The menu lists more than a dozen preparations of beef, including the time-tested favorite, *tafelspitz,* as well as mixed grills, all kinds of steaks, and fish that includes lobster, salmon, crab, and zander. Homage to the cuisine of Franz Josef appears in the form of very large Wiener schnitzels, a creamy goulash, and even a very old-fashioned form of braised calf's head. Wine is available, but by far the most popular beverage here is a foaming stein of the local brew, Hietzinger.

Auhofstrasse 1. © **01/87770870.** Reservations not necessary. Main courses 16€–23€. DC, MC, V. Daily 11:30am–3pm and 6–11:30pm. U-Bahn: Hietzing.

IN THE OUTER DISTRICTS
Inexpensive

Blaustern CONTINENTAL   It's well managed, hip, and stylish, but because of its location in Vienna's outlying 19th District, Blaustern almost exclusively attracts local residents. The Sunday-morning breakfast crowd might include local celebrity and race-car champ Niki Lauda. Expect bacon and eggs, light fare such as pastas and salads, and daily specials that include braised scampi with vegetable beignets and avocado sauce. The name comes from the *blau stern* (blue star) that used to adorn sacks of coffee imported from South America by the restaurant's owners.

Döblinger Gürtel 2. © **01/369-6564.** www.blaustern.at. Main courses 7.50€–12€. No credit cards. Mon–Fri 7am–1am; Sat–Sun 8am–1am. U-Bahn: Nussdorfer Strasse.

EXPLORING VIENNA

❝The Balkans begin at Rennweg," Austria's renowned statesman, Prince Klemens von Metternich, said at the Congress of Vienna in 1814, referring to the power and influence of the far-flung Austrian Empire which the Habsburg dynasty controlled from 1273 to 1918.

Viennese prosperity under the Habsburgs reached its peak during the long reign of Maria Theresa in the late-18th century, yet continued to shape the character and future of Europe for another two centuries, culminating in an explosion of creative energy in its final half-decade in science, in philosophy, the new field of psychology, literature, art, and music; setting in motion the ideas and trends—both the best and the worst—that shaped the 20th century. Many of the sights described below originated under the great empress who escorted Vienna through the Age of Enlightenment, a woman who welcomed the prodigy Mozart to her court at Schönbrunn when he was just 6 years old.

With the collapse of the Napoleonic Empire, Vienna took over Paris's long-held position as "the center of Europe." At the Congress of Vienna, the crowned heads of Europe met to restructure the continent's political boundaries. But they devoted so much time to galas that little was being accomplished, leading Prince de Ligne to remark memorably, "The Congress isn't taking a single step, it's dancing!"

In this chapter we'll explore many of Vienna's historic sights and the extraordinary richness of its contemporary urban life. It's possible to spend a week here and only scratch the surface of this multifaceted city. We'll take you through the highlights, but even this venture will take more than a week of fast-paced walking.

THE HOFBURG PALACE COMPLEX ★★★

Once the winter palace of the Habsburgs, the vast and impressive **Hofburg** sits in the heart of Vienna. To reach it (you can hardly miss it), head up Kohlmarkt to Michaelerplatz 1, Burgring, where you'll stumble across two enormous fountains embellished with statuary. You can also take the U-Bahn to Stephansplatz, Herrengasse, or Mariahilferstrasse, or Tram nos. 1, 2, D, or J to Burgring.

The Hofburg

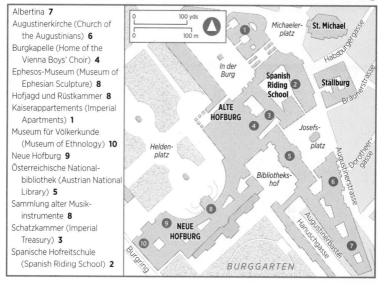

Albertina **7**
Augustinerkirche (Church of the Augustinians) **6**
Burgkapelle (Home of the Vienna Boys' Choir) **4**
Ephesos-Museum (Museum of Ephesian Sculpture) **8**
Hofjagd und Rüstkammer **8**
Kaiserappartements (Imperial Apartments) **1**
Museum für Völkerkunde (Museum of Ethnology) **10**
Neue Hofburg **9**
Österreichische National-bibliothek (Austrian National Library) **5**
Sammlung alter Musik-instrumente **8**
Schatzkammer (Imperial Treasury) **3**
Spanische Hofreitschule (Spanish Riding School) **2**

This complex of imperial edifices, the first of which was constructed in 1279, grew with the empire; and today the palace is virtually a city within a city. The earliest parts surround the **Swiss Court,** a courtyard named for the Swiss mercenaries who performed guard duty here. The Hofburg's styles, which are not always harmonious, result from each emperor's opting to add to or take away some of the work done by his predecessors. Called simply *die Burg,* or "the Palace," by the Viennese, the Hofburg has withstood three major sieges and a great fire. Of its more than 2,600 rooms, some two dozen are open to the public.

Albertina ★   This Hofburg museum, named for a son-in-law of Maria Theresa, houses one of the world's great graphic art collections, spanning 6 centuries. The museum underwent an extensive renovation at the beginning of the century that restored the magnificent statuary, fountain, and facade and opened three major exhibition spaces that have put the Albertina on the map as one of the most exciting museums in Europe. Its permanent collection includes Dürer's *Hare* and *Clasped Hands,* which the Albertina has owned for centuries, as well as some 60,000 drawings and one million prints; the best known include Ruben's children's studies. In addition, the museum owns masterpieces of Schiele, Cézanne, Klimt, Kokoschka, Picasso, and Rauschenberg. The collection was badly threatened in 2008 in the unprecedented flooding that submerged towns all along the Danube, when its high security depot, thought to be waterproof, began leaking. Some 950,000 works, including Dürer's *Rabbit,* were evacuated until the damage could be repaired and the site dried out. The Albertina is also considered one of the most beautiful classical palaces in the world, its state apartments among the most admired examples of classical architecture.

THE singing AMBASSADORS

The Vienna Boys' Choir is one of the oldest of its kind in the world, and has been an institution in Austria for more than 5 centuries. In 1498, Emperor Maximilian I, a great music lover, moved his court orchestra from Innsbruck to Vienna and added a dozen choirboys to the new musical group, to sing Mass at the Imperial Chapel in the Hofburg every Sunday. Since that time, the Vienna Boys' Choir has occupied a prominent position in Austrian musical life. Its first-class training has produced many highly-qualified vocalists, string players, conductors, and pianists. A number of famous composers also have emerged from its ranks.

Joseph Haydn, a member of the Cathedral Choir of St. Stephan's, sang with the court choirboys in the chapel of the Hofburg and in the newly-built palace of Schönbrunn. **Franz Schubert** wrote his first compositions as a member of the Court Choir Boys. He was often in trouble because he was more interested in composing and making music than in studying. After Schubert's voice broke in 1812 and he had to leave the choir, he noted on a musical score (now in the National Library) *F. Schubert, zum letzten Mal gekräht* (F. Schubert has crowed for the last time).

Many of Austria's leading composers and teachers worked with the Boys' Choir, including Johann Joseph Fux, Antonio Salieri, and Joseph and Michael Haydn. As court organist, **Anton Bruckner** rehearsed his Masses with the choir. If a performance went particularly well, he rewarded the boys with cake.

With the end of the monarchy in 1918, the choir changed its name and relinquished the imperial uniform (complete with swords), replacing them with sailor suits. As early as 1924, the Vienna Boys' Choir, now consisting of four separate choirs, was performing in most of the world's famous concert halls. In the days of the First Republic, between 1918 and 1938, they acquired the sobriquet "Austria's singing ambassadors." Since then, the Vienna Boys' Choir has performed with some of the world's top orchestras and nearly all the great conductors, including Claudio Abbado, Leonard Bernstein, Herbert von Karajan, Carlos Kleiber, Lorin Maazel, Riccardo Muti, and Sir Georg Solti. The choir has also made innumerable recordings and participated in opera and film productions. And the long tradition continues, with the Vienna Boys' Choir performing every Sunday during the solemn Mass in Vienna's Imperial Chapel.

Albertinaplatz 1. ℂ **01/534830.** www.albertina.at. Admission 9.50€ adults, 8 € senior citizens, 7€ students, free for those under 19. Thurs-Tues 10am–6pm; Wed 10am–9pm.

Augustinerkirche (Church of the Augustinians) ★ This 14th-century church was built within the Hofburg complex to serve as the parish church for the imperial court. In the latter part of the 18th century, it was stripped of its baroque embellishments and returned to the original Gothic features. Enter the Chapel of St. George, dating from 1337, from the right aisle. The **Tomb of Maria Christina** ★, the favorite daughter of Maria Theresa, is housed in the main nave near the rear entrance; but there's no body in it. (The princess was actually buried in the Imperial Crypt, described later in this section.) This richly-ornamented empty tomb is one of Canova's masterpieces. A small room in the Loreto Chapel is filled with urns containing the hearts of the imperial Habsburg family. They are visible through a window in an iron door. The Chapel of St. George and the Loreto Chapel are open to the public by prearranged guided tour.

The Augustinerkirche was also where Maria Theresa married her beloved François of Lorraine in 1736, with whom she had 16 children. Other royal weddings included Marie Antoinette to Louis XVI of France in 1770, Marie-Louise of Austria to Louis Napoleon in 1810 (by proxy—he didn't show up), and Franz Joseph to Elisabeth of Bavaria in 1854.

The best time to visit is on Sunday at 11am, for High Masses of Mozart, Haydn, Schubert, Gounod, Kodaly, or Faure, with full choir and orchestra.

Augustinerstrasse 3. ✆ **01/533-70-99.** Free admission. Daily 6:30am–6pm. U-Bahn: Stephansplatz.

Burgkapelle (Home of the Vienna Boys' Choir) Construction of this Gothic chapel began in 1447 during the reign of Emperor Frederick III, but it was later massively renovated. Today, the Burgkapelle hosts the **Hofburgkapelle ★★**, an ensemble of the Vienna Boys' Choir and members of the Vienna State Opera chorus and orchestra, which performs works by classical and modern composers. Send written applications for reserved seats at least 8 weeks in advance. Use a credit card; do not send cash or checks. For reservations, write to **Verwaltung der Hofmusikka-pelle,** Hofburg, A-1010 Vienna. If you failed to reserve in advance, you might be lucky enough to secure tickets from a block sold at the Burgkapelle box office every Friday from 11am to 1pm or 3 to 5pm. The line starts forming a half an hour before. If you're willing to settle for standing room, it's free.

Hofburg (entrance on Schweizerhof). ✆ **01/533-9927.** Mass: Seats and concerts 5€–29€; standing room free. Masses (performances) held only Jan–June and mid-Sept to Dec, Sun and holidays 9:15am. Concerts held May–June and Sept–Oct Fri 4pm.

Kaiserappartements (Imperial Apartments) ★★ These were the Imperial family residence of the Franz Joseph and Elisabeth and their children, reached through the rotunda of Michaelerplatz. Here you can see not only their reception, dining and living rooms, but also their bedrooms and private studies, the nursery, and bathrooms. In the reception rooms, wall panels are filled with huge oil paintings of life at court; the more private rooms are covered with deep red moiré, which, while beautiful, also helped insulate against the cold. The court tableware and silver is of breath-taking opulence, reflecting the pomp of a court whose lands included two-thirds of all Europe. You'll see the narrow "iron bed" of Franz Joseph, who claimed he slept like his soldiers, and the exercise equipment the Empress used to stay fit for the riding she loved. A separate "Sissi Museum" has six rooms devoted to the life and complex personality of this tragic empress.

The remaining Imperial quarters, once occupied by the Empress Maria Theresa, are now used by the president of Austria and are not open to the public. However, the **Imperial Silver and Porcelain Collection** from the Habsburg household of the 18th and 19th centuries, also on view downstairs, provides a window into the court etiquette of Maria Theresa's time.

Michaelerplatz 1 (inside the Ring, about a 7-min. walk from Stephansplatz; entrance via the Kaisertor in the Inneren Burghof). ✆ **01/533-7570.** www.hofburg-wien.at. Admission 9.90€ adults, 8.90 € students and seniors, 5.90€ children 6–18, free for children 5 and under. Open daily, Sept–Jun 9am–5.30pm, Jul–Aug 9am–6pm. U-Bahn: U1 or U3 to Stephansplatz. Tram: 1, 2, to Burgring.

'SISSI—ETERNAL beauty

Empress Elisabeth of Austria (1837–98), called "Sissi," is remembered as one of history's most tragic and fascinating women. An "empress against her will," she was at once a fairytale princess and a liberated woman, and recently compared to Britain's Princess Diana—both were elegant women, dedicated to social causes, who suffered through unhappy marriages and won a special place in the hearts of their subjects.

Born in Munich on Christmas Day 1837, Elisabeth grew up away from the ceremony of court and developed a freedom-loving spirit. When Emperor Franz Joseph of Austria met her as a 15 year old, he fell in love, and they were married on April 24, 1854, in Vienna, when she was 17 and he was 24. With her beauty and natural grace, Elisabeth soon charmed the public. But in private, she bridled under a strict court regime and a domineering mother-in-law, the Grand Duchess Sophie. She saw little of her husband; "I wish he were not emperor," she once declared.

She was liberal and forward-minded, and in the nationality conflict with Hungary she was decisively for the Hungarians, and is remembered warmly to this day.

Personal blows left heavy marks, the worst, perhaps the death of her son, Rudolf, in 1889 in an apparent double suicide. From that time on, she dressed only in black and turned her back on the pomp and ceremony of the Viennese court.

On September 10, 1898, as Elisabeth was walking along the promenade by Lake Geneva, a 24-year-old anarchist stabbed her to death, unaware that her contempt for the monarchy, which she considered a "ruin," matched his own.

Even a century after her death, Sissi's hold on the popular imagination remains undiminished. A TV series about her life achieved unprecedented popularity, and the musical *Elisabeth* ran in Vienna for some 15 years.

Neue Burg   The most recent addition to the Hofburg complex is the Neue Hofburg. Construction was started in 1881 and continued through 1913. The palace was the residence of Archduke Franz Ferdinand, the nephew and heir apparent of Franz Joseph, whose assassination at Sarajevo by Serbian nationalists set off the chain of events that led to World War I.

The arms and armor collection, said to be second only to the Metropolitan Museum in New York, is in the **Hofjagd und Rüstkammer ★★**, on the second floor of the Neue Burg. On display are crossbows, swords, helmets, pistols, and other armor, mostly of Habsburg emperors and princes, some disarmingly small. Some of the items, such as scimitars, were captured from the Turks as they fled their unsuccessful siege.

The **Sammlung alter Musikinstrumente ★** is devoted to old instruments, from the 17th and 18th centuries, with some as early as the 16th century. Some pianos and harpsichords were played by Brahms, Schubert, Mahler, Beethoven, and Austrian emperors who, like Joseph II, were also devoted musicians.

In the **Ephesos-Museum (Museum of Ephesian Sculpture),** with an entrance behind the Prince Eugene monument, you'll see high-quality finds from Ephesus in Turkey and the Greek island of Samothrace. Here the prize is the Parthian monument, the most important relief frieze from Roman times ever found in Asia Minor, erected to celebrate Rome's victory in the Parthian wars (A.D. 161–65).

The **Museum für Völkerkunde (Museum of Ethnology)** holds the only original Aztec feather headdress in the world. Also Benin bronzes, Cook's collections of Polynesian art, Indonesian, African and pre-Columbian exhibits.

1 Heldenplatz. ✆ **01/525-24-0.** Admission: 12 € adults , 9 € students and seniors, under 19s free. Sammlung alter Musikinstrumente and Ephesos-Museum: Wed–Sun 10am–6pm. Museum für Völkerkunde: Wed–Mon 10am–6pm. Admission: 8€ adults, 6€ students and seniors, under 19s free.

Österreichische Nationalbibliothek (Austrian National Library)   The royal library of the Habsburgs dates from the 14th century; and the library building, developed on the premises of the court from 1723 on, is still expanding to the Neue Hofburg. The **Great Hall ★★** of the present-day library was ordered by Karl VI and designed by those masters of the baroque, the Fischer von Erlachs, father and son. The complete collection of Prince Eugene of Savoy is the core of the holdings. With its manuscripts, rare autographs, globes, maps, and other historic memorabilia, this is among the finest libraries in the world.

Josefsplatz 1. ✆ **01/53410.** www.onb.ac.at. Admission 7€, 4.50 € students and seniors, 12 € family (2 adults and children under 19) . Thurs 10am–9pm; Fri–Sun and Tues–Wed 10am–6pm.

Ringstrasse ★★★   In 1857 Emperor Franz Josef ordered that all the foundations of the medieval fortifications around the *Altstadt* (Old Town) be removed and that a grand circular boulevard or belt of boulevards replace them.

This transformation, which turned Vienna into a building site that rivaled Paris under Baron Haussmann, created the Vienna we know today. Work on this ambitious project began in 1859 and stretched to 1888, when the grand boulevard reached a distance of 4km (2½ miles).

You can take the yellow Ring Trams to circle the Ring, changing from Trams 1 or 2, or the U1 or U4 at **Schwedenplatz.** This special tram (leaving every 30 minutes at quarter past and quarter to the hour, from 10am to 6pm) has taken over the old

---

IMPRESSIONS

In May of 1889, Mark Twain was granted a private audience with Emperor Franz Joseph. He met the Emperor in his study, and although he had spent hours learning a speech in German, when the moment came, he was speechless. The Emperor was understanding: "He was amused that I couldn't now recall what had taken me so many hours to memorize, and he assured me such a speech was quite unnecessary," Twain later told a reporter. And when he had regained his composure, the Emperor asked him how he had liked his stay in Austria. He replied in glowing terms: "I can truthfully say that, in all my travels, I have never felt so well as in this wonderful gemütlich Vienna, a city from whose splendid yet graceful proportions I have derived so much inspiration that I could put to good use." Twain issued an apology for his clumsy pronunciation, but the Emperor said that he understood him well. The interview lasted only 15 minutes, but Twain described it as "one of the finest moments of my life."

—"Twain in Vienna", *The Vienna Review*, Mar. 2008

route passing the dozen monumental buildings that were constructed along the Ring during the *Gründerzeit,* meaning "Founders Time," of the 1860s to 1880s when the Ring replaced the old city wall. The boulevard changes its defining name as it goes along, each stretch ending in the word "Ring."

Extending south from the Danube Canal, the first lap of the Ring is **Schottenring,** taking in the Italianate Börse (the former Stock Exchange), and the Votivkirche or Votive Church (p. 147). Running from the university, with its bookstores, bars, and cafes to Rathausplatz, the next lap of the Ring is **Karl-Lueger Ring.** The chief attraction along this stretch is the Universität Wien, dating from 1365. In the 1800s the massive new building you see today was constructed in an Italian Renaissance style.

The **Dr.-Karl-Renner Ring** begins at the Rathausplatz. Here stands the Rathaus or town hall, evoking a Gothic fantasy castle, the dream work of Friedrich Schmidt. Constructed between 1872 and 1883, the town hall is the setting of summer concerts and the Opera Film Festival, as well as the *Christkindlmarkts,* from mid-November until New Year's Eve.

Across from this imposing building is the Burgtheater or the Imperial Court Theater, constructed between 1874 and 1888 in the Italian Renaissance style. Mozart's *The Marriage of Figaro,* were premiered here and frescoes by Gustav Klimt, and his brother, Ernest, draw visitors inside.

Next to the town hall stands Parliament, its elegant neoclassic facade decked out with winged chariots and a splendid statue of the goddess Athena.

Moving on, we next enter the **Burgring,** opposite the Hofburg Palace on either side of Maria-Theresien-Platz. Two of the city's largest and finest museums lie here along the boulevard: the Kunsthistorisches Museum (Museum of Art History, see p. 139) and Naturhistorisches Museum (Natural History Museum; see p. 148).

Opernring begins at the Burggarten or Palace Gardens; in this tranquil retreat in the heart of the city, you'll find magnificent statues of Mozart, Goethe, and the only one of the Emperor Franz Josef. This Ring runs to Schwarzenbergstrasse with its equestrian statue of Prince Karl Philipp von Schwarzenberg, and behind the strange monument to the Russian "Liberators" of Vienna in 1945, so disliked that the Viennese make sure that the fountain in front of it spouts high enough to effectively conceal it from view. Throughout the Russian occupation, a tank stood next to the statue and the Schwarzenbergplatz was renamed Stalin Square. The architectural highlight of this Ring is the Staatsoper (State Opera; p.196).

Finally, the **Schubertring/Stubenring** stretch of the Ring goes from Schwarzenbergstrasse to the Danube Canal. This Ring borders the Stadtpark; established in 1862, it was the first city municipal park to be laid out outside the former fortifications. The highlight along this stretch is the Postsparkasse or Post Office Savings Bank, near the end of the Stubenring at George-Coch-Platz 2. This Art Nouveau building was designed at the beginning of the 20th century by Otto Wagner, and it remains a showpiece of modernist Jugendstil architecture.

Schatzkammer (Imperial Treasury) ★★★

Reached by a staircase from the Swiss Court, the Schatzkammer is the greatest treasury in the world. It's divided into two sections: the Imperial Profane and the Sacerdotal Treasuries. The first displays the crown jewels and an assortment of imperial riches, while the other contains ecclesiastical treasures.

The most outstanding exhibit in the Schatzkammer is the Imperial crown, which dates from 962. It's so big that, though padded, it probably slipped down over the ears of many a Habsburg at his coronation. Studded with emeralds, sapphires, diamonds, and rubies, this 1,000-year-old symbol of sovereignty is a priceless treasure. That fact was not lost on Adolf Hitler, who had it taken to Nürnberg in 1938 (the American army returned it to Vienna after World War II). Be sure to have a look at the coronation robes of the Imperial family, some of which date from the 12th century, which are depicted in a portrait of Francis I with the robes and insignia themselves in the glass case beside it.

You can also view the 9th-century saber of Charlemagne and the 8th-century holy lance, a sacred emblem of imperial authority thought in medieval times to be the weapon that pierced the side of Christ on the cross. Among the great Schatzkammer prizes is the Burgundian Treasure. Seized in the 15th century, it is rich in vestments, oil paintings, and gems. Highlighting this collection are artifacts connected with the Order of the Golden Fleece, the medieval order of chivalry.

Hofburg, Schweizerhof. ✆ **01/525-240.** www.khm.at. Admission 12€ adults, 9 € students and seniors, under 19s free . Wed–Mon 10am–6pm.

Spanische Hofreitschule (Spanish Riding School) ★★

Few other rituals are as evocative of the power and majesty of the 18th-century Habsburg Empire as the Spanish Riding School, whose horse-breeding savvy was once firmly entrenched as part of the military bedrock of Europe. It's headquartered within an opulent and baroque section of the enormous Hofburg Palace, in the section closest to the Michaelertor, the magnificent "back" entrance to the old Hofburg.

During their twice-per-week performances, as many as 25 Lipizzaner stallions move with suspended elegance through complex dressage routines, weaving in and out of complicated formations, sometimes between or around barriers. Their riders and trainers are outfitted in rakish 18th-century uniforms, the kind that once made ladies of the court (and leaders of lesser cavalries in other parts of Europe) tremble. Many aspects of the show haven't changed very much in 430 years, except that some kind of recorded music now accompanies the show—invariably a polonaise or a waltz by Chopin or one of the Strausses.

Some aspects of the performances almost attain the surreal. One example involves massive crystal chandeliers poised in midair above the raked turf of the dressage ring. At regular intervals, the chandeliers are lowered on their chains to positions just above the sand and mud for meticulous cleanings.

The easiest way to guarantee a seat at one of these performances involves prepayment through the Internet several weeks in advance. Except for midsummer, when the horses are taken to pastures in the Austrian countryside, "regular" performances are conducted every Sunday as well as either Friday or Saturday, depending on a complicated series of factors having to do with the well-being of the horses. Depending on what's being emphasized that particular week, performances last from 80 to 100 minutes each, with tickets for seats selling for between 23€ and 116€.

During July and August, performances are abbreviated, not particularly flashy 60-minute routines with less emphasis on the high-stepping dressage (the Piaffe or the Levade) for which the Lipizzaner breed is famous. Summer performances showcase relatively docile mares and foals, and not the high-tempered stallions that are featured during the more elaborate winter performances. Seats for summer performances cost 23€ to 130€ each.

Michaelerplatz 1. ✆ **01/533-9031.** www.srs.at or email your requirements to order@oeticket.com. You can also order tickets via telephone: 01/96096.

MORNING exercise WITH THE LIPIZZANERS

Like any athletes, Lipizzaners need regular exercise to stay fit. And you are invited to witness what goes into preparing the perfection you see in performance. The trainers of these elegant animals put them through their paces within the Hofburg stables every day of the week except Monday and during the July to August period when the horses are off in the countryside. For 12€ adults, 9€ seniors, 6€ students and under 18s, you can sit quietly beneath the baroque ceilings of the Hofburg's riding ring, most Tuesdays to Sundays between 10am and noon.

The emphasis is on the horses and their training, without any particular concern for whomever might be in the stands. Interruptions will occur, and the trainers might go into huddles to discuss this or that particular animal. Classical music may or may not be playing. It pays, the trainers think, to accustom the animals to the sounds of Chopin in advance of the more elaborate full-dress performances, a reminder that this is, in some ways, closer to dance than sport.

From these morning training sessions, you'll get an idea of what all the fuss is about. But be warned: they might be cancelled on short notice and positively will not include the elaborate ritual of a full-blown performance. Advance reservations are not accepted for the morning training, and tickets are sold only on the day.

For more information, contact the **Spanische Hofreitschule** at Michaelerplatz 1 (✆ **01/553-9032**); www.srs.at or email your question to tickets@srs.at.

THE MUSEUMSQUARTIER COMPLEX ★★★

The giant modern art complex **MuseumsQuartier** (www.mqw.at; U-Bahn: MuseumsQuartier) opened in 2001. Art critics proclaimed that the assemblage of art installed in former Habsburg stables tipped the city's cultural center of gravity from Habsburgian pomp into the new millennium. One of the 10 largest cultural complexes in the world, it is like combining New York's Guggenheim Museum, Museum of Modern Art, and Brooklyn Academy of Music, plus a children's museum, an architecture and design center, theaters, art galleries, video workshops, an ecology workshop, and a museum of digital culture and fashion.

Kunsthalle Wien ★ This is a showcase for cutting-edge contemporary and classic modern art. You'll find works by everyone from Picasso, Joán Miró, and Jackson Pollock to Paul Klee, Andy Warhol, and Yoko Ono. From expressionism to cubism, exhibits reveal the major movements in contemporary art since the mid-20th century. Exploring the 5 floors takes 1 to 2 hours.

Museumsplatz 1. ✆ **01/521-89-33.** Admission 11.50€ adults, 4.60 € students, 2€ 10–18, children under 10 free. Fri-Wed 10am–7pm; Thurs 10am–9pm.

Leopold Museum ★★ This extensive collection of Austrian art includes the world's largest trove of the works of Egon Schiele (1890–1918), who has been rediscovered by the art world and now stands alongside Gustav Klimt and Oskar Kokoschka as one of the preeminent artists of the Wiener Modern. The Leopold's collection includes more than 2,500 Schiele drawings and watercolors and 330 oil canvases. Other Austrian modernist masterpieces include paintings by Kokoschka, Klimt, Anton Romaki, and Richard Gerstl, and Klimt's Secessionist colleagues Josef Hoffmann, Kolo Moser, Adolf Loos, and Franz Hagenauer.

Museumsplatz 1. ℂ **01/525-700.** www.leopoldmuseum.org. Admission 11€ adults, 7€ students, 8€ senior citizens, 7€ students and children over 7. Fri–Wed 10am–6pm; Thurs 10am–9pm.

MUMOK (Museum Moderner Kunst Stiftung Ludwig Wien) ★   This gallery presents one of the most outstanding collections of contemporary art in Central Europe. It exhibits mainly American pop art, mixed with concurrent Continental movements such as hyperrealism of the 1960s and 1970s. Five exhibition levels.

Museumsplatz 1. ℂ **01/525-00.** www.mumok.at. 9€ adults, 7.20€ seniors. Free admission for those under 19 and students up to 27. Fri–Wed 10am–6pm; Thurs 10am–9pm.

OTHER TOP ATTRACTIONS
The Inner Districts

Belvedere ★★   Southeast of Karlsplatz, the **Österreichische Galerie Belvedere** sits on a slope above Vienna. The approach to the palace is memorable—through a long garden with a huge circular pond that reflects the sky and the looming palace buildings. Designed by Johann Lukas von Hildebrandt, the last major Austrian baroque architect, the Belvedere was built as a summer home for Prince Eugene of Savoy. It consists of two palatial buildings made up of a series of interlocking cubes. Two great, flowing staircases dominate the interior. The Gold Salon in Lower Belvedere is one of the most beautiful rooms in the palace. A regal French-style garden lies between the two buildings.

Unteres Belvedere (Lower Belvedere), Rennweg 6A, was constructed from 1714 to 1716. **Oberes Belvedere (Upper Belvedere)** was started in 1721 and completed in 1723. Anton Bruckner, the composer, lived in one of the buildings until his death in 1896. The palace was the residence of Archduke Franz Ferdinand, whose assassination sparked World War I. In May 1955, the Allied powers signed the peace treaty recognizing Austria as a sovereign state in Upper Belvedere. The treaty is on display in a large salon decorated in red marble.

The lower Belvedere houses the **Barockmuseum (Museum of Baroque Art).** Displayed here are the original sculptures from the Neuer Markt fountain (replaced now by copies), the work of Georg Raphael Donner, who died in 1741. During his life, Donner dominated the development of Austrian sculpture. The fountain's four figures represent the four major tributaries of the Danube. Works by Franz Anton Maulbertsch, an 18th-century painter strongly influenced by Tiepolo, and the greatest and most original Austrian painter of his day. He was best known for his iridescent colors and flowing brushwork.

Museum Mittelalterlicher Kunst (Museum of Medieval Art) is in the Orangery at Lower Belvedere. Here you'll see art from the Gothic period as well as a Tyrolean Romanesque crucifix that dates from the 12th century.

The upper **Belvedere** houses the **Galerie des 19. und 20. Jahrhunderts (Gallery of 19th- and 20th-Century Art) ★**. Here you also find works by the artists of the 1897 Secessionist movement. Most outstanding are those by Gustav Klimt (1862–1918), one of the movement's founders. Sharing almost equal billing

Vienna Attractions

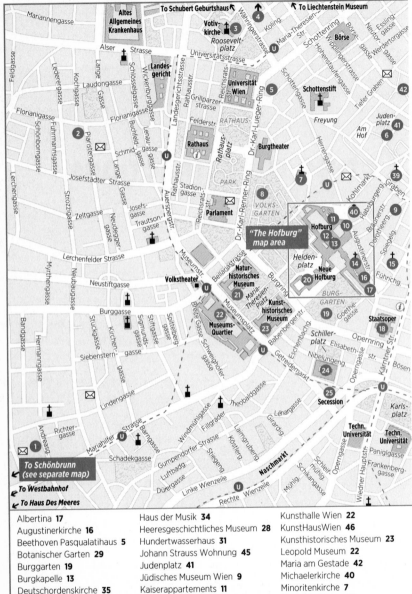

Albertina **17**
Augustinerkirche **16**
Beethoven Pasqualatihaus **5**
Botanischer Garten **29**
Burggarten **19**
Burgkapelle **13**
Deutschordenskirche **35**
Domkirche St. Stephan **36**
Gemäldegalerie der Akademie
  der Bildenden Künste **24**

Haus der Musik **34**
Heeresgeschichtliches Museum **28**
Hundertwasserhaus **31**
Johann Strauss Wohnung **45**
Judenplatz **41**
Jüdisches Museum Wien **9**
Kaiserappartements **11**
Kaiserliches Hofmobiliendepot **1**
Kapuzinerkirche **15**
Karlskirche **26**

Kunsthalle Wien **22**
KunstHausWien **46**
Kunsthistorisches Museum **23**
Leopold Museum **22**
Maria am Gestade **42**
Michaelerkirche **40**
Minoritenkirche **7**
Mozartwohnung **37**
MUMOK (Museum Moderner Kunst
  Stiftung Ludwig Wien) **22**

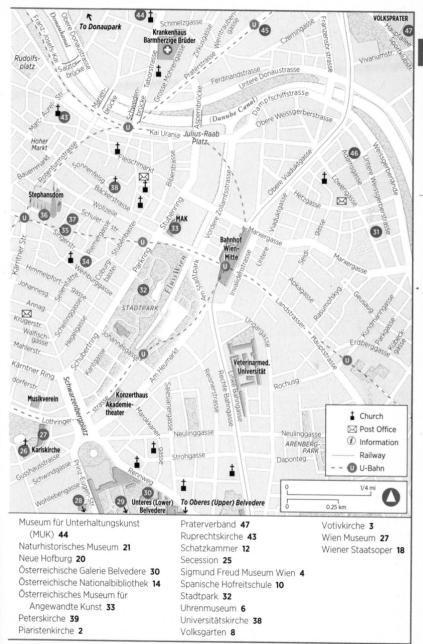

Art-School Reject

One Austrian painter whose canvases will never grace any museum wall is Adolf Hitler. An aspiring artist, Hitler had his traditional paintings, including one of the Auersberg Palace, rejected by the Academy of Fine Arts in Vienna. The building was accurate but the figures out of proportion, the judges said. Hitler did not take this well, denouncing the board as a "lot of old-fashioned fossilized civil servants, bureaucrats, devoid lumps of officials. The whole academy ought to be blown up!" Later, when he had the chance, his mind was apparently on other things…

with Klimt is Egon Schiele (1890–1918), whose masterpieces here include *The Wife of an Artist*.

Prinz-Eugen-Strasse 27. ✆ **01/79557-0.** www.belvedere.at. Admission 9.50€ adults, free for young people up to 19. Tues–Sun 10am–6pm. Tram: D to Schloss Belvedere.

Gemäldegalerie der Akademie der Bildenden Künste (Painting Gallery of the Academy of Fine Arts) ★ This gallery is home to the *Last Judgment* ★★ triptych by Hieronymus Bosch. In this masterpiece, the artist conjured up all the demons of hell for a terrifying view of the suffering and sins that humankind must endure. You'll also be able to view many Dutch and Flemish paintings, some from as far back as the 15th century, although the academy is noted for its 17th-century art. The gallery boasts works by Van Dyck, Rembrandt, and a host of others. There are several works by Lucas Cranach the Elder, the most outstanding being his *Lucretia* from 1532. Some say it's as enigmatic as *Mona Lisa*. Rubens is represented here by more than a dozen oil sketches. You can see Rembrandt's *Portrait of a Woman* and Guardi's scenes from 18th-century Venice.

Schillerplatz 3. ✆ **01/58816-2222.** www.akademiegalerie.at. Admission 8€ adults, 5€ students and seniors, under 19s free. Tues–Sun 10am–6pm. U-Bahn: Karlsplatz.

Haus der Musik ★ This full-scale museum devoted to music is both hands-on and high-tech. Wandering the building's halls and niches, you encounter reminders of the great composers who have lived in Vienna—not only Mozart, but also Beethoven, Schubert, Brahms, and others. In the rooms, you can listen to your favorite renditions of their works or explore memorabilia. You can even take to the podium and conduct the Vienna Philharmonic that responds to your baton. A memorial, "Exodus," pays tribute to the Viennese musicians driven into exile or murdered by the Nazis. The Musicantino Restaurant on the top floor has a panoramic view of the city and good food. There's a coffee house on street level.

Seilerstätte 30. ✆ **01/5134850.** www.hdm.at. Admission 10€ adults, 8.50€ students and seniors, 5.50€ children 3–12, children under 3 free. Open daily 10am–10pm.

Hundertwasserhaus In a city filled with baroque palaces and numerous architectural adornments, this sprawling public-housing project in the rather bleak 3rd District is visited—or at least seen from the window of a tour bus—by about a million visitors annually. Completed in 1985, it was the work of self-styled "eco-architect" Friedensreich Hundertwasser. The complex has a facade like a gigantic black-and-white game board, relieved by scattered splotches of red, yellow, and blue. Trees stick out at 45-degree angles from apartments among the foliage.

There are 50 apartments here, and signs warn not to go inside. However, there's a tiny gift shop (© 01/715-15-53) at the entrance where you can buy Hundertwasser posters and postcards, plus a coffee shop on the first floor.

Löwengasse and Kegelgasse 3. © **01/715-15-53.** www.hundertwasserhaus.info. U-Bahn: Landstrasse. Tram:1.

Kunsthistorisches Museum (Museum of Fine Arts) ★★★ Across from Hofburg Palace, this huge building houses many of the fabulous art collections gathered by the Habsburgs as they added new territories to their empire. One highlight is the fine collection of ancient Egyptian and Greek art. The museum also has works by many of the great European masters, such as Velásquez and Titian.

On display here are Roger van der Weyden's *Crucifixion* triptych, a Memling altarpiece, and Jan van Eyck's portrait of Cardinal Albergati. The museum is renowned for the works of **Pieter Bruegel the Elder,** known for his sensitive yet vigorous landscapes and lively studies of peasant life. Don't leave without a glimpse of Bruegel's *Children's Games* and his *Hunters in the Snow,* one of his most celebrated works.

Don't miss the work of Van Dyck, especially his *Venus in the Forge of Vulcan,* or Peter Paul Rubens's *Self-Portrait* and *Woman with a Cape,* for which he is said to have used the face of his second wife, Helen Fourment. The Rembrandt collection includes two remarkable self-portraits as well as a moving portrait of his mother and one of his sons, Titus.

A highlight of any trip to Vienna is the museum's **Albrecht Dürer** collection. The Renaissance German painter and engraver (1471–1528) is known for his innovative art and his painstakingly-detailed workmanship. *Blue Madonna* is here, as are some of his landscapes, such as *Martyrdom of 10,000 Christians.*

Maria-Theresien-Platz, Burgring 5. © **01/525-24-4025.** www.khm.at. Admission 12€ adults, 9€ students and seniors, under 19s free. Tue-Sun 10am–6pm; Thurs 10am–9pm. U-Bahn: Mariahilferstrasse. Tram: 1, 2, or D.

Liechtenstein Museum ★★★ The rare collection of art treasures from the Liechtenstein's princely collections is on display in a renovated family palace in the

---

An Indestructible Legacy of the Third Reich

As you stroll about Vienna, you'll come across six massive anti-aircraft towers with walls up to 5m (16 ft.) thick, a legacy of the Third Reich. These Flaktürme ("Flak" is short for *Flugabwehrkanone*) were built during World War II. After the war, there was some attempt to dismantle the giant bunkers, but the citadels proved indestructible, their proportions as thick as the Arc de Triomphe in Paris. So other uses were sought: one in the 6th District has been transformed into the Haus des Meeres, an aqua-terra zoo (© 01/587-1417. www.haus-des-meeres.at.) Another, in the Augarten, is an IT data center, little altered. Locals have mixed feelings. To some the towers are important reminders of the disaster of war, others would rather they were gone, and the scar allowed to heal.

9th District. For the first time, visitors can see the Raphaels, Rubens, and Rembrandts, one of the world's greatest private art collections.

Works by Frans Hals and Van Dyck are displayed in the neoclassical Garden Palace, and here are some 1,700 works of art in the collection, in rotating display.

On your visit you're likely to see some 200 works spread over eight galleries. Works range from the 13th to the 19th centuries. Peter Paul Rubens is one of the stars of the museum, including his remarkable *Venus in Front of the Mirror* (ca. 1613). Of spectacular beauty is the splendid **Hercules Hall** ★, the largest secular baroque room in Vienna. Frescoes were painted between 1704 and 1708 by Andrea Pozzo.

The palace also has two new restaurants, including Ruben's Brasserie, serving both traditional Viennese and Liechtenstein fare (some based on princely recipes) and Ruben's Palais, offering more haute cuisine. Both restaurants have gardens in the palace's baroque courtyard.

Liechtenstein Garden Palace, Fürstengasse 1. © **01/3195767-0.** www.liechtensteinmuseum.at. Admission 10€ adults, 5€ students and seniors, under 19s free. Fri–Tues 10am–5pm. U-Bahn: Rossauer Lände. Tram: D to Bauernfeldplatz.

Secession ★   This artistic statement was constructed in 1898 and is crowned by a magnificent dome once called "outrageous in its useless luxury." The empty dome—covered in triumphal laurel leaves—echoes that of the Karlskirche on the other side of Karlsplatz. It stands south of the Opernring, beside the Academy of Fine Arts. The Secession was the home of the Viennese avant-garde, which extolled the glories of Jugendstil (Art Nouveau). A young group of painters and architects launched the Secessionist movement, led by Gustav Klimt, in 1897 in rebellion against the strict, conservative ideas of the official Academy of Fine Arts. Kokoschka was featured here, as was the "barbarian" Paul Gauguin.

Come here to see Klimt's *Beethoven Frieze,* a 30m (98-ft.) visual interpretation of Beethoven's *Ninth Symphony.* Most other works by the Secessionist artists are on display in the Belvedere Palace, and the Secession building itself, as much art as any of the paintings, is used for substantial contemporary exhibits.

Friedrichstrasse 12 (on the western side of Karlsplatz). © **01/587-530711.** www.secession.at. Admission 5€ adults, 4€ students and seniors, children under 10 free. Tues–Sun 10am–6pm; Thurs 10am–8pm. U-Bahn: Karlsplatz.

Wiener Staatsoper (Vienna State Opera) ★   This is one of the most important opera houses in the world. When it was built in the 1860s, critics apparently upset one of the architects, Eduard van der Null, so much that he killed himself. In 1945, at the end of World War II, Vienna started restoration work on the theater; despite many other pressing needs such as public housing, the spiritual need to return the opera to the center of the city's life was considered essential. It was finished in time to celebrate the country's independence from occupation forces in 1955. (See also Chapter 9, "Vienna After Dark.")

Opernring 2. © **01/5144-42250.** www.staatsoper.at. Tours daily year-round, 2–5 times a day, depending on demand. Tour times are posted on a board outside the entrance. Tours 6.50€ per person, 5.50€ senior citizens, 3.50€ students. U-Bahn: Karlsplatz.

Outside the Inner City

Schönbrunn Palace ★★★   The 1,441-room Schönbrunn Palace was designed for the Habsburgs by those masters of the baroque, the von Erlachs. It was built

Schönbrunn Park & Palace

THE PARK

1 Main Gate
2 Courtyard & Wagenburg
   (Carriage Museum)
3 Schlosstheater
4 Café Restaurant Residenz ☕
5 Mews
6 Chapel
7 Kutscher Gwölb &
   Schönbrunner Stöckl ☕
8 Hietzing Church
9 Naiad's Fountains
10 Joseph II Monument
11 Palm House
12 Neptune's Fountain
13 Schöner Brunnen
14 Gloriette
15 Small Gloriette
16 Spring
17 Octagonal Pavilion

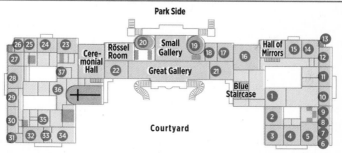

THE PALACE

1 Guard Room
2 Billiard Room
3 Walnut Room
4 Franz Joseph's Study
5 Franz Joseph's Bedroom
6 Cabinet
7 Stairs Cabinet
8 Dressing Room
9 Bedroom of Franz
   Joseph I & Elisabeth
10 Empress Elisabeth's Salon
11 Marie Antoinette's Room
12 Nursery
13 Breakfast Room
14 Yellow Salon
15 Balcony Room
16 17 18 Rosa Rooms
19 20 Round & Oval
   Chinese Cabinets
21 Lantern Room
22 Carousel Room
23 Blue Chinese Salon
24 Vieux-Laque Room
25 Napoleon Room
26 Porcelain Room
27 Millions Room
28 Gobelin Tapestry
   Room
29 Archduchess
   Sophie's Study
30 Red Drawing Room
31 East Terrace Cabinet
32 Bed-of-State Room
33 Writing Room
34 Drawing Room
35 Wild Boar Room
36 Passage Chamber
37 Bergl-Zimmer

between 1696 and 1712 at the request of Emperor Leopold I for his son, Joseph I. Leopold envisioned a palace whose grandeur would surpass that of Versailles. However, Austria's treasury, drained by the cost of wars, would not support the ambitious undertaking; the original plans were never carried out.

When Maria Theresa became empress, she changed the original plans, and Schönbrunn looks today much as she conceived it. Done in "Maria Theresa ochre," with delicate rococo touches designed for her by Austrian Nikolaus Pacassi, the palace is in complete contrast to the grim, forbidding Hofburg. Schönbrunn was the Imperial summer palace during Maria Theresa's 40-year reign, and it was the scene of great ceremonial balls, lavish banquets, and fabulous receptions held during the Congress of Vienna. At the age of 6, Mozart performed in the Hall of Mirrors before Maria Theresa and her court. The Empress held secret meetings with her chancellor, Prince Kaunitz, in the round Chinese Room.

Franz Joseph was born within the palace walls. It was the setting for the lavish court life associated with his reign, and he spent the final years of his life here. The last of the Habsburg rulers, Karl I, signed a document here on November 11, 1918, renouncing his participation in affairs of state—not quite an abdication, but tantamount to one. Allied bombs damaged the palace during World War II, but restoration has covered the scars.

The **Gloriette ★★**, a marble summerhouse topped by a stone canopy with an imperial eagle, embellishes the palace's **Imperial Gardens ★**. The so-called Roman Ruins (a collection of marble statues and fountains) date from the late-18th century, when it was fashionable to simulate the ravaged grandeur of Rome. Adria van Steckhoven laid out the park, which contains many fountains and heroic statues, often depicting Greek mythological characters. It is open to visitors until sunset daily.

The **State Apartments ★★★** are the most stunning display in the palace. Much of the interior ornamentation is in the rococo style, with red, white, and 23½-karat gold predominating. Of the 40 rooms that you can visit, particularly fascinating is the Room of Millions, decorated with Indian and Persian miniatures—a truly grand rococo salon. English-language guided tours of many of the palace rooms, lasting 50 minutes, start every half-hour beginning at 9:30am. You should tip the guide 1€.

Also in the grounds is the baroque **Schlosstheater (Palace Theater;** *℃* **01/876-4272**), which stages summer performances. The **Wagenburg (Carriage Museum) ★** (*℃* **01/877-3244**) is also worth a visit. It contains a fine display of imperial coaches from the 17th to 20th centuries.

The **Schloss Schönbrunn Experience** is a 60- to 90-minute children's tour. First, kids are dressed in imperial clothing, then led by English-speaking guides through rooms that offer hands-on displays.

Admission price to the palace includes a tour (the Grand Tour) of 40 state rooms with audio guide.

Schönbrunner Schlossstrasse. *℃* **01/811-132-39.** www.schoenbrunn.at. Admission 9.50€ adults, 8.50€ students and seniors, 6.50€ children 6–18, free for children under 6; Wagenburg Nov–March 10am–4pm, Apr–Oct 9am–6pm, 6€ adults, 4€ students and seniors, under 19s free. Schloss Schönbrunn Experience 4.90€ children (3–18). Apr–June and Sept–Oct daily 8:30am–5pm; July–Aug daily 8:30am–6pm; Nov–Mar daily 8:30am–4:30pm. U-Bahn: Schönbrunn.

Kaiserliches Hofmobiliendepot (Imperial Furniture Collection) ★ A collection spanning 3 centuries of royal acquisitions, this museum is a treasure-house of the Habsburg attics. Exhibits range from the throne of the Emperor Francis Joseph and Prince Rudolf's cradle, to a forest of coat racks and some 15,000 chairs. At the end of World War I, with the collapse of the Empire, the new republic inherited the collection established by Maria Theresa in 1747; it now totals some 55,000 objects.

In all, the collection includes prized examples of decorative and applied arts; it is particularly rich in Biedermeier furnishings, which characterized the era from 1815 to 1848. Particularly stunning is Maria Theresa's imposing desk of palissander (an exotic wood) marquetry with a delicate bone inlay. The modern world also intrudes, with pieces designed by such 20th-century Viennese architects as Adolf Loos and Otto Wagner. The material occupies a century-old warehouse complex halfway between Hofburg Palace and Schönbrunn Palace. Allow about 2½ hours to visit the three floors. Expect cheek-by-jowl bric-a-brac.

Andreasgasse 7. ✆ **01/524-33570.** www.hofmobiliendepot.at. Admission 6.90€ adults, 5.50€ students and seniors, 4.50€ children 6–18. Tues–Sun 10am–6pm. U-Bahn: Zieglergasse.

CHURCHES

See section 1 of this chapter for information on the Burgkapelle, where the Vienna Boys' Choir performs, and the Augustinerkirche.

The Inner City

Deutschordenskirche (Church of the Teutonic Order)   The Order of the Teutonic Knights was a German society founded in 1190 in the Holy Land. The order came to Vienna in 1205, and the church dates from 1395. The building never fell prey to the baroque madness that swept the city after the Counter-Reformation, so you see it pretty much in its original form, a Gothic church dedicated to St. Elisabeth. The 16th-century Flemish altarpiece standing at the main altar is richly decorated with woodcarving, gilt, and painted panel inserts. Many knights of the Teutonic Order are buried here, their heraldic shields still mounted on some of the upper walls.

In the knights' treasury, on the second floor of the church, you'll see mementos such as seals and coins illustrating the history of the order, as well as a collection of arms, vases, gold, crystal, and precious stones. Also on display are the charter given to the Teutonic Order by Henry IV of England and a collection of medieval paintings. A curious exhibit is the Viper Tongue Credenza, said to have the power to detect poison in food and render it harmless.

Singerstrasse 7. ✆ **01/512-1065-214.** www.deutscher-orden.at. Free admission to church; treasury: 4€ adults, [3€ students and seniors, children under 6 free. Church daily 7am–6pm; treasury Tue, Thurs, Sat 10am–noon, Wed, Fri 3pm–5pm. Closed Mon, Sun, and holidays. U-Bahn: Stephansplatz.

Domkirche St. Stephan (St. Stephan's Cathedral) ★★★ ☺   A basilica built on the site of a Romanesque sanctuary, this cathedral was founded in the 12th century in what was, even in the Middle Ages, the town's heart.

A fire that swept through Vienna in 1258 virtually destroyed Stephansdom; and toward the dawn of the 14th century a Gothic building replaced the basilica's ruins. The cathedral suffered terribly during the Turkish siege of 1683, then experienced peace until Russian bombardments in 1945. Destruction continued when the Germans fired on Vienna as they fled the city at the close of World War II. Restored and reopened in 1948, the cathedral is one of the greatest Gothic structures in Europe, rich in woodcarvings, altars, sculptures, and paintings. The 135m (450-ft.) steeple has come to symbolize the spirit of Vienna.

The 106m-long (352-ft.) cathedral is inextricably entwined with Viennese and Austrian history. Mourners attended Mozart's "pauper's funeral" here in 1791, and Napoleon posted his farewell edict on the door in 1805.

The **pulpit** of St. Stephan's is the enduring masterpiece of stone carver Anton Pilgrim, but the chief treasure of the cathedral is the carved wooden **Wiener Neustadt altarpiece ★★**, which dates from 1447. The richly painted and gilded altar, in the left chapel of the choir, depicts the Virgin Mary between St. Catherine and St. Barbara. In the Apostles' Choir, look for the curious **tomb of Emperor Frederick III ★★**. Made of pinkish Salzburg marble in the 17th century, the carved tomb depicts hideous hobgoblins trying to wake the emperor from his eternal sleep. The entrance to the catacombs or crypt is on the north side next to the Capistran pulpit. Here you'll see the funeral urns that contain remains of 56 members of the Habsburg family. You can climb the 343-step South Tower of St. Stephan's for a view of the Vienna Woods. Called **Alter Steffl (Old Steve),** the tower, marked by a needlelike spire, dominates the city's skyline. It was built between 1350 and 1433, and reconstructed after heavy damage in World War II. The North Tower (Nordturm), reached by elevator, was never finished to match the South Tower, but was crowned in the Renaissance style in 1579. From here you get a panoramic view of the city and the Danube.

Stephansplatz 1. ⓒ **01/515-523526.** www.stephanskirche.at. Cathedral free admission; tour of catacombs 4.50€ adults, 1.50€ children under 14. Guided tour of cathedral 4.50€ adults, 1.50€ children under 15. South Tower 3.50€ adults, 1€ children 6–14. Evening tours, including tour of the roof, 10€ adults, 4€ children under 15. Cathedral daily 6am–10pm except times of service. Tour of catacombs Mon–Sat 10–11.30am and 1.30–4.30pm; Sun and holidays 1:30–4:30pm. Guided tour of cathedral Mon–Sat 10:30am and 3pm; Sun and holidays at 3pm. Guided tour in English daily 3.45pm Apr–Oct. Special evening tour Sat 7pm (June–Sept). South Tower daily 9am–5:30pm. Bus: 1A, 2A, or 3A. U-Bahn: Stephansplatz.

Kapuzinerkirche The Kapuziner Church (just inside the ring behind the Opera) has housed the Imperial Crypt, the burial vault of the Habsburgs, for some 3 centuries. Capuchin friars guard the final resting place of 12 emperors, 17 empresses, and dozens of archdukes. Only their bodies are here: their hearts are in urns in the Loreto Chapel of the Augustinerkirche in the Hofburg complex, and their entrails are similarly enshrined in a crypt below St. Stephan's Cathedral.

Most outstanding of the imperial tombs is the double sarcophagus of Maria Theresa and her consort, Francis Stephen (François, duke of Lorraine, or, in German, Franz von Lothringen, 1708–65), the parents of Marie Antoinette. The "King of Rome," the ill-fated son of Napoleon and Marie-Louise of Austria, was buried here in a bronze coffin after his death at age 21. (Hitler managed to anger both the Austrians and the French by having the remains of Napoleon's son transferred to Paris in 1940.)

Emperor Franz Joseph was interred here in 1916. He was a frail old man who had outlived his time and died just before the final collapse of his empire. His wife, Empress Elisabeth, was also buried here after her assassination in Geneva in 1898, as was their son, Crown Prince Rudolf, who died at Mayerling (see the "Twilight of the Habsburgs" box, in Chapter 10).

Impressions

This is one of the most perplexing cities that I was ever in. It is extensive, irregular, crowded, dusty, dissipated, magnificent, and to me disagreeable. It has immense palaces, superb galleries of paintings, several theaters, public walks, and drives crowded with equipages. In short, everything bears the stamp of luxury and ostentation; for here is assembled and concentrated all the wealth, fashion, and nobility of the Austrian empire.

—Washington Irving, letter to his sister, from *Tales of a Traveller*, 1824

Neuer Markt. ☏ **01/512-6853-16.** www.kaisergruft.at. Admission 5€ adults, 4€ students and seniors, 2€ children up to 14. Daily 10am–6pm. Closed Nov 1, 2. U-Bahn: Stephansplatz.

Maria am Gestade (St. Mary's on the Bank)   This church, also known as the Church of Our Lady of the Riverbank, was once just that. With an arm of the Danube flowing by, it was a place of worship for fishermen. The river was redirected, and now the church relies on its beauty to draw people. A Romanesque church on this site was rebuilt in the Gothic style between 1394 and 1427. The western facade is flamboyant, with a remarkable seven-sided Gothic tower surmounted by a dome that culminates in a lacelike crown.

Salvatorgasse/Passauer Platz. ☏ **01/5339-5940.** Free admission. Daily 9am–5pm. U-Bahn: Stephansplatz.

Michaelerkirche (Church of St. Michael)   Over its long history this church has felt the hand of many architects and designers, resulting in a medley of styles, not all harmonious. Some of the remaining Romanesque sections date to the early 1200s. The exact date of the chancel is not known, but it's probably from the mid-14th century. The catacombs remain as they were in the Middle Ages.

Most of St. Michael's as it appears today dates from 1792, when the facade was redone in neoclassical style; the spire is from the 16th century. The main altar is richly decorated in baroque style, and the altarpiece, entitled *The Collapse of the Angels* (1781), was the last major baroque work completed in Vienna.

Michaelerplatz. ☏ **01/533-8000.** www.michaelerkirche.at. Free admission. Mon–Sat 6:45am–8pm; Sun 8am–6:30pm. Information on guided tours: 0650/533-8003. U-Bahn: Herrengasse. Bus: 2A or 3A.

Minoritenkirche (Church of the Minorites)   If you're tired of baroque ornamentation, visit this church of the Friar Minor Conventual, a Franciscan order also called the Minorite friars (inferior brothers). Construction began in 1250 but was not completed until the early-14th century. The Turks damaged the tower in their two sieges of Vienna, and the church later fell prey to baroque architects and designers. But in 1784, Ferdinand von Hohenberg ordered the baroque additions removed; and the simple lines of the original Gothic church returned, complete with cloisters. Inside you'll see a full-sized mosaic copy of da Vinci's *The Last Supper*, by Giacomo Raffailli, commissioned by Napoleon, who abdicated before it was finished. Emperor Francis II bought it and, too large for the Belvedere, he hung it in the church. Masses are held on Sunday at 8:30am (in German) and 11am (in Italian).

Minoritenplatz 2A. ☏ **01/533-4162.** www.minoritenkirche-wien.info. Free admission. Apr–Oct Mon–Sat 8am–6pm; Nov–Mar Mon–Sat 9am–5pm. U-Bahn: Herrengasse.

Peterskirche (St. Peter's Church)   This is the second-oldest church in Vienna, and the spot on which it stands could well be Vienna's oldest Christian church site. It is believed that a place of worship stood here in the second half of the 4th century, and Charlemagne is credited with having founded a church on the site when he conquered what is now Vienna in 803.

The present St. Peter's is the most lavishly decorated baroque church in Vienna. Gabriel Montani designed it in 1702. Hildebrandt, the noted architect of the Belvedere Palace, is believed to have finished the building in 1732. The fresco in the dome is a masterpiece by J. M. Rottmayr, painter of the frescoes in the Liechtenstein Museum, depicting the coronation of the Virgin. The church contains many frescoes and much gilded carved wood, plus altarpieces done by well-known artists of the period.

Peterplatz. ℂ **01/533-6433.** www.peterskirche.at. Free admission. Mon–Fri 7am–8pm, Sat, Sun, holidays 9am–9pm. U-Bahn: Stephansplatz.

Ruprechtskirche (St. Rupert's Church)   The oldest church in Vienna, Ruprechtskirche has stood here since 740, although much that you see now, such as the aisle, is from the 11th century. Beautiful new stained-glass windows, the work of Lydia Roppolt, were installed in 1993. Much of the masonry from a Roman shrine on this spot is believed to have been used in the present church. The tower and nave are Romanesque; the rest of the church is Gothic. St. Rupert is the patron saint of the Danube's salt merchants.

Ruprechtsplatz. ℂ **01/535-6003.** www.ruprechtskirche.at. Free admission. Easter Monday to Oct Mon–Fri 10am–noon, Mon, Wed, Fri 3–5pm. Closed Nov–Easter. U-Bahn: Schwedenplatz.

Universitätskirche (Church of the Jesuits)   Built at the time of the Counter-Reformation, this church is rich in baroque embellishments. This was the university church, dedicated to the Jesuit saints Ignatius of Loyola and Franciscus Xaverius. The high-baroque decorations—galleries, columns, and the *trompe l'oeil* painting on the ceiling, which gives the illusion of a dome—were added from 1703 to 1705. The embellishments were the work of a Jesuit lay brother, Andrea Pozzo, on the orders of Emperor Leopold I. Look for Pozzo's painting of Mary behind the main altar. The church has a superb choir and orchestra (that emigrated from the Augustinerkirche) that performs classical and romantic Masses on Sundays and holy days at 10am.

Dr.-Ignaz-Seipel-Platz 1. ℂ **01/512-52320.** Free admission. Mon–Sat 7am–7pm, Sun 8am–7pm. U-Bahn: Stephansplatz or Stubentor. Tram: 2. Bus: 1A.

Outside the Inner City

Karlskirche (Church of St. Charles)   The Black Plague swept Vienna in 1713, and Emperor Charles VI vowed to build a church if the disease abated. Dedicated to St. Charles Borromeo, the church was designed by baroque master, Johann Bernard Fischer von Erlach, who did the original work from 1716 to 1722 and completed by his son Joseph Emanuel by 1737. Frescoes by J. M. Rottmayr.

The green copper dome is 72m (236-ft.) high, a dramatic landmark on the Viennese skyline. Two columns, spin-offs from Trajan's Column in Rome, flank the front, opening on to Resselpark, and a sculpture by Henry Moore in the pool.

Karlsplatz. ℂ **01/504-6187.** www.karlskirche.at. Admission 6€ adults, 4€ students and seniors, free for children up to 10. Mon–Sat 9am–12:30pm and 1–6pm; Sun noon–5.45pm. U-Bahn: Karlsplatz.

A beautiful CORPSE

The Viennese are fascinated with death, something foreigners tend to find bizarre and possibly disturbing. People plan quite openly for their eventual demise (anathema in more youth-obsessed cultures) discussing reserving burial plots, designing headstones, joining death associations (*Sterbeverein*) that ensure somebody shows up and also pays the bill.

All this is summed up by an ever-popular cabaret song of Georg Kreisler: "Death must be Viennese, as surely as Love is French." This song in fact heads up a collection of satirical and melancholy Viennese songs performed to sell-out houses each year for All Souls Day, November 1, (of which American Halloween was originally the preamble), the occasion when the Viennese make ritual trips to the cemetery to pay a call on the grandparents. But it's not the only time, and in fact many pleasant Sunday afternoons involve outings to the Wiener Zentralfriedhof, the rambling inter-denominational Vienna Central Cemetery, a pleasant tram ride (no. 71) into the 11th District of Simmering.

In short, like Shakespeare's Thane of Cawdor, nothing in life becomes the Viennese like the leaving of it! Death is a major production, and its rituals big business, with the Austrian funeral industry said to be the largest per capita in Europe. Like the Irish Wake, the gatherings that follow (the Trauerfeier, literally a "celebration of mourning") have a festive quality.

And also ironic: The loved one is being celebrated, but as with the Shakespeare's Thane, perhaps with just the slightest suggestion that scoundrel got what's coming to him. Coming back from a funeral, one is sure to hear that it was "eine schöne Leiche," a beautiful corpse! In a city that loves theater, this is one more fine occasion to put on a good show.

Piaristenkirche (Church of the Piarist Order)   A Roman Catholic teaching congregation known as the Piarists (fathers of religious schools) launched work on the Piaristenkirche in 1716. The church, more popularly known as Piaristenplatz, was not consecrated until 1771. Some of the designs submitted during that long period are believed to have been drawn by von Hildebrandt, the noted architect who designed the Belvedere Palace, but many builders had a hand in its construction. This church has a fine classic facade as well as the frescoes by F.A. Maulbertsch that adorn the cupolas.

Piaristengasse 54. © **01/405-0425.** www.mariatreu.at. Free admission. Mon–Fri 9–11am; Sat 10am-noon. U-Bahn: Rathaus.Tram: 2.

Votivkirche   After a failed assassination attempt on Emperor Franz Joseph, grateful subjects took up a collection to construct the Votive Church, across from the site of the attempt. Heinrich von Ferstel began work on the neo-Gothic church in 1856, consecrated in 1879, creating a magnificent facade of lacy spires and intricate sculpture.

Rooseveltplatz 8. © **01/406-1192.** www.votivkirche.at. Opening hours church: Tue–Sun 9am–1pm. Opening hours museum: Tue–Fri 4–6pm, Sat 10am–1pm. Admission 3.90€ adults, 2.90€ students and seniors. U-Bahn: Schottenor.

MUSEUMS & GALLERIES

The Inner City

Jüdisches Museum Wien   This is the main museum tracing the history of Viennese Jewry, not to be confused with its annex at Judenplatz (p. 149). It opened in
1993 in the former Eskeles Palace, among the most elegant town houses in Vienna,
with both temporary and permanent exhibitions. The permanent exhibitions trace
the major role that Jews played in the history of Vienna until their expulsion or death
in the Holocaust beginning in 1938. Displays note their extraordinary contributions
in such fields as philosophy, music, medicine, and, of course, psychiatry. Sigmund
Freud, although already frail, escaped to London, where he died the following year.
Many objects were rescued from Vienna's private synagogues and prayer houses,
concealed from the Nazis throughout the war. Many other exhibits are from Vienna's
old Jewish Museum, which closed in 1938.

Dorotheergasse 11. ℂ **01/535-0431.** www.jmw.at. Admission 6.50€ adults, 4€ children and seniors;
school classes are free. Sun–Fri 10am–6pm. U-Bahn: Stephansplatz.

Naturhistorisches Museum (Natural History Museum) ☺   Housed in a handsome neo-Renaissance building near the Museum of Fine Arts, this is the third-largest
natural history museum (after its counterparts in New York and London) in the world,
and holds the oldest collections. It was established by the husband of Empress Maria
Theresa (Franz Stephan von Lothringen) in 1748, who donated one of its major art
objects (a personal gift to him from his wife) to the collections at the time of his death.
Located in Room no. 4 of the Mineralogy Department, and known as Der Juwelen
Strauss, it's a 60cm-tall (24-in.) bouquet of flowers crafted from more than 2,000
gemstones, each of which was even rarer at the time of the object's creation than it is
today. The museum also holds an important collection of early Stone Age artifacts, the
best-known and most evocative of which is the **Venus of Willendorf,** whose discovery in Lower Austria in 1906 attests to the area's ancient habitation.

Maria-Theresien-Platz, Burgring 7. ℂ **01/521770.** www.nhm-wien.ac.at. Admission 10€ adults, 5€
seniors and students, under 19s free. Thurs–Mon 9am–6:30pm; Wed 9am–9pm. U-Bahn: Volkstheater.
Tram: 1, 2, D, or J.

**Österreichisches Museum für Angewandte Kunst (Museum of Applied
Art)**   Of special interest here is a rich collection of tapestries, some from the 16th
century, and the most outstanding assemblage of Viennese porcelain in the world.
Look for a Persian carpet depicting *The Hunt,* as well as the group of 13th-century
Limoges enamels. Biedermeier furniture and other antiques, glassware, crystal, and
large collections of lace and textiles are also on display. An entire hall is devoted to
Art Nouveau. There are outstanding objects from the Wiener Werkstätte (Vienna
Workshop), founded in 1903 by architect Josef Hoffman. In the workshop, many
well-known artists and craftsmen created a variety of objects—glass, porcelain, tex-
tiles, wooden articles, and jewelry.

Stubenring 5. ℂ **01/711360.** www.mak.at. Admission 7.90€ adults, 5.50€ seniors and students, under
19s free. Wed–Sun 10am–6pm; Tues 10am–midnight. Free admission on Sat. U-Bahn: Stubentor. Tram: 2.

Uhrenmuseum (Municipal Clock Museum)   A wide-ranging group of timepieces—some ancient, some modern—is on view here. Housed in what was once

IN memory OF VIENNA'S JEWISH GHETTO

Judenplatz (U-Bahn: Stephansplatz), between Wipplingerstrasse and Tuchlauben, was the heart of the Jewish ghetto from the 13th to the 15th centuries. Archeologists excavating the square in 1995 found, as in other parts of the city, the remains of an earlier community, and a synagogue that contemporary records revealed to be one of the largest of its time, attracting renowned religious scholars to Vienna as a thriving Jewish community grew.

The Holocaust memorial on this square (by architect Rachel Whitehead, and opened in 2000) pays tribute to the tradition of books and learning, as well as the closed doors on a lost culture. Around the base of the monument are engraved the names of the places in which Austrian Jews were put to death during the Nazi era. Nearby is a statue of Gotthold Ephraim Lessing (1729–81), the Jewish playwright. Together, the excavations, the memorials, and the new museum have re-created a center of Jewish culture on Judenplatz, and a place of remembrance at the center of the city's daily life unique to Europe.

Museum Judenplatz, Judenplatz 8 (✆ 01/535-0431), is a new annex of Vienna's Jewish Museum. The main exhibition features a multimedia presentation on the religious, cultural, and social life of the Viennese Jews in the Middle Ages until their expulsion in 1420 and 1421. Other exhibits tell of the defining role Viennese Jews played in all aspects of city life, from music to medicine, until a reign of terror began in 1938. The three exhibition rooms are in the basement of the Misrachi house, where an underground passage connects them to the exhibitions of the medieval synagogue. The museum is open Sunday through Thursday from 10am to 6pm and Friday from 10am to 2pm; admission is 4€ for adults and 2.50€ for children under 15, students and seniors. School classes are welcomed at no charge.

An exhibition room has been installed in the **Mittelalterliche Synagogue (Medieval Synagogue)** nearby, open during the same hours as the Jewish Museum. Built around the middle of the 13th century, it was one of the largest synagogues of its time. After the pogrom in 1420 to 1421, the synagogue was systematically destroyed, so that only the foundations and the floor remained. These were excavated by the City of Vienna Department of Urban Archaeology from 1995 to 1998. The exhibition room shows the remnants of the central room, or "shul," the room where men studied and prayed, and a smaller room annexed to it, which might have been used by women. In the middle of the central room is the foundation of the hexagonal bimah, the raised podium from which the Torah was read. Admission is 4€ adults, 2.50€ ages 14 and under; school classes are welcomed at no charge.

the Obizzi town house, the museum dates from 1917 and attracts clock collectors from all over Europe and North America. Check out Rutschmann's 18th-century astronomical clock. Also here are several interesting cuckoo clocks and a gigantic timepiece that was once mounted in the tower of St. Stephan's.

Schulhof 2.✆ **01/533-2265.** www.museum.vienna.at. Admission 4€ adults, 2€ seniors and students, under 19s free. Tues–Sun 10am–6pm. U-Bahn: Stephansplatz. Bus: 1A, 2A, 3A.

Outside the Inner City

Heeresgeschichtliches Museum (Museum of Military History) The oldest state museum in Vienna, this building was constructed from 1850 to 1856 and is a precursor to the Ringstrasse style. Inside, exhibits delineate Habsburg military history—defeats as well as triumphs.

A special display case in front of the Franz Josef Hall contains the six orders of the House of Habsburg that Franz Josef sported on all public occasions, the Sarajevo room, mementos of the assassination of Archduke Franz Ferdinand and his wife on June 28, 1914, the event that sparked World War I. The archduke's bloodstained uniform is on display, along with the bullet-scarred car in which the couple rode. Many exhibits focus on the Austro-Hungarian navy, and frescoes depict important battles, including those against the Turks in and around Vienna.

Arsenal 3. © **01/795610.** www.hgm.or.at. Admission 5.10€ adults, 3.30€ seniors and students, under 19s free. Daily 9am–5pm. Closed Jan 1, Easter, May 1, Nov 1, and Dec 24–25 and 31. Tram: 18 or D. Bus: 69A.

KunstHausWien ★ 🎁 Vienna's most whimsical museum, a former Thonet chair factory, shows the imaginative, fantastical works of painter and designer Friedensreich Hundertwasser (1928–2000). Hundertwasser was one of the world's most famous architects, and this is a fitting memorial. It's filled with his paintings, drawings, and architectural projects (many of which were never built). The museum is also a venue for temporary exhibitions of international artists. Previous shows have focused on such artists as Chagall, Picasso, and Cecil Beaton.

The tiled black-and-white checkerboard exterior has been compared to a Klimt painting seen through a kaleidoscope. Inside, the architect created uneven floors, irregular corners, trees growing out of the roof and windows, and oddly-shaped, different-size windows. After leaving the museum, you can walk 5 minutes to the **Hundertwasserhaus** (see listing earlier in this chapter).

Untere Weissgerberstrasse 13. © **01/712-04-91.** www.kunsthauswien.com. Admission 9€ adults, 7€ students and seniors, 4.50€ for children 11–18, free for children up to 10. Extra charge for temporary exhibits. Daily 10am–7pm. Tram: 1 or O.

Sigmund Freud Museum Wien Walking through this museum, you can almost imagine the good doctor ushering you in and telling you to make yourself comfortable on the couch. Antiques and mementos, including his velour hat and dark walking stick with ivory handle, fill the study and waiting room he used during his residence here from 1891 to 1938. The museum bookshop with a variety of postcards of the apartment, books by Freud, posters, prints, and pens.

Berggasse 19. © **01/319-1596.** www.freud-museum.at. Admission 7€ adults, 5.50€ seniors, 4.50€ students, 2.50€ children 12–18, under 11s free. Open daily. Jul–Sept 9am–6pm, Oct–Jun 9am–5pm. Tram: D to Schlickgasse.

Wien Museum (Museum of the History of Vienna) History buffs should seek out this fascinating but little-visited collection. Here the full panorama of Old Vienna's history unfolds, beginning with the settlement of prehistoric tribes in the Danube basin. Roman relics, artifacts from the reign of the dukes of Babenberg, and a wealth of leftovers from the Habsburg sovereignty are on display, as well as arms and armor from various eras. A scale model shows Vienna as it looked in the Habsburg heyday. You'll see pottery and ceramics dating from the Roman era,

14th-century stained-glass windows, mementos of the Turkish sieges of 1529 and 1683, and Biedermeier furniture. There's also a section on Vienna's Art Nouveau.

Karlsplatz 4. ☏ **01/505-87470.** www.museum.vienna.at. Admission 6€ adults, 4€ seniors, 3€ students, under 19s free. Tues–Sun 10am–6pm. U-Bahn: Karlsplatz.

PARKS & GARDENS

When the weather is fine, Vienna's residents shun city parks and head for the **Wienerwald (Vienna Woods),** a wide arc of forested countryside that surrounds northwest and southwest Vienna (for more details, see Chapter 9, "Side Trips from Vienna"). If you love parks, you'll find some magnificent ones in Vienna. Within the city limits are more than 1,600 hectares (3,952 acres) of gardens and parks, and no fewer than 770 sports fields and playgrounds. You can, of course, visit the grounds of **Schönbrunn Park** and **Belvedere Park** when you tour those palaces. Below, we highlight Vienna's most popular parks.

The Inner City

Burggarten   These are the former gardens of the Habsburg emperors. They were laid out soon after the Volksgarten (see below) was completed. Look for the monument to Mozart, as well as an equestrian statue of Francis Stephen, Maria Theresa's beloved husband. The only open-air statue of Franz Joseph in Vienna is also here, and there's a statue of Goethe at the park entrance.

Opernring-Burgring, next to the Hofburg. UBahn: U1, U2, U4 Opera. Tram: 1, 2, or D.

Stadtpark   This lovely park lies on the slope where the Danube used to overflow into the Inner City before the construction of the Danube Canal. Of the many statues, the best known is of Johann Strauss, Jr., composer of operettas and waltzes like *The Blue Danube Waltz.* Here, too, are monuments to Franz Schubert and Hans Makart, a well-known artist whose work you'll see in churches and museums throughout Vienna. Verdant squares of grass, well-manicured flower gardens, and plenty of benches surround the monuments. Open 24 hours daily.

Parkring. U-Bahn: U4 Stadtpark. Tram: 2, Ringtram from Schwedenplatz.

Volksgarten (People's Park)   Laid out in 1820 on the site of the old city wall fortifications, this is Vienna's oldest public garden. It's dotted with monuments, including a 1907 memorial to assassinated Empress Elisabeth and the so-called Temple of Theseus, a copy of the Theseion in Athens.

Dr.-Karl-Renner-Ring, between the Hofburg & the Burgtheater. U-Bahn: U2 Herrengasse. Tram: 1, 2, or D.

Outside the Inner City

Botanischer Garten (Botanical Garden of the University of Vienna)   These lush gardens contain exotic and sometimes rare plants from all over the world. Located in Landstrasse (3rd District) right next to the Belvedere Park, the Botanical Garden was developed on a spot where Maria Theresa once ordered medicinal herbs to be planted. Always call in advance if the weather is doubtful.

Rennweg 14. ☏ **01/4277-54100.** www.botanik.univie.ac.at. Free admission. Opening hours vary according to season. Tram: D to Schloss Belvedere or Südbahnhof, 71 to Unteres Belvedere.

Donaupark This park, in the 22nd District between the Danube Canal and the Alte Donau (Old Danube), was converted in 1964 from a garbage dump to a park with flowers, shrubs, and walks, as well as a bird sanctuary. You'll find a bee house, an aviary with native and exotic birds, a small-animal paddock, a horse-riding course, playgrounds, and games. An outstanding feature of the park is the **Donauturm (Danube Tower),** Donauturmstrasse 4 (✆ **01/2633-5720;** www.donauturm.at), a 253m (830-ft.) tower with 2 rotating cafe-restaurants—one at the 161m (528-ft.), the other at 171m (561 ft.)—and a panoramic view of Vienna. Menues indlude international dishes and Viennese cuisine. There's also a sightseeing terrace at 151m (495 ft.) plus two express elevators to the tower.

Daily from 10am to 11.30pm. Elevator: 6.90€ adults, 5.50€ seniors, 4.90€ children 6–14 years, under 6 free. Wagramer Strasse. U-Bahn to Reichsbrücke.

Praterverband (The Prater) ★ ☺ This extensive tract of woods and meadowland in the 2nd District has been Vienna's leading recreation area since 1766, when Emperor Joseph II opened this imperial hunting ground to the public.

The Prater is an amusement park, fairground, and recreation area without barricades or an entrance gate. Its paid attractions in the *Würstlprater* are independently operated and maintained by individual entrepreneurs who determine their own hours, prices, and, to a large extent, policies and priorities. In addition, there are tennis clubs and riding stables, two racetracks, a golf course, a bowling alley and billiard hall, two swimming pools, bicycles, rowboats and canoes, and a soccer stadium. The vast parkland of meadows, woods, and water beyond has countless opportunities for sport and relaxation, and absorbs thousands of people without ever feeling crowded.

Few other spots in Vienna convey such a sense of the decadent end of the Habsburg Empire—it's turn-of-the-century nostalgia, with a touch of 1950s-era tawdriness. The Prater is the birthplace of the waltz, first introduced here in 1820 by Johann Strauss, Sr., and Josef Lanner. However, it was under Johann Strauss, Jr., "the King of the Waltz," that the musical form reached its greatest popularity.

The best-known part of the huge park is at the end nearest the entrance from the Ring. Here you'll find the **Riesenrad** (✆ **01/729-5430;** www.wienerriesenrad. com), the giant observation wheel, which reaches 64.75m (232 ft.) at its highest point. It remains, after St. Stephan's Cathedral, the most famous landmark in Vienna. Erected in 1897 when European engineers were flexing their mechanical muscles, the wheel was designed by British engineer Walter Basset, for the Universal Exhibition (1896–97), marking the golden anniversary of Franz Joseph's coronation in 1848. Like the Eiffel Tower a decade earlier, it was supposed to be a temporary exhibition. But except for World War II damage, the Riesenrad has been going around without interruption ever since.

Just below is the terminus of the Lilliputian railroad, the 4km (2.5 mile) narrow-gauge line that operates in summer using vintage steam locomotives. The amusement park, right behind the giant wheel, has all the typical attractions—roller coasters, merry-go-rounds, tunnels of love, and games arcades. Another attraction is "Volare—The Flying Coaster," which flies facedown along a 435m (1,437-ft.) labyrinth of track at a height of 23m (75 ft.); and "Starflyer," a tower ride where passengers are whirled around at 70m (230 ft.) above the ground at speeds of up to 70kmph (43 mph).

But while the Prater is always open, not all amusements are open throughout the year. The season lasts from March or April to October, although the wheel operates

TALES OF THE VIENNA woods

The Vienna Woods (*Wienerwald* in German) are often called the lungs of Vienna, a wondrous, hilly retreat of gentle paths, forests and streams bordering the city on the southwest and northwest. It is a deeply evocative landscape somewhere between mountain and meadow, ancient hillsides, vineyards, and the occasional ruin, in whose soft contours even the angst-ridden Kafka could find love with Milena, where the troubled Beethoven, when his hearing was failing, thought the chirping of birds, the sheltering trees, and leafy vineyards of the Wienerwald made it easier for him to compose. There is something special about the light streaming in at an odd angle between the crags across a leaf-trodden lane, about the special smells of the damp earth and the crisp snap of a blue autumn sky.

A round-trip through the woods takes about 3 1/2 hours by car, a distance of some 80km (50 miles). However, if you want to go native, head for the Wienerwald by tram, either the "D" to **Nußdorf**, the 43 to **Neuwaldegg** or the 38 (the same ticket is valid) to **Grinzing**, home of the beloved *heuriger* (wine taverns). At each of these, the woods are at your feet, or you can board bus no. 38A in Grinzing, and go through the Wienerwald to the top of the **Kahlenberg**, from where you can head back down the mountain in almost any direction. The whole trip takes about 1 hour each way. You might also rent a bicycle nearby to explore the woods.

Kahlenberg is on a hill that is part of the northeastern-most spur of the Alps (483m/1,584 ft.). If the weather is clear, you can see all the way to Hungary and Slovakia. At the top is the small Church of St. Joseph, where the Polish King Jan Sobieski stopped to pray before leading his troops to save Vienna from the Turks. For one of the best views, go to the right of the Kahlenberg restaurant. From the terrace of the Modul Hotel School, you'll have a panoramic sweep, including the spires of St. Stephan's. You can go directly to Kahlenberg in about 20 minutes by U-Bahn to Heiligenstadt; then take bus no. 38A.

Anywhere you find yourself in the Vienna Woods, there'll be inviting *hütte*, *beisl*, or *heuriger* around the next bend, where you can stop for a beer or a glass of new wine, and a sausage or a spicy Liptauer cheese spread on a thick slice of *meterbrot*, a hearty tavern loaf that comes a full meter long. Rested and restored, you can then head back out on any of the many inviting footpaths that will eventually lead you back to the bright lights.

For more about the Wienerwald, see Chapter 9, "Side Trips from Vienna."

all year round. Some of the more than 150 booths and restaurants stay open in winter, including the pony merry-go-round and the gambling venues. If you drive here, don't forget to observe the no-entry and no-parking signs, which apply daily after 3pm. The place is usually jammed on Sunday afternoons in summer. Admission to the park is free, but you'll pay for games and rides.

Prater 9. ☎ **01/728-0516.** www.prater.at. Free admission; price for rides and amusements varies. Ferris wheel 8.50€ adults; 3.50€ children 3 to 14; infants and toddlers, free. Park May–Sept daily 10am–1am; Oct–Nov 3 daily 10am–10pm; Nov 4–Dec 1 daily 10am–8pm. Closed Dec 2–April. U-Bahn: U1, U2 Praterstern. Tram: O, 5, Praterstern, 2 Prater Hauptallee.

ESPECIALLY FOR CHILDREN

The greatest attraction for youngsters is the **Prater Amusement Park** (p. 152), but children will also enjoy performances at the **Spanish Riding School** (p. 133), climbing the tower of **St. Stephan's Cathedral** (p. 143), and visiting the exhibition at the **Natural History Museum** (p. 148). And nothing quite tops a day like a picnic in the **Vienna Woods** (p. 210).

Other worthwhile museums for children include the **Museum für Unterhaltungskunst (MUK)**, Karmelitergasse 9 (© **0676 460 4794**), a tribute to clowns and circus performers throughout the centuries. It is open every Sunday 10am to 1pm and on the first and third Thursday of every month from 7 to 9pm. Closed July and August. Admission is free.

In addition, see "Sports & Active Pursuits," at the end of this chapter.

Haus des Meeres ☺   A highly successful conversion of a World War II anti-aircraft tower into an aquarium has resulted in what is called an aqua-terra zoo with 10,000 water, reptile, and land creatures. In the terrarium are crocodiles and giant snakes. One of the best parts is the fresh-water aquarium hall with exotic, giant turtles and coral reefs, and, in the Mediterranean section, crabs, starfish, and sea anemones. Visitors can stroke the snakes on Wednesdays at 2pm, and watch the piranhas being fed at 3pm. Other times are listed on the website. And that's just the beginning.

Haus des Meeres. © **01/587 1417.** www.haus-des-meeres.at. Admission 12.60€ adults, 9.60€ students and seniors, 5.90€children under 15. Mar–Sept daily 9am–6pm; Thurs, 9am–9pm. No dogs allowed. U-Bahn: U3 Neubaugasse, Bus 13A, 14A, 57A Haus-des-Meeres.

Schönbrunner Tiergarten ☺   The world's oldest zoo was founded by the husband of Empress Maria Theresa. She liked to have breakfast here with her brood, enjoying animal antics with her eggs. The baroque buildings in the historic park landscape make a unique setting for modern animal-keeping; the tranquility makes for a relaxing yet interesting outing.

Schönbrunn Gardens. © **01/8779-2940.** www.zoovienna.at. Admission 12€ adults, 5€ students and children, free for children under 3. Mar–Sept daily 9am–6:30pm; Oct–Feb daily 9am–5pm. U-Bahn: Hietzing.

MUSICAL LANDMARKS

Nearly all of the great composers who lived in Vienna lived at a number of addresses during their years there. Mozart probably wins hands down with 14. ("He threw too many parties and made *much* too much noise," one of the curators confided.) Schubert was born in one where he lived a few years, and died in one where he stayed only a few months. Beethoven was far more settled with only four or so, and Strauss and Haydn actually lived established family lives. With the music everywhere, it can be fun to see some of the sites where it was conceived and written. But be warned: many of these houses suffer from a bad case of museum purism— pristine, empty rooms with display cases. Only the Strauss apartment on Praterstrasse and, after much public complaint, the re-thinking of the Mozart apartment on Domgasse, give a real feel for the lives of the composers. The displays are interesting, but it's not the same. Still, it will help you picture the pattern of life, and you will still be able to hear their music in the concert halls and palaces where they performed, as well as the cemeteries where they are buried.

Beethoven Pasqualati House (Beethoven Pasqualatihaus) Beethoven (1770–1827) lived in this building on and off from 1804 to 1814. Beethoven is known to have composed his Fourth, Fifth, and Seventh symphonies here, as well as *Fidelio* and other works. There isn't much to see except some family portraits and the composer's scores, but you might feel it's worth the climb to the fourth floor. At least the chamber pot by the door, which his visitors complained about, is gone.

Mölker Bastei 8. © **01/535-8905.** Admission 2€ adults, 1€ children 6-18. Tues-Sun 10am-1pm and 2-6pm. U-Bahn: Schottentor.

Haydnhaus (Haydn's House) This is where (Franz) Joseph Haydn (1732–1809) conceived and wrote his magnificent later oratorios *The Seasons* and *The Creation*. He lived in this house from 1797 until his death and gave lessons to Beethoven here. The house also contains a room celebrating Johannes Brahms.

Haydngasse 19. © **01/596-1307.** Admission 2€ adults, 1€ students and children 10-16. Wed-Thurs 10am-1pm and 2-6pm; Fri-Sun 10am-1pm. Closed Mon and Tues. U-Bahn: Zieglergasse.

Johann Strauss Memorial Rooms (Johann Strauss Wohnung) "The King of the Waltz," Johann Strauss, Jr. (1825–99), lived at this address for a number of years, composing *The Blue Danube Waltz* here in 1867. Here the wine red moiré wall coverings, paintings, and Strauss's own surprisingly small piano give a sense of his life.

Praterstrasse 54. © **01/214-0121.** Admission 2€ adults, 1€ children 10-18. Tues-Thurs 2-6pm; Fri-Sun 10am-1pm. U-Bahn: Nestroyplatz.

Mozartwohnung (Mozart's Apartment) This 17th-century house is called the House of Figaro because Mozart (1756–91) composed his opera *The Marriage of Figaro* here. The composer lived here from 1784 to 1787, a relatively happy period during which he often played chamber music concerts with Haydn. Over the years he lived in 14 apartments in all, which became more squalid as he aged. He died in poverty and was given a pauper's blessing at St. Stephan's Cathedral and then buried in St. Marx Cemetery. The museum was reinvented in 2006 for the Mozart Year, the 250th anniversary of his birth, and is now an imaginative journey into the composer's life, well worth a visit.

Domgasse 5. © **01/512-1791.** www.mozarthausvienna.at. Admission 10€ adults, 7.50€ students and children. Daily 10am-7pm. U-Bahn: Stephansplatz.

Schubert Museum (Schubert Gerburtshaus) The son of a poor schoolmaster, Franz Schubert (1797–1828) was born here in a house built earlier in that century. Many Schubert mementos are on view. You can also visit the house at Kettenbrückengasse 6, where he died at age 31.

Nussdorferstrasse 54. © **01/317-3601.** Admission 2€ adults, 1€ students and children 10-16. Tues-Sun 10am-1pm and 2-6pm. S-Bahn: Canisiusgasse.

TOURS

Wiener Rundfahrten (Vienna Sightseeing Tours), Starhemberggasse 25 (© **01/7124-6830**; www.viennasightseeingtours.com), offers the best tours, including a 1-day motor-coach excursion to Budapest for 99€ per person. The historical city tour costs 36€ for adults and is free for children 12 and under, ideal for visitors who want to be shown the major (and most frequently photographed) monuments of Vienna in a compact visit. Tours leave the Staatsoper daily at 9:45 and 10:30am and 2:45pm. The tour lasts 3½ hours (U-Bahn: Karlsplatz).

"Vienna Woods–Mayerling," another popular excursion, leaves from the Staatsoper and takes you to the towns of Perchtoldsdorf and Mödling, and to the Abbey of Heiligenkreuz, a center of Christian culture since medieval times. The approximately 4-hour tour also takes you for a short walk through Baden, the spa that was once a favorite summer resort of the aristocracy. Tours cost 43€ for adults and 15€ for children ages 10 to 16.

A **"Historical City Tour,"** which includes visits to Schönbrunn and Belvedere palaces, leaves the Staatsoper daily at 9:45 and 10:30am and 2:45pm. It lasts about 3 hours and costs 36€ for adults and 15€ for children ages 10 to 18.

A variation on the city tour includes an optional visit to the Spanish Riding School. This tour is offered Tuesday through Saturday, leaving from the Staatsoper building at 8:30am. Tickets are 61€ for adults, 30€ for children 13 and older, and free for children 3 to 12.

Information and booking for these tours can be obtained either through Vienna Sightseeing Tours (see above) or through its affiliate, **Elite Tours,** Operngasse 4 (✆ **01/5132225;** www.elitetours.at).

SPORTS & ACTIVE PURSUITS
Active Sports

BIKING   Vienna maintains almost 322km (200 miles) of cycling lanes and paths, many of which meander through some of the most elegant parks in Europe. Depending on their location, they're identified by a yellow image of a cyclist either stenciled directly onto the pavement or crafted from rows of red bricks set amid the cobblestones or concrete of the busy boulevards of the city. Some of the most popular bike paths run parallel to both the Danube and the Danube Canal.

You can carry your bike on to specially marked cars of the Vienna subway system, but only during non-rush hours. Subway cars marked with a blue shield are the ones you should use for this purpose. Bicycles are *not* permitted on the system's escalators—take the stairs.

You can rent a bike for 3€ to 5€ per hour. You'll usually be asked to leave either your passport or a form of ID as a deposit. One rental possibility is **Pedal Power,** Ausstellungsstrasse 3 (✆ **01/729-7234;** www.pedalpower.at). There are rental shops at the Prater and along the banks of the Danube Canal. You can also rent a bike at **Bicycle Rental Hochschaubahn,** Prater 113 (✆ **01/729-5888;** www.wien.gv.at/english/leisure/bike/bikerental.htm).

One terrific bike itinerary (quite popular since it has almost no interruptions) encompasses the long, skinny island that separates the Danube from the Neue Donau Canal. Low-lying and occasionally marshy, but with paved paths along most of its length, it provides clear views of central Europe's industrial landscape and the endless river traffic that flows by on either side. But there are many more. Pick up a copy of the fine Radatlas Wien at most book stores, a narrow, easy-to-handle guide to bike paths in and around Vienna. In German, but maps are maps, and these are good ones.

Radatlas Wien, Verlag Esterbauer; ✆ **02983/28982-500.** www.esterbauer.com.

CRUISING THE Danube

The Danube is the quintessential European river of so many nations, and peoples from Passau, Vienna, Budapest and Belgrade, Galati and Selena all encounter each other. It was this idea of a "multi-peopled land" that was embraced by the Austro-Hungarian Empire, making it perhaps the gentler heir of the Roman Empire. It was this river that carried ships, and soldiers, courtiers, and culture from one end of the Empire to the other, and by the 19th century, the Austro-Hungarian army marched to commands in 11 languages. This was the river of the Empire, and today it is the river of a reunited Europe, as central to its new, cooperative identity as it was to the old.

Cynics aside, the Danube is really blue, at least on sunny days, and visitors to Austria will view a day cruise as a highlight of their trip. Until the advent of railroads and highways, the Danube played a vital role in Austria's history, helping to build the complex mercantile society that eventually became the Habsburg Empire.

The most professional of the cruises are operated by the **DDSG Blue Danube Shipping Co.,** whose main offices are at Handelskai 265, A-1020 Vienna (✆ **01/588800;** www.ddsg-blue-danube.at). The most appealing cruise focuses on the Wachau region east of Vienna, between Vienna and Dürnstein. The cruise departs April to October every Sunday at 8:30am from the company's piers at Handelskai 265, 1020 Vienna (U-Bahn: Vorgartenstrasse), arriving in Dürnstein 6 hours later. The cost is 25€ to 38€ for adults; half-price for children aged 10 to 15.

For longer Danube cruises see "Side Trips from Vienna," p. 209.

BOATING   Wear a straw boating hat and hum a few bars of a Strauss waltz as you paddle your way around the quiet eddies of the Alte Donau. This gently curving stream bisects residential areas to the north of the Danube and is preferable to the muddy and swift-moving currents of the river itself.

Along the old Danube, you'll find some kiosks in summer, where you can negotiate for the rental of a boat, perhaps a canoe, or a kayak. There are, of course, tours of the Danube, but it's more fun to do it yourself.

GOLF   The two golf courses in or near Vienna are chronically overbooked, forcing even long-term members to be highly flexible about their starting times. The busier, and more challenging, of the region's two golf courses lies within a 15-minute drive north of Vienna, on the grounds of the Prater, at the 18-hole **Golfplatz Wien-Freudenau 65A** (✆ **01/728-9564**). If there's an available tee-off time, nonmembers with a minimum handicap of 28 can play for a fee of 75€ per person. More likely to have an available tee-off time on a weekday (but rarely on a weekend), is **Golfplatz Föhrenwald** (✆ **02622/29171**), an 18-hole course that's positioned about 48km (30 miles) south of Vienna, at Bodenstrasse 54 in the hamlet of Klein Wolkersdorf, just outside the suburb of Wiener Neustadt. If space is available, green fees there cost 55€ for tee-offs Monday to Friday, 85€ for tee-offs on Saturday or Sunday, and require that prospective players have a handicap of at least 45.

HEALTH CLUBS   Even if you're not registered there, you may use the exercise facilities at the popular health club, **Health & Fitness (Living Well Express),** in the Vienna Hilton, Am Stadtpark (✆ **01/717-00-12800**). Positioned on the third floor (designed in the access elevators as level "M1") of the also-recommended hotel, it charges nonresidents of the hotel 19€. Know in advance that men and women share the same sauna and steam-room facilities, either with or without the discreet covering of a towel, so if you're feeling shy or modest at the time of your visit, plan your sauna rituals accordingly. (Women who prefer to have their sauna alone are directed, by appointment only, to a private room.) Open daily from 10am to 10pm. Hotel residents can use the exercise facilities at this place 24 hours and at no charge.

HIKING   You're likely to expend plenty of shoe leather simply walking around Vienna, but if you yearn for a more isolated setting, the city tourist offices will provide information about its eight **Stadtwanderwege.** These marked hiking paths usually originate at a stop on the city's far-flung network of trams.

You can also head east of town into the vast precincts of the **Lainzer Tiergarten,** where hiking trails meander amid forested hills, colonies of deer, and abundant bird life. To get there, first take the U-Bahn to the Kennedy Brücke/Hietzing station, which lies a few steps from the entrance to Schönbrunn Palace. Take tram no. 60, then bus no. 60B.

SKIING   We strongly recommend that if you're an avid skier, avoid the flatlands of Vienna completely and head for mountainous regions in western and southern Austria, particularly the Tyrol, Land Salzburg, the Vorarlberg, or perhaps Styria. (For more about the ski resorts of those regions, refer to this edition's companion guide, *Frommer's Austria.*)

If you're absolutely dying to go skiing and you're not able to wander far from the relatively flat landscapes in and around Vienna, there's a limited amount of skiing within about an hour's drive of the city, on the gentle slopes of Mount Semmering (the Hirschenkogl Ski Lifts) and Mount Schneeberg (the Rax am Schneeberg Lifts; ✆ **02664/20025** for information about either venue). Most visitors find it infinitely easier to reach these areas by car, but at a serious pinch, you can ride the U4 subway to the Hütteldorf station, then take bus no. 49B to the city's far-flung 14th District. For additional information about skiing in Austria, either near Vienna or within the more appealing zones of the country's western regions, contact the Austrian National Tourist Office, Margaretenstrasse 1, A-1040 Vienna (✆ **01/588660**).

SWIMMING   Despite the popularity of beaches on islands in the Alte Donau Canal in summer, swimming in either the Danube or any of its canals is not recommended because of pollution and a dangerous undertow in the main river.

To compensate, Vienna has dozens of swimming pools. Your hotel receptionist can tell you about nearby options. One of the most modern is **Stadionbad** in the Prater. For locations of any of the city's many indoor or outdoor pools, contact the Vienna Tourist Office on Albertinaplatz (✆ **01/24-555**).

TENNIS   Your hotel might have a connection to a tennis court in Vienna, or might be able to steer you to a court nearby. The **Askö-Sport-Centrum-Schmelz,** Auf der Schmelz 10 (✆ **01/982-1333;** take U3 to Jungstrasse), is a modern, publicly-supported complex with about 6 outdoor courts. Depending on the time of day, prices range from 11€ to 17€ per hour. The center also hosts soccer clubs, and the Vienna Vikings (American football); it has ping-pong, billiards, an Olympic-sized pool, and more. Even closer by in the Prater is HTC Wien, ✆ **(01) 7286891,** www.

htcwien.at, in a quiet corner right along the Hauptallee, surrounded by the park grounds and the many diversions nearby. This private tennis club offers outdoor courts, a hockey rink, and showers, and is easy to reach with the Tram: no. 2, the U1 or the U2. If nothing is available, we recommend that you contact one of the city's largest tennis agencies, including **Askö Wien,** Hafenleitengasse 73, in the 11th District (© **01/545-3131**). It will direct you to one of several tennis centers it manages and might charge a small referral fee.

Spectator Sports

HORSE RACING   There are three racetracks in Vienna, but by far the oldest, most venerable, and most prestigious is the **Rennbahn Freudenau,** at **Freudenau 65** on the grounds of the Prater (© **01/728-9531**). Established in 1836, this lovely flat track normally operates April to November for traditional thoroughbred racing, with the Vienna Derby in late June. A second trotting track, the **Rennbahn Krieau** (© **01/728-0046**) lies farther down the Prater fairgrounds, offering a range of options for families and groups with considerable creature comforts and attentive service toward town. This more modern facility operates trotting races every week of the year, except July and August, when trotters race in the outlying resort of Baden for a 2-month season. Newer still, and permeated with deliberate hypermodern chic, is the **Magna Racino** racetrack and casino complex in the suburb of A-2483 Ebreichsdorf (© **02254/9000-1410;** www.magnaracino.at), 30km (19 miles) south of Vienna. Inaugurated in 2004 by Frank Stronach, a Canadian billionaire of Austrian descent, it's open from 11:30am to 9pm and is the site of a casino, several restaurants, cabaret shows, and both flat track and trotting races, April through October. Entry is 4€, with children under 15 free. It's the home of the **Austrian Derby,** in late June.

SOCCER   Football, as it's known in Europe, tends to draw a slightly less impassioned response in Austria than it does in Germany or Italy, but it still exerts a powerful appeal. The city's team is **Rapid-Wien** (Hannappi Stadion, Keisslergasse, © **01/72743-0;** www.skrapid.at. U-Bahn: Hütteldorf), who have a season from July to May. The Austrian national team (Österreichische National Team) are based at the **Horr Stadion,** Fischhofgasse (© **01/688-0150;** U-Bahn: Reumannplatz). Bigger than either of those stadiums, and usually used for soccer matches of above-average international interest drawing massive crowds, is the **Ernst-Happel-Stadion** (sometimes known simply as **Wiener Stadion**), Meiereistrasse 7; for information, call the Wiener Stadthalle: (© **01/728-0854;** to reach the Stadion: U-Bahn: Praterstern, then tram no. 21 to Meiereistrasse). For tickets and information about upcoming events, call the stadiums.

VIENNA WALKING TOURS

One of the best ways to get to know Vienna is from the street. Simply heading off on foot, eyes open and guide book in hand, you will find its history, its passions and ideals reveal themselves in the buildings, parks and squares, in the pattern of the streets and the use of space—all this a living 3-D portrait of a culture and a people. Stroll down the wide Graben, and around the corner along the Kohlmarkt, past the facades of 7 centuries lined up like books on a shelf, it's like a research library to the story of the city's rich past.

There are few cars in central Vienna, where half the city seems to be out walking, and the other half at a cafe, sitting outside or in. Turn off on one of the narrow cobbled lanes and immediately the intimacy of Vienna greets you like a friend; shops and restaurants are small and welcoming, the scale is personal. Through a doorway you peek into a courtyard planted with a couple of trees and some ivy, encircled with iron balconies, that double as corridors set out with flower boxes and a couple of chairs.

Vienna's architecture is the story of the city's history. Although it suffered extensive damage during World War II, it retained many of its important buildings, and reconstruction has been meticulous.

Each of the three walking tours below is geared toward a different kind of experience. Note that many of the streets in the 1st District are pedestrian zones, where cars have been banished except for early morning deliveries. And keep looking up; much of what is special about Vienna is above eye level.

WALKING TOUR: IMPERIAL VIENNA

START:	**Staatsoper (State Opera House).**
FINISH:	**Staatsoper.**
TIME:	**3 hours.**

Walking Tour: Imperial Vienna

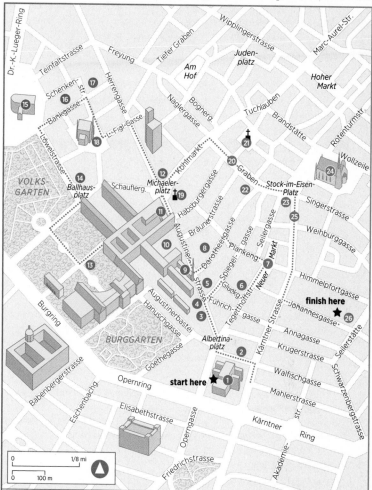

1   Wiener Staatsoper (Vienna
    State Opera House)
2   Hotel Sacher
3   Augustinerkeller
4   Albertina
5   Lobkowitz Palace
6   Church of the Capuchin Friars
7   Donner Fountain
8   Dorotheum
9   Hofburg
10 Josefsplatz

11 Spanish Riding School
    (Spanische Hofreitschule)
12 Loos House
13 Heldenplatz
14 Federal Chancellery
15 Burgtheater
16 Palais Liechtenstein
17 Hungarian Embassy
18 Minoritenkirche (Church of
    the Minorites)
19 St. Michael's Church

20 Pestsäule (Plague Column)
21 Peterskirche
22 Buffet Trzesniewski
23 Stock-im-Eisen
24 St. Stephan's Cathedral
25 Kärntnerstrasse
26 Savoy Foundation for
    Noblewomen (Savoysches
    Damenstift)

BEST TIME:	**During daylight hours or at dusk.**
WORST TIME:	**Rainy days.**

One of dozens of potential paths through Vienna's historic heart, this meandering tour will give you a street-scape view of the Habsburgs' urban haunts. This tour also reveals lesser-known sights best seen on foot. Later, you can pick the attractions you want to revisit. (For details on many of these sights, see Chapter 7.)

Our tour begins at the southernmost portion of the Ringstrasse, the boulevard that replaced the old city wall and encircles most of the historic urban core. It is an appropriate place to start, in the shadow of the very symbol of Austrian culture, the:

1 Wiener Staatsoper (Vienna State Opera House)

This French Renaissance opera house launchedthe massive Ringstrasse project, begun in 1863 on land reclaimed at the razing of city's medieval fortifications.

Controversy and cost overruns plagued the construction of the opera house from the first. Bad planning left the street several feet higher than the foundation, on the south side. This error, coupled with an offhand—but widely reported—criticism by Franz Joseph, is believed to have contributed to the suicide (by hanging) of one of the building's architects, Eduard van der Null, and the death by a stroke a few weeks later of the other, August von Sicardsburg.

The roof and much of the interior were largely rebuilt after a night bombing raid on March 12, 1945, sent the building up in flames. Afterward, it was rumored the Allies claimed to have mistaken the magnificent opera house for a train station, which might be more plausible if there were a rail yard nearby!

Ironically, the last performance before the bombing was a rousing version of Richard Wagner's *Götterdammerung,* (*The Twilight of the Gods*), complete with immolation scene. Since its reconstruction, the Staatsoper has hosted luminaries like Karl Böhm, Herbert von Karajan, Claudio Abbado, and Seiji Ozawa.

From Opernring, walk one block north toward Austria's most famous pedestrian street, **Kärntner Strasse.** We'll later walk past the glamorous shops and famous houses, but for the moment, turn left behind the arcaded bulk of the State Opera onto Philharmonikerstrasse. On the right side, you'll see the door-men and globe lights of Vienna's best-known hotel, the:

2 Hotel Sacher

This famous hotel has been a signature of Vienna since its opening in 1876. At the death of Eduard Sacher in 1892, his emancipated, cigar-smoking wife Anna took over running the hotel, which became the "in" meeting place before or after the opera, for deal making and discrete encounters of all kinds.

Before and during World War II, it became the favored haunt of spies, who found the famed separées useful for many purposes. In 1945, it was taken over as an Allied headquarters hotel, and became a set for the 1949 film noir classic, *The Third Man* (see Chapter 2 p. 31). If you're dressed well, take a look inside.

A confectionery store, with a separate street entrance around the corner to the right, sells the hotel's namesake, Sachertorte, to ship anywhere in the world.

A few steps farther you'll find yourself amid the irregular angles of Albertinaplatz. In its middle is the *Memorial Against War and Fascism* by the Austrian artist Alfred Hrdlicka. Its various elements include 'The Gateway of Violence,' 'The Streetwashing Jew,' 'Orpheus Enters Hell,' and the 'Stone of the Republic,' with portions of Austria's postwar declaration of independence.

3 Augustinerkeller

If you'd like something hearty to eat, try the Augustinerkeller, Augustinerstrasse 1 (℃ 01/533-1026), in the basement of the Hofburg palace wing sheltering the Albertina collection. This popular wine tavern, open daily from 11am to midnight, offers wine, beer, and Austrian food, and has live music daily.

In the same building as your rest stop is the:

4 Albertina

This rambling 1744 palace-museum gets its name from the Archduke Albert von Sachsen-Teschen. A gift from his cousin Kaiser Franz II, it houses one of the world's most important collections of master drawings and prints, some 1.6 million in all, plus significant temporary exhibits. In the curved wall to the left are statues representing all the rivers of Austria, and the terrace may be familiar from an important scene in the 1995 film *Before Sunrise*. The building was transformed from 2000 to 2003, through an extensive renovation that not only restored the statuary, fountain, and baroque facade, but added the dramatic marquis reaching out over the street, by architect Hans Hollein, also designer of the Haas Haus on Stephansplatz.

Adjacent to Albertinaplatz, at Lobkowitzplatz 2, is one of the many baroque jewels of Vienna. It lies across the street and about 50 paces to the right of the Albertina. This is the:

5 Lobkowitz Palace

Now the home of the Austrian Theatre Museum, this is one of the oldest palaces in Vienna, built in 1665–87, 2 years after the Turks were driven from the outskirts of the city. In 1745, it was purchased by the Lobkowitz family and was later enlarged by the reigning architect of the day, Fischer von Erlach. Franz Joseph Maximilian, Prince of Lobkowitz, was a great patron of the arts; Beethoven's *Third Symphony* was dedicated to him and had its first Vienna performance in the palace's festival hall, now called the "Eroica Hall."

At the end of Lobkowitzplatz, take Gluckgasse past a couple of antique shops and boutiques filled with Art Deco jewelry and silverware. At the end of the block, at Tegetthoffstrasse, go left. About 50 steps later, you'll be in front of the deceptively simple facade of the:

6 Church of the Capuchin Friars

Originally constructed in the 1630s, its facade was restored in 1935 along the simple original lines following old illustrations. Behind the rather severe facade, the Kapuzinerkirche contains the burial vaults of every Habsburg ruler since 1633. This is not a coincidence: the traditional royal burial ritual asks "Who comes here?" and on the monarch's behalf is answered, all titles left behind, "We come with a sinful mortal." Nonetheless, the heavily sculpted double casket of Maria Theresa and Francis is flanked with weeping nymphs and skulls, and capped with a triumphant cherub reuniting the couple.

The portal of this church marks the beginning of the Neuer Markt, whose perimeter is lined with rows of elegant baroque houses. The square's centerpiece is one of the most beautiful works of outdoor art in Austria, the:

7 Donner Fountain

Holding a snake, the graceful, half-draped figure of Providentia is a symbol of the welfare of the city's citizens, symbolized by fresh water for all. She is attended by four laughing cherubs struggling with fish. Around the fountain's basin are four allegorical figures representing nearby tributaries of the Danube, all a copy of a 1737 original by Georg Raphael Donner now housed in the Lower Belvedere Museum. The figures were removed by Maria Theresa, who found them obscene. Today it's judged a masterpiece.

Down the street stretching west, Plankengasse reveals a yellow baroque church filling the space at the end of the street, housing one of Vienna's international Protestant congregations. You'll pass a number of antique shops and an ancient apothecary at the corner of Spiegelgasse, with a vaulted ceiling and rows of antique bottles. Museum-quality antique clocks fill the window at Plankengasse 6 at Dorotheergasse.

Turn left when you reach Dorotheergasse, to the impressive building at no. 17, one of the most famous auction houses of Europe, the:

8 Dorotheum

Named after the former monastery upon whose grounds it now stands, it was established in 1707 and rebuilt in the neoclassical style in 1901. More that 600 auctions are held yearly, the most prominent being that of old master paintings. Take a peak at the lobby.

After about half a block, turn right onto Augustinerstrasse, which borders the labyrinth of palaces, museums, and public buildings known as the:

9 Hofburg

The traffic is a bit too heavy along this narrow street. Still, the huge Hofburg, the group of buildings ahead and to the left, is the single most impressive symbol of the majesty and might of the Habsburgs.

In about half a block you'll arrive at:

10 Josefsplatz

The first thing you see is the equestrian statue of Joseph II on his pedestal behind a guard rail of loose black chain. This is where Harry Lime's body was carried by his friends, after the so-called accident in *The Third Man* (see Chapter 2, p. 31). At the back of the square is the entrance to the Grand Reading Room of the National Library. The child prodigies "Wolfi" Mozart and his sister "Nanerl" performed at the Palais Palffy, at no. 6, in 1762. Heavily damaged in World War II, it was rebuilt and its renaissance facade restored. Two pairs of mighty caryatids guard the entrance of the Pallavicini Palace, next door at no. 5, completed in 1784. It is still the private residence of the Pallavicini family; the magnificent rooms up on the first floor, the *bel étage*, are only slightly faded and are still used for receptions and state events.

A few steps further, the arcades lead past the:

11 Spanish Riding School (Spanische Hofreitschule)

Here on the right are the Renaissance arches of the Stallburg, the stables of the famous Lipizzaner horses of the Spanish Riding School. If you are lucky, while you are watching, a white horse will be led across to the training and performance halls on the other side of the street.

Michaelerplatz now opens to view. At Michaelerplatz 3, opposite the magnificent curve of the Hofburg entrance to the left, is a streamlined building with an elegant yet simple green marble entrance. This is the:

12 Loos House

Designed in 1909, Vienna's very first modernist building caused a shock in a city whose architecture was steeped in historicism. It was an unabashed contrast to the lavishly ornamented facade of the Michaelerplatz entrance to the Hofburg. Soon called the "house without eyebrows," referring to its unadorned windows, contemporary critics compared the entrance to "a gutter grid." Emperor Franz Joseph disliked the building so much that he kept the shades drawn and left the Hofburg through this gate.

At the center of Michaelerplatz is an open archeological excavation site, revealing stone walls from Roman times.

The splendid baroque entrance to the Hofburg complex was only completed in the late-19th century, a mere 25 years before Austria's Imperial age came to an end. It is flanked on either side by four Hercules figures and two allegorical fountains, to the left Austria's Power at Sea and, to the right, its Power on Land. Singing groups love the perfect acoustics of the ornate dome that rises above like a huge imperial canopy. Continuing inside brings you to a large courtyard with a statue of Francis I portrayed as a Roman emperor. To the left, a red gate leads to the Swiss Court, the oldest part of the Hofburg. Tucked into its corner is the gothic Hofburg Chapel, venue of the Vienna Choir Boys since 1498.

Back to the courtyard of Francis I and continuing through another passageway, you find yourself in the sudden expanse of the:

13 Heldenplatz

To the left is the grand semi-circle sweep of the Neue Burg (the new palace), completed in 1913, just a year before the assassination of the Arch Duke Franz Ferdinand in Sarajevo that launched World War I. A parallel building was planned to the right, but never built. The Neue Burg now houses the OSCE, the reading rooms of the National Library, and a number of small museums, including the Ethnographic Museum. On its balcony Adolf Hitler announced his "Anschluss" of Austria in 1938 to a crowd of 200,000 cheering well-wishers.

A wonderful view can be had to the west, over the grassy lawns of the Heldenplatz. "Heroes' Square," gets its name from two giant equestrian statues; on the right, the Archduke Charles of Austria, the horse springing from its hind legs, and to the left, the less successful statue of Prince Eugene of Savoy, which has to sit on its tail. The view, from left to right over the grass, of the Art History Museum, the Natural History Museum, the Parliament, and the City Hall is especially splendid from this point.

Enjoy the lawns and the gardens behind them if you want, but to continue the tour, put the rhythmically spaced columns of the Hofburg's curved facade behind you, and walk right to the far end of the palace's right wing. At Ballhausplatz 2, see the:

14 Federal Chancellery

This elegant building was erected in between 1717 and 1719. Its address, Ballhausplatz, is shorthand for Austria's seat of power, much like Downing St. or the White House. The square takes its name from the "ball house" that once stood here, a sports club where the aristocracy could play tennis and badminton. Prince Klemens von Metternich used these rooms as his headquarters during the Congress of Vienna (1814–15). In 1934, Austrian Nazis murdered Chancellor Dollfuss here, and, 4 years later when Austria was annexed by Germany, his successor Kurt von Schuschnigg gave a speech here, stating the famous words, "God save Austria." Since 1945 it has held the offices of the federal chancellor and Austria's Foreign Ministry.

Walk along the gardens adjacent to the Chancellery, along Lowelstrasse. Behind the fence is the Volksgarten, the People's Garden. It was laid out where the city walls destroyed by Napoleon once stood. Famous for its rose garden, it has been open to the public since 1823. Continue until you reach the:

15 Burgtheater

The national theater of Austria is one of the world's leading theaters. It is the second oldest theater in Europe (founded in 1741 by Maria Theresa) after the Comédie-Française, and the largest theater in the German-speaking world. Its current home was built in 1888, a large double-winged building with elegant stairways decorated with ceiling frescoes by Gustav Klimt. Among its many claims to fame, the premieres of three Mozart operas, (*Abduction from the Seralio, Marriage of Figaro,* and *Cosi Fan Tutti*) were performed there, as was George Bernard Shaw's *Pygmalion* (see "Theater," Chapter 10, p. 198).

After a walk once around the Burgtheater, turn onto Bankgasse. On your right at no. 9 is the:

16 Palais Liechtenstein

One of two Liechtenstein palaces in Vienna, this exquisite baroque jewel was begun in 1692 and completed in 1705 based on plans by the Italian architect Domenico Martinelli. It holds the Biedermeier portion of the Liechtenstein art collection.

A little farther on, pause at nos. 4–6, the:

17 Hungarian Embassy

Designed by the most influential architect of the baroque era in Vienna, Johann Bernhard Fischer von Erlach, this charming city palace has housed diplomats from the Empire's second most powerful kingdom since 1747.

Now retrace your steps for about half a block until you reach Abraham-a-Sancta-Clara-Gasse. At its end, on Minoritenplatz, you'll see the severe Gothic facade of the:

18 Minoritenkirche (Church of the Minorites)

The first gothic church in eastern Austria, its foundation stone was placed in 1276. Its design follows the scheme of French cathedrals of the period, rare for Austria. In the late-18th century the church was renamed The Italian National

Church of Mary of the Snow, and still today the high masses are held in Italian. If the doors are open, look inside for a huge mosaic copy of da Vinci's *Last Supper* (see Chapter 7, p. 145).

Walk behind the church to the curve of the building's rear. At this point some maps may lead you astray. Look for Leopold-Figl-Gasse, under the two large buildings linked by a bridge housing government offices. A block later, turn right onto Herrengasse. Within a few minutes, you'll be back at the now-familiar Michaelerplatz. This time you'll be facing:

19 St. Michael's Church

The Romanesque Michaelerkirche is one of the oldest churches in Vienna; the building of today's church probably began around 1220. The present neoclassical facade dates to 1792. Above the entranceway are winged angels and the figure of St. Michael slaying Lucifer, carved by Lorenzo Mattielli, who also sculpted the four Hercules figures at the Hofburg entrance.

Turn left (north) along Kohlmarkt, with its elegant buildings and shops, the luxury mile of Vienna. Earlier many of the shops were purveyors to the court, including **Demel** at no. 14, the most famous Konditorei (confectionary) in Vienna. Its windows display remarkable scenes or figures, entirely made of sugar, that comment on the news of the day.

At the broad pedestrian street known as the Graben, turn right. In its center stands the:

20 Pestsäule (Plague Column)

This high baroque column was erected by Emperor Leopold I in thanks to God for deliverance from the last Black Plague epidemic in Vienna, which broke out in 1679 and may have killed as many as 150,000 people. The column is divided into three clear sections, the human realm at the bottom with gruesome dying bodies falling into Hades and the kneeling, praying figure of Emperor Leopold I, who was the sponsor of the column. Above this is a pyramid of clouds full of angels, the mediators between men and God, who is seen as the Trinity at the top. Carved between 1682 and 1693 by a team of the most famous artists of the era, the column inspired many similar monuments across Austria.

Just before the Plague Column, turn left onto Jungferngasse and enter the lovely:

21 Peterskirche

Believed to be on the site of a crude wooden church built during the conversion of Austria around A.D. 350, legend has it rebuilt by Charlemagne in around 810. It was lavishly reinvented in 1712–14 by a team of baroque artists, the frescoes by the famed J. M. Rottmayr.

Return to the Graben, passing the Plague Column. You might, after all this, enjoy a sandwich. Leave the Graben at one of the first intersections on the right, Dorotheergasse, where you'll find a fine choice.

22 Buffet Trzesniewski

Despite its functional simplicity, Buffet Trzesniewski, Dorotheergasse 1 (© 01/512-3291), has, with a tasty nibble and an *"achtl"* of house wine, satisfied everybody who was anybody in Vienna since 1902. For more info, see Chapter 6, "Where to Dine."

After your break, continue right down the Graben to its terminus. Here you'll find a vaguely defined section of pavement that signs identify as:

23 Stock-im-Eisen

Here two pedestrian thoroughfares, the Graben and Kärntnerstrasse, meet at the southernmost corner of Stephansplatz. To your right, notice the curved piece of glass in the corner of an elegant building on the periphery of the square. Behind it are the remains of a tree into which hundreds of hand-forged nails have been hammered. For journeyman smithies or carpenters arriving in the Middle Ages, this was an act of putting down roots in Vienna, and believed to bring good luck. Carbon dating has shown that the tree lived from 1400 to 1440, thus some of the nails were pounded in while it was still alive. One of the iron bands holding the trunk bears the date 1575.

It has certainly been difficult to avoid taking in the full view of Vienna's most famous building:

24 St. Stephan's Cathedral

A walk around the entire cathedral will allow you to take in the enormous size of this Gothic wonder. The oldest-standing portion is the wall of the main entrance on the west, which was built from 1230 to 1245. The cathedral is laid out on an east–west axis, designed to have the rising sun shine directly into the east windows over the altar on the feast day of St. Stephan, December 26. The south tower is 136.7m (448 feet) tall; built from 1368 to 1433, it was a masterpiece of engineering in its time. In the entire Austro-Hungarian Empire, Alps to Black Sea, no church was allowed to be taller.

> **Impressions**
>
> *The streets of Vienna are paved with culture, the way other cities pave with asphalt. In Berlin, people walk on papier mâché, in Vienna they bite into granite.*
> Austrian journalist Karl Kraus, ca.1910

After a visit inside the cathedral, exit through the main door, turn left and head down the most famous street in Vienna's Inner City, the pedestrian-only:

25 Kärntnerstrasse

As you wander through the street, don't miss the mini-museum of glassmaking that decorates the second floor of the world-famous glassmaker **Lobmeyr,** at no. 26, and the windows of the Österreichische Werkstätte at no. 6.

If you still have the energy, detour off Kärntnerstrasse, turning left on Johannesgasse. You'll pass some old and interesting facades before reaching the baroque carvings and stone lions that guard the 17th-century portals of the:

26 Savoy Foundation for Noblewomen (Savoysches Damenstift)

In a palace built in 1688, the foundation was established by the duchess of Savoy-Carignan, Princess of Liechtenstein, in 1769 as a home for orphaned aristocratic women with fewer than 4,000 Gulden. The foundation still exists today, although no orphans live in the building now. The facade is adorned with a lead statue by the baroque sculptor F. X. Messerschmidt.

As you retrace your steps to the shops and pedestrian crush of Kärntnerstrasse, you might hear strains of Beethoven or Schubert cascading into the street from the **Vienna Music University (Universität für Musik und darstellende**

Kunst), which occupies a building on Johannesgasse. Turn left as on Kärntnerstrasse, and return to your point of origin, the **State Opera House.**

WALKING TOUR: SOUTH OF THE RING

START:	**Staatsoper (State Opera House).**
FINISH:	**Gumpendorferstrasse (on Sat, at the flea market).**
TIME:	**3½ hours, not counting visits to museums.**
BEST TIME:	**Saturday morning, when the flea market is held.**
WORST TIME:	**After dark or in the rain.**

The temptation is strong, especially for first-time visitors to Vienna, to limit exploration to the area within the Ring—the city's medieval core, the 1st District.

You'll discover a different side of Vienna by following this tour, past some of the dazzling at at times surreal manifestations of *fin-de-siècle* Vienna just south of the Ring. The tour also includes several less-celebrated, late-19th-century buildings that for their era were almost revolutionary.

Parts of the 6th District, the area of this tour, were heavily damaged during World War II and have had to be rebuilt, leaving an interesting contrast of old and new. A network of underground passageways, designed by city planners as part of Vienna's subway system, makes navigating the densest traffic a bit easier.

Begin your tour near the southern facade of:

1 Wiener Staatsoper (Vienna State Opera)

Built between 1861 and 1865 in a style inspired by the French Renaissance (and faithfully reconstructed after World War II), it was so severely attacked when it was unveiled that one of its architects, Eduard van der Null, committed suicide. (See "Walking Tour 1," earlier in this chapter, for a more extensive discussion.)

Now walk west along the Opernring, crossing Operngasse, past a row of shops and across another narrow street to arrive at a statue of the great German poet and playwright Johann Wolfgang von Goethe, brooding in a bronze chair, usually garnished with a roosting pigeon. If you look across the Ring, you can see him face to face with the other giant of German literature, Friedrich Schiller, whom we'll meet later. And just beyond Goethe, is a gateway into the always populated:

2 Burggarten (Castle Garden)

Since 1881, Hercules has been struggling with a lion in the middle of Burggarten. But he is about the only one who is, in this oasis of relaxed pleasure on the edge of the busiest part of Vienna. Here, in what was once the Emperor's private garden, spring, summer, and early fall afternoons see the gentle contours of the park strewn with free-spirited students, working people on a lunch break, or visitors taking in the sun. All find an untroubled, yet scenic place to unwind here, stretched out on a blanket with a book or chatting with a friend, amid games of Frisbee or hacky sack. Head up the handsome classical stone staircase to the terrace of the Palmenhaus, a tropical green house whose soaring glass roof is magnificently framed in ornate wrought iron, and is now an exotic setting for a restaurant pavilion. After you peek inside, turn right as you face the garden and follow the terrace around, past the main entrance to the National Library and pass through the iron gates to the street.

Heading across Opernring you come to Robert-Stolz-Platz, named for an Austrian composer who died in 1975.Here you turn right into Schillerplatz, where a statue of German poet Friedrich Schiller stands (eyeing Goethe across the road) surrounded by a company of other writers and artists. The building on the square's southern edge is the:

3 Akademie der bildenden Künste (Academy of Fine Arts)

Designed by the Danish architect, Theophil Hansen, the Akademie der bildenden Künste was established by Emperor Franz Joseph as the supreme authority on fine art in Austria. Built between 1872 and 1876, it was in a mix of Greek Revival and Italian Renaissance, symbolizing the sources of great art. Here the artistic dreams of a struggling 18-year-old Adolf Hitler were dashed in 1907 and again in 1908 when he twice failed to gain admission to what was at the time the ultimate arbiter of the nation's artistic taste and vision. A few years later, the young Egon Schiele, an artist of Hitler's age, withdrew from the academy frustrated by the restrictions and pomposity. A look inside at the imposing entry and grand staircase help explain both young men's reactions (for exhibits, see Chapter 7, p. 138).

Now walk east for a half block along the Niebelungengasse and then south along the Makartgasse, named for painter and decorative artist Hans Makart, best known today for his influence on Gustav Klimt, but revered in his day, the darling of Academy Exhibitions with huge historical canvases that attracted large crowds. Young Adolf Hitler is said to have idolized Makart's grandiloquent style; Klimt and Schiele of the Secessionist school at first admired him, then abandoned his presuppositions and forged a bold new path. Stories and innuendo swirled about the identities of the models, who appeared as artfully undressed figures in the handsome and promiscuous artist's paintings. He fell from grace by marrying a ballet dancer and contracting the syphilis that killed him at age 44.

At the end of Makartgasse, turn left (east) and go a half block. Then turn right onto the Friedrichstrasse. Before the end of the block, at Friedrichstrasse 12, is the Jugendstil (Art Nouveau) facade of a building that was the aftermath of the artistic changes wrought by the rebels, one of the most admired and envied artistic statements of the early-20th century:

4 The Secession

At the time of its construction in 1898, Olbrich's design was much more controversial than it is today, and hundreds of passersby would literally gawk. Its severe cubic lines, Assyrian-Egyptian looking corner towers, and chaotically covered gold leaf dome caused its detractors to refer to it as the Gilded Cabbage and Mahdi's Tomb. Purposefully built near the Fine Arts Academy to defy everything it stood for, it was immediately interpreted as an insult to bourgeois sensibilities. Both for and against the controversy, 57,000 people attended the inaugural exhibition. The inscription above the door reads *Jeder Zeit sein Kunst, Jeder Kunst sein Freiheit,* which translates as, "To every age its art, to every art its freedom."

Even today, the spirit of rebellion embodied in the "Jugendstil" art of Secessionists is seen all over Vienna ornamenting facades, on simple garden gates, or peering out from a bas-relief.

Walking Tour: South of the Ring

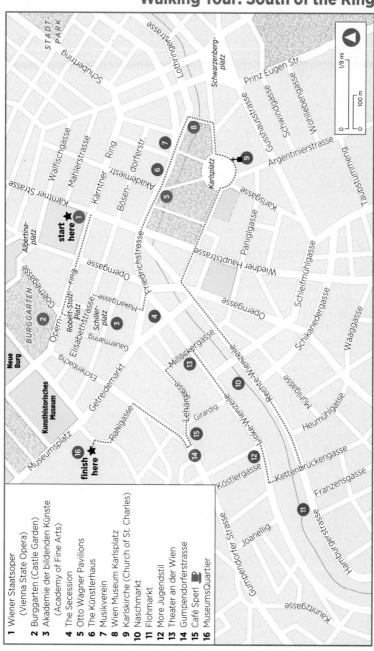

1 Wiener Staatsoper
   (Vienna State Opera)
2 Burggarten (Castle Garden)
3 Akademie der bildenden Künste
   (Academy of Fine Arts)
4 The Secession
5 Otto Wagner Pavilions
6 The Künstlerhaus
7 Musikverein
8 Wien Museum Karlsplatz
9 Karlskirche (Church of St. Charles)
10 Naschmarkt
11 Flohmarkt
12 More Jugendstil
13 Theater an der Wien
14 Gumpendorferstrasse
15 Café Sperl
16 MuseumsQuartier

From the Secession, look for the large U marking the entrance to the subway and follow the underground concourse to Karlsplatz. Turn right at the first major underground intersection, and follow signs to the Wiedner Hauptstrasse. You'll ascend into daylight near the sprawling and sunken perimeter of the Karlsplatz. From there climb up a flight of stone steps to the platform that skirts the Karlsplatz's northern edge, and walk east to the pair of Jugendstil (Art Nouveau) houses:

5 Otto Wagner Pavilions

Originally designed by Otto Wagner as stations for his *Stadtbahn*, they are jewels of applied Secessionist theory and have been preserved as monuments by the city. After their construction, many of their decorative adornments were copied throughout other districts of the Austro-Hungarian Empire as part of the late-19th-century building boom. Regrettably many were later demolished as part of the Soviet regime's suppression of so-called decadent architecture during the Cold War. In Vienna, the pavilions were nearly lost in the subway expansion, until a public outcry pushed the city to renovate them and raise them 2 meters (ca. 6 feet) higher at the new grade level, reincarnated as a cafe. If you are not in a hurry, take a seat on the terrace; it's a lovely spot.

From here, continue walking east. The first building on your left, at Friedrichstrasse 5, is:

6 The Künstlerhaus

Around 1900, its name was associated with conservative art and tended to enrage the iconoclastic rebels who later formed the Secessionist movement. Completed in 1868, the building served for years as the exhibition hall for students at the Fine Arts Academy. The building was nearly lost in 1966 to plans to build IBM offices on its site that met with widespread criticism from the media and the public. Today, the building is used for exhibitions, experimental theater and film, including screening some of the Viennale Film Festival.

Immediately to the right (east) of the Künstlerhaus, at Karlsplatz 13, is the Renaissance-inspired:

7 Musikverein

Home of the Vienna Philharmonic, this is the site of concerts that often sell out years in advance, through fiercely-protected private subscriptions and the famed New Year's Concert. Constructed between 1867 and 1869, and designed by the same Theophil Hansen who built the Fine Arts Academy (stop no. 3), it's a particularly fine example of the way architects dabbled in the great styles of the past during the late-19th-century revitalization of the Ringstrasse.

At Karlsplatz 4, a short walk southeast from the Musikverein, is a monument that serves, better than any other, to bind the complicated worlds, subcultures, and historic periods that form the city of Vienna, the:

8 Wien Museum Karlsplatz

Since the appointment of Director Wolfgang Kos, the Museum of the History of Vienna has been reinvented into a dynamic, creative place of theatrical energy, hosting one blockbuster show after another. Even its bland main building has been transformed into a glistening setting for the ideas and events on its cultural calendar. So be sure to plan a separate visit. (See p. 150.)

Continue your clockwise circumnavigation of the Karlsplatz to the divine confines of the:

9 Karlskirche (Church of St. Charles)

Mourning the loss of Austria's vast domains in Spain, Maria Theresa's father Charles VI is thought to have built the Karlskirche as a means of recapturing some of Vienna's imperial glory. It is certainly the monument for which Austria's leading architect of the time, Johann Fischer von Erlach, is best remembered. The Ringstrasse was not yet in place, and it lay within an easy stroll of the emperor's residence in the Hofburg.

Built between 1716 and 1737, it was occasioned by another disastrous bout with the plague, and named after St. Charles Borromeo, who had shown special compassion to plague sufferers and was thus considered a patron saint of healing, although the confusion that ensued over which Charles had given his name to the church was almost certainly deliberate.

The twin pillars in front were inspired by Trajan's Column in Rome, and the reflecting pool (won back from a parking lot) holds a statue by Henry Moore. On a fair day, you can grab a sausage at a Würstelstand, pick out a spot on the curbed edge of the fountain, and enjoy the generous view of the square and the glories of the house of God before you.

Now continue walking clockwise around the perimeter of the square to the southern edge of the Karlsplatz, crossing a short side street running into the Karlsplatz. Continue walking west along the southern perimeter of the Karlsplatz, along Resselpark, and across the Wiedner Hauptstrasse that was, in ancient times, the road that originally linked Vienna to the Empire's Mediterranean port cities of Venice and Trieste. Cross the Wiedner Hauptstrasse and continue along Treitlstrasse and along the westward extension of Resselpark, until you reach the Rechte Wienzeile, a broad boulevard that once flanked the quays of the Danube before the river was tamed and covered over as part of 19th-century urban renewal. On the new surface, you'll see the congested stalls, booths, and lanes of Vienna's largest food-and-produce market, the:

10 Naschmarkt

Wandering through the narrow and filled alleys of the Naschmarkt it is easy to get lost among the 120-odd stands in the ancient market place. Among the many stalls and permanent stores, there are profusions of bright red and yellow spices, mounds of baby onions, rows of carrots, and lengths of leaks, followed by a mouth-watering array of cold cuts and iced bins of fish, and even larger selections of cheeses, olives, and finger foods. Be prepared to bargain with sellers from Burgenland south of Vienna or Marchfeld to the east, from Poland, Hungary, Greece, Bulgaria, Turkey, Iran, Egypt or Morocco, with exotic snack shops or restaurants spliced in between. Follow your eyes and your nose through the market, a world tour all its own.

Further down, nearing Kettenbrückengasse, the food stands dissolve and are replaced by racks and bins of apparel and handbags of various cultures, to another of Otto Wagner's Jungendstil pavilions, the Kettenbrückengasse underground station, and the:

11 Flohmarkt

Don't expect glamour, or even merchants who are particularly polite. Instead be prepared for swarms of people rummaging through so much junk in hopes of finding treasure. Which, with a little patience, you probably will. Scattered amid the racks of clothing, musical instruments, old china, glass- and hardware, there are priceless things, old postcards, a typewriter, a pair of riding boots, a hunting horn. Haggling is in, and don't forget your weight limits.

12 More Jugendstil

Back on the Linke Wienzeile at Köstlergasse (at nos. 1 and 3) are apartment houses designed by Otto Wagner. At Linke Wienzeile 40, you'll see yet another of his designs, an apartment house referred to by architecture students around the world as the **Majolikahaus.** Adjacent to the Majolikahaus, at 38 Linke Wienzeile, is the **Medallion House,** with a Secession-style floral display crafted from tiles set into its facade.

At the corner of the Millöckergasse, at Linke Wienzeile 6, you'll see a historic theater that, during the decade-long renovation of the State Opera House, functioned as Vienna's primary venue for the performing arts, the:

13 Theater an der Wien

Despite its unadorned facade, this is the oldest theater in Vienna, dating to 1801. To get an idea of its age, bypass the front entrance and walk northwest along Millöckergasse. At no. 8 is the theater's famous *Pappagenotor,* a homage to the Pan-like character in Mozart's *Magic Flute.* The likeness was deliberately modeled after Emanuel Schikaneder, the first actor to play the role, the author of most of the libretto, and the first manager, in 1801, of the theater. Beethoven lived upstairs and composed parts of his *Third Symphony* and the *Kreuzer* Sonata here, and *Fidelio* premiered here. If you come by in the mornings you may be allowed to peek inside the lovely old theater itself.

Continue walking northwest along Millöckergasse, then turn left onto the Lehárgasse. Within about 3 blocks, Lehárgasse merges into the:

14 Gumpendorferstrasse

Here you see the same sort of historically eclectic mix, on a smaller scale, that you'll find on the Ringstrasse. Previously the medieval village of Gumpendorf, the neighborhood was incorporated into the city of Vienna as the 6th District of Mariahilf in 1850. Now, it's time to:

15 Café Sperl

Café Sperl, Gumpendorferstrasse 11 (✆ 01/586-4158), is one of the most beautiful cafes in Vienna. From the time of its opening in 1880 until World War II, it was a hub of social and intellectual life, the Stammcafe of Secession artists Josef Hoffmann and Josef Maria Olbrich, a role it has gradually regained. Carefully restored under historic preservation protection in 1983, it is the haunt of intellectuals and theater people, where, coffee at hand, newspaper in hand, and a cigarette hanging from your mouth, you'll fit right in! (And as everywhere in Vienna, half the cafe is smoke free.)

After your break, walk back east along Gumpendorferstrasse, admiring the eclectic Ringstrasse-style houses that line the sidewalks. At the next corner, Rahlgasse, turn left into the cul-de-sac, and head for the handsome 1870 Rahlstiege, a double staircase leading up to a lovely "goose-girl" fountain and Mariahilferstrasse. **Now walk back across Mariahilferstrasse and enter the:**

16 MuseumsQuartier

The MuseumsQuartier is housed in what were originally the Imperial stables, built in 1713 for Karl VI by lead architects Johann and Josef Fischer von

Erlach, father and son. Later parts were sold off, and then in 1920 it was rededicated as the *Messepalast*, used for major arts and industrial expositions by the Nazi propaganda machine, and returned to its public uses after the war. In the 1980s, it became the setting for the Vienna Festival, the *Wiener Festwochen*, leading to the decision to turn it into a permanent arts center complex.

The competition for a design finally went to star architects Laurids and Manfred Ortner, under heated public debate, resulting in the abandonment of a central tower that supporters saw as the needed reach for the modern and others as a betrayal of the elegant proportions of the original Fischer von Erlach building. In the end, however, the brilliant use of space in a nearly perfect balance of old and new has resulted in what many say is the most successful arts and cultural center in Europe. A joy to be in, it attracts young and old, and has become the "in" place to be in Vienna.

WALKING TOUR: VIENNA'S BACK STREETS

START:	**Maria am Gestade.**
FINISH:	**St. Virgil's Chapel.**
TIME:	**2½ hours (not counting visits to interiors).**
BEST TIME:	**Daylight hours, when you can visit shops and cafes.**
WORST TIME:	**In the rain and after dark.**

When the English King Richard I, the 'Lion-Hearted,' was captured on his way back from the Third Crusade in 1192, he was apprehended trespassing on Babenberg lands in the village of Erdberg—now part of Vienna's 3rd District. (Disguised as a monk, he gave himself away by paying for his dinner with a gold sovereign.) The funds the English handed over for his ransom were used for the enlargement of Vienna's fortifications, which eventually incorporated some of the areas you'll cover on this walking tour. Thus, some of medieval London was mortgaged to pay for Vienna's city walls.

Much of this tour focuses on smaller buildings and lesser-known landmarks on distinctive streets where some of the most influential characters of Viennese history have walked, a labyrinth of medieval streets with quirky insights into lives past. Covered passages, and tiny streets lead you through the age-old Viennese congestion that sociologists claim helped inspire the artistic output of the Habsburg Empire.

Begin your promenade slightly northwest of Stephansplatz, a short walk and upstairs from the Schottenring U-Bahn, and explore one of the least-visited churches of central Vienna:

1 Maria am Gestade

At Salvatorgasse 1, this is also known as "Maria-Stiegen-Kirche," or the Church of St. Mary on the Strand; it replaced an 800s wooden church, with the 14th-century stonework you see today. Designated centuries ago as the Czech national church in Vienna, the narrowness of the medieval streets around it restricted the floor plan to only 9m (30 feet) in width, capped with an elaborate, pierced Gothic steeple. It has also been a film location, including Carol Reed's *The Third Man* (1949), and Richard Linklater's 1995 film *Before Sunrise*.

From here, take a left after exiting the church and walk south along Schwertgasse, turning left (east) on Wipplingerstrasse to the:

2 Altes Rathaus

The Habsburg ruler Duke Frederick the Fair confiscated this marvelous *palais* in 1316 from the leader of an anti-Habsburg revolt and donated it to the city. The baroque facade was added about 1700 and a courtyard fountain in 1741, one of the last works of Raphael Donner, designer of the great Providence Fountain at Neuermarkt. The building, at Wipplingerstrasse 3, served as the city hall until the offices moved to new, neo-Gothic quarters on the Ring. Today, the Altes Rathaus contains a museum on the Austrian resistance of the Turks.

Continue down Wipplingerstrasse east to the:

3 Hoher Markt

The city's oldest marketplace, this was the location of a public gallows until the early 1700s, and of a pillory for dishonest bakers until the early 1800s. But its history actually goes back to Roman times, when it was the forum of the ancient settlement of Vindobona. Some excavations of what's believed to be a Roman barracks are visible in the courtyard of the building at no. 3. Most visitors, though, go straight for the Jugendstil Ankeruhr, which somehow escaped destruction during aerial bombardments of the square in 1945 and was an important location in *The Third Man*, filmed here in 1948. But don't miss the plague memorial, which replaced the instruments of torture that dominated the square. The present version was designed by Josef Emanuele von Ehrlach in 1732, sculpted by Italian Antonio Corradini.

From here, walk a short block east along the Lichtensteg, then turn left and walk northeast along one of Vienna's most prominent shopping streets, Rotenturmstrasse, for 2 blocks. Then turn right (east) onto the:

4 Griechengasse

You will not find a more concentrated collection of quirky oddities than on Griechengasse and Fleischmarkt (see no. 5). The construction of this narrow street in the 1100s was representative of the almost desperate need for expansion away from the city's earlier perimeter, which more or less followed the ancient configuration of the Roman settlement of Vindobona. Griechengasse's name comes from the 18th-century influx of Greek merchants, precursor of the waves of immigrants flooding into modern Vienna from Eastern Europe and the Middle East today.

At Griechengasse 5, the unpretentious exterior of the 1805 Greek Orthodox church was legally required of all non-Catholic churches until the 19th century, and at the point where the street turns sharply stands a 14th-century watchtower. One of the few medieval vestiges of the old city walls, it was incorporated long ago into the architecture that surrounds it.

The Griechengasse narrows at this point, and in some places buttresses supporting the walls of the buildings on either side span it. Griechengasse soon intersects with a thoroughfare where, during the 12th century, you'd have been confronted with the stench of rancid blood from the nearby slaughterhouses.

Turn right and head to:

5 Fleischmarkt

This former meat market also retains many clues to its turbulent past. Notice the heroic frieze above the facade of the antique apartment house at no. 18 ("The

Walking Tour: Vienna's Back Streets

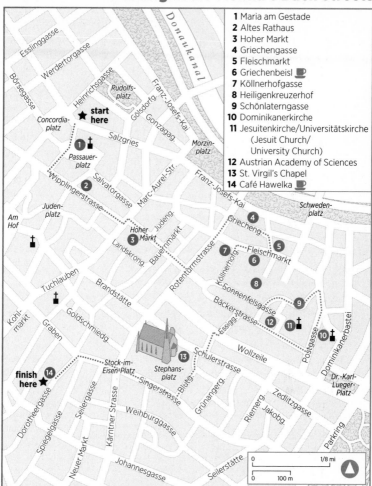

1 Maria am Gestade
2 Altes Rathaus
3 Hoher Markt
4 Griechengasse
5 Fleischmarkt
6 Griechenbeisl ☕
7 Köllnerhofgasse
8 Heiligenkreuzerhof
9 Schönlaterngasse
10 Dominikanerkirche
11 Jesuitenkirche/Universitätskirche
   (Jesuit Church/
   University Church)
12 Austrian Academy of Sciences
13 St. Virgil's Chapel
14 Café Hawelka ☕

Tolerance House"), which depicts in symbolic form Joseph II, son of Maria Theresa, granting freedom of worship to what was at the time a mostly Greek Orthodox neighborhood. No. 9, opened in the 1400s and improved and enlarged during the next 300 years, was used as an inn (or, more likely, a flophouse) and warehouse for traders from the Balkans and the Middle East in Mozart's time.

6 Griechenbeisl

Griechenbeisl, Fleischmarkt 11 (✆ 01/533-1941), is an inn named for the many Greeks who made it their regular dining spot for hundreds of years. Established in 1450, it's divided into a warren of cozy dining rooms, where there are no right angles or level floors. See Chapter 6, "Where to Dine" for details.

The walls of another Greek Orthodox church rise next to the Griechenbeisl, embellished in 1858 by Theophil Hansen, the Danish-born architect of several of the grand buildings of the Ringstrasse.

Also notice the plaque at no. 9, a warning to pedestrians to watch out for cartwheels. Coach drivers are asked to keep tight hold of their reigns and send an adult ahead of the carriage to alert pedestrians before entering the street.

The passage is also lined with stone bollards, some with iron bands, designed to protect the walls from wheel damage.

A branch of the Vienna post office is at no. 19, on the premises of a monastery confiscated from the Dominicans by Joseph II, as part of his campaign to secularize the Austrian government. The only ecclesiastical trappings left in this bureaucratic setting are the skeletons of dozens of dead brethren, buried in the building's crypt many generations ago.

Turn left and walk for about a half block onto:

7 Köllnerhofgasse

Nos. 1–3 served long ago as the headquarters of a group of merchants, based in Cologne on the Rhine, who set up a trading operation in Vienna in response to privileges granted to merchants during medieval times. The building you'll see today—remarkable for the number of windows in its facade—dates from 1792.

At this point, turn left into a cul-de-sac Grashofgasse, whose far wall is painted with a restored fresco of the Stift Heiligenkreuz (Holy Cross Abbey), a 12th-century Cistercian monastery 24km (15 miles) in the Wienerwald. A covered arcade, which is usually open, leads into the cobbled public courtyard of the:

8 Heiligenkreuzerhof

This ecclesiastical complex incorporates a 17th-century cluster of monks' apartments, lodging for an abbot, and the diminutive baroque chapel of St. Bernard (Bernardinenkapelle), closed to the public since the recent renovation except for weddings. The courtyard's continued existence in the heart of Vienna is unusual: many equivalent tracts owned by abbeys were converted long ago into building sites and public parks after sale or confiscation by the government.

Exit the monastery's courtyard from its opposite (southeastern) edge onto:

9 Schönlaterngasse

Its name derives from the wrought-iron street lamp that adorns the facade of the 16th-century building at no. 6, a copy of the original hanging in the Wien Museum. This lovely street is part of a designated historic district, in which renovation loans are available at rock-bottom interest rates.

At Schönlaterngasse 7 lies the Basilikenhaus, a 13th-century bakery supported by 12th-century foundations. When foul odors began emanating from the building's well, the medieval residents of the building assumed that it was sheltering a basilisk, a mythological reptile from the Sahara Desert whose breath and gaze were believed to be fatal. The facade features a stone replica of a beast that was killed, according to a wall plaque, by a brave baker who showed the creature its own reflection in a mirror. A modern interpretation involves the possibility of methane gas or sulfurous vapors seeping out of the building's well.

Schönlaterngasse 7A was the home of Robert Schumann from 1838 to 1839, the winter he rediscovered some of the unpublished compositions of Franz

Schubert. Basking in the glory of a successful musical and social career, Schumann did more than anyone else to elevate the relatively unknown Schubert to posthumous star status.

The Alte Schmiede at no. 9 (the Old Forge) on the same street, dating from the Middle Ages, was made into a smithie in 1880, and since 1975 has been one of Vienna's most important literary societies. From outside, you can glimpse a collection of antique tools on the far wall of the preserved forge.

Continue east along Schönlaterngasse, where you'll see the back of the Jesuit Church (Jesuitenkirche), which you'll visit in a moment. Continue as the street turns sharply right until it widens into the broad plaza of Postgasse, where you again turn right. The building that rises in front of you, at Postgasse 4, is the:

10 Dominikanerkirche

This is the third of three Dominican churches on this site. The earliest, constructed around 1237, burned down. The Turks demolished the second, completed around 1300, during the siege of 1529. The building you see today was completed in 1632 and is the most important early-baroque church in Vienna. The rather murky-looking frescoes in the side chapels are artistically noteworthy; some are the 1726 statement of baroque artist Françoise Roettiers. However, the church is mainly attractive as an example of baroque architecture and for the pomp of its high altar. Elevated to the rank of what the Viennese clergy calls a "minor basilica" in 1927, it's officially the "Rosary Basilica ad S. Mariam Rotundam." Beethoven lived for about a year in Postgasse 8 adjacent to the simple facade of St. Barbara's at no. 10.

Now, walk south along the Postgasse until the street narrows and turn right into a small alley that widens within a few paces into Bäckerstrasse. Houses at nos. 8 and 10 have lovely details, take a close look. If the doors are open, take a stroll into the courtyard of no. 7, which dates back to 1587 and the Italian Renaissance, with balcony walls hung with the ornamental ironwork of the artist Friedrich Amerling. Behind the columns are the original stables containing the horses' stone watering troughs. Other Renaissance houses can be found at no. 12 and no. 14.

Follow Bäckerstrasse for about a block until you reach the confines of the square that's referred to by locals as Universitätsplatz, but by virtually every map as Dr. Ignaz Seipel-Platz (named for a theologian and priest who functioned twice as chancellor of Austria between the two world wars). The building that dominates the square is the:

11 Jesuitenkirche/Universitätskirche (Jesuit Church/University Church)

This magnificent church was built between 1623 and 1627, and adorned with twin towers and an enhanced baroque facade in the early 1700s by those workhorses of the Austrian Counter-Reformation, the Jesuits. The Spanish-born and fervently Catholic Emperor Ferdinand invited the Jesuits to Vienna at a time when about three-quarters of the population had turned Protestant. It was estimated that only four Catholic priests remained at their posts in the entire city. From this building, the Jesuits spearheaded the 18th-century conversion of Austria back to Catholicism and more or less dominated the curriculum at the university next door. These intellectual clerics built a wonderful ornate church, with allegorical frescoes and all the aesthetic tricks that evoke a transitional world midway between earth and heaven.

The western edge of Dr. Ignaz Seipel-Platz borders one of the showcase buildings of Vienna's university, the:

12 Austrian Academy of Sciences

One of Vienna's premier rococo attractions, the Aula of the Academy of Sciences is a precursor of the great concert halls that dot the city today. In the 18th century, orchestral and choral works were presented in halls such as this one, and chamber works in private homes of wealthy patrons. Haydn's oratorio *The Creation* had its premiere here, as did Beethoven's *Seventh Symphony*.

This square was also the scene of one of the major uprisings of 1848 when, on March 13, university professors and students, booksellers, and coffee house intellectuals joined in protest against the police state of Metternich, the "Iron Chancellor," demanding freedom of the press and other political and civil rights. Army detachments were called out and, by evening, 50 people had been killed. Old and frail, Metternich fled the city, hidden in a laundry cart.

Exit the Dr. Ignaz Seipel-Platz at its northwest corner, and walk right along Sonnenfelsgasse. Flanked with 15th- and 16th-century houses (until recently still operating open bordellos) a few that shouldn't be missed include nos. 3, 15, 17, and 19. Don't be afraid to look into the courtyards if the front doors are open.

The street is named for Josef von Sonnenfels, of one of the few advisors who could ever win an argument with Maria Theresa. Sonnenfels had learned a dozen languages as a foot soldier in the Austrian army, and later used his influence to abolish torture in the prisons and particularly cruel methods of capital punishment. Beethoven dedicated his *Piano Sonata in D Major* to him.

Walk west down Sonnenfelsgasse until it ends in a square called Lugeck, then turn left and back along Bäckerstrasse. You will, in effect, have circumnavigated an entire medieval block. Then turn south into a narrow alleyway, Essiggasse, and cross over Wollzeile, centerpiece of the wool merchants and weavers' guild during the Middle Ages and now a noted shopping district.

Continuing southward along Strobelgasse, you arrive at Schulerstrasse. Turn right onto Schulerstrasse, which leads to Stephansplatz and an ancient, almost forgotten, church:

13 St. Virgil's Chapel

Most visitors to Vienna walk over an interesting and curious piece of Viennese history without even realizing it. Hidden for 200 years, this chapel was uncovered in 1973 during excavations for the Stephansplatz U-Bahn station. Built on the cemetery grounds of St. Stephan's in the 14th century, it was used for consecration masses and funerals until 1781, when it was demolished in a fire. Downstairs, in the Stephansplatz U-Bahn station you can view the interior.

Here we are at the end of your walk! Well done!

Now cross Stephansplatz, and take a short walk down The Graben to Dorotheergasse, and:

14 Café Hawelka

Café Hawelka, Dorotheergasse 6 (✆ 01/512-8230), is one of the most authentic of the remaining traditional literary cafes, in the same family since 1939, whose interior was designed by a protégé of Adolf Loos and has been maintained unchanged. Appealingly threadbare and plastered with posters, and dozens of newspapers, this place serves great coffee and is open late. The real thing. See Chapter 6, "Where to Dine" for details.

SHOPPING

When it comes to fine art and good taste the Viennese go much farther than the music for which they are legend. While traditional attire and handicrafts are part of a long-established tradition of skilled craftsmanship, Austrian design, both traditional and modern, is also famous all over the world. Visitors can spend many happy hours browsing in antiques stores and galleries of fine art, and in shops selling unique design pieces and original fashion.

9

The traditional products have not lost their allure, of course, like the *dirndl* and *lederhosen* that many Viennese still wear in summer and to the *Jägerball* (Hunters' Ball) each January (although it's probably unlikely that you'll want to take them home with you). The traditions of the Wiener Werkstätte designs from the 1900s also continue and are available at selected shops. Other local specials are petit-point linens, hand-painted Augarten porcelain, gold and silver work, ceramics, enamel jewel work, wrought-iron art, and leather goods. Shopping in Vienna is fun and most vendors know their products well.

THE SHOPPING SCENE

In general there are two main shopping areas. One is the Inner City (1st District). Here you'll find **Kärntnerstrasse,** between the State Opera and Stock-im-Eisen-Platz (U-Bahn: Karlsplatz or Stephansplatz); The **Graben,** between Stock-im-Eisen-Platz and Kohlmarkt (U-Bahn: Stephansplatz); **Kohlmarkt,** between The Graben and Michaelerplatz (U-Bahn: Herrengasse); and **Rotenturmstrasse,** between Stephans-platz and Schwedenplatz (U-Bahn: Stephansplatz or Schwedenplatz). The side streets off The Graben, especially Dorotheergasse, are lots of fun to browse through, with their high concentration of antiques stores.

In addition to this upmarket area, there's the more mainstream stretch on **Mariahilferstrasse,** between MuseumsQuartier and Westbahnhof, one of the longest (and often busiest) shopping streets in Europe (U-Bahn: MuseumsQuartier, Neubaugasse, Zieglergasse, or Westbahn-hof). Off this boulevard there are many hidden treasures, such as the so-called Furniture Mile on Siebensterngasse, or between Mariahilfer-strasse and the Naschmarkt, where you'll find Gumpendorferstrasse with fine boutiques, good restaurants, and stylish hairdressers at every turn.

Vienna Shopping

Church
Post office
Information
Railway
U-Bahn line
RATHAUS & station

0   200 yds
0   200 m

To Westbahnhof
and Schönbrunn

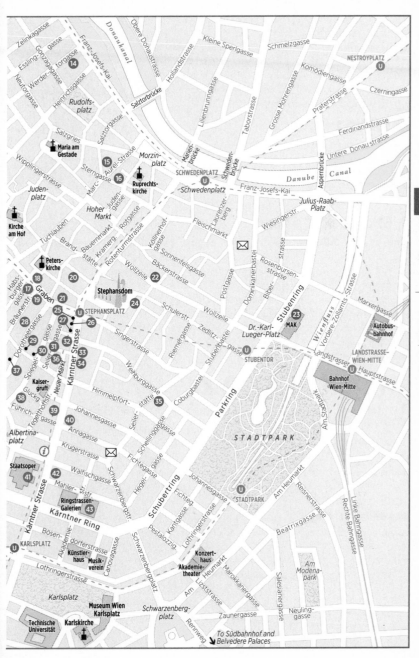

The **Naschmarkt** itself is an international fine foods market with a lively scene every day. To visit, head south of the opera district. It joins the Linke and Rechte Wienzeile (U-Bahn: Karlsplatz or Kettenbrückengasse; see the box, "Open-Air Markets," later in this chapter).

The larger shopping streets have elegant department stores, which are wonderful to browse in on colder days. On Kärntnerstrasse it is the **Steffl,** a glass tower from which an elevator sticks out into the street. On Mariahilferstrasse, the place to find everything under one roof is **Gerngross,** the renovated, century-old shopping palace (see "Department Stores" below).

Shopping Hours

Shops are normally open Monday to Friday from 9am to 6pm, and Saturday from 9am to 1pm. On Thursdays many shops stay open longer, generally until 7pm. Small shops usually close between noon and 2pm for lunch. Shops in the Westbahnhof and Südbahnhof rail stations are open daily from 7am to 11pm, offering groceries, stationery, books, and flowers.

A Shopping Center

Ringstrassen Galerien   Renting shop space in central Vienna is wildly expensive. As a result, about 70 tasteful boutique-ish emporiums selling everything from bric-a-brac to eveningwear have pooled their resources and moved to labyrinthine quarters on the Ring, near the State Opera House, and linked to the Grand Hotel. The prominent location guarantees glamour, though the cramped dimensions of some stores might be a turnoff. The selection, however, is usually good and each shop is operated independently. Most are open Monday to Friday, 10am to 7pm, and Saturday, 10am to 6pm. In the Palais Corso and in the Kärntnerringhof, Kärntner Ring 5-13. ℰ **01/512-81-11.** www.ringstrassen-galerien.at.

SHOPPING A TO Z

Antiques

Vienna's antiques shops are a limitless source of treasures. You can find valuable old books, engravings, etchings, and paintings in second-hand shops, bookshops, and picture galleries. Along the Dorotheergasse and Stallburggasse area you're sure to find eye-catching items. If you're looking for more contemporary antiques, say Art Deco or 50s–80s flair, head over to the Spittelberg area and along Burggasse in the 7th District area (U-Bahn: 4 to Neubaugasse).

D&S Antiques ★ 🎁   Some of the greatest breakthroughs in clock-making technology occurred in Vienna between 1800 and 1840. This store, established in 1979, seeks out antique Viennese clocks and repairs them ready for sale, stocking an awesome collection worthy of many world-class museums. The shop even stocks a "masterpiece" (each craftsman made only one such piece in his lifetime, to accompany his bid for entrance into the clockmakers' guild)—in this case, the work of a well-known craftsman of the early 1800s, Benedict Scheisel. Don't come here expecting a bargain—prices are astronomical—but devotees of timepieces from around the world flock to this emporium, treating it like a virtual museum. Dorotheergasse 13. ℰ **01/512-5885-0.** www.ds-antiques.com.

Dorotheum ★★   Dating from 1707, this is the oldest auction house in Europe. Emperor Joseph I established it so that impoverished aristocrats could fairly (and anonymously) get good value for their heirlooms. Today the Dorotheum holds regular auctions of art, antiques, jewels, and musical instruments. If you're interested in an item, you give a small fee to a *Sensal,* or licensed bidder, and he or she bids in your name. The vast array of objects for sale includes exquisite furniture and carpets, delicate *objets d'art,* and valuable paintings, as well as necklaces and the like. If you're unable to attend an auction, you can browse the salerooms, selecting items you want to purchase directly to take home with you the same day. Around 30 auctions take place each July alone; over the course of a year, the Dorotheum handles some 250,000 pieces of art and antiques. Dorotheergasse 17. ℰ **01/51560-0.** www.dorotheum.at.

Flohmarkt ★ 👜   You can find a little of everything at this flea market near the Naschmarkt (see the box "Open-Air Markets," below) and the Kettenbrückengasse U-Bahn station. It's held every Saturday from 6:30am to 6pm, except on public holidays. The Viennese have perfected the skill of haggling, and the Flohmarkt is one of their top arenas. It takes a trained eye to spot the antique treasures scattered among the junk. Everything you've ever wanted is here, especially if you're seeking chunky Swiss watches from the 1970s, glassware from the Czech Republic (sold as "Venetian glassware"), and even Russian icons. Believe it or not, some of this stuff is original; other merchandise is merely knockoff. Linke Wienzeile. No phone. www.flohmarkt.at.

Galerie bei der Albertina   Come here for ceramics and furniture made during the early 20th century by the iconoclastic crafts group Wiener Werkstätte. Its members made good use of the machinery of the emerging industrial age in the fabrication of domestic furnishings and decor. The inventory incorporates decorative objects, sculpture, paintings from the Jugendstil (Art Nouveau) age, etchings, plus an occasional drawing by Egon Schiele or Gustav Klimt. Lobkowitzplatz 1. ℰ **01/513-1416.** www.galerie-albertina.at.

Glasgalerie Kovacek   Antique glass collected from estate sales and private collections throughout Austria takes up the ground floor of this showroom around the corner from the Dorotheum. Most items date to the 19th and early 20th centuries, some to the 17th century. The most appealing pieces boast heraldic symbols, sometimes from branches of the Habsburg family. Also here is a collection of cunning glass paperweights imported from Bohemia, France, Italy, and other parts of Austria. The upper floor holds the kind of classical paintings against which the Secessionists revolted. Look for canvases by Franz Makart, foremost of the 19th-century historic academics, as well as some Secessionist works. Spiegelgasse 12. ℰ **01/512-9954.** www.kovacek.at.

Zeitloos 👜   This pun means both timeless (*zeitlos*) and recalls the famous turn-of-the-century architect Adolf Loos whose artistic influence still shapes the industry. This shop has more to offer than just furniture, you'll find unique statuettes, ceramics, candlesticks, and enchanting lamps. The proprietor is very accommodating and is glad to arrange shipping for larger items. Kirchengasse 39/Burggasse 47. ℰ **0676/526-1956.** www.zeitloos.at.

Art

M-ARS ★ 👜   You can stroll around with a shopping cart, selecting a future Picasso, a Matisse, or perhaps a Klimt? Well, maybe not, but this unique supermarket is stocked with works of fine art by Austrian artists—not groceries. And you just might find for 15€ the Gustav Klimt of 2050. Only a 5-minute walk from MuseumsQuartier, the M-ARS offers more than 1,000 paintings, sculptures, and photographs, the work of some 50 artists selected by a panel of art historians and directors from Austrian museums. Westbahnstrasse 9. ✆ **01/890-5803.** www.m-ars.at.

MAK(Museum für angewandte Kunst) Design Shop ★   The creators of the unique pieces at the MAK design shop in the Museum of Applied Arts are among the best up-and-coming Austrian and Central European designers and architects. Here you'll find everything from clothing and handbags to office decor and silverware. Perhaps you'll find a washable breadbasket or magnetic bird paperweight, India-inspired scarves or a 3-D picture frame. And no one at home will have anything like it. 9 Stubenring 5. ✆ **01/711-36-228.** www.makdesignshop.at.

Ö.W. (Österreichische Werkstätten) ★★   Even if you skip every other store in Vienna, check this one out. This fascinating shop sells hundreds of handmade art and design pieces. It was set up by leading artists and craftspeople around the country as a co-operative to showcase their wares. The location is easy to find, only half a minute's walk from St. Stephan's Cathedral. There's an especially good selection of pewter, along with modern glassware, brass, baskets, ceramics, and serving spoons fashioned from deer horn and bone. Take some time to wander through this cavernous, three-floor Aladdin's cave, also frequented by discriminating locals. Kärntnerstrasse 6. ✆ **01/512-2418.** www.austrianarts.com.

VAT Refunds

For non-EU visitors to Austria, the country's Value-Added Tax (*Mehrwertsteuer,* or VAT), which can be as high as 34% on some luxury goods, is refundable. See "Taxes" under the section 'Fast Facts: Vienna' in chapter 12 to learn the refund procedure.

Books

The British Bookshop   This is the largest and most comprehensive emporium of English-language books in Austria, with a sprawling ground-floor showroom loaded with American, Australian, and British books just off the Ring next to the Marriott Hotel. It's especially strong in fiction (there's a good section of audio books), language-learning materials and phrase books for teaching English as a second language. Regular readings feature local authors and visiting writers on Vienna and the region. Weihburggasse 24–26. ✆ **01/512-1945.** www.britishbookshop.at.

Buchhandlung Walter König   Just inside the main entrance of the Museums-Quartier, this is the Austrian branch of the leading purveyor of books on art and architecture in the German-speaking world. Emphasis is on art, architecture, photography, and design and includes current international publications and bargain books. Many books are in English. There is also an excellent bistro, Kantine, attached. Open Monday to Saturday 10am to 7pm, Sunday 1pm to 7pm. Museums-Quartier. ✆ **01/ 512 85 880.** www.mqw.at/de/shopping/buchhandlung+walther+koenig.

Morawa   This is the well-stocked main branch of one of Austria's largest bookstore chains. Although its collection is mostly German-language, there is a decent selection of English and other foreign-language books, including much on contemporary

The empire of the kingdom of Austria and Hungary faded into history at the end of World War I, and Austria is only a tiny republic today. But you wouldn't know that by looking into the windows of certain shops. Many proudly display the initials "K & K," or *Kaiserlich und Königlich*. The anachronistic symbol translates as "by appointment of the Imperial and Royal Household."

life and politics. Also be sure to check out the Press Centre at the back (2nd entry on Bäckerstrasse) that carries leading newspapers and magazines in many languages from around the world. Wollzeile 11. ✆ **01/910-76276.** www.morawa.at.

Satyr Filmwelt 🎁 Feted by insiders as the best-stocked bookstore on film in Europe, this is a remarkable place and carries everything from histories, biographies, and memoirs, to screenplays, original posters, and a connoisseur's DVD shop. Books and films in every relevant language, including a strong section on film music, with hard-to-find books on the great Austrian film composers. Marc-Aurel-Strassee 5 (entrance Vorlaufstrasse) ✆ **01/ 535 53 26-27-28.** satyr.filmwelt@netway.at.

Shakespeare & Company ★★ 🎁 Established in the 1980s, this is a book lovers' haven, packed from floor to ceiling in a creaky building enhanced by age. Fashioned to some degree after its namesake in Paris, this store carries well-chosen English-language books on Vienna and Austria, plus a general selection of fiction, and non-fiction and magazines on politics, culture, and world affairs. A knowledgeable staff can guide you through the fine selection of literature.Sterngasse 2. ✆ **01/535-5053.** www.shakespeare.co.at.

Confectionery

Altmann & Kühne Many older Viennese fondly recall the marzipan, hazelnut, or nougat confections their parents bought for them during strolls along the Graben. Established in 1928, this little shop stocks virtually nothing good for your waistline or your teeth, but plenty that's great for the soul, and undeniably scrumptious. The visual display of all things sweet is almost as appealing. The pastries and tarts filled with fresh seasonal raspberries are, quite simply, delectable. Graben 30. ✆ **01/533-0927.** www.altmann-kuehne.at.

Gerstner Gerstner competes with Café Demel (see Chapter 6) as one of the city's great pastry makers and chocolatiers, selling some of the most scrumptious cakes, petits fours, and chocolates anywhere. Kärntnerstrasse 11-15. ✆ **01/512-49630.** www.gersnter.at.

Department Stores

Gerngross The younger and more price-sensitive crowd likes to go to Gerngross at the U3 station Neubaugasse. Built in 1904 this building has never gone out of date. Today there is an entire floor dedicated to sportswear and one to electronics. When you're all shopped-out, relax over tea and cake at Demmers Teehaus on the ground floor or go up to the 5th for a great view and sushi at Akakiko. Mariahilfer Strasse 42-48 ✆ **01/521800.** www.gerngross.at.

9

SHOPPING | Shopping A to Z

Steffl Kaufhaus This five-level department store is one of Vienna's most visible and well advertised. You'll find rambling racks of cosmetics and perfumes, a noteworthy section devoted to books and periodicals, household items, and clothing. If you forgot to pack something for your trip, chances are very good that Steffl Kaufhaus will have it. Kärntnerstrasse 19. ℂ **01/514310.** www.kaufhaus-steffl.at.

Fashion

Fürnkranz Everything from tennis skirts to fur coats; Fürnkranz not only carries its own label but a mixture of top European designers. The mélange of Austrian, French, and Italian is all incorporated in Viennese style. The mannequins show the care with which a Cavalli dress is accentuated by a Tahiliani scarf and topped off with a hat by Jean Paul Gaultier. The couture team is gracious and accommodating and will help you put together an outfit from shoes to hairpiece. Kärntnerstrasse 39. ℂ **01/488-4426.** www.fuerenkranz.at.

Nachbarin ★ For a real taste of modern Austrian design check out this slick joint right across from Café Sperl on Gumpendorferstrasse. This is the place to go for ultra chic women's wear by Anna Aichinger and other Euro stars that every Viennese fashionista will covet. The handbags and scarves are also very desirable. Gumpendorferstrasse 17. ℂ **01/587-2169.** www.nachbarin.co.at.

PARK This is where the chic Viennese of today shop. The minimalist storefront encloses brand names and sought-after young designers galore. You'll find hard-to-get combos for both men and women along with accessories and fun gift items such as books on fashion or photography. Mondscheingasse 20, 1070. ℂ **01/526-4414.** www.park.at.

Popp & Kretschmer When Ball season comes to Vienna the employees of Popp & Kretschmer have their hands full dressing the world's finest ball-goers in the trendiest or most utterly timeless gowns. The employees know their products and fit each gown to Italian shoes and delectable accessories. In the off-season the fashion is not as decadent, but the light-hearted attitude translates into Pucci and Cavalli get-ups that will have heads turning. Three floors of dresses, along with shoes, handbags, belts, plus men's briefcases and travel bags, await you at this boutique opposite the State Opera. Kärntnerstrasse 51. ℂ **01/512-78010.** www.popp-kretschmer.at.

Traditional Clothing

Lanz A well-known and rustically-elegant Austrian store, Lanz deals in dirndls and other folk clothing. It is mostly for women, with a limited selection of men's jackets, neckties, and hats. There are also clothes for young children. Kärntnerstrasse 10. ℂ **01/512-2456.** www.lanztrachten.at.

Loden Plankl ★★ Established in 1830 by the Plankl family, this store is the oldest and most reputable outlet in Vienna for traditional Austrian clothing for men, women, and children. Michaelerplatz 6. ℂ **01/533-8032.**

Hats

Mühlbauer ★★ Mühlbauer has been at the head of Vienna's headwear hierarchy since the early 1900s, and today produces everything from outrageous leopardskin print numbers to variations on the traditional Austrian trilby with feather. And yet it's a family affair, the new look coming when Klaus Mühlbauer and sister Marlies

OPEN-AIR markets

Since the Middle Ages, Viennese merchants have thrived by hauling produce, dairy products, and meats from the fertile farms of Lower Austria and Burgenland into the city. The tradition of buying the day's provisions directly from street stalls is still strong, and in summer months the bug hits and markets spring up all over the Inner City, just like the Christmas markets in winter. However, the main outlets of this wonderful way to shop are also hidden in lesser-known areas.

The largest of the city's permanent outdoor food markets is the **Naschmarkt,** Wienzeile, in the 6th District (U-Bahn: Karlsplatz), just south of the Ring. It occupies what was originally the river bed of a branch of the Danube, which was diverted and paved over during the massive public works projects of the 19th century. It's the most popular, international, and flamboyant of the markets, as well as the most comprehensive.

Entire books have been written about the subcultures and linguistic dialects that flourish among the Naschmarkt's denizens. You'll find Austrian and international cuisine, as well as fruit and vegetables, baked goods, meat, poultry, game, and fish, not to mention flowers, soaps, honey, and unusual stands like a vinegar brewery. Get there early in the morning and wander through the labyrinth of stalls and, at the end of your tour, head for the nearby **Café Drechsler** for breakfast or a cup of coffee. Or pick from the many restaurants flanking the market.

Somewhat smaller and less varied are the: **Karmelitermarkt,** recently revived and very "hot," and Vienna's oldest existing market. Alongside fruit, vegetables, and kosher meat (not to mention horse butchers) there are an array of popular new cafes and restaurants, right across the canal from Schottenring (U-Bahn: Schottenring, exit Herminengasse; no. 2 Tram); **Rochusmarkt,** at Landstrasser Hauptstrasse at the corner of the Erdbergstrasse, in the 3rd District (U-Bahn: Rochusgasse), a short distance east of the Ring. This market is one of the most popular, offering a little bit of everything a gourmet could ask for; and the **Brunnenmarkt,** on the Brunnengasse, in the 16th District (U-Bahn: Josefstädterstrasse), a subway ride west of the middle of the city and a short walk north of the Westbahnhof. This is the only market where you can truly practise old school oriental haggling.

Most merchants in these markets maintain approximately the same hours: Monday to Friday from 8am to 6pm, Saturday from 8am to noon.

(the 4th generation of the founding family) took over in 2001. The store has begun producing a clothing line. All over the world, the fashion elite wears Mühlbauer headwear, nearly 80% of which comes from Vienna. The flagship store is in the 1st District. 10 Seilergasse. ✆ **01/5335269;** www.muehlbauer.at.

Jewelry

A. E. Köchert ★   The 6th generation of the family, which served the court at the end of the Habsburg Empire, continues its tradition of fine workmanship here. The store, founded in 1814, occupies a 16th-century landmark building. The firm designed many of the crown jewels of Europe, but the staff gives equal attention to customers looking only at charms for a bracelet. Neuer Markt 15. ✆ **01/512-5828.** www.koechert.com.

Frey Wille Necklaces, rings, and bangles from this Austrian creator combine exotic designs with impressive craftsmanship. Every detail is inspired by an art epoch or by famous artists such as Klimt or Hundertwasser. Although there are shops all over the world (including new openings in New York and London), the pieces are only produced in Vienna. Stephansplatz 5. ✆ **01/513-4892.** www.frey-wille.com.

Swarovski In Vienna, crystals are a girl's best friend. Almost any self-respecting Viennese lady has a pair of Swarovski earrings, a necklace, or bracelet. Some even cover their iPods or phones in Swarovski crystals. Not only can you find the famed figurines from this enterprise all over the globe, the shop has something for everyone. From watches, belts, and crystal-covered rings to the masses of decorations, chandeliers, and collectables. The store is usually a hub of activity, and even if you don't buy anything, the sparkling display windows are worth a look. Kärntnerstrasse 8. ✆ **01/512-9032-33.** www.swarovski.at.

Rozet & Fischmeister ★ Owned by the same family since 1770, this store focuses on gold, gemstones in artful settings, and both antique and modern silver tableware. If you opt to buy an engagement ring or a bauble for a friend, you'll be following in the footsteps of Franz Joseph I. The staff will even quietly admit that the Emperor made several discreet purchases for his legendary mistress, actress Katharina Schratt. Kohlmarkt 11. ✆ **01/533-8061;** www.rozet-fischmeister.com.

Lace & Needlework

Zur Schwäbischen Jungfrau ★★ This is one of the most illustrious shops in Austria, with a reputation that goes back almost 300 years. Empress Maria Theresa bought her first handkerchiefs and thousands of debutantes have shopped here for dresses. Come for towels, bed linens, lace tablecloths, and some of the most elaborate needlepoint and embroidery anywhere. Service is impeccable, courtly, and cordial. Graben 26. ✆ **01/535-5356;** www.schwaebische-jungfrau.at.

Music

Arcadia Opera Shop This respected record store is one of the best for classical music. The well-educated staff knows the music and performers (as well as the availability of recordings), and is usually eager to share that knowledge. The shop also carries books on art, music, architecture, and opera, as well as an assortment of musical memorabilia. The shop is on the street level of the Vienna State Opera, with a separate entrance on Kärntnerstrasse. Guided tours of the splendid opera house end here. Wiener Staatsoper, Kärntnerstrasse 40. ✆ **01/513-95680;** www.arcadia.at.

Da Caruso Almost adjacent to the Vienna State Opera, this store is known to music fans and musicologists worldwide. Its inventory includes rare and unusual recordings of historic performances by the Vienna Opera and the Vienna Philharmonic. If you're looking for a magical or particularly emotional performance by Maria Callas, Herbert von Karajan, or Bruno Walter, chances are you can get it here, on CD. The people here are hip, alert, and obviously in love with music. Operngasse 4. ✆ **01/513-1326;** www.dacaruso.at.

Doblinger Classical and jazz lovers beware: it's easy to get stuck in this sheet music paradise, where you can browse the drawers to discover chamber music, Wiener Lieder, cabaret, stage and choral music, or jazz masters you thought forever lost to time. Not only does it have a vast selection of new editions of sheet music as well as CDs, there's also a back room filled with antiques from Vienna's musical past. Stroll through the shop and you'll start itching to go to the Musikverein or the opera, to which the employees are happy to direct you. Dorotheergasse 10. ℭ **01/515-03-0.** www.doblinger.at.

EMI ★ This is where music buffs go when they die. It's hard to live up to the motto "good music is better" when the selection is so vast, but the employees really know their stuff. These are music lovers selling to music lovers, and whatever you're looking for you are certain to find it in the endless shelves on these four floors in downtown Vienna. Whether it's a Snoop Dog single or a rare recording of a Mahler symphony, this place has it. Kärntnerstrasse 30. ℭ **01/512-3675;** www.emimusic.at.

Musiktank ★ 📇 The strangest souvenir of all, a personal CD of Austrian pop songs. You can listen to the music at the MuseumsQuartier and then have your choices burned on to CD—all at an affordable price and totally legal. Here you'll find a pool of more than 3,000 Austrian pop tunes, from hits to out-of-print rarities, and tracks from the vinyl era that have never been released on CD, even in Austria. MuseumsQuartier, Electric Avenue, Museumsplatz. ℭ 01/5264715; www.musiktank.at.

Porcelain & Pottery

Albin Denk ★★ The oldest continuously operating porcelain store in Vienna (since 1702). Its clients have included the Empress Elisabeth, and the shop you see today looks almost the same as it did when she visited. The three low-ceilinged rooms are beautifully decorated with thousands of objects from Meissen, Dresden, and other regions. Graben 13. ℭ **01/512-44390;** www.albindenk.at.

Augarten Porzellan ★★ The history of one of the oldest porcelain manufacturers in Europe goes back almost 300 years. Exquisitely crafted, Vienna porcelain is famous for its delicate and graceful shape and the purity of its lines. Here, every step of production, from mixing the paste to the finishing touches, is carried out by hand. Both manufacturer and shop may be a little out of the way, but the trip is worth it. You can watch the master craftsmen at work and also see the former hunting lodge of Kaiser Franz Joseph, surrounded by the beautiful Augarten Park, and the Augarten Palace, home of the Vienna Boys' Choir. Stock-im-Eisenplatz 3-4, 1010. Shop: Obere Augartenstrasse 1, 1020. ℭ **01/512-14940;** www.augarten.at.

Toys

Kober ★ ☺ Kober has been a household name in Vienna, especially at Christmastime, for more than 100 years. It carries old-fashioned wooden toys, teddy bears straight out of a Styrian storybook, go-carts (assembly required), building sets, and car and airplane models. The occasional set of toy soldiers is more *Nutcracker Suite* than G.I. Joe. Graben 14-15. ℭ **01/533-60180.** www.kobertoys.com.

Spielwaren Bannert ☺ This place prides itself in having toys for people from 0 to 99 years old and the sheer size of the shop makes it believable. It's not a warehouse, more a family store, but the 50,000 products are bound to include something you or your children will want to play with. From old-school rocking horses and model trains to Barbie dolls and SpongeBob, this store has it all. Werdertorgasse 14. ℭ **01/533-2530.** www.spielwarenbannert.at.

THE supermarket OF YOUR DREAMS

Julius Meinl am Graben At the corner of Graben and Kohlmarkt (Graben 19. www.meinlamgraben.at. U-Bahn: Stephansplatz), is one of the most beautiful supermarkets in the world. In essence it's like London's Harrod's and New York's Zabar's combined, but with an imperial touch. From hundreds of cheeses and meats, to internationally renowned caviars, this two-floor gourmet's paradise has an in-house bakery, confiserie, seafood counter, wine bar, and endless mahogany shelves full of fine foods from all parts of the globe. The store is also dedicated to organic and local delights. Sauntering through the aisles of Meinl am Graben is perhaps the most fun you'll ever have food shopping. And then you get to the register, where reality kicks in...

Vinegars & Oils

Gegenbauer ★★ 🎁   More than 50 artisan vinegars and 20 oils are available from this unique store. This is a family business operating since 1929 and its boss, Erwin Gegenbauer, may be the world's leading expert on vinegar. There's vinegar made from tomatoes as well as elderberry, asparagus, lemongrass, sour cherry, cucumber, and even beer. Rare oils come from fruit kernels, wine grapes, and much more. Gegenbauer 14, Naschmarkt. ✆ **01/6041088.** www.gegenbauer.at.

Wine

Wein & Co.   Since the establishment of Vindobona, the original Vienna, by the ancient Romans, the Viennese have always taken their wines seriously. Wein & Co. is Vienna's largest wine outlet, a sprawling cellar-level ode to the joys of the grape and the bounty of Bacchus. You'll also find wines from around the world. Jasomirgott-strasse 3–5. ✆ **01/535-0916;** www.weinco.at.

Weinquartier Wien ★ 🎁   Right between the opera and the Burggarten there's a small but stylish wine bar. Not only does it have 20 wines to be tasted each week, but 50 different vineyards from the *Weinviertel* (wine region in lower Austria) are on offer and even the snacks are worth the visit. This is a newly opened and well-kept locals' secret. *Prost!* Hanuschgasse 3. ✆ **01/513-4319.** www.weinquartier.at.

VIENNA AFTER DARK

At 6pm, the Viennese close the office door behind them and head off into the evening. There's no time to waste! A light meal and then it's off to the theater or a concert, doll up for the opera, a festival, or dance into the wee hours; you can try your luck at roulette, or simply sit and talk over a drink at a local *beisl*.

While the Viennese love their culture, that's far from the whole story. So take a look around; whatever you like to do, you can probably find it somewhere in this dynamic city.

The best source of constantly updated information about cultural events is the *Wien Monatsprogramm*, which is distributed free at tourist information offices and at many hotel reception desks. Or find it at www. vienna.at. Also, check out *The Vienna Review*, a monthly English-language newspaper available at bookstores and many *Tabak-Trafiken*, which has a detailed listings calendar full of insider tips. If you read German, the weekly *Falter* is the choice of locals.

Be alert: booking tickets in advance can reduce the price significantly. And if you're not eligible for a student or senior discount and don't want to go bankrupt to see a performance at the Staatsoper, Burgtheater, Volk-soper, or Musikverein you can purchase standing-room tickets at a cost of about 5€.

Students under 27 with valid IDs are eligible for many discounts. The Burgtheater, Akademietheater, and Staatsoper sell student tickets for just 10€ on the night of the performance. Theaters routinely grant students about 20% off the regular ticket price.

In general the Viennese are avid partygoers; age, interests, and occupation alone play a role in choosing the venue. This selection of nightspots should give you a good foundation to chase the dawn in whichever way you enjoy most.

THE PERFORMING ARTS

Music is at the heart of Vienna's cultural life. This has been true for centuries, and the city continues to lure composers, librettists, musicians, and music lovers. You can find places to enjoy everything from orchestras, chamber music, and pop, to jazz, gypsy music, alternative, electro, and anything else in between. You'll find small discos and large

A Note on Evening Dress

People like to dress in Vienna, a change from the informality of North America or some parts of Europe. Not only do locals wear evening clothes for concerts and theater visits, they also get quite dolled up to go clubbing. No clubs require jackets or eveningwear, but you won't be let in if you don't look the part. For especially festive occasions—such as opera premieres, receptions, and balls—tails or dinner jackets and evening dresses are *de rigueur*. And while few will force the issue, it's best not to reek "tourist" in jeans and flip-flops. If you want to dress up and didn't bring the right clothes, you can rent evening wear (as well as carnival costumes) from several places. Consult your hotel concierge or the telephone classified section under "Kleiderleihanstalten" also available online at www.herold.at.

concert halls, as well as musical theaters, cabaret, clubs, and piano bars. If you tire of listening, you'll find no shortage of stage shows, from classical to avant-garde. Below we describe just a few of the better-known spots for cultural diversion; if you're in Vienna long enough, you'll find many others on your own.

Just for the record, Vienna is the home of four major symphony orchestras, including the world-acclaimed Vienna Philharmonic and the Vienna Symphony. In addition to the ORF Radio Symphony Orchestra and the Niederösterreichische Tonkünstler, there are dozens of others, ranging from smaller orchestras to chamber orchestras.

Major Orchestras & Ensembles

Concentus Musicus   Founded in 1953 by Nikolas Harnencourt, who still serves as the principal director and inspiration for the group, it is a baroque orchestra of such authenticity and joie de vivre that its members have often left other supposedly more prestigious orchestras to join it. Consentus Musicus Wien, Musikverein, Grosser Saal. Karlsplatz 6. ℂ **01/5058190.** tickets@musikverein.at. www.musikverein.at.

KlangForum   Ever since its first concert in 1985, under founder Beat Furrer at the Palais Liechtenstein, these 24 musicians from 9 countries have written musical history. Klangforum Wien has premiered roughly 500 new pieces by living composers from three continents, and recorded more than 70 CDs, giving a voice to the notes for the first time. Klangforum Wien, Diehlgasse 51. ℂ **01/521670.** info@klangforum.at. www.klangforum.at.

Radio Symphony Orchestra   The orchestra of the ORF Austrian National Radio, the RSO under Bertrand de Billy has joined the ranks of Vienna's top orchestras, a high-energy, high-polish ensemble that brings audiences to their feet. A massive public campaign is credited with turning ORF budget discussions around and assuring the orchestra's future. It's also the resident orchestra at Theater an der Wien. ORF Radio-Symphonieorchester, Argentinierstraße 30a. ℂ **01/50101-18420.** rso-wien@orf.at.

Vienna Philharmonic   Among the world's great orchestras, some would say this is the greatest. There is no ensemble that has played as important a role in the development of European classical music. Over its 160-year history, it has helped define the sound and performance practises of classical, romantic, and modern orchestral literature, translating the Viennese aesthetic into music. Composer Richard Strauss said: "All praise of the Vienna Philharmonic reveals itself as understatement." The Vienna Philharmonic plays a series of 10 regular concerts (most performed twice) and six soirees, at the Musikverein (see below), plus 20 other concerts at other venues around the city. It also doubles as the orchestra of the Vienna State Opera. Wiener Philharmoniker Karten- & Ballbüro Kärntner Ring 12. ℂ **01/505 6525.** www.wienerphilharmoniker.at.

Vienna Symphony Formed at the turn of the century to supplement the schedule of the Philharmonic, since World War II the Wiener Symphoniker has played an increasingly important role in Vienna's love for music. With more than 150 performances a year it is one of the busiest orchestras in the world, appearing not only at its home Wiener Konzerthaus, but also at the Musikverein, Theater an der Wien, and at a dozen other cities and venues around Europe. Wiener Symphoniker, Lehárgasse 11. ℂ **01/58979-0.** office@wiener-symphoniker.at. www.wiener-symphoniker.at.

THE TOUGHEST ticket IN TOWN

Reservations and information for the Wiener Staatsoper (Vienna State Opera), Volksoper, Burgtheater (National Theater), and Akademietheater can be obtained by contacting **Österreichische Bundestheater (Austrian Federal Theaters),** the office that co-ordinates reservations and information for all four state theaters (ℂ **01/5144-42959;** www.bundestheater.at). Call Monday to Friday 8am to 5pm. **Note:** The number is often busy; it's easier to get information and order tickets online. The major season is September to June, with more limited presentations in summer. Many tickets are issued to subscribers before the box office opens. For all four theaters, box-office sales are made only 1 month before each performance at the Bundestheaterkasse, Goethegasse 1 (ℂ **01/51-44-40**), open Monday to Friday, 8am to 6pm; Saturday, 9am to 2pm; Sunday and holidays, 9am to noon. Credit card sales can be arranged by telephone within 6 days of a performance by calling ℂ **01/513-1513** Monday to Friday, 10am to 6pm; and Saturday and Sunday, 10am to noon. Tickets for all performances, including the opera, are also available by

writing to the Österreichischer Bundestheaterverband, Goethegasse 1, A-1010 Vienna, from outside Vienna. Orders must be received at least 3 weeks in advance of the performance to be booked, but do not send money through the mail.

Note: The single most oft-repeated complaint of music lovers in Vienna is about the lack of tickets for the high-demand performances. If the suggestions above don't produce the desired tickets, you could consult a broker. Their surcharge usually won't exceed 25%, except for very rare items, when the surcharge can double or triple. One of the most reputable agencies is **Liener Brünn** (ℂ **01/533-09-61**), which sometimes has tickets months in advance or as little as a few hours before the event.

As a final resort, remember that the concierge of virtually any top hotel in Vienna long ago learned a few tricks for acquiring hard-to-come-by tickets. (A gratuity of at least 10€ can work wonders, and will generally be expected anyway for the time and phoning involved. You'll pay a hefty surcharge as well.)

The Sound of Music at the Philharmonic

Almost immediately after the orchestra of the Wiener Hofburgtheater (the Vienna Court Theater) began offering symphonic concerts on March 28, 1842, the Wiener Philharmoniker attracted lavish accolades. By 1845, the French composer Hector Berlioz had already declared that the orchestra "may have its equal, but it certainly has no superior." In 1863, Richard Wagner gushed: "I heard expressive and tonal beauty, which no other orchestra has offered me." Twelve years later, Verdi described the Wiener Philharmoniker as "a wonderful orchestra." Anton Bruckner, himself regarded as "God's musician," exclaimed that the musicians "played like gods," and Leonard Bernstein thought their excellence came from the fact that "they perform totally out of love."

Wiener Kammerorchester   Made its debut in 1946 after World War II, and performed a 40-concert series in Vienna in 2010 under principal conductor Stefan Vladar. He took over as artistic director from Heinrich Schiff, who now conducts the orchestra's concerts in New York. Vienna Chamber Orchester, Schachnerstrasse 27, Diehlgasse 51. ℂ **01/2903 6357.** wiener@kammerorchester.com. www.kammerorchester.com.

Other Ensembles   There are so many fine ensembles active on the Vienna musical scene, it is impossible to present them all here. However a short list needs to include: the Bach Consort Wien (www.bachconsort.com), which plays baroque chamber ensemble music; the Clemencic Consort of early music (www.clemencic. at); The Schönberg Chor, the only professional concert choir in Europe (www.asc. at); and the Orchester der Wiener Akademie (www.wienerakademie.at). There are also numerous chamber ensembles: the Aron Quartet (www.georghamann.at/aronquartett), the Artis String Quartet Wien (www.artis-quartet.at), and the Quatuor Mosaiques, (members of the Concentus Musicus) among the very best.

Opera & Classical Music Venues

Musikverein ★   Count yourself fortunate if you get to hear a concert here. The Goldenensaal is regarded as acoustically one of the four best concert halls in the world. Some 600 concerts per season (September to June) are presented here, of which only about two dozen are by the Vienna Philharmonic, nearly all of which are subscription concerts, sold out long in advance. The box office is open August 16 to September 3, Monday to Friday, 9am to noon (Monday to Friday 9am to 8pm and Saturday 9am to 1pm the rest of the year; closed from July to August 15). Bösendorferstrasse 12. ℂ **01/5058190** for the box office. www.musikverein.at. Tickets up to 120€ for seats, 3€ for standing room. U-Bahn: Karlsplatz.

Wiener Staatsoper (State Opera) ★★★   Opera is sacred in Vienna: when World War II was over, the city's top priority was the restoration of the heavily damaged Staatsoper. With musicians from Vienna Philharmonic Orchestra in the pit, and the leading opera stars of the world on stage, combined with the generous budgets of a government-supported house, the results are legendary. In their day, Richard Strauss and Gustav Mahler were artistic directors. The Staatsoper stages more than 60 productions a year of opera and ballet and, with 1,700 seats and 560 standing room places, performs for about 10,000 concert-goers a week. Daily performances run from September 1 until the end of June; with a little planning, tickets are to be had for almost any performance, although many sell out. (Also see "Other Top Attractions," in Chapter 7.) Opernring 2. (*) **01/5144-42960.** www.staatsoper.at. Tickets 10€–220€. Tours 6.50€ per person. U-Bahn: Karlsplatz.

Schönbrunn Palace Theater ★ A small gem that opened in 1749 for the court of Maria Theresa. The architecture is a medley of baroque and rococo, and there's a large, plush box where the Imperial family sat to enjoy the shows. Operettas and comic operas are performed in July and August. A wide variety of different art groups perform here, each responsible for its own ticket sales. At Schönbrunn Palace, Schönbrunner Schlossstrasse. (*) **01/512-01-00.** www.musik-theater-schoenbrunn.at. Tickets 35€–85€. U-Bahn: Schönbrunn.

Theater an der Wien Since opening on June 13, 1801, this has been a leading venue for opera and operetta. After a mistaken re-positioning for musicals, it was returned to its true calling as a boutique opera house in 2006, to celebrate the 250th

---

 HAVING A ball

The Viennese of all ages and walks of life love to dress up and go dancing. So besides the legendary **Opera Ball**, there are dozens of others, less celebrity-packed, eminently affordable, and not sold out months ahead of time. And they're all fun. Prime ball season takes place during the weeks between New Year and *Fasching*, the Austrian version of Carnival and the last fling before the beginning of Lent. Thus it begins with the **Kaiserball** on New Year's Eve and mostly ends in March. In the dark winter nights the gaiety of the costuming, the champagne, music, dancing, and general carrying-on are just the thing to ward off the cold. And remember: this is for everyone. A good third of any ball crowd is under 30, and one Viennese expression for a "party animal" is "Ball Tier!" Some of the great ones are the **Jägerball,** (Hunters' Ball) where the dress code is *dirdl* and *lederhosen*—far more rustic and Oktoberfest-like than the others. Also there is the **Juristenball** (Lawyers' Ball), the **Bonbonball**, **Ball der Wiener Kaffeesieder** (Coffee Roasters' ball), **Finanzball** (Finance Ball), and next to the Opera ball the most famous and popular is of course the **Philharmonikerball** (Ball of the Vienna Philharmonic). Just pick the crowd with whom you'd like to mingle. And be prepared for a late night: balls don't begin till 9pm and cruise on through till 4 or 5am. After the madness of the midnight *Galopp* and morning dance-floor antics have taken their toll on your feet, it is traditional to go for breakfast with your date or a group of friends. Try **Café Schwarzenberg** (Kärntnerring 17. (*) **01/512 8998**) on the edge of Schwarzenbergplatz, or the Landtmann, Dr. Karl Lueger-Ring (*) **01/24 100-100** by the Burgtheater. You'll find a comprehensive ball season calendar at www.austria.info. Tickets range from 60€–500€ and availability is also varied. While evening clothes (black tie and long gowns) are usually the rule, the dress code does vary, so do make sure you know what's expected. One good rental place for ball attire is on the inner side of the 9th District, **Rottenberg** (Porzellangasse 8, (*)**01/317 61 55**), which will do you fine for starters, or check with your concierge for closer options.

anniversary of Mozart's birth. The house hosted the 1805 premiere of *Fidelio,* by Ludwig van Beethoven (who lived upstairs) and of Johann Strauss, Jr.'s *Die Fledermaus* in 1874. Linke Wienzeile 6. ✆ **01/588-300.** www.theateranderwien.at. Tickets 30€–140€. U-Bahn: Karlsplatz.

Volksoper   This opera house presents lavish productions of Viennese operettas, light opera, as well as 18th, 19th, and 20th century operas (*The Magic Flute, Tosca, La Boheme,* etc.), classical musicals (*My Fair Lady*), and ballet from September 1 until the end of June. The season consists of some 300 performances divided among some 35 different productions and revivals from previous years. Tickets go on sale at the Volksoper only 1 hour before performances. Währingerstrasse 78. ✆ **01/514-443670.** www.volksoper.at. Tickets 7€–150€ for seats, 2.50€–4€ for standing room. U-Bahn: Volksoper.

Wiener Konzerthaus   This major concert hall, built in 1912, is home to the Wiener Symphoniker. It's the venue for a wide range of musical events, including orchestral concerts, chamber music recitals, choir concerts, piano recitals, and opera stage performances. The box office is open Monday to Friday, 9am to 7:45pm; and Saturday, 9am to 1pm. August hours are Monday to Friday, 9am to 1pm. Lothringerstrasse 20. ✆ **01/242-002.** www.konzerthaus.at. Ticket prices depend on the event. U-Bahn: Stadtpark.

Theater

Akademietheater   Specializes in both classic and contemporary works. The Burgtheater Company often performs here; it's the world-famous troupe's second, smaller house. Lisztstrasse 3. ✆ **01/5144-44740.** www.burgtheater.at. Tickets 4€–48€ for seats, 1.50€ for standing room. U-Bahn: Stadtpark.

Burgtheater (National Theater)   The Burgtheater produces classical and modern plays in German, universally accepted as the leading stage in the German-speaking world. Work started on the original structure in 1776; it moved to the Ring in 1857, was badly damaged in World War II, and re-opened in 1955. Among its permanent company today are Oscar winners Klaus Maria Brandauer (*Mephisto, Out of Africa*) and Christoph Waltz (*Inglourious Basterds*), and Sonke Workmann (*Pope Joan*). Dr.-Karl-Lueger-Ring 2. ✆ **01/5144-4140.** www.burgtheater.at. Tickets 5€–48€ for seats, 1.50€ for standing room. Tram: 1, 2, or D to Burgtheater.

English Lovers 👫   This group of charmers does improvisational theater every second Friday night at 10:30p.m. The Late Night Theater Jam begins with asking the audience for a theme and characters, from which they create a drama. The troupe is very gifted and is a joy to watch. If you have a good grasp of German you can see them *auf Deutsch* on the Fridays in between. Theater Drachengasse 26. Fleischmarkt 22. ✆ **01/513-1444.** www.english-lovers.at. Tickets 16€, 10€ for students. U-Bahn: Schwedenplatz.

International Theater & Fundus   First a touring company, the International Theater found a permanent home in 1980, continuing as a repertory company of a dozen actors who put on 6 to 8 productions a season from the leading playwrights of British and American theatre, from Noel Coward and Eugene O'Neill, to Lillian Hellman and Woody Allen. Their annual production of *The Christmas Carol* has become a Vienna institution. The season runs from September to May. The box office is open Monday to Saturday, 10am to 7:30pm. Prozellangasse 8. ✆ **01/319-6272.** www.internationaltheater.at. Tickets 20€–25€, 15 € students and seniors. D Tram: Schlickplatz.

Theater in der Josefstadt   One of the most influential theaters in the German-speaking world, this institution reached legendary heights under the aegis of Max

The Austrian Solution

In 1913, George Bernard Shaw was fearful of the reception he would get in London for his new play *Pygmalion*. Instead of risking it, he booked the premiere at Vienna's Burgtheater, in a translated version with the London dialects paralleled with the equally rich Viennese. It took the German-speaking audiences by storm and two weeks later he brought it to Berlin. It was almost a year later he dared open in London. Vienna, and especially the Burgtheater, is known for being receptive to new productions and, who knows, you may just be there when the next big hit is tested on a Viennese audience.

Reinhardt, beginning in 1924. Built in 1776, it presents a variety of comedies and dramas. The current actor/director, Helmut Lohner, is also credited with leading the theater through another era of consistent excellence. The box office is open daily 10am to 7:30pm. Josefstädterstrasse 26. ℂ **01/42700.** www.josefstadt.org. Tickets 3€–65€. U-Bahn: Rathaus. Tram: J. Bus: 13A.

Vienna's English Theatre This popular English-speaking theater was established in 1963. Many international actors and celebrities from Joan Fontaine, Anthony Quinn, and Princess Grace of Monaco, to Siobhan McKenna and Judi Dench have appeared on the neo-baroque boutique stage. The seasons are a mix of comedy and drama, classics and premieres, that in recent years have included Yazmina Reza's *Art*, winner of the Prix Molière, and the Austrian premiere of *Old Wicked Songs*. The box office is open Monday to Friday, 10am to 7:30pm. Josefsgasse 12. ℂ **01/402-1260-0.** www.englishtheatre.at. Tickets 20€–38€. U-Bahn: Rathaus. Tram: J. Bus: 13A.

Volkstheater Built in 1889, this theater presents classical works of European theater. Modern plays and comedies are also presented. The theater's season runs September through May. The box office is open Monday to Saturday 10am to 7:30pm. Neustiftgasse 1. ℂ **01/521-110.** www.volkstheater.at. Tickets 8€–40€. U-Bahn: Volkstheater. Tram: 1, 2, 49, D, or J. Bus: 48A.

THE CLUB & MUSIC SCENE

Although the Viennese are not known to be overly outgoing or demonstrative people, they do their fair share of stepping out after the sun goes down. Unlike many club cultures, you can dance almost everywhere there is music in Vienna, including jazz clubs like **Porgy & Bess.** Besides concerts, bars, and after-work parties, Vienna's nights begin late. While in other cities the evening starts at 8pm, the Viennese won't start the evening until close to 11pm unless they're attending a concert or performance, in which case they'll try for a second wind. On the other hand, clubs and bars stay open longer than in most cities, so as long as you can sleep in you'll be fine.

Night Clubs

Aux Gazelles This place is a multi-tasker. A Turkish spa and restaurant by day, the flair of these rooms literally downstairs from the Maria Hilferstrasse is unequaled. One loud room with a dance floor is balanced by a number of side areas with lots of cushions, with Turkish lamps and alcoves for a more intimate atmosphere, and a long bar area with tables in front. Despite the foreign theme and decor the place has become a staple of Viennese nightlife, perhaps the only place in Vienna where the Turks laid siege and succeeded! Rahlgasse 5. © **01/5856645.** www. auxgazelles.at. Cover varies. U-Bahn: MuseumsQuartier.

Belmar (Havana Club) Many a twitchy behind has been set in motion by the legendary Latinpop at this watering hole. La Vida takes the form of everything from merengue to hip-hop. On select evenings a professional dancer will give salsa lessons in a very laid-back fashion, with caipirinha in hand. The club is located a minute's walk from the Opera House behind the Ringstrassengalerien. Open nightly from 7pm to 4am. Depending on the night, you might be hit with a cover charge. Otherwise, cocktails start at 8.90€. Mahlerstrasse 11. © **01/5132075.** www.clubhavana.at. Cover varies. U-Bahn: Karlsplatz.

Café Leopold No one ever expected that the city's homage to Viennese expressionism (the Leopold Museum) would ever pulsate with the echos of dancing feet and high-energy music. But that's exactly what happens here every night but Sunday. The museum's restaurant fills up with drinkers, wits, gossips, dancers, and people of all ilk on the make. There's a revolving cycle of DJs, each vying for local fame and approval, and a wide selection of cocktails, priced at around 10€ each. The cafe/restaurant section is open Sunday to Wednesday, 10am to 2pm; Friday and Saturday, 10am to 4pm. The disco operates only Thursday to Saturday, 9:30pm until between 2 and 3am, depending on business. In the Leopold Museum, Museumsplatz 1. © **01/523-67-32.** www.cafe-leopold.at. U-Bahn: Volkstheater or Babenbergstrasse/MuseumsQuartier.

Chelsea ★ This is the city's hottest venue for underground music. From all over the continent, the best bands and DJs are imported to entertain the gyrating throngs who gather here in a sort of rock-and-pop atmosphere. The pulsating club lies in one of the arches of the old railway train tracks that divide the north of the city from the historic core. Open Monday to Thursday, 6pm to 4am; Friday and Saturday, 6pm to 5am; and Sunday 4pm to 3am. Lerchenfelder-Gürtel (Stadtbahnbögen 29–31). © **01/407-93-09.** www.chelsea.co.at. Cover 6€–12€. U-Bahn: Josefstädterstrasse/Thaliastrasse.

Klub Kinsky ★ This gem of a location just reopened and is all about quality rather than quantity. The rooms inhabited by this classy establishment are in the Palais Kinsky, between The Graben and Schottentor. The renovation has yielded state-of-the-art technology and Italian designer furniture; in short a private and elegant ambiance with great service. The vibes are great as the bass reverberates through the archways of this baroque palace. In Palais Kinsky, Freyung 4. © **01/5353435.** www.palaisklub.at. Cover varies. U-Bahn: Schottentor.

Passage ★ This club has been a raging success ever since it opened its catacombs to the public in 2003. At the point where The Ring joins Mariahilferstrasse, literally underneath the Ringstrasse, this hot spot has a reputation for having a strict door policy, so no sneakers for gents and snazzy party attire a must for the ladies. The lighting concept is inspired and the layout of the space lets different moods all weld together in one open space, broken up only by lounge sofas and cocktail bars. Just watch your bag. This is a night spot that seems to attract sticky fingers. Open Tuesday to Saturday, 10pm to 6am. Ringstrasse at Babenbergerstrasse. © **01/9618800.** www.sunshine.at. Cover 13€. U-Bahn: MuseumsQuartier.

Rock, Salsa, Jazz, & Blues

Jazzland ★   One of the oldest and probably the most famous jazz club in Austria, noted for the quality of its U.S. and Central European-based performers. It's in a deep 200-year-old cellar below the Ruprechtskirche, unheard on the street. Platters of classic Viennese *beisl* food, such as Wiener schnitzel or spicy *cevapcici* meat patties and roulades of beef cost 5€ to 10€. Open Monday to Saturday 7:30pm to 1:30am. Music is from 9pm to 1am, in three sets. No reservations, so best to arrive by 8pm or before. Franz-Josefs-Kai 29. © **01/533-2575.** www.jazzland.at. Cover 11€–18€. U-Bahn: Schwedenplatz.

Porgy & Bess ★★   Its name may suggest George Gershwin's great all-black classic musical back in the States, but in Vienna this is actually the best jazz club in town. Its array of performers from Europe and around the world is absolutely first class. Established in 1993, the club became an instant hit and has been going strong ever since, patronized by Vienna's most avid jazz aficionados. The club opens Monday to Saturday at 7pm, and Sunday at 8pm; closing times vary, often 3am or 4am. Riembergasse 11. © **01/5128811.** www.porgy.at. U-Bahn: Stubentor. Tram: 1A to Riemerg.

Reigen ★   This Jugendstil-themed venue has been a highlight of the live music scene for 10 years, but is a little out of the way. In Hietzing, almost at Schönbrunn, this downstairs location is a must for jazz lovers. On Session Nights a concert is followed by an open-ended jam session, or on Saturdays you can practise your salsa moves at the Latin Club. Hadikgasse 62. © **01/8940094.** www.reigen.at. U-Bahn: Hietzing.

Szene Wien   Szene is a direct competitor of the also-recommended Tunnel (see below). As such, it attracts some of the same clientele, has some of the same energy, with perhaps a higher percentage of hip hop, reggae, heavy metal, and new wave artists. It's also about twice as large as the Tunnel, which contributes to larger crowds and louder volumes. Szene rocks every day of the week with live concerts, stand-up, or electro. Call ahead or check online for the live music schedule. Hauffgasse 26. © **01/749-1775.** www.szenewien.com. Cover charge 9€–30€. U-Bahn: Enkplatz.

Tunnel   Experiences like the ones created in the 1960s and 1970s by Jimi Hendrix are alive and well, if in less dramatic form, at Tunnel. In a smoke-filled cellar near Town Hall, it showcases musical groups from virtually everywhere. You'll never know quite what to expect, as the only hint of what's on or off is a recorded German-language announcement of what's about to appear and occasional advertisements in local newspapers. It's open daily, 9pm to 2am, with live music beginning around 10pm. Florianigasse 39. © **01/405-3465.** www.tunnel-vienna-live.at. Cover 3€–15€. U-Bahn: Rathaus.

Zwe 📖   This intimate, insider jazz joint is run by the Koberer family and frequented by jazz students and faculty members from the conservatory who jam together on Tuesday nights in open session. The performers are local and there is no cover charge but the musicians pass a hat, and you know what to do. Floßgasse 4 39. © **01/405-3465.** www.zwe.cc. U-Bahn: Schottenring.

Dance Clubs

Camera Club 📖   This joint, celebrating 30 years, is as infamous as New York's Studio 54 when it comes to urban legend. The sound system is very powerful and exudes house, deep house, minimal, electro, techno, and drum'n'bass on multiple levels and in two separate floors. Don't miss the craziest night of the week when

Heaven takes over on Saturdays, letting Vienna's gay crowd rule the dance floor. Neubaugasse 2. *©* **01/523-323063.** www.camera-club.at. Cover 10€. U-Bahn: Neubaugasse.

Flex ★   No other dance club in Vienna has a history as long, as notorious, and as "flexible" as this one. This industrial-looking venue is set between the edge of the canal and the subway tracks. With exterior graffiti that is redone every year mostly by locals, and both an indoor and outdoor chill area, it's a prime venue for post-millennium fans of electronic music. Inside, you'll find a beer-soaked, congenially-battered venue. It's where the young and the restless (some of them teenagers) of Vienna go for access to music that's the rage and the rave in places such as Berlin, London, NYC, and Los Angeles. Open daily 9pm to 2am. Am Donaukanal. *©* **01/533-7525.** Cover 10€. U-Bahn: Schottenring.

Praterdome ♨   At the entrance to the Prater amusement park, this new addition to the club scene is overwhelming. When you arrive you are given a card on which you credit your drink and pay when you leave. On the 8 floors you'll find a techno dance floor with a very impressive light show, alongside house, and soul floors. There is an outdoor chill area in summer and parts of the club are theme-inspired, like the castle corner or ski lodge bar. The club is very impressive, but not worth the teenage bar fights and spilled drinks that seem to be inevitable here. Am Riesenradplatz 7. *©* **01/9081192900.** www.praterdome.at. Cover 10€. U-Bahn: Praterstern.

Pratersauna ★   As the name suggests, this location used to be a fitness club and sauna and although the pool remains the patrons are not there for their health. The self-dubbed "social life and art space" is the new vintage. Many complain about the inconsistent door policy but, all in all, the place is a big hit, especially for the art and fashion crowd. In the Prater. *©* **01/729-1927.** www.pratersauna.tv. Cover 10€–15€. U-Bahn: Messe Prater. Tram: 1 Prater Hauptalle.

Volksgarten Disco   A club since the 1950s, this has stayed abreast of the times, offering everything today from hip hop, to house and break-beat remixes of current hits. There is a great vibe on the dance floor and in the warm months you can step into the garden area behind the DJ where an enormous swirling bar leads you straight to a pool and lounge chairs. Also, the summer-only Volksgarten Pavilion next door is a garden bar and a great place to finish off a hot summer's day (see "Only in Vienna" below). Friday and Saturday are the most popular nights, although the club is open Tuesday to Saturday, 10pm to 5am. Inside the Ring at Volksgarten. *©* **01/5330518.** www.volksgarten.at. Cover charge 5€–15€. U-Bahn: Volkstheater.

U-4 ★   This is one of the most famous nightclubs in Vienna, with a history going back 30 years, and a gift for re-inventing itself with each new generation of night owls. Its name has even surfaced in songs by rockers throughout Europe and the world; the high-profile roster has included Kurt Cobain and David Bowie. Set on the city's western edge, it offers two floors, and three fast-moving bars. There are often live acts on Mondays; Fridays are Addicted to Rock. Tuesday and Thursday nights are the most youth-oriented (that is, the late-teen end of 20-something). A somewhat more mature crowd (emotionally-available20-30-year-olds) is there on Saturday when disco fever takes over for Behave. U-4 is open nightly from 10pm until around 5am, depending on demand, and closed every Sunday between June and September. Schönbrunner Strasse 222. *©* **01/817-1192.** www.U-4.at. Cover charge 8€–11€. U-Bahn: Meidlinger Hauptstrasse.

THE BAR SCENE

Vienna's bar scene clusters at the **Bermuda Triangle,** an area roughly bordered by Judengasse, Seitenstettengasse Rabensteig, and Franz-Josefs-Kai. You'll find everything from intimate watering holes to large bars with live music, a sample of which we list below. The closest U-Bahn stop is Schwedenplatz. But there are others:

Barfly's ★ 🎁 This is the most urbane and sophisticated cocktail bar in town, frequented by journalists, actors, and politicians. It's got a laissez-faire ambience that combines aspects of Vienna's *grande bourgeoisie* with its discreet avant-garde. A menu lists about 370 cocktails that include every kind of mixed drink imaginable. The only food served is "toast" (grilled sandwiches). It's open daily 6pm to between 2 and 4am, depending on the night. In the Hotel Fürst Metternich, Esterházygasse 33. ✆ **01/586-0825.** http://barflys.at. U-Bahn: Zieglergasse or Neubaugasse. Tram: 5.

Bar Italia The fashion and society crowd flocks here after dark to sip on cocktails, wine or beer and look good. The intimate atmosphere of the place is part of what makes it popular as eavesdropping is made easy. Even if you don't speak German, there is plenty to see and stylish snacks are available for small appetites. Mariahilfer-strasse 19-21. ✆ **01/585-2838.** www.baritalia.net. U-Bahn: Museumsquartier. Tram: 5.

First Floor 🎁 At the bottom of the hill leading to the Bermuda Triangle, an unassuming doorway leads you to, you guessed it, the first floor, where dimmed lighting and a fishless aquarium with swaying sea grass sets the back drop for one of the best bars in the city. More than 200 cocktails are served by competent but unobtrusive staff to a mixture of jazz and blues. Great place for a quiet chat or one for the road. Seitenstettengasse 5. ✆ **01/533-7866.** U-Bahn: Schwedenplatz.

Krah Krah This place is the most animated and well-known beer joint in the area. An attractive, and sometimes available, after-work crowd fills this somewhat battered space. There are more than 60 kinds of beer available. Sandwiches, snacks, and simple platters, including hefty portions of Wiener schnitzel, start at 8.50€. It's open daily 11am to 2am, often with live music. Rabensteig 8. ✆ **01/533-8193.** www.krah-krah.at. U-Bahn: Schwedenplatz.

Loos American Bar ★ 🎁 One of the most unusual and interesting bars in Vienna, this very dark, sometimes mysterious bar was designed by the noteworthy architect, Adolf Loos, in 1908. At the time, it was the drinking room of a private men's club. Today, it's more democratic and welcomes a mostly bilingual crowd of hip singles from Vienna's arts-and-media scene; and in these cramped quarters you can't help making new acquaintances. Walls, floors, and ceilings sport layers of dark marble and black onyx, making this one of the most expensive small-scale decors in the city. No food is served, but the mixologist's specials include six kinds of martinis, plus five kinds of Manhattans, each 10€. Beer starts at 2.60€. It's open daily, from noon to 4am. Kärntnerdurchgang 10. ✆ **01/512-3283.** U-Bahn: Stephansplatz.

Onyx Bar One of the most visible and best known, though crowded, bars on Stephansplatz is on the sixth (next-to-uppermost) floor of one of Vienna's most controversial buildings—Haas Haus. Lunch is served from noon to 3pm daily; dinner is from 6pm to midnight. There's a long and varied cocktail menu from 6pm to 2am, including strawberry margaritas and caipirinhas, each priced from 10€ to 15€. Live or recorded music usually begins after 8:30pm. In the Haas Haus, Stephansplatz 12. ✆ **01/53539690.** U-Bahn: Stephansplatz.

Rhiz Bar Modern ★ Hip, multicultural, and electronically sophisticated, this bar is nestled into the vaulted, century-old niches created by the trusses of the U6 subway line, a few blocks west of the Ring. Drinks include Austrian wine, Scotch, and beer from across Europe. It's open Monday to Saturday, 6pm to 4am; and Sunday, 6pm to 2am. Llerchenfeldergürtel 37-38, Stadtbahnbögen. ✆ **01/409-2505.** www.rhiz.org. U-Bahn: Josefstädterstrasse.

Schikaneder If you're young and hot, and you want to meet locals who share those same traits, come here. Through the door past the sofa chairs, the atmosphere is intimate at the 10m (30 ft) bar. There's plenty of conversation, good drinks, and sympathetic company. The bar starts filling up by 9:30pm and by midnight it's packed, often with university students. Don't dare tell anyone in this hip crowd you're a tourist. Open daily, 6pm to 4am. Margaretenstrasse 22-24. ✆ **01/5855888.** www. schikaneder.at. U-Bahn: Margaretengürtel.

Sky Bar ★ Local hipsters ridicule this top-floor place as a posh see-and-be-seen venue for Vienna's socially-striving nouveaux riches. We think the place is well designed and, under the right circumstances, can be a lot of fun, particularly when we remind ourselves that the Steffl building was erected on the site of the (long-ago demolished) house where Mozart died. Sip your drink and take in the sweeping view over the city. Open Monday to Saturday, 6pm to 2am. Kärntnerstrasse 19. ✆ **01/513-1712.** www.skybar.at. U-Bahn: Karlsplatz.

Weinquartier ★★ Anyone who thought drinking wine in Vienna meant accordion players and dirndl-clad servers has a surprise in store. This newly-opened establishment is Vienna's embassy for the *Weinviertel* (Austria's wine region). Subdued lighting, chic waiters and slightly kitschy black-and-whites of the vineyards whose wares you're sampling somehow fit with the location between the Opera and the Albertina. Hanuschgasse 3. ✆ **01/513-43-19.** www.weinquartier.at. U-Bahn: Karlsplatz.

The Wine Bar at Julius Meinl Part of its allure derives from its role as a showcase for the wine-buying savvy of Vienna's most comprehensive delicatessen (Julius Meinl) and wine shop. It's small and set in the cellar of a gourmet food shop, and accessible through a separate entrance that's open long after the delicatessen has closed. The decor evokes the interior of a farmhouse on, say, the Austro–Italian border. You'll be amply satisfied with the dozens of wines listed on the blackboard or on the menu, but if there's a particular bottle you're hankering for in the stacks of wine within the street-level deli, a staff member will sell it to you at shop price and uncork it at a surcharge of only 10%. Open Monday to Saturday, 11am to midnight. Graben 19. ✆ **01/532-3334-6100.** www.meinlamgraben.at. U-Bahn: Stephansplatz.

Gay & Lesbian Bars

In addition to the permanent gay bars, cafes, and restaurants there are also a number of notable gay club events. The most prominent and popular of these is Heaven, every Saturday at **Camera Club** (see above). This is the hottest party in town and many hetero men and women love it because this scene just knows how to party.

Alfi's Goldener Spiegel The most enduring gay restaurant in Vienna (p. 120) is also its most popular gay bar, attracting mostly male clients to its position near Vienna's Naschmarkt. You don't need to come here to dine to enjoy the bar, where almost any gay male from abroad drops in for a look-see. The place is very cruisy, and the bar is open Wednesday to Monday, 7pm to 2am. Linke Wienzeile 46. © **01/586-6608.** U-Bahn: Kettenbruckengasse.

Café Berg ★   This stylish establishment is known for hosting wild events, such as fashion shows and before- and after-parties surrounding the annual Life Ball AIDS gala. For 18 years it's been a staple of gay, lesbian, and transgender life in Vienna. Most notably they serve a great breakfast. Berggasse 8. © **01/3195720.** www.café-berg.at. U-Bahn: Kettenbruckengasse.

Café Savoy   Soaring frescoed ceilings and a smoke-stained beaux-arts decor make this cruisy cafe/bar an appealing setting. The clientele are mostly men and the mood is always jovial, no loud music just a pleasant atmosphere and echoes of laughter and conversation. Open Monday to Friday, 5pm to 2am; Saturday, 9am to 2am. Linke Wienzeile 36. © **01/586-7348.** U-Bahn: Kettenbruckengasse.

Eagle Bar   This is one of the premier leather and denim bars for gay men in Vienna. There's no dancing, and the bar even offers a back room where free condoms are distributed. It's open daily, 9pm to 4am. Blümelgasse 1. © **01/587-26-61.** www.eagle-vienna.com. U-Bahn: Neubaugasse.

Felixx ★   It's the classiest gay bar and cafe in town, thanks to a refurbishment. The decor emphasizes turn-of-the-20th-century cove moldings, a crystal chandelier that could proudly grace any Opera Ball, and a huge late-1800s portrait of the female cabaret entertainer, Mela Mars, who introduced *lieder* (Austrian *chansons*) for the first time to a generation of wine and coffee-drinkers. Ironically, the venue is less kitschy than you'd think, managing to pull off a lasting impression of elegance and good taste. On Saturday and Sunday breakfast is served here from 10am to 4pm. Open daily, 7pm to 3am. Gumpendorferstrasse 5. © **01/920-4714.** U-Bahn: Babenbergerstrasse or MuseumsQuartier.

Frauencafé   Frauencafé is exactly what its name implies: a politically conscious cafe for women, lesbian or otherwise, who appreciate the company of other women. Established in 1977 in a century-old building, it's filled with magazines, newspapers, modern paintings, and a clientele of Austrian and international women. Next door is a feminist bookstore loosely affiliated with the cafe. Frauencafé is open Tuesday to Saturday, 6:30pm to 2am. Glasses of wine begin at 2.50€. Langegasse 11. © **01/4063754.** U-Bahn: Lerchenfelderstrasse.

THE HEURIGER

These *Heuriger,* or wine taverns, on the outskirts of Vienna have long been celebrated in operetta, film, and song. Grinzing and Nussdorf are probably the most-visited but there are many other *Heuriger*-rich areas include Sievering, Neustift am Walde, Stammersdorf, and Heiligenstadt.

Grinzing lies at the edge of the Vienna Woods, a short distance northwest of the center. Much of Grinzing looks the way it did when Beethoven lived nearby. It's a district of crooked old streets and houses, with thick walls surrounding inner court-yards where grape arbors shelter wine-drinkers. The sound of zithers and accordions lasts long into the summer night. Take public transport, as police patrols are very strict, and it is illegal to drive with more than 0.8% alcohol in your blood. Most *Heuriger* are within 30 to 40 minutes of downtown, an easy tram ride away. So start at Schottentor, and take tram no. 38 to Grinzing, no. 41 to Neustift, or no. 38 to Sievering (which is also accessible by bus no. 39A). Heiligenstadt is the last stop on U-Bahn line U4.

Der Rudolfshof ★   One of the most appealing wine restaurants in Grinzing dates back to 1848, when it was little more than a shack within a garden. Its real fame came around the turn of the 20th century, when it was adopted by the Crown Prince Rudolf. A verdant garden, scattered with tables, is frequented by Viennese apartment dwellers on warm summer evenings. Come here for pitchers of the fruity white wine Grüner Veltliner and light red Roter Bok. A glass of wine costs 3€ to 5€. The menu features schnitzels, roasts, and soups, but the house special is shish kabob. Main courses cost 10€ to 13€. Open daily, 3 to 11pm. Cobenzlgasse 8, Grinzing. ✆ **01/32021-08.** www.rudolfshof.at.

Heurige Mayer ★   This historic house was some 130 years old back in 1817 when Beethoven composed sections of his *Ninth Symphony* while living here. The same kind of fruity dry wine is still sold to guests in the shady courtyard of the rose garden. The menu includes grilled chicken, pork, and a buffet of well-prepared country food. Reservations are suggested. It's open Sunday to Friday, 4pm to midnight. Closed Saturday. There's live music every Sunday and Friday, 7pm to midnight. Wine sells for 1.40€ a glass, with meals beginning at 13€. It's closed December 21 to January 15. Am Pfarrplatz 2, Heiligenstadt. ✆ **01/3703361,** or 01/370-1287 after 4pm.

Reinprecht   This staple of the *heurigen* scene in Grinzing is a fun choice. Not only does the 300-year-old former monastery have its ancient charm, but this place has live *schrammel* music (folk) every day. Besides the new wines that are the staples of every such establishment there is also a sparkling wine that is worth a toast. The place is utterly appealing, and has a small garden. Cobenzlgasse 22, Grinzing. ✆ **01/320-6345.**

Sirbu   Some of the *heuriger* in Grinzing can be overly touristy, but some hide the most beautiful gardens and the best wine. *Heuriger* Sirbu is one such. The drive up the Nussberg, with vineyards on either side, is sensational. Inside, the decor is simple but warm and the kitchen offers real treats in the salad and cheese departments. The only catch is that it's a bit of a hike to get there. Take the bus no. 38A to the last station (Kahlenberg) and then it's a 15 minute walk downhill. Kahlenbergstrasse 210, Nussdorf. ✆ **01/3205928.**

Weingut Wolff   Although aficionados claim that the best *heuriger* are "deep in the countryside" of lower Austria, this one comes closest to offering an authentic experience, just 20 minutes from the 1st District of Vienna. In summer, you're welcomed into a flower-decked garden set against a backdrop of ancient vineyards. You can fill up your platter with some of the best wursts and roast meats (especially the delectable pork), along with freshly made salads. Save room for one of the velvety-smooth Austrian cakes. Find a table under a cluster of grapes and sample the fruity young wines, especially the Chardonnay, Sylvaner, or Grüner Veltliner. The tavern is open daily 11am to 1am, with main courses ranging from 8€ to 15€. Rathstrasse 50, Neustift. ✆ **01/440-3727.** www.wienerheuriger.at.

MORE ENTERTAINMENT

A Casino

Casino Wien   You'll need to show your passport to get into this casino, opened in 1968. There are gaming tables for French and American roulette, blackjack, and

The Third Man Lives

At **Burg Kino,** Opernring 19 (☎ 01/587-8406; www.burgkino.at), they still feature English-language presentations of *The Third Man,* with the names of the stars, Joseph Cotten and Orson Welles, in lights. When it was first released, the postwar Viennese were horrified at the depiction of their city as a "rat-infested rubble heap." Over decades they have come to love the film, which this cinema shows twice a week. Many young Viennese, as well as visitors from abroad, flock to screenings (in English) on Friday at 10:45pm, Sunday at 3:30pm, and Tuesday 4:15pm. Tickets cost 6€ to 8€. U-Bahn: Karlsplatz.

chemin de fer, as well as the ever-present slot machines. The casino is open daily, 11am to 3am. Esterházy Palace, Kärntnerstrasse 41. ☎ **01/512-4836.** www.casinos.at.

Film

Artis International   Besides the Burg Kino, this is the other English-language cinema in the 1st District. The place is frequented by the international community and Austrian cinema buffs who want to avoid the dubbed versions. It is quite small, but shows both blockbusters and independent films and is 3-D digital equipped. Schultergasse 5. ☎ **01/533-7054.** www.cineplexx.at. For movie listings: www.film.at/artis_international/. U-Bahn: Karlsplatz.

Filmmuseum   This cinema shows films in their original languages and presents retrospectives of directors from Fritz Lang to Richard Linklater. The museum presents avant-garde, experimental, and classic films. A monthly list is available free inside the Albertina, and a copy is posted outside. The film library inside the government-funded museum includes more than 11,000 book titles, and the still collection numbers more than 100,000. Admission costs 9.50€ for non-members. Membership for 24 hours costs 5.50€. In the Albertina, Augustinerstrasse 1. ☎ **01/533-7054.** www.filmmuseum.at. U-Bahn: Karlsplatz.

ONLY IN VIENNA

If the above nightspots aren't *Wien* enough for you, take a look at these establishments to get a truly Viennese experience.

Café Alt Wien   Set on one of the oldest, narrowest streets of medieval Vienna, a short walk north of the cathedral, this is the kind of smoky, mysterious, and shadowy cafe that evokes subversive plots, doomed romances, and revolutionary movements being hatched and plotted. During the day it's a busy workaday restaurant used by virtually everybody. But as the night progresses you're likely to rub elbows with denizens of late-night Wien who get more sentimental and schmaltzy with each beer. Foaming mugs sell for 3€ each and can be accompanied by heaped platters of goulash and schnitzel. Main courses range from 6€ to 10€. It's open daily, 10am to 2am. Bäckerstrasse 9 (1). ☎ **01/512-5222.** U-Bahn: Stephansplatz.

Pavillion   Even the Viennese stumble when trying to describe this civic monument from the Sputnik-era of the 1950s. Only open in warm weather, during the day it's a cafe with a multi-generational clientele and a sweeping garden overlooking the Heldenplatz (forecourt to the Hofburg). Come here to peruse the newspapers, chat with locals, and drink coffee, wine, beer, or schnapps. The place grows much more animated after the music (funk, soul, blues, and jazz) begins around 8pm. Platters of Viennese food are priced from 6.50€ to 12€. It's open daily, 9am to 2am, between April and October. Burgring 2. ✆ **01/532-0907.** U-Bahn: Volkstheater.

Phil 🎁   Whether it's a cafe where you can shop, or a shop where you can order coffee and snacks, is unimportant. At Phil you can take old and new books as well as the furniture home with you. Readings and live performances complete the repertoire of this unique address. Except of course, for the conversation. Arrive early for performances, before all the chairs are filled. Gumpdendorferstrasse 10-12. ✆ **01/581-0489.** www.phil.info. U-Bahn: MuseumsQuartier.

Schnitzelwirt Schmidt   The waitresses wear dirndls, the portions are huge, and the cuisine—only pork and some chicken—celebrates the culinary folklore of Central Europe. The setting is rustic, a kind of tongue-in-cheek bucolic homage to the Old Vienna Woods, and schnitzels are almost guaranteed to hang over the sides of the plates. Regardless of what you order, it will be accompanied by fries (*pommes*), salad, and copious quantities of beer and wine. Go for the good value, unmistakably Viennese ambience, and great people-watching. Main courses cost 6€ to 10€. It's open Monday to Saturday, 11am to 10pm. Neubaugasse 52 (7). ✆ **01/523-3771.** U-Bahn: Neubaugasse. Tram: 49.

Schweizerhaus ★   References to this old-fashioned eating house are about as old as the Prater itself. Awash with beer and central European kitsch, it sprawls across a *biergarten* landscape. Indulgence is indeed the word—the huge main dishes could feed a 19th-century army. The menu stresses old-fashioned schnitzels and its house special, roasted pork hocks (*hintere Schweinsstelze*) served with dollops of mustard and horseradish. Wash it all down with mugs of Czech Budweiser. A half-liter of beer costs 3.70€; main courses range from 5€ to 12€. It's open from March 15 to October 31, daily, 11am to 11pm. In the Prater, Strasse des Ersten Mai 116. ✆ **01/728-01-52.** U-Bahn: Praterstern.

Wiener Stamperl (The Viennese Dram)   Named after the unit of drink otherwise known as a shot, this is about as beer-soaked and as rowdy a night time venue as one can recommend. It occupies a battered room decorated with wood panels and reeking of spilled beer. At the horseshoe-shaped bar, order foaming steins of Ottakinger beer, new wine from nearby vineyards served from an old-fashioned barrel. Make sure you take a look at the legendary urinal, a bit of a cult. The menu starts with coarse bread, slathered with various meats and cheeses. It's open Monday to Thursday, 11am to 2am; and Friday and Saturday, 11pm to 4am. Sterngasse 1. ✆ **01/533-6230.** U-Bahn: Schwedenplatz.

SIDE TRIPS FROM VIENNA

Exciting day trips are on Vienna's doorstep in almost any direction. Among the best: the Vienna Woods; the villages along the Danube, particularly the vineyards of the Wachau; and the small province of Burgenland, between Vienna and the Hungarian border.

Lower Austria (Niederösterreich), known as the cradle of Austria's history, is the largest of the nine federal states that make up the country. The province is bordered on the north by the Czech Republic, on the east by Slovakia, on the south by the provinces of Styria and Burgenland, and on the west by Upper Austria.

This historic area was once heavily fortified, as some 550 castles and battlements (often in ruins) testify. The medieval Künringer and Babenburger families had their hereditary estates here. Vineyards cover the province, among historic monasteries, churches, and abbeys. In summer it booms with music festivals and both classical and contemporary stage productions.

Lower Austria consists of four regions, or quarters (Viertel). From the **Industrieviertel,** which borders much of southern Vienna, moving clockwise you hit the **Mostviertel,** the **Waldviertel,** and the **Weinviertel,** which borders Vienna's northeastern corner. Together the Wine and Woods quarters contain thousands of miles of marked hiking paths and plenty of mellow old wine cellars. The Wienerwald, or **Vienna Woods** (see "Tales of the Vienna Woods" box, in Chapter 7), spreads across borders between the Most and Industrie quarters and is a great place for anything from walking to biking to feasting.

The **foothills of the Alps** begin about 48km (30 miles) west of Vienna and extend to the borders of Styria and Upper Austria. This area has some 50 open-air swimming pools and nine chairlifts to the higher peaks, such as Ötscher and Hochkar (both around 2,100m/6,890 ft.).

Lower Austria, from the rolling hillsides of the Wienerwald to the terraces of the Wachau, produces some 60% of Austria's grape harvest. Many visitors like to take a **wine route** through the province, stopping at taverns to sample the vintages from Krems, Klosterneuburg, Dürnstein, Langenlois, Retz, Gumpoldskirchen, Poysdorf, and other nearby towns.

Lower Austria is also home to more than a dozen **spa** resorts, such as Baden and Oberlaa, two of the most popular. These resorts are family-friendly, and most hotels accommodate children up to 6 years old free;

those between the ages of 7 and 12 generally stay for half price. Many towns and villages have attractions designed just for kids.

A side trip to Lower Austria can ease your budget, as prices there are about 30% lower than those in Vienna. And finding a hotel in these small towns isn't usually a problem; they're signposted at the approaches to the resorts and villages, and if one is full, they'll send you to a friend down the road. You might not always find a room with a private bathroom; but unless otherwise noted, all recommended hotels have them. Parking is also easier and, unless otherwise noted, free. Don't worry that some hotels have only a postal code as an address. If you're contacting them by post, this will be enough.

Burgenland, the easternmost province of Austria, is a stark contrast to Lower Austria. It's a border region, formed in 1921 from German-speaking areas of what was once Hungary. Burgenland voted to join Austria in the aftermath of World War I. When the vote was taken in 1919 its capital, Ödenburg, now called Sopron, chose to remain with Hungary. It lies west of Lake Neusiedl (Neusiedlersee), a popular haven for the Viennese.

The province marks the beginning of a flat steppe (*Puszta*) that reaches from Vienna almost to Budapest. It shares a western border with Styria and Lower Austria, and the long eastern boundary separates Burgenland from Hungary. Called "the vegetable garden of Vienna," Burgenland is mostly an agricultural province producing, among other things, more than one-third of all the wine made in Austria. Its climate translates into hot summers with little rainfall and moderate winters. You can usually enjoy sunny days from early spring until late autumn.

The capital of Burgenland is **Eisenstadt,** the small provincial city that was for many years the home of Joseph Haydn where he was kapellmeister for the Esterházy family, and where he is buried. Each summer there's a festival in Mörbisch, using **Lake Neusiedl** as a theatrical backdrop. It's the only steppe lake in Central Europe. If you're visiting in summer, you'll most certainly want to explore it by motorboat or sail boat. Lots of Viennese flock to Burgenland on weekends for sailing, birding, and other outdoor activities.

Hotels in the province are extremely limited, but they're among the least expensive in the country. The area is relatively unknown to non-Austrians, which means fewer tourists. Like Lower Austria, Burgenland contains many fortresses and castles, often in ruins; but you'll find a few castle hotels. The touring season in Burgenland lasts from April to October.

THE WIENERWALD (VIENNA WOODS) ★

The Vienna Woods, featured in operetta, literature, and the famous Strauss waltz, stretch south from Vienna's city limits to the foothills of the Alps. For an introduction, see Chapter 7, "Exploring Vienna."

You can hike through the woods along marked paths or drive through, stopping at country towns to sample the wine and the local cuisine, which is usually hearty and reasonably priced. The Viennese and a horde of foreign visitors, principally German, usually descend on the wine taverns and cellars here on weekends. So if you can, plan your summer visit on a weekday. The best time of year to go is in September and October, when the grapes are harvested from the terraced hills.

Lower Austria, Burgenland, & the Danube Valley

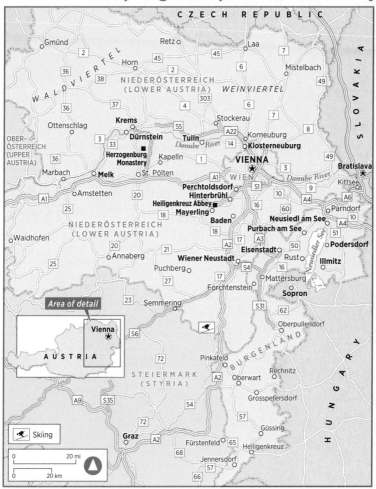

TIPS ON EXPLORING

You can get around the Vienna Woods by car or by public transportation. We recommend renting a car if you are pressed for time so you can still stop and explore some of the villages and vineyards along the way. Public transportation will get you around, but it will take longer, although a train can also be part of the adventure. Either way, you can easily reach all of the destinations below within a day's trip from Vienna. If you have more time, spend the night in one or more of the lovely Austrian towns along the way.

VISITOR INFORMATION   Before you go, visit the tourist office for **Klosterneuburg** at Niedermarkt 4, A-3400 (© **02243/32038;** www.klosterneuburg.com).

It's the best source of information for outings to the Vienna Woods, open daily 10am to 7pm.

TOURS **Vienna Sightseeing Tours,** Weyringergasse 28A-30, Entrance at Goldeggasse 29, A-1040 (© **01/712-4683-0;** fax 01/714-11-41; www.viennasight seeingtours.com), runs a popular 4-hour tour called Vienna Woods–Mayerling. It goes through the Vienna Woods, past Burg Liechtenstein and the old Roman city of Baden. There's an excursion to Mayerling. You'll pay a short visit to the Cistercian abbey of Heiligenkreuz and take a boat ride on Seegrotte, the largest subterranean lake in Europe. The office is open daily for regular tours April to October 6:30am to 7:30pm, and November to March daily 6:30am to 5pm. It costs 44€ for adults and 15€ for children, including admission fees and a guide.

Klosterneuburg

On the northwestern outskirts of Vienna, Klosterneuburg is an old market town in the major wine-producing heart of Austria. The Babenburgs established the town on the eastern foothills of the Vienna Woods, making it an ideal spot to stay if you want to enjoy the countryside and Vienna, 11km (7 miles) southeast. Austrians gather in Klosterneuburg annually on November 15 to celebrate St. Leopold's Day with music, banquets, and a parade.

ESSENTIALS

GETTING THERE By **car** from Vienna, take Route 14 northwest, following the south bank of the Danube (Donaustrasse/Brigittenauer Lände) and take the exit for Klosterneuburg. If you opt for public transportation, take the **U-Bahn** (U4, U6) to Heiligenstadt, and catch **bus** no. 239 or 341 to Klosterneuburg. By **train,** catch the Schnellbahn (S-Train) from Franz-Josef Bahnhof to Klosterneuburg-Kierling.

VISITOR INFORMATION Contact the Klosterneuburg **tourist information office** at Niedermarkt 4, A-3400 (© **02243/32038;** fax 02243/32038; www. klosterneuburg.com). It's open daily 10am to 7pm.

VISITING THE ABBEY

Klosterneuburg Abbey (Stift Klosterneuburg) ★ , Stiftsplatz 1 (© **02243/4110**; www.stift-klosterneuburg.at), is one of the most significant abbeys in Austria. It was founded in 1114 by the Babenberg margrave Leopold III and was once the residence of the famous Hapsburg emperor Charles VI.

The abbey is visited not only for its history, but also for its art treasures. The most valuable piece is the world-famous altar of Nikolaus of Verdun, created in 1181. The monastery also boasts the largest private library in Austria, with more than 1,250 handwritten books and many antique paintings. Guided tours of the monastery are given daily year-round. On the tour, you visit the Cathedral of the Monastery (unless Masses are underway), the cloister, St. Leopold's Chapel (with the Verdun altar), the former well house, and the residential apartments of the emperors.

The monastery itself remains open year-round, but the museum of the monastery is closed from mid-November to April. The museum can be visited without a guide from May to mid-November, Tuesday to Sunday, 10am to 5pm. Visits to the monastery itself, however, require a guided tour. These are available at hourly intervals year-round daily from 9am to noon and 1:30 to 4:30pm. Except for a specially designated English-language tour conducted every Sunday at 2pm most tours are conducted in German, with occasional snippets of English if the guide is able. The price is 8€ for adults and 5€ for children. Additional English-language tours can be arranged in advance. You can get a cost-effective combination monastery/museum ticket for 12€ for adults and 7€ for children 6 to 14.

WHERE TO STAY & DINE

Hotel Schrannenhof This building dates from the Middle Ages, but has modern comforts. There are guest rooms with large living and sleeping rooms and small kitchens, as well as quiet and comfortable double rooms with showers. The hotel's cafe-restaurant serves international and Austrian dishes. The hotel also runs the Pension Alte Mühle (see below).

Niedermarkt 17–19, A-3400 Klosterneuburg. © **02243/32072.** Fax 02243/320-7213. www.schrannenhof. at. 14 units. 92€–108€ double; 128€ suite. Rates include buffet breakfast. AE, DC, MC. Free parking. **Amenities:** Breakfast room; lounge. *In room:* A/C (in some), TV, kitchenette (in some), minibar, hair dryer, free Wi-Fi.

Park Inn Klosterneuburg This brand new hotel is only a 5-minute drive from the center of Klosterneuburg. It's also right next to the large and well-equipped Donaupark campsite, which is popular with cyclists and a good place to meet fellow explorers. The hotel is a cross between an office building and a minimalist modern art museum. The rooms are spacious and echo the functionality and decoration of early Bauhaus.

In der Au 6, A-3400 Klosterneuburg. © **02243/229220.** Fax 02243/22922390. www.parkinn.de/ hotel-klosterneuburg. 130 units. 79€–89€ double. Buffet breakfast 12€ extra. AE, DC, MC, V. Free parking. Closed Dec 15–Jan 15. **Amenities:** Restaurant; bar; 24-hour front desk; garden; kitchenette (in suites); room-service. *In room:* A/C, TV, free Wi-Fi.

Pension Alte Mühle A gracious and hospitable bed-and-breakfast which offers a bountiful morning buffet, while the restaurant-cafe, Veit, is a several-minute stroll away. Bedrooms are furnished in a traditional style. Quaint and comfortable.

Mühlengasse 36, A-3400 Klosterneuburg. © **02243/37788.** Fax 02243/377-8822. www.hotel-altemuehle.at. 13 units. 80€ double. Rates include breakfast. AE, DC, MC. Free parking. **Amenities:** Breakfast room; laundry service. *In room:* TV, minibar, hair dryer, free Wi-Fi.

Perchtoldsdorf: A Stop on the Wine Tour

This old market town with brightly-painted buildings, referred to locally as Petersdorf, is one of the most-visited spots in Lower Austria for Viennese wine tours. You'll find many *Heuriger* here, where you can sample local wines and enjoy good, hearty cuisine. Perchtoldsdorf is not as well known as Grinzing, which is actually within the city limits of Vienna, but many therefore find it less touristy. It has a Gothic church, and part of its tower dates from the early 16th century. A vintners' festival, held annually in early November, attracts many Viennese for the county fair atmosphere of music and dancing, crafts and other festivities. Local growers make a "goat" from grapes for this occasion.

GETTING THERE Perchtoldsdorf lies 18km (11 miles) from the middle of Vienna (it's actually at the southwestern city limits) and 14km (8¾ miles) north of Baden. From Vienna's Westbahnhof, you can take the S-Bahn to Liesing. From here, Perchtoldsdorf is just a short taxi ride away (there are cabs at the train station).

VISITOR INFORMATION The **tourist information office,** in the middle of Perchtoldsdorf (𝄢 **01/536100;** www.noe.co.at), is open Monday to Friday, 8:30am to 4pm.

WHERE TO DINE

Restaurant Jahreszeiten ★ AUSTRIAN/FRENCH/INTERNATIONAL In what was a private villa in the 1800s, this restaurant, the best in town, provides a haven for those looking for a romantic night with flickering candles. Enjoy well-crafted dishes, such as poached salmon with herbs and truffled noodles, Chinese-style prawns in an Asiatic sauce prepared by the kitchen's Japanese cooks, and filet of turbot with morels and asparagus-studded risotto. Try a soufflé for dessert. A tremendous effort is made to secure the freshest produce. Service is polite, attentive, and discreet.

Hochstrasse 17. 𝄢 **01/8656080.** Reservations recommended. Main courses 14€–20€. Set menus 30€. AE, DC, MC, V. Daily 11:30am–11pm. Closed 3 weeks in Aug.

Hinterbrühl

You'll find both good places to stay and food in this hamlet, a cluster of rustic homes, frequented by Viennese who like to escape the city for a long weekend. Franz Schubert retreated here in the summer of 1826 and produced the exquisite tune *Der Linden-baum,* to words by Wilhelm Mueller for the cycle *Der Winterreise,* (The Voyage in Winter). This tiny area is also home to Europe's largest subterranean lake (see below).

GETTING THERE The village is 26km (16 miles) south of Vienna and 3km (2 miles) south of Mödling, the nearest large town. To reach Hinterbrühl from Vienna, take the S-Bahn from the Südbahnhof to Mödling (trip time: 15 min.) and then catch a connecting bus to Hinterbrühl, the last stop (12 min.). By car, drive south-west along the A-21, exiting at the signs to Gisshubel. From there, follow the signs to Hinterbrühl and Mödling.

VISITOR INFORMATION The **tourist information office** in Kaiserin-Elisa-beth 2, Mödling (𝄢 **02236/26727**), is open Monday to Friday 9am to 5pm.

AN UNDERGROUND LAKE

Seegrotte Hinterbrühl Some of the village of Hinterbrühl was built directly above the stalactite-covered waters of Europe's largest underground lake. From the entrance a few hundred yards from the edge of town, you'll descend a steep flight of stairs before facing the extensively illuminated waters of a shallow, very still, and very cold underground lake. The famous natural marvel was the site of the construction of the world's first jet plane and other aircraft during World War II. Expect a running commentary in German and broken English during the 20-minute boat ride.

Grutschgasse 2A, Hinterbrühl. 𝄢 **02235/26364.** Admission and boat ride 9€ adult, 6€ children under 14 and students. Apr–Oct daily 9am–5pm; Nov–Mar Mon–Fri 9am–noon and 1–3pm, Sat–Sun 9am–3:30pm.

WHERE TO STAY

Hotel Beethoven This hotel in the heart of the hamlet boasts one of the village's oldest buildings, a private house built around 1785. In 1992, the hotel renovated most of the interior and built a new wing. It has been renovated since. The average-size bedrooms are traditional, with good beds and adequate bathrooms. There's no formal restaurant, but there is an all-day cafe where coffee, drinks, pastries, ice cream, salads, and platters of regional food are served daily.

Beethovengasse 8, A-2371 Hinterbrühl. ℂ **02236/26252.** Fax 02236/277017. www.hotel-beethoven.at. 25 rooms. 78€–98€ double. Rates include buffet breakfast. AE, DC, MC, V. Free parking. **Amenities:** Cafe; bar. *In room:* TV, minibar, hair dryer, free Wi-Fi.

WHERE TO DINE

Restaurant Hexensitz ★ AUSTRIAN/INTERNATIONAL   Featuring impeccable service, this restaurant celebrates the subtleties of Austrian country cooking. Its grand setting is a century-old building whose trio of dining rooms is outfitted in the Lower Austrian style with wood panels and country antiques. In summer, the restaurant expands into a well-kept garden. It offers dishes that change daily, such as Styrian venison with kohlrabi, wine sauce, and homemade noodles; medallions of pork with spinach and herbs; and sea bass with forest mushrooms. The traditional desserts are luscious.

Johannesstrasse 35. ℂ **02236/22937.** www.hexensitz.at. Reservations recommended. Main courses 12€–22€; fixed-price lunch 25€ available on Sun; fixed-price dinner 40€. MC, V. Tues 6–10pm; Wed–Sat 11:30am–2pm and 6–10pm; Sun 11:30am–2pm.

Mayerling

This beautiful spot, 29km (18 miles) west of Vienna in the heart of the Wienerwald, is best known for the unresolved deaths of Archduke Rudolf, son of Emperor Franz Joseph, and his young lover Marie Vetsera in 1889. The event, which took place in a hunting lodge (now a Carmelite convent), altered the line of Austro-Hungarian succession. The heir apparent became Franz Joseph's nephew, Archduke Ferdinand, whose murder in Sarajevo sparked World War I. Mayerling, incidentally, is only a small hamlet, not even a village.

ESSENTIALS

GETTING THERE   By **car,** head southwest on A-21 to Alland and take exit 17 to Mayerling. At the roundabout take the Mödlinger-Bundesstrasse/B11 exit. Turn right towards Mayerling. Or take **bus** no. 1123, 1124, or 1127, marked ALLAND, from Wien Meidling (trip time: 75 min.). From Baden, hop on bus no. 1140 or 1141.

VISITOR INFORMATION   Pop into the **Rathaus,** in nearby Heiligenkreuz (ℂ **02258/8720**; www.heiligenkreuz.at). It's open Monday to Friday 8am to noon and 2 to 5pm.

SEEING THE SIGHTS

Abbey Heiligenkreuz (Abbey of the Holy Cross)   This sprawling 12th-century Abbey is a spiritual place, with more relics of the Holy Cross than anywhere but Rome. The 50 Cistercian monks make a highly reputable wine and sing God's praises each day at Matins and Evensong in the haunting resonance of Gregorian Chant.

And thus the Abbot Gregor Henckel Donnersmark invited his nephew, Florian, to the Abbey to work on his next film script. Hearing the chant, Florian suggested the monks audition for film. They submitted a video over YouTube and, overnight, had signed a contract with Universal Music. Suddenly, they were at the top of the UK classical charts. And Florian? His script became *Das Leben der Anderen,* winning a 2006 Oscar for Best Foreign Film.

Today, things have settled down in Heiligenkreuz, but the monks still make great wine. And the music? Well, it's among the best we have on earth. In summer at noon and 6pm daily, visitors can attend the solemn choir prayers.

TWILIGHT OF the HABSBURGS

On January 30, 1889, a hunting lodge in Mayerling was the setting of a grim tragedy that altered the line of succession of the Austro-Hungarian Empire and shocked the world. On a snowy night, Archduke Rudolf, the only son of Emperor Franz Joseph and Empress Elisabeth, and his 18-year-old mistress, Maria Vetsera, were found dead. It was announced that they had shot themselves, although no weapon ever surfaced for examination. All doors and windows to the room had been locked when the bodies were discovered. All evidence that might have shed light on the deaths was subsequently destroyed. Had it been a double suicide or an assassination?

Rudolf, a passionate intellectual, chafed under the suffocating indifference of his father while also trapped in an unhappy marriage. Neither the Emperor nor Pope Leo XIII would allow an annulment. He had fallen in love with Maria at a German embassy ball when she was only 17. Her public snubbing of the Prince's wife, the Archduchess Stephanie of Belgium, led to a heated argument between Rudolf and his

father. Because of Rudolf's liberal leanings and, like his mother, a sympathy for Hungarian nationalist aspirations, he was not trusted by some of his father's court, which gave rise to lurid speculation about a cleverly-designed plot.

Supporters of the assassination theory included Empress Zita von Habsburg, the last Habsburg heir, who in 1982 told the Vienna daily, the *Kronen Zeitung,* that she believed their deaths were the culmination of a conspiracy against the family. Whatever their differences, Franz Joseph was grief-stricken at the loss of his only son, and ordered the hunting lodge torn down and an unspectacular Carmelite nunnery built on the site.

Maria Vetsera was buried in a village cemetery in Heiligenkreuz. The inscription over her tomb reads, *Wie eine Blume sprosst der mensch auf und wird gebrochen.* (Human beings, like flowers, bloom and are crushed.) In a curious incident in 1988, her coffin was exhumed and stolen by a Linz executive, who was distraught at the death of his wife and obsessed with the Mayerling affair. It took police 4 years to recover the coffin.

Heiligenkreuz. ☎ **02258/8703.** Admission 7€ adults, 3.50€ children. Daily 9am–noon and 1:30–5pm (until 4pm Nov–Feb). Tours Mon–Sat 10 and 11am plus 2, 3, 4pm (also at 5pm with groups of 6 or more, reservation required). From Mayerling, take Heiligenkreuzstrasse 4.8km (3 miles) to Heiligenkreuz.

Jagdschloss A Carmelite abbey, Karmeliterkloster Mayerling, stands on the site of the infamous hunting lodge where Archduke Rudolf and his mistress supposedly committed suicide (see "Twilight of the Habsburgs," below). If it hadn't been torn down, the hunting lodge would be a much more fascinating, if macabre, attraction. Although nothing remains of the lodge, history buffs enjoy visiting the abbey.

Mayerling. ☎ **02258/2275.** Admission 3€ adults, 1.50€ children under 14. Mon–Sat 9am–6pm (5pm Oct–Mar); Sun 10am–6pm (5pm Oct–Mar).

WHERE TO STAY & DINE
Hotel Hanner The best hotel in town; it is conservative but with a very modern format. Bedrooms are streamlined and comfortable, with varying decor. Guests appreciate the quiet, and the proximity to the region's natural beauty.

Mayerling 1, A-2534 Mayerling. ☏ **02258/2378.** www.hanner.cc. Fax 02258/237841. 27 rooms. 142€–208€ double. Rates include breakfast. AE, DC, MC, V. Free parking. **Amenities:** Restaurant; bar; fitness center; sauna; room service. *In room:* TV, minibar, hair dryer.

Restaurant Hanner AUSTRIAN   Dignified and conservatively modern, this is the best restaurant in a town not noted for lots of competition. Large windows have a panoramic view of the surrounding forests, and dishes change with the seasons and the whim of the chef. Examples include fresh fish, goulash soup, chicken breast with paprika noodles, and filets of venison in port-wine sauce.

In the Hotel Hanner, Mayerling 1. ☏ **02258/2378.** Reservations not necessary. Main courses 15€–40€, 5-course tasting menu 98€; 7-course tasting menu 118€. AE, DC, MC, V. Daily noon–2pm and 6–10pm.

THE SPA TOWN OF BADEN BEI WIEN ★

Baden was once known as "the dowager empress of health spas in Europe." Tsar Peter the Great of Russia ushered in the town's golden age by establishing a spa here at the beginning of the 18th century. The Soviet army used the resort city as its headquarters from the end of World War II to the end of the Allied occupation of Austria in 1955.

The Romans began to visit what they called Aquae in A.D. 100. It had 15 thermal springs whose temperatures reached 95°F (35°C). You can still see the Römerquelle (Roman Springs) in the Kurpark, which is the heart of Baden today.

This lively casino town and spa in the eastern sector of the Vienna Woods was at its most fashionable in the early 18th century, but it continued to lure royalty, musicians, and intellectuals for much of the 19th century. For years the resort was the summer retreat of the Habsburg court. In 1803, when he was still Francis II of the Holy Roman Empire, the emperor began summer visits to Baden. It was a tradition he continued as Francis I of Austria after the Holy Roman Empire ended in 1806.

During the Biedermeier era (mid-late 1800s), Baden became known for its ochre buildings, a deeper, more coral shade than the Schönbrunner yellow of the baroque, which still contribute to the spa city's charm. The **Kurpark** is handsomely laid out and beautifully maintained.

Emperor Karl made this town the Austrian army headquarters in World War I, but still a certain lightheartedness persisted. It was the presence of the Russians during the post-World War II years that brought the resort's fortunes to their lowest ebb. It was here that Wilhelm von Habsburg became a spy during the inter-war years for the British and French. If things had turned out differently he might have become King of Ukraine, but he was hauled off into custody by the Russians, and died soon after from the tuberculosis they refused to treat.

The **bathing complex** in Baden bei Wien is constructed over more than a dozen sulfur springs. There are some half-dozen indoor bath establishments, plus four outdoor thermal springs. These thermal springs reach temperatures ranging from 75°–95°F (24°–35°C). The thermal complex also has a "sandy beach" and a restaurant. It lies west of the town in the Doblhoffpark, a natural park with a lake where you can rent sail boats and cross the water for lunch on the other side. There's also a garden restaurant in the park.

ESSENTIALS

GETTING THERE   If you're driving from Vienna, head south on Autobahn A2, take exit 21 onto the B210, which leads to Baden. By train, Baden is a local rather than an express stop. Trains depart daily at 15 to 30 minute intervals from Wien Meidling (trip time: 30 min.). For schedules, call ☎ **05/1717** in Vienna, or check **www.oebb.at**. By bus, the Badner Bahn leaves every 15 minutes from the Staatsoper (trip time: 1 hr.).

VISITOR INFORMATION   The **tourist information office,** at Brusattiplatz 3 (☎ **02252/22-600-600;** www.baden.at), is open Monday to Friday 9am to 6pm, Saturday 9am to 2pm. From October to April the office is closed on both Saturday and Sunday.

SEEING THE SIGHTS

In the Hauptplatz (Main Square) is the **Trinity Column,** built in 1714, which commemorates the lifting of the plague that swept over Vienna and the Wienerwald in the Middle Ages. Also here are the **Rathaus** (☎ **02252/86800**) and, at no. 17, the **Kaiserhaus,** Franz II's summer residence from 1813 to 1834.

Every summer between 1821 and 1823, Beethoven rented the upper floor of a modest house, above what used to be a shop on the Rathausgasse, for about 2 weeks, hoping to find a cure for his increasing deafness. The site has been reconfigured by the city of Baden into the **Beethovenhaus,** a small museum commemorating the time he spent here, at Rathausgasse 10 (☎ **02252/868-00230**). Inside you'll find a trio of small, relatively modest rooms, furnished with one of Beethoven's pianos, his bed, several pieces of porcelain, photographs of others of his residences around the German-speaking world, some mementos, and copies of the musical folios he completed (or at least worked on) during his time in Baden. The museum is open year-round Tuesday to Friday 4 to 6pm, and Saturday and Sunday 10am to noon and 4 to 6pm. Admission costs 3€ for adults and 1.50€ for students and children under 18. Entrance is free for children under 6.

Among the other sights in Baden, a celebrated death-mask collection resides at the **Stadtisches Rolletmuseum,** Weikersdorfer-Platz 1 (☎ **02252/48255**). The museum possesses many items of historic and artistic interest. Furniture and the art of the Biedermeier period are especially well represented. It's open every day (except Tuesday) from 3 to 6pm. Admission is 3€ for adults and 1.50€ for children. To reach the museum from Hauptplatz, go south to Josefs Platz and then continue south along Vöslauer Strasse, turning right when you come to Elisabeth Strasse, which leads directly to Weikersdorfer-Platz.

The **Stadttheater,** at Theaterplatz 7 (☎ **02252/253253**), is a 5-minute walk from Hauptplatz, and on nearby Pfarrgasse, you'll find the 15th-century parish church of **St. Stephan's** (☎ **02252/48426**). Inside there's a commemorative plaque to Mozart who, it is claimed, composed his *Ave Verum* here for the parish choirmaster.

The real reason to come to Baden, though, is the sprawling and beautiful **Kurpark ★**. Here you can attend concerts, plays, and operas at an open-air theater, or try your luck at the casino (see "Baden After Dark," below).

TAKING A BATH

Taking a bath is not a simple thing in Baden; as you might expect from a place that has lured so many for so long, there are several different ways you can experience the mineral waters. The **Kurhaus** (also known sometimes as the **Kurzentrum**), at Pelzgasse 30 (✆ 02252/48580), in the heart of town, is a strictly medical facility, which requires doctors' appointments. The less structured enterprise nearby (at Brussatiplatz 4; **02252/45030**), is the *Römertherme*, a complex of hot mineral baths, which are open, with no reservations needed, to anyone who shows up. The *Römertherme* charges according to how long you spend inside. Two hours (the minimum charge) costs 9.50€, with each additional hour priced at 1.70€. A full day is 14€ per person, unless you opt to enter after 8pm, in which event you'll pay 4.80€. Access to any of the saunas inside costs an additional 4€, and access to the exercise and fitness area is 12.20€ per person.

WHERE TO STAY
Expensive
Grand Hotel Sauerhof zu Rauhenstein ★   Although this estate dates back to 1583, it became famous in 1757, when a sulfur-enriched spring bubbled up after a cataclysmic earthquake in faraway Portugal. The present building was constructed in 1810 on the site of that spring, which continues to supply water to its spa facilities today. In the past, the property served as an army rehabilitation building, a sanatorium during the two world wars, and headquarters for the Russian army. In 1978, after extravagant renovations, the Sauerhof reopened as one of the region's most prestigious spa hotels. The rooms, though comfortable and bright, have many vintage furnishings, which verge on the worn. Expect average food from the restaurant.

Weilburgstrasse 11-13, A-2500 Baden bei Wien. ✆ **02252/412510.** Fax 02252/43626. www.sauerhof.at. 88 units. 220€ double; from 650€ suite. Rates include buffet breakfast; half-board 25€ per person extra. AE, DC, MC, V. Free parking. **Amenities:** Restaurant; bar; indoor heated pool; 2 tennis courts; fitness center; spa; sauna; room service; solarium. *In room:* TV, minibar, hair dryer, free Wi-Fi.

MODERATE
Krainerhütte ☺   Very zen. This hotel stands on tree-filled grounds 8km (5 miles) west of Baden at Helenental. It's a large A-frame chalet with rows of wooden balconies. The interior has more details than you might expect in such a modern hotel. There are separate children's rooms and play areas. You can dine on international and Austrian cuisine in the restaurant or on the terrace; the fish and deer come from the hotel grounds. Hiking in the owner's forests, hunting, and fishing are possible. *Postbus* service to Baden is available all day.

Helenental 41, A-2500 Baden bei Wien. ✆ **02252/44511.** Fax 02252/44514. www.krainerhuette.at. 62 rooms. 68€-89€ double; from 89€ suite. Rates include breakfast; half-board 15€ per person extra. AE, MC, V. Free parking. **Amenities:** Restaurant; bar; indoor heated pool; fitness center; tennis court; sauna; room service; babysitting. *In room:* TV, minibar, hair dryer, free Wi-Fi.

Parkhotel Baden   You can't beat this location. The *Römertherme*, Kurpark, and Casino are all within a few minutes walking distance. Most of the good-size, sunny guest rooms have their own loggia overlooking century-old trees; each contains a good bathroom with tub/shower combination and plenty of shelf space. The TVs and some of the furniture are old and will hopefully be updated soon.

Kaiser-Franz-Ring 5, A-2500 Baden bei Wien. ✆ **02252/443860.** Fax 02252/80578. www. niederoesterreich.at/parkhotel-baden. 87 rooms. 170€ double; 280€ suite. Rates include breakfast. AE, DC, MC, V. Free parking. **Amenities:** 2 restaurants; bar; indoor heated pool; health club; sauna; room service; massage; babysitting; laundry service. *In room:* TV, minibar, hair dryer, free Wi-Fi.

Schloss Weikersdorf   Vaulted ceilings, a terrace leading down into parkland with a rose garden, and a courtyard arcade with a skylight … it's delightful. The 77 bedrooms in the main house, plus 27 in the annex, are handsomely furnished and very comfortable. The rooms in the newer section tastefully echo the older section's style. Great location and a nice walk into town.

Schlossgasse 9–11, A-2500 Baden bei Wien. ✆ **02252/48301.** Fax 02252/4830-1150. www.hotel schlossweikersdorf.at. 104 rooms. 124€–150€ double; 250€ suite. Rates include breakfast. AE, DC, MC, V. Free parking. **Amenities:** Restaurant; bar; indoor heated pool; sauna; room service; massage; bowling alley; rooms for those w/limited mobility; Wi-Fi in the lobby. *In room:* TV, minibar, hair dryer, free Wi-Fi.

WHERE TO DINE
Kupferdachl AUSTRIAN   A local cornerstone since 1966, this moderately-priced family spot serves rib-sticking Austrian fare that the locals adore, everything from cabbage soup to *apfelstrudel*. The chefs make the town's best Wiener schnitzel, served with a fresh salad and rice. The veal cutlets with potatoes are also worth trying. The hotel is about a 15-minute drive from Baden.

Heiligenkreuzegasse 2. ✆ **02252/41617.** Reservations recommended. Main courses 10€–14€. No credit cards. Mon–Fri 8am–6:30pm; Sat–Sun 9:30am–4pm.

BADEN AFTER DARK
Casino Baden   The town's major evening attraction is the casino, where you can play roulette, blackjack, baccarat, poker (seven-card stud), money wheel, and slot machines. Many visitors from Vienna come down to Baden for a night of gambling, eating, and drinking; there are two bars and a restaurant. Guests are often fashionably dressed, and you'll feel more comfortable if you are too (men should wear jackets and ties, at least). It's open daily 3pm to 3am. A less formal casino on the premises, the Casino Leger, is open daily noon to midnight.

In the Kurpark. ✆ **02252/444960.** www.casinos.at. Free admission; 25€ worth of chips for 23€.

WIENER NEUSTADT

Wiener Neustadt was once the official residence of Habsburg emperor Friedrich III, and this thriving city between the foothills of the Alps and the edge of the Pannonian lowland has an interesting historic background.

The town was founded in 1192, when Duke Leopold V of the ruling house of Babenburg built its castle. He had it constructed as a citadel to ward off attacks by the Magyars from the east. From 1440 to 1493, Austrian emperors lived in this fortress, in the southeast corner of what is now the old town. Maximilian I, called "the last of the knights," was born here in 1459 and buried in the castle's Church of St. George. In 1752, on Maria Theresa's orders, the castle became a military academy.

In 1903 Paul Daimler started building his 2-cylinder engine factory in Wiener Neustadt and in 1906 hired Ferdinand Porsche as his technical director. A half a dozen years later, the engines were purring and they began hiring young mechanical engineers from the Benz factory in Munich.

Wiener Neustadt was a target for Allied bombs during World War II. It's where the routes from Vienna diverge, one going to the Semmering Pass and the other to Hungary via the Sopron Gate. The 200-year-old military academy that traditionally turned out officers for the Austrian army might have been an added attraction to bombers; German general Erwin Rommel ("the Desert Fox") was the academy's first commandant after the Nazi Anschluss. At any rate, the city was the target of more Allied bombing than any other in the country. It leveled an estimated 60% of Wiener Neustadt's buildings. Luckily some of its most beautiful were spared.

ESSENTIALS

GETTING THERE   If you're driving from Vienna, head south along the A2 and take exit 44 marked Wiener Neustadt, west onto B26. Follow B26 to Wiener Neustadt.

Trains to Wiener Neustadt leave every 10 to 15 minutes from Wien Meidling (trip time: 25–45 min.). For schedules, call ℂ **05/1717** in Vienna or check www.oebb.at.

VISITOR INFORMATION   The Wiener Neustadt **tourist information office,** at Hauptplatz in Rathaus (ℂ **02622/29551**), is open Monday to Friday 8am to 5pm, Saturday 8am to noon.

SEEING THE SIGHTS

You can visit the **Church of St. George (St. Georgenkirche),** Burgplatz 1 (ℂ **02622/3810**), daily from 8am to 6pm. The gable of the church is adorned with more than 100 heraldic shields of the Habsburgs. It's noted for its handsome late-Gothic interior.

Neukloster, Neuklostergasse 1 (ℂ **02622/23102**), a Cistercian abbey, was founded in 1250 and reconstructed in the 18th century. The New Abbey Church (Neuklosterkirche), near Hauptplatz, is also Gothic and happens to have a wonderful choir. It contains the tomb of Empress Eleanor of Portugal, wife of Friedrich III and mother of Maximilian I. Mozart's *Requiem* was first presented here in 1793. Admission is free, and, while the church is always open to visitors, the abbey's office hours are Monday, Tuesday, Wednesday, and Friday from 8 to 11am and 3 to 6pm.

Liebfrauenkirche, Domplatz (ℂ **02622/23202**), was once the headquarters of an Episcopal seat. It's graced by a 13th-century Romanesque nave, but the choir is Gothic. The west towers have been rebuilt. Admission is free, and the church is open daily 8am to noon and 2 to 6pm.

In the town is a **Recturm,** Babenberger Ring (ℂ **02622/279-24**), a Gothic tower said to have been built with the ransom money paid for Richard the Lionheart. It's open March to October, Tuesday to Thursday, 10am to noon and 2 to 4pm, and Saturday and Sunday, 10am to noon only. Admission is free.

WHERE TO STAY

Hotel Zentral ★   The best hotel in town, right on the main square. The staff is competent, very friendly and make up for the somewhat out-dated, yet comfortable, furnishings. It's small, so we recommend reserving way in advance. Due to its location, parking places are scarce, but you can load and unload in front of the hotel anytime and there is a parking garage 250m (820ft.) away that costs 3€ per day, if you buy your ticket at the hotel.

Hauptplatz 27, A-2700 Wiener Neustadt. ℂ **02622/23169.** Fax 02622/237935. www.hotelzentral.at. 68 rooms. 150-190€ double. Rates include buffet breakfast. AE, DC, MC, V. Free parking. **Amenities:** Restaurant; bar; room service. *In room:* TV, minibar, hair dryer, free Wi-Fi.

WHERE TO DINE

Stachl's Gaststube ★ CONTINENTAL   Set within the city's pedestrian zone in the heart of town, this is one of the most popular and well-respected restaurants in the region. Dishes are well presented and tasty, served in an intimate environment that includes a busy bar area independent of the restaurant. We would recommend the carpaccio of Styrian beef with wild mushrooms and arugula, or strips of marinated salmon with pesto sauce and a truffled version of mushroom risotto. You could also try Wiener Schnitzel with salad, *tafelspitz* (boiled beef) with chive sauce and horseradish or perhaps a local lakefish (*zander*) with herbed noodles. For dessert, consider a platter containing light and dark versions of chocolate mousse topped with berry sauce.

Lange Gasse 20. ✆ **02622/25221.** www.stachl.at. Reservations recommended. Main courses 12€–20€. MC, V. Mon–Fri 5pm–12:30am; Sat 5pm–midnight.

THE DANUBE VALLEY ★★★

The Danube is one of Europe's legendary rivers, rich in scenic wonders and surrounded by history and architecture. The Wachau, a section of the Danube Valley northwest of Vienna, is one of the most beautiful and historic areas of Austria. Traveling through the rolling hills and fertile soil of the Wachau, you'll pass ruins of castles reminiscent of the Rhine Valley, some of the most celebrated vineyards in Austria, famous medieval monasteries, and ruins from the Stone Age, the Celts, the Romans, and the Habsburgs. Unrelentingly prosperous, the district has won many awards for the authenticity of its historic renovations.

Recent research has revealed a history of the Danube Valley even older than previously believed, preceding the civilizations of the Fertile Crescent which were the first cities of Mesopotamia and the Nile. For 1,500 years, starting earlier than 5000 B.C. say researchers, people in these old Danube cultures farmed and built sizable towns, a few with as many as 2,000 dwellings. They mastered copper smelting and wore the earliest gold artifacts to be found anywhere in the world. These ancient cultures, known in part by isolated scholars in Iron Curtain countries, are only now attracting attention from a wider world and historians are able to pool their knowledge to make the pieces of the puzzle fit. An initial show at New York University in 2009–10, was followed by a second exhibition of the most important finds at the Ashmolean Museum in Oxford, England, and another exhibition at the Museum of Cycladic Art in Athens. This new work will change the understanding of the Danube's effect on the history of European civilization.

Tips on Exploring the Danube Valley

If you have only a day to see the Danube Valley, we highly recommend the tours listed below. If you have more time, rent a car and explore this district yourself, driving inland from the river now and then to visit the towns and sights listed below. You can also take public transportation to the towns we've highlighted (see individual listings).

The Wachau and the rest of the Danube Valley contain some of the most impressive monuments in Austria, but because of their far-flung locations, many prefer to participate in an organized tour. The best of these are conducted by **Vienna Sightseeing Tours,** Goldeggasse 29 (✆ **01/712-4683-0;** fax 01/714-1141; www.vienna sightseeingtours.com), which offers guided tours by coach in winter and by both coach and boat in summer. Stops on this 8-hour trip include Krems, Dürnstein, and Melk Abbey. Prices are 61€ for adults and 30€ for children under 12, and do not include lunch, except in winter. Advance reservations are required.

RIVER cruises

If you're really "doing the Danube," you can get week-long trips (some even two weeks) which go the length of the river. It's possible to see the valley by starting at Nuremberg or Passau, in Germany, passing through Vienna (with sightseeing tour and concert included), and going all the way to the Black Sea and across to the Crimean Peninsula, stopping over at Yalta. Some of the best river cruise companies include AMAWaterways (www. amawaterways.com in the U.S. or www. amawaterways.co.uk in Britain), Viking River Cruises (www.vikingrivercruises. com/www.vikingrivercruises.co.uk) and Cosmos and Avalon Waterways (www.avalonwaterways.com/ www. avaloncruises.co.uk). The cruises are aboard startlingly luxurious vessels with wonderful cabins, gourmet food, and sundecks from which you can watch the world go by. It's possible to see the sights with excursions, and often to borrow bikes which the ships have on board.

This is a luxury if you have the time; sadly most visitors limit themselves to one of the short trips from Vienna. Most of these operate only between April 1 and October 31. You can take in the countryside from an armchair on the ship's deck. (See the "Cruising the Danube" box in Chapter 7.)

Before you venture into the Danube Valley, pick up maps and other helpful information at the **tourist office for Lower Austria,** Postfach 10,000, A-1010 Vienna (© **01/536-106200;** fax 01/536-106-060; www.niederoesterreich.at).

Tulln

This is one of the most ancient towns in Austria. Originally a naval base called Comagena and later a focus for the Babenburg dynasty, Tulln, on the right bank of the Danube, is "the flower town" because of the masses of blossoms you'll see in spring and summer. It's the place, according to the Nibelungen saga, where Kriemhild, the Burgundian princess of Worms, met Etzel, king of the Huns. A famous "son of Tulln" was Kurt Waldheim, former secretary-general of the United Nations and one of Austria's most controversial former presidents, due to his previous Nazi affiliations.

ESSENTIALS

GETTING THERE Tulln lies 42km (26 miles) west of Vienna, on the south bank of the Danube, and 13km (8 miles) southwest of Stockerau, the next big town, on the north bank of the Danube. If you're driving from Vienna, head along the Danube Canal (Brigittenauer Lände/B227) and take the exit marked Klosterneuburger-Bundesstrsse/B14. Follow B14 to Tulln.

Direct S-Bahn trains depart from Wien Franz-Josefs Bahnhof daily from 5am to noon (trip time: 27–45 min.). You can also catch these trains at the U4 stops Spittelau and Heiligenstadt. Tulln lies on the busy main rail lines linking Vienna with Prague, and most local timetables list Gmund, an Austrian city on the border of the Czech Republic, as the final destination. For more information, call © **05/1717,** or check **www.oebb.at**. We don't recommend taking the bus from Vienna, as it requires multiple transfers.

VISITOR INFORMATION   The **tourist office** in Tulln, at Minoritenplatz 2 (☎ 02272/67566; www.tulln.at), is open November to April, Monday to Friday, 8am to 3pm; and May to October, Monday to Friday, 9am to 7pm, Saturday and Sunday, 10am to 7pm.

SEEING THE SIGHTS

The **Pfarrkirche (parish church)** of St. Stephan on Wiener Strasse grew out of a 12th-century Romanesque basilica dedicated to the Protomartyr. Its west portal was built in the 13th century. The Gothic overlay that followed fell victim to a baroque craze that swept the country during the 1700s. The 1786 altarpiece depicts the Saint's death by stoning.

Adjoining the church is the **Karner (Charnel House) ★★**, Wiener Strasse 20 (☎ 02272/62338). This 11-sided polygonal structure, which was built sometime between 1240 and 1250, is not only a strikingly well-preserved example of late Romanesque, you can also visit the basement of the former bone house, where they would dump those who had outstayed their welcome in the cemetery.

In a restored former prison, Tulln has opened the **Egon Schiele Museum ★★**, Donaulände 28 (☎ 02272/64570), devoted to its other famous son, born here in 1890. Schiele is one of the most influential Austrian artists of the early 1900s. The prison setting might be appropriate, as the expressionist painter spent 24 days in jail in 1912 in the town of Neulengbach for possession of what back then was regarded as pornography. While awaiting trial, he produced 13 watercolors, most of which are now in The Albertina in Vienna. The Tulln museum has more than 90 of his oil paintings, watercolors, and designs, along with lots of memorabilia. The museum is open Tuesday to Sunday, 10am to noon and 1pm to 5pm, April 1 to November 1. It's also open on public holiday Mondays. Admission is 5€ for adults and 3.50€ for seniors, students, and children.

WHERE TO STAY

Hotel Römerhof   This ultra new hotel near the river is easily accessible from the B14 and about a 15-minute walk from St. Stephan's. Its furnishings are pure functionality, but with the benefit of modern comforts. If you book half-board be sure to ask for an upgrade.

Hafenstrasse 3, A-3430 Tulln an der Donau. ☎ 02272/62954. www.hotel-roemerhof.at. 51 rooms. 76€–90€ double. Rates include buffet breakfast. MC, V. Free parking. Amenities: Breakfast room; bar; beer garden; sauna. In room: TV, minibar, hair dryer, Wi-Fi: 3€/hour.

WHERE TO DINE

Gasthaus zur Sonne (Gasthaus Sodoma) ★ AUSTRIAN   This is Tulln's finest and most famous restaurant. The 1940s building, on the main street and a short walk from the railway station, looks like a cross between a chalet and a villa. Under the direction of the Sodoma family since 1968, it consists of two dining rooms lined with oil paintings. The menu invariably includes well-prepared versions of dumplings stuffed with minced meat, pumpkin soup, a marvelous Wiener schnitzel, onion-studded roast beef, *Tafelspitz* (boiled beef), and perfectly cooked *zander* (a freshwater lake fish similar to perch) served with potatoes and butter sauce.

Bahnhofstrasse 48. ☎ 02272/64616. Reservations recommended. Main courses 9€–27€. No credit cards. Tues–Sat 11:30am–1:30pm and 6–9pm.

Herzogenburg

To reach Herzogenburg from Vienna, drive 65km (40 miles) west on the A1 to St. Pölten. The monastery is 11km (6¾ miles) north of St. Pölten. Take Wiener Strasse (Rte. 1) east from St. Pölten to Kapelln (13km/8 miles), go left at the sign onto a minor road to Herzogenburg, and follow signs.

Herzogenburger Augustiner Chorherrenstift (Augustinian Herzogenburg Monastery)   A-3130 Herzogenburg (ℂ 02782/83113), a German bishop from Passau founded the Augustinian Monastery in the early 12th century. The present complex of buildings comprising the church and the abbey was reconstructed in the baroque style (1714–40). Jakob Prandtauer and Josef Munggenast, along with Fischer von Erlach, designed the buildings. The magnificent baroque church has a sumptuous interior, with an altarpiece by Daniel Gran and a beautiful organ loft. The most outstanding art owned by the abbey is a series of 16th-century paintings on wood ★; they are on display in a room devoted to Gothic art. You can wander around on your own or join a guided tour. There's a wine tavern in the complex where you can eat Austrian dishes.

A-3130 Herzogenburg. ℂ **02782/83113.** Admission 7€ adults, 5€ seniors and students. Apr–Oct daily 9am–6pm. Tours daily 9:30, 11am, 1:30, 2:30, and 3pm. Closed Nov–Mar.

Krems ★

In the eastern part of the Wachau, on the left bank of the Danube, lies the 1,000-year-old city of Krems. The city today encompasses Stein and Mautern, once separate towns. Krems is a mellow town of old churches, courtyards, and cobblestones in the heart of vineyard country, with some partially preserved town walls. Just as the Viennese flock to Grinzing and other suburbs to sample new wine in the *heurigen*, so the people of the Wachau come here to taste the fruit of the vine that appears in Krems earlier in the year.

ESSENTIALS

GETTING THERE   Krems is 80km (50 miles) west of Vienna and 35km (22 miles) north of St. Pölten. If you're driving from Vienna, drive north along the A22 until you approach the town of Stockerau. Here, exit on to the S5 and drive due west, following the signs to Krems.

A train with non-stop service to Krems departs daily from the Franz-Josefs Bahnhof every hour from 6:51am to 9:51pm (trip time: 60–95 min.). Trains with transfers at Absdorf-Hippersdorf or St. Pölten are available from Wien Nord (Praterstern) or Westbahnhof, respectively. For schedules, call ℂ **05/1717** in Vienna, or check **www.oebb.at**. We don't recommend going from Vienna to Krems by bus because of the many transfers required. Krems, however, is well connected by local bus lines to surrounding villages.

Between mid-May and late September, the Linz-based **Wurm & Köck Donau Schiffahrt** (ℂ 0732/783607; www.donauschiffahrt.de) runs river cruises, which depart from Vienna every Sunday morning at 7:30am, arriving in Krems around 12:20pm. After a tour through the abbey at Krems, most passengers take any of the frequent trains back to Vienna.

VISITOR INFORMATION The Krems **tourist office,** at Utzstrasse 1 (✆ **02732/82676;** www.krems.gv.at), is open Monday to Friday 9am to 6pm, Saturday 11am to 5pm, Sunday 11am to 4pm.

SEEING THE SIGHTS

The most scenic part of Krems today is what used to be the village of **Stein.** Now called Stein an der Donau, its narrow streets run above the river, and the single main street, **Steinerlandstrasse,** is flanked by houses, many from the 16th century. The **Grosser Passauerhof,** Steinlanderstrasse 76 (✆ **02732/82188**), is a Gothic structure decorated with an oriel. Another house, at Steinerlandstrasse 84, combines Byzantine and Venetian elements among other architectural influences; it was once the imperial tollhouse. Centuries ago the aristocrats of Krems barricaded the Danube and extracted heavy tolls from the river traffic. When the tolls were more than the hapless victims could pay, the townspeople just confiscated the cargo. In the old city (*Altstadt*), the **Steiner Tor,** a 1480 gate, is a landmark.

Pfarrkirche St. Viet (✆ **02732/857100**), the parish church of Krems, stands in the middle of town at Pfarrplatz 5, where the Untere Landstrasse and Obere Landstrasse meet. The overtly ornate church is rich with gilt and statuary. Construction on this, one of the oldest baroque churches in the province, began in 1616. In the 18th century, Martin Johann Schmidt, better known as Kremser Schmidt, painted many of the frescoes inside the church.

Visit the **Weinstadt Museum Krems (The Wine City Museum of Krems),** Körnermarkt 14 (✆ **02732/801567**) for a comprehensive survey of the city's cultural and commercial history. Arranged inside a restored 13th-century Dominican monastery, this historic collection, ranging from wine barrels to broad swords and furniture, offers an insight into the region. The museum is laid out on three levels, from the stone cellar to the upstairs art gallery, and includes a few works by the painter Martin Johann Schmidt. Admission is 4€ for adults and 2€ for children. It's open March to November, Wednesday to Saturday, 10am to 6pm, Sundays and holidays 1pm to 6pm.

For those interested in a more in-depth look at modern wine production, we recommend visiting **Winzer Krems**, Sandgrube 13 (✆ **02732/85511**). You can take an informative hour-long guided tour of the winery, which includes a look at the vineyard, wine presses, the cellar (where a couple of pre-recorded ghosts talk about how to store old wine), and a short film. The tour includes 3 wine samples with bread. Admission is 11€ for adults but it's free for children under 16.

Nearby Attractions

Twenty-nine kilometers (18 miles) north of Krems at St. Pölten is the Museum of Lower Austria, formerly located in Vienna. Now called **Landes Museum,** it's at Franz-Schubert-Platz (✆ **2742/908-090-999**). This museum exhibits the geology, flora, and fauna of the area surrounding Vienna. It also exhibits a collection of arts and crafts, including baroque and Biedermeier; temporary shows featuring 20th-century works are presented as well. Admission is 8€ for adults and 7€ for children. It's open Tuesday to Sunday 9am to 5pm.

WHERE TO STAY

Gourmethotel am Förthof ★ 📷 A charming hotel with all the elements of a romantic country getaway. It boasts exceptional food, all from local farmers, and a friendly atmosphere indicative of traditional Austrian hospitality. Each of the high-ceilinged bedrooms has a foyer and a shared balcony. Most bedrooms are fairly spacious.

Donaulände 8, A-3500 Krems. © **02732/83345.** Fax 02732/833-4540. www.gourmethotel-foerthof. at. 20 rooms. 100€–150€ double. Rates include breakfast; half-board 25€ per person extra. AE, DC, MC, V. Free parking. **Amenities:** Restaurant; bar; outdoor pool; room service (7am–10pm); babysitting. *In room:* TV, minibar, hair dryer, free Wi-Fi.

Hotel Goldener Engel This family-run, multi-cultural bed-and-breakfast offers a convenient base from which to explore Krems. The rooms are modest, comfortable, and well maintained. Other perks include a small outdoor swimming pool on a grassy terrace above the hotel with a view of the valley. An affordable suite with its own balcony is also available. The German-language section of the website includes a collection of panorama photographs, under "weitere Infos."

Wiener Strasse 41, A-3500 Krems. © **02732/82067.** Fax 02732/77261. www.hotel-ehrenreich-krems. at. 21 rooms. 80€–114€ double. Rates include buffet breakfast; half-board 12€ extra per person. MC, V. Free parking. **Amenities:** Bar; outdoor pool; bike rental. *In room:* TV, free Wi-Fi.

WHERE TO DINE

Restaurant Bacher ★ AUSTRIAN/INTERNATIONAL   Lisl and Klaus Wagner-Bacher operate this excellent restaurant-hotel, with an elegant dining room and a well-kept garden. Specials include crabmeat salad dressed with nut oil. Dessert might be beignets with apricot sauce and vanilla ice cream. Lisl has won awards for her cuisine, as her enthusiastic clientele will tell you. The wine list has more than 600 selections. There are also eight double and three single rooms (134€ to 190€ for a double with buffet breakfast). The Bacher is just across the river, 4km (2½ miles) from Krems. Follow the signs from the bridge to Landhaus-Bacher.

Südtiroler Platz 208, A-2352 Mautern. © **02732/82937.** Fax 02732/74337. Reservations required. Main courses 24€–39€; fixed-price menus 72€–99€. DC, V. Wed–Sat 11:30am–1:30pm and 6:30–9pm; Sun 11:30am–9pm. Closed mid-Jan to mid-Feb.

Dürnstein ★★

Less than 8km (5 miles) west of Krems, Dürnstein is arguably the loveliest town in the Wachau and, accordingly, draws throngs of visitors in summer. The ruins of Dürnstein Castle and the hiking paths around the mountain to the left of the ruins make this an essential visit.

ESSENTIALS

GETTING THERE   The town is 80km (50 miles) west of Vienna. If you're driving, take the A22 to S5 west. From Krems, continue driving west along the S5 (which becomes Route 3 or B3) for 8km (5 miles). Train travel to Dürnstein from Vienna requires a transfer in Krems (see above). In Krems, trains depart approximately every 2 hours on river-running routes; it's a 6km (4-mile) trip to Dürnstein. For schedules, call © **05/1717** in Vienna, or check **www.oebb.at.** There's also a bus between Krems and Dürnstein (trip time: 20 min.).

VISITOR INFORMATION   A little **tourist office,** housed in a tiny shed in the east parking lot called Parkplatz Ost (© **02711/200**), is open April to October 19 only. Hours are daily 11am to 1pm and 2pm to 6:30pm.

SEEING THE SIGHTS

The ruins of a **castle fortress,** 159m (522 ft.) above town, are inextricably linked to the Crusades. Here Leopold V, the Babenberg duke ruling the country at that time, held Richard the Lionheart of England prisoner in 1193. For a while, nobody knew exactly where in Austria Richard had been incarcerated. His loyal minstrel companion, Blondel, so the story goes, had a clever idea. He went from castle to castle, playing his lute and singing the songs Richard loved. The tactic worked and Richard heard Blondel's singing and sang the lyrics in reply. The discovery forced Leopold to transfer Richard to a castle in the Rhineland Palatinate, but by then everybody knew where he was. So Leopold set a high ransom for the king's release, which was eventually met and Richard was set free. The castle was virtually demolished by the Swedes in 1645, but you can visit the ruins if you don't mind a climb (allow an hour). Little is left of the castle, but the view of Dürnstein and the Wachau is more than worth the effort.

Back in town, take in the principal artery, **Hauptstrasse ★**, which is flanked by richly adorned old residences. Many of these date from the 1500s and have been well maintained through the centuries.

The 15th-century **Pfarrkirche (parish church)** merits a visit. The building was originally an Augustinian monastery and was reconstructed when the baroque style swept Austria. The church tower is a prominent landmark in the Danube Valley. Kremser Schmidt, the noted baroque painter, did some of the altar paintings.

WHERE TO STAY & DINE

Gartenhotel Weinhof Pfeffel 🍃   This black-roofed, white-walled hotel is partially concealed by well-landscaped shrubbery. One of the best bargains in town, the hotel takes its name from its garden courtyard with flowering trees, where tasty but simple meals are served. The public rooms are furnished with traditional pieces. The bedrooms are handsomely furnished in a traditional Austrian motif, with comfortable armchairs and good beds. Leopold Pfeffel, your host, serves wine from his own terraced vineyard.

A-3601 Dürnstein. ✆ **02711/206.** Fax 02711/12068. www.pfeffel.at. 40 rooms. 112€–132€ double; from 136€ suite. Rates include breakfast. MC, V. Free parking. Closed Dec–Feb. **Amenities:** Restaurant; bar; outdoor pool; sauna; room service. *In room:* TV, minibar, hair dryer, free Wi-Fi in older rooms.

Hotel-Restaurant Sänger Blondel ★ 🎁   Lemon-painted and charmingly old-fashioned, with green shutters and clusters of flowers at the windows, this hotel is named after the faithful minstrel who searched the countryside for Richard the Lionheart. Bedrooms are furnished in a rustic style and are comfortable with good beds. Each Thursday evening there's zither music. If the weather is good, the music is played outside in the flowery chestnut garden near the baroque church tower. There's a good and reasonably-priced restaurant serving regional cuisine.

A-3601 Dürnstein. ✆ **02711/253.** Fax 02711/2537. www.saengerblondel.at. 15 units. 69€ single; 49€–57€ double; 67€ suite with balcony. Rates include breakfast. MC, V. Parking 7€. Closed Dec–Feb. **Amenities:** Restaurant; lounge. *In room:* TV, hair dryer.

Hotel Schloss Dürnstein ★★   The perfect place for a fancy romantic dinner. This throwback villa has a stone terrace that overlooks the river. Elegantly-furnished bedrooms come in a wide variety of styles, ranging from the large and palatial to others that are rather small and modern. The restaurant serves well-prepared dishes.

A-3601 Dürnstein. © **02711/212.** Fax 02711/212-30. www.schloss.at. 41 rooms. 235€–253€ double; from 338€–365€ suite. Rates include breakfast. AE, DC, MC, V. Free parking. Closed Nov 1–Easter. A pick-up can be arranged at the Dürnstein rail station. **Amenities:** Restaurant; bar; 2 pools (1 heated indoor); fitness center; gym; sauna; room service; babysitting; free Wi-Fi in lobby. *In room:* TV, minibar, hair dryer.

Romantik Hotel Richard Löwenherz ★★   This hotel was built on the site of a 700-year-old nunnery, originally dedicated to the sisters of Santa Clara in 1289. Its richly-adorned interior is filled with antiques, Renaissance sculpture, chandeliers, stone vaulting, and wood panels that have acquired a mellow patina over years of polishing. An arbor-covered sun terrace with restaurant tables extends toward the Danube. The bedrooms, especially those in the balconied modern section, are filled with cheerful furniture. The duvet-covered beds are the finest in the area. Each bedroom also has a beautifully kept bathroom. The restaurant offers a fine selection of local wines and regional specials.

A-3601 Dürnstein. © **02711/222.** Fax 02711/22218. www.richardloewenherz.at. 38 rooms. 166€–191€ double; 310€ suite. Rates include buffet breakfast. AE, MC, V. Free parking. Closed Nov to mid-Apr. **Amenities:** Restaurant; lounge; outdoor heated pool; room service. *In room:* TV, hair dryer, free Internet.

Melk

The words of Empress Maria Theresa speak volumes about Melk: "If I had never come here, I would have regretted it." The main attraction is Melk Abbey, a sprawling baroque building overlooking the Danube basin. Melk marks the western terminus of the Wachau and lies upstream from Krems.

ESSENTIALS

GETTING THERE   Melk is 89km (55 miles) west of Vienna. **Motorists** can follow the A1 (Link/St. Pölten), taking exit 80 to Melk. If you prefer a more romantic and scenic road, try the B3 from Krems, which parallels the Danube but takes 30 to 45 minutes longer. **Trains** leave frequently from Vienna's Westbahnhof to Melk, with two brief stops en route (trip time: about 1 hr.).

VISITOR INFORMATION   The **Melk tourist office** at Babenbergerstrasse 1 (© **02752/52307410;** www.stadt-melk.at), in the middle of town, is open April and October Monday to Friday 9am to noon and 2 to 5pm, Saturday 10am to 2pm. Hours from May to August are Monday to Friday 9am to noon and 2 to 6pm, Saturday and Sunday 10am to 2pm; in September, Monday to Friday 9am to noon and 2 to 5pm, Saturday 10am to 2pm.

SEEING THE SIGHTS

Melk Abbey ★★   One of the finest baroque buildings in the world, the abbey and its **Stiftskirche (abbey church)** ★ are the major attractions in Melk today. The town has been an important location in the Danube Basin ever since the Romans built a fortress over this tiny "branch" of the Danube. Melk is also featured in the German epic poem, *Nibelungenlied,* in which it is called *Medelike.*

The rock-strewn bluff where the abbey now stands overlooking the river was the seat of the Babenbergs, who ruled Austria from 976 until the Hapsburgs took over. In the 11th century, Leopold II of the House of Babenberg presented Melk to the Benedictine monks, who turned it into a fortified abbey. Its influence and renown as a place of learning and culture began to spread all over Austria. The Italian philosopher Umberto Eco, no doubt aware of its reputation at the time, named the narrator of his

1980 novel, *The Name of the Rose,* after the town. The Reformation and the 1683 Turkish invasion took a toll on the abbey, although it was spared from direct attack when the Ottoman armies were repelled outside Vienna. The construction of the new building began in 1702, just in time to be given the full baroque treatment.

Most of the design of the present abbey was by the architect Jakob Prandtauer. Its marble hall, called the Marmorsaal, contains pilasters coated in red marble. A richly-painted allegorical picture on the ceiling is the work of Paul Troger. The library, rising two floors, again with a Troger ceiling, contains some 80,000 volumes. The Kaisergang, or emperors' gallery, 198m (650-ft.) long, is decorated with portraits of Austrian rulers.

Despite all the adornment in the abbey, it is still surpassed in lavish glory by the Stiftskirche, the golden abbey church. Damaged by fire in 1947, the church has been fully restored, including regilding the statues and altars with gold. The church has an astonishing number of windows, and it is richly embellished with marble and frescoes. Many of the paintings are by Johann Michael Rottmayr, but Troger also contributed.

Melk is still a working abbey, and you might see black-robed Benedictine monks going about their business or students rushing out of the gates. Visitors head for the terrace to see a view of the river. Napoleon probably used it for a lookout when he made Melk his headquarters during the campaign against Austria.

Throughout the year, the abbey is open every day. From May to September tours depart at intervals of 15 to 20 minutes. The first tour begins at 9am and the last is at 5pm. Guides make efforts to translate into English a running commentary that is otherwise German.

Dietmayerstrasse 1, A-3390 Melk. ℂ **02752/555-225** for tour information. www.stiftmelk.at. Guided tours 9.30€ adults, 5.90€ children; unguided tours 7.50€ adults, 4.10€ children.

WHERE TO STAY

Hotel Stadt Melk ★ 🍴 Just below the town's palace, this hotel, with a gabled roof and stucco walls, was built a century ago as a private home. It was eventually converted into this family-run hotel, and now has simply-furnished bedrooms that are clean and comfortable, with sturdy beds. Rooms in the rear open on to views of the abbey. The amiable restaurant has leaded-glass windows in round, ripple patterns of greenish glass. Meals, beginning at 40€, are also served on a balcony at the front of the hotel.

Hauptplatz 1, A-3390 Melk. ℂ **02752/52475.** Fax 02752/524-7519. www.tiscover.at/hotel-stadt-melk. 14 rooms. 93€ double; 180€ suite. Rates include breakfast. AE, DC, MC, V. Free parking. **Amenities:** 2 restaurants; bar. *In room:* TV, minibar, hair dryer.

WHERE TO DINE

Stiftsrestaurant Melk BURGENLANDER If you're visiting Melk, this place is required dining. Sitting right at the entrance to the abbey, don't let its cafeteria-like dimensions sway you from its fine cuisine. This modern restaurant is well equipped to handle large groups—some 3,000 visitors a day frequent the establishment during peak season. From the reasonable fixed-price menu you might opt for the asparagus and ham soup with crispy dumplings; hunter's roast with mushrooms, potato croquettes, and cranberry sauce; and pretty decent Sachertorte for dessert.

Abt-Berthold-Dietmayrstrasse 3. ℂ **02752/52555.** www.stiftmelk.at. Main courses 10€–14€. AE, MC, V. Mid-Mar to Dec daily 8am–7pm. Closed otherwise.

EISENSTADT: HAYDN'S HOME

When Burgenland joined Austria in the 1920s, it was a province without a capital. In 1924, its citizens agreed to give Eisenstadt the honor. The small town lies at the foot of the Leitha mountains, at the beginning of the Little Hungarian Plain. Surrounded by vineyards, forests, and fruit trees, it's a convenient stopover for exploring Lake Neusiedl, 9.6km (6 miles) east.

Even before assuming its new administrative role, Eisenstadt was renowned as the place where the great composer Joseph Haydn lived and worked while under the patronage of the aristocratic Esterházy family.

ESSENTIALS

GETTING THERE While Südbahnhof remains under construction, many of the trains departing for Eisenstadt have been rerouted to Meidling in the southwest of Vienna. This station can be reached with the U6 U-Bahn line. From Südbahnhof connections now continue directly to Eisenstadt through Neusiedl am See (trip time: 90 min.). From Meidling the connection is made at Wulkaprodersdorf. A bus from the station at Südtirolerplatz is another option, which will bring you directly to Eisenstadt's Domplatz. For schedules, call ✆ **05/1717** in Vienna, or check **www.oebb.at**.

Many visitors prefer to go by bus leaving Vienna from Südtiroler Platz (on the U1 U-Bahn line). Suburban buses begin their runs at this huge depot. A bus leaves during the day for Eisenstadt on an hourly basis, the trip taking anywhere from 47 to 70 minutes, bringing you directly to Domplatz.

If you're driving from Vienna, take Route 10 east to Parndorf Ort, and then head southwest along Route 50 to Eisenstadt. A more convenient, if less scenic, route takes drivers south out of the city on the A2, switching to the A3 that goes directly to Eisenstadt.

VISITOR INFORMATION The **Eisenstadt tourist office,** Schloss Esterházy (✆ **02682/67390**), will make hotel reservations for you at no charge and distributes information (in English).

SEEING THE SIGHTS

Bergkirche (Church of the Calvary) If you want to pay your final respects to Haydn, follow Hauptstrasse to Esterházystrasse, which leads to this church containing Haydn's white marble tomb. Until 1954, only the composer's headless body was here. His skull was in Vienna's Sammlung alter Musikinstrumente (p. 130), where curious spectators were actually allowed to touch it. It was stolen a few days after his death and wasn't reunited with his body for 145 years. The church itself contains an architectural distinctiveness: a spiral ramp on the outside perimeter of the building leads up to the steeple, taking visitors on a tour of the passion of the Christ on the way to Calvary.

Josef-Haydn-Platz 1. ✆ **02682/62638.** Church free admission; Haydn's mausoleum, treasure chamber and Kalvarienberg 3€ adults, 2€ seniors, 1€ students. Daily 9am-5pm. Closed Nov-Mar. From Esterházy Platz at the castle, head directly west along Esterházystrasse, a slightly uphill walk.

Haydn Museum The home of the composer from 1766 to 1778 is now a museum. Reconstructed rooms give viewers an intimate perspective of Haydn's life, using personal letters and other memoirs. Although he appeared in court nearly every night, Haydn actually lived very modestly when he was at home. A little flower-filled courtyard is one of the few luxuries. He was one of the more productive composers, creating over 107 symphonies and 24 operas among numerous solo pieces and concerts. Haydn also composed Germany's current national anthem, albeit unintentionally.

Joseph-Haydn-Gasse 19 and 21. ✆ **02682/7193900.** www.haydnhaus.at. Admission 4€ adults; 3.50€ children, seniors, and students. Daily 9am–5pm. Closed Nov–Mar. Pass Schloss Esterházy and turn left onto Joseph-Haydn-Gasse.

Schloss Esterházy ★   Haydn worked in this château built on the site of a medieval castle and owned by the Esterházy princes. The Esterházy clan was a great Hungarian family with vast estates that ruled over Eisenstadt and its surrounding area. They claimed descent from Attila the Hun. The Esterházys helped the Hapsburgs gain control of Hungary; so great was their loyalty to Austria, in fact, that when Napoleon offered the crown of Hungary to Nic Esterházy in 1809, he refused it.

The castle, built around an inner courtyard, was designed by the Italian architect Carlo Antonio Carlone, who began work on it in 1663. Subsequently, many other architects remodeled it, resulting in sweeping alterations to its appearance. In the late 17th and early 18th centuries, it was given a baroque pastel facade. On the first floor, the great baronial hall was made into the Haydnsaal, where the composer conducted the orchestra Prince Esterházy had provided for him. The walls and ceilings of this concert hall are elaborately decorated, but the floor is of bare wood, which, it is claimed, is the reason for the room's acoustic perfection. Part of the castle provides rooms for the provincial parliament.

Esterházy Platz. ✆ **02682/6385412.** www.schloss-esterhazy.at. Admission 7.50€ adults; 6.50€ children, seniors, and students; 16€ family ticket. Jul–Aug daily 9am–7pm; Mar–Jun and Sept–Nov daily 9am–6pm; Nov–Dec Thurs–Sun 9am–6pm; closed Jan–Feb. From the bus station at Domplatz, follow the sign to the castle (a 10 min. walk).

WHERE TO STAY & DINE

Gasthof Öhr   Although the rooms of this pleasant inn are clean and comfortable, with exposed panels, comfortable beds, and a sense of old-fashioned charm, the place is more famous and more consistently popular as a restaurant, where main courses cost 12€ to 20€ each, and where the kitchen consistently turns out excellent *tafelspitz*, freshwater fish dishes including *zander* in white wine and capers, as well as seasonal and regional delights such as wild boar and asparagus. These are served in any of four traditional dining rooms accented with wood trim, or in the garden. The restaurant is open from June to September, Monday 11am to 2pm and 6 to 9pm. Tuesday to Saturday, 11am to 3pm and 5:30 to 10pm. Sunday from 11am to 9pm. Check the website for hours during the colder months. This inn is just across from Eisenstadt's bus station.

Rusterstrasse 51, A-7000 Eisenstadt. ✆ **02682/62460.** Fax 02682/624609. www.hotelohr.at. 40 units. 90€–145€ double. DC, MC, V. Parking 7€. **Amenities:** Restaurant; room service; babysitting. *In room:* TV, Wi-Fi: 10€/hour.

Hotel Burgenland   The best hotel in Eisenstadt, and pretty too, with white stucco walls and big windows. The rooms have lots of light, comfortable beds and functional furniture. One of the best restaurants in Burgenland is the hotel's sleek and modern Bienenkorb. Bright and airy, it serves traditional Austrian dishes, Pannonia cuisine (Hungarian), as well as dishes with a Mediterranean feel.

Schubertplatz 1, A-7000 Eisenstadt. © **02682/6960.** Fax 02682/65531. www.hotelburgenland.at. 88 rooms. 120€–165€ double; from 200€ suite. Rates include buffet breakfast. AE, DC, MC, V. Parking 10€. **Amenities:** restaurant; bar; indoor heated pool; exercise room; sauna; room service; babysitting. *In room:* TV, minibar, hair dryer, Wi-Fi: 10€/hour, 17€/24hours.

LAKE NEUSIEDL ★

The region encompassing Neusiedlersee (Lake Neusiedl) is a famous getaway for the Viennese, and others will find it just as desirable. The lake offers countless diversions, making it an ideal destination for families or active travelers. You can play in and around the lake all day, and then relax over a fine meal of Burgenland cuisine in the evening. The geological anomaly of the Neusiedler (see "The Capricious Lake," below) and the steppe landscape make for intriguing hikes, strolls, and bike tours. Steady winds make the lake ideal for sailing, kite surfing and windsurfing; in fact, the lake hosts a Professional Windsurfers' Association World Cup competition every spring. The surrounding towns tend to be small, sleepy hamlets offering little more than lakeside relaxation, but they are ideal bases for exploring the surrounding countryside.

Neusiedl am See

On the northern shore of Lake Neusiedl lies this popular summer weekend spot where water sports prevail. You can rent sail boats, take windsurfing lessons, rent a bike or even go for a horseback ride at a nearby stable. The town's Gothic parish church is noted for its "ship pulpit." A watchtower from the Middle Ages still stands guard over the town with a sweeping view of the lake. Vineyards cover the nearby fields. If you plan to be here on a summer weekend, be sure to make reservations in advance.

ESSENTIALS

GETTING THERE   Neusiedl am See lies 45km (28 miles) southeast of Vienna, 359km (223 miles) east of Salzburg, and 34km (21 miles) northeast of Eisenstadt. This town is your gateway to the lake, as it's less than an hour by express train from Vienna. If you're driving from Vienna, take the A4 or B10 east. If you're in Eisenstadt, head northeast along B50, cutting east along B51 for a short distance. It's better to have a car if you're exploring Lake Neusiedl, although bus connections depart several times daily from the Domplatz bus station at Eisenstadt.

VISITOR INFORMATION   The **Neusiedl am See tourist office,** Untere Haupstrasse 7 (© **02167/2229**), distributes information about accommodations and boat rentals. Open July and August, Monday to Friday, 8am to 6pm; Saturday 10am to noon and 2 to 6pm, Sunday 9am to noon; May and June, Monday to Friday, 8am to 5pm; September, Monday to Friday, 8am to noon and 1 to 5pm; October to April, Monday to Thursday, 8am to noon and 1 to 4:30pm, Fridays, 8am to 1pm.

WHERE TO STAY & DINE

Gasthof zur Traube   This small hotel stands on the town's bustling main street. The pleasant ground-floor restaurant is filled with rustic decorations and wrought-iron table dividers. You can stop for a meal any time between 11am to 10pm, when

THE capricious LAKE

Neusiedler See (Lake Neusiedl) is a popular steppe lake lying in the northern part of Burgenland. But this strange lake should never be taken for granted—in fact, from 1868 to 1872, it completely dried up, as it has done periodically throughout its known history. The lake was once part of a body of water that blanketed all of the Pannonian Plain. Today its greatest depth is about 1.8m (6 ft.), and the wind can shift the water dramatically, even causing parts of the lake to dry up. The lake is between 7 and 15km (4¼–9¼ miles) wide and about 35km (22 miles) long.

A broad belt of reeds encircles the huge expanse. This thicket is an ideal habitat for waterfowl. Some 250 different species of birds inhabit the lake,

including the usual collection of storks, geese, ducks, and herons. The plant and animal life in the lake is unique in Europe. Within its slightly salty waters, alpine, Baltic, and Pannonian flora and fauna meet.

Viennese flock to the lake throughout the year, in summer to fish, sail, and windsurf, and in winter to skate. Nearly every lakeside village has a beach (although on any given day it might be swallowed up by the lake or be miles from the shore, depending on which way the wind blows). The temperate climate and fertile soil surrounding the west bank are ideal for vineyards. Washed in sun, the orchards in Rust produce famous award-winning vintages.

they serve locally-caught venison and wild boar. Rooms and shower-only bathrooms are a bit on the small size, but in summer you can relax in the garden.

Hauptplatz 9, A-7100 Neusiedl am See. ✆ **02167/2423.** Fax 02167/24236. www.zur-traube.at. 7 rooms. 68€ double. Rates include breakfast. MC, V. Free parking. **Amenities:** Restaurant; bar. *In room:* A/C, TV.

Hotel Wende ★   More a complex of three sprawling buildings interconnected by rambling corridors, this hotel is set at the edge of town on the road leading to the water. There's a swimming pool, spa, and gym. The restaurant, bar, and daytime cafe are a renowned culinary set-up, with a winter garden providing a bright, airy accompaniment. In summer, tables are placed outside overlooking the grounds. The bountiful table of Burgenland is presented under a wood-beamed ceiling indoors, reflecting the border-state personality of the area with cuisines of Hungary and Austria. An in-house confectionery supplies visitors with desserts, sweets, and cakes. Homemade jams are sold by the jar.

Seestrasse 40-50, A-7100 Neusiedl am See. ✆ **02167/8111.** Fax 02167/811-1649. www.hotel-wende.at. 105 rooms. 140€–170€ double; 316€–320€ suite. Rates include half-board. AE, DC, MC, V. Parking garage 10€. Closed first 2 weeks in Feb. Free pickup from the Neusiedl am See train station. **Amenities:** Restaurant; bar; indoor heated pool; gym; Jacuzzi; sauna; children's room; room service. *In room:* TV, minibar, hair dryer, free Wi-Fi.

Purbach am See

If you take B50 south from the northern tip of Lake Neusiedl, your first stop might be this little resort village, which has some decent accommodation. Purbach is also a market town, and you can buy Burgenland wine in the shops. Some of the town walls, built against invading Turks, still stand.

ESSENTIALS

GETTING THERE Purbach is 50km (31 miles) southeast of Vienna and 18km (11 miles) northeast of Eisenstadt. From Eisenstadt, you can take a daily bus that leaves from the station at Domplatz. If you're driving from Eisenstadt, head northeast along B50; if you're coming from Vienna, cut southeast along B10.

VISITOR INFORMATION Contact the **Neusiedler See tourist office** in Neusiedl am See, Untere Hauptstrasse 7 (✆ **02167/2229**). See p. 233 for opening hours.

WHERE TO STAY

Am Spitz A hotel has stood here for more than 600 years, and the current version has a gable trim with baroque embellishments and wonderful views of the lake and surrounding vineyards. Rooms and shower-only bathrooms are average-size. The adjoining restaurant (see below) is one of the best places in the region for Burgenland cuisine. The Spitz is 2km (1¼ miles) from town.

Waldsiedlung 2, A-7083 Purbach am See. ✆ **02683/5519.** Fax 02683/551920. www.klosteramspitz.at. 18 rooms. 100€–120€ double, from 120€ suite. Rates include buffet breakfast. MC, V. Free parking. Closed Jan 1–Mar 5. The hotel will pick up guests at the bus station. **Amenities:** Restaurant; lounge; room service. *In room:* A/C, TV, minibar, hair dryer, free Wi-Fi.

WHERE TO DINE

Am Spitz Restaurant BURGENLAND/PANNONIAN Regional decor, excellent staff, and dishes which cross the borders of Burgenland and Pannonia. The setting is a former 17th-century abbey with a flower garden open in summer to the lake itself. The menu changes daily but always features the catch of the day (from the nearby lake) prepared to your liking. Veal and wild game are also on offer. Most diners begin with a bowl of the spicy Hungarian-inspired Spitz fish soup. Also available are 5- and 6-course menus with or without wine accompaniment. The wine cellar stocks hundreds of bottles, including wines from the hotel's own vineyards.

Waldsiedlung 2. ✆ **02683/5519.** Reservations recommended. Main courses 13€–22€; 5- and 6-course menus 50€–55€, with wine accompaniment 23€. Closed Jan–Feb. Mar to Dec Wed 5–9pm; Thurs–Fri noon–2pm and 5–9pm; Sat–Sun (and holidays) noon–9pm.

Rust

South of Purbach, this small village *is* full of stork nests perched on chimneys and a charming *Altstadt,* which is well preserved. Some sections date back to the 17th century, such as the walls built in 1614 for protection against the Turks. Rust is tucked in a rich setting of vineyards famed for the Burgenlander grape, specifically dessert wines such as the Beerenauslese and the Ruster Ausbruch. The Blaufränkisch is a local red wine loved by the locals and Viennese who escape to the area. At certain times, you can go right up to the door of a vintner's farmhouse, especially if a green bough is displayed, to sample and buy wine on the spot. The town holds a wine festival in late July, called the *Ruster Goldene Weinwoche,* (Rust's Golden Week of Wine) where the ancient wine cellars of the main street cater to wine-loving visitors, and local craftsmen offer baskets made from lake reeds.

ESSENTIALS

GETTING THERE The village is 18km (11 miles) northeast of Eisenstadt, 71km (44 miles) southeast of Vienna, and 349km (217 miles) east of Salzburg. There's no train station, but buses connect Eisenstadt with Rust. For bus information, call the regional public transportation office (☏ **0810/222324**). From Eisenstadt by car, head east on Route 52. From Purbach, take Route 50 south toward Eisenstadt. At Seehof, take a left fork to Oggau and Rust.

VISITOR INFORMATION   The **Rust tourist office,** Conradplatz 1, in the middle of town (☏ **02685/502**), can arrange inexpensive stays with English-speaking families. Opening hours: April and October, Monday to Saturday, 9am to noon and 1 to 4pm; May, June and September, Monday to Friday, 9am to noon and 1 to 5pm; Saturday, 9am to noon and 1 to 4pm; July and August, Monday to Friday, 9am to noon and 1 to 6pm; Saturday, 9am to noon and 1 to 4pm; Sunday, 9am to noon; November to February, Monday to Thursday, 9am to noon and 1 to 4pm; Friday 9am to noon.

WHERE TO STAY & DINE

Hotel-Restaurant Sifkovitz ★   Attracting summer visitors from Vienna and Hungary, this hotel consists of an older building with a new wing. Rooms get a lot of sun and are functional but comfortable. There's no great style here, but the beds are firm. The hotel's large garden gives guests space to relax in the fresh air. There is access to tennis courts, but they're in the grounds of another hotel nearby (the staff will make arrangements). A wine bar serves locally-produced varieties, while the restaurant supplies local fare.

Am Seekanal 8, A-7071 Rust. ☏ **02685/276.** Fax 02685/36012. www.sifkovits.at. 33 rooms. 80€–130€ double. Rates include buffet breakfast. AE, DC, MC, V. Closed Dec–Mar. **Amenities:** Restaurant; bar; fitness room; sauna; room service. *In room:* TV, minibar, hair dryer, free Wi-Fi.

Mooslechner's Burgerhaus ★ AUSTRIAN/CONTINENTAL   Rust has several restaurants fixated on innovative and more expensive cuisine, but this middle-bracket tavern in the heart of town is one of the most charming. The building dates from the 1530s and provides plenty of old-fashioned charm. The food, focused on traditional preparations of *zander*, goose, and in-season game dishes, evokes traditional Austria at its best. The cook here is particularly proud of his terrines of goose-liver. The venue is welcoming with a lovely atmosphere.

Hauptstrasse 1. ☏ **02685/6416.** Reservations recommended only in midsummer. 3- 4- and 5-course menus 42€–72€. DC, MC, V. Daily noon–2pm and 6–10pm. Closed Jan–Feb.

Seehotel Rust ★   Seehotel Rust is one of the most attractive hotels in the lake district, set on a grassy lawn at the edge of the lake. This well-designed hotel remains open year-round, and offers pleasantly-furnished bedrooms and clean bathrooms equipped with a shower unit. Most rooms have balconies with a view over the lake. The restaurant features every type of fish from the lake as well as the hearty, meaty dishes from the land.

Am Seekanal 2-4, A-7071 Rust. ☏ **02685/3810.** Fax 02685/381419. www.seehotel-rust.at. 110 rooms. 166€–201 double; from 220€ suite. Rates include half-board. DC, MC, V. Free parking. **Amenities:** Restaurant; bar; indoor heated pool; squash court; 4 tennis courts (2 indoor); fitness room; spa; room service; babysitting; boat rental; free Wi-Fi in lobby. *In room:* TV, minibar, hair dryer, free Wi-Fi in rooms (signal often weak).

Illmitz

This old *puszta* village on the east side of the lake has grown into a town with a moderate tourist business in summer. From Eisenstadt, take B50 northeast, through Purbach, cutting southeast on B51, via Podersdorf, to Illmitz. It's a 61km (38-mile) drive, which seems long because traffic must swing around the lake's northern perimeter before heading south to Illmitz. There are a number of horse stables in the area, and horse riding on the grassy plains next to the lake has become popular with tourists.

NEARBY ATTRACTIONS

Leaving Illmitz, head east on the main route and then cut north at the junction with Route 51. From Route 51, the little villages of Frauenkirchen, St. Andrä bei Frauenkirchen, and Andau are signposted.

Frauenkirchen has a lovely pedestrian zone with a number of shops, a basilica, a Franciscan monastery, and great *Vinotheken* (wine bars). One winery from this town has risen to the ranks of the French and Italian: Weingut Umathum. The estate is located right outside the village and is open Monday to Friday, 9am to 6pm; Saturdays, 10am to 5pm. You can go on a tour of the vineyards and cellars and afterward enjoy a wine tasting.

Near the Hungarian border, the tiny village of **St. Andrä bei Frauenkirchen** is filled with thatched houses. The town is known for its basket weaving, so a shopping expedition can be planned when exploring the area.

A short drive will take you to **Andau,** which became the focus of world attention in 1956 during the Hungarian uprising. It was through this point that hundreds of Hungarians dashed to freedom in the west, fleeing the grim Soviet invasion of Budapest. Starting in the late 1940s, the border with Hungary was closely guarded and people who tried to escape into Austria were shot from the Communist-controlled watchtowers. But time has rendered the region's bleak past obsolete. In 1989, the fortifications were broken down and before the year was out the once fortified border was completely opened.

The surrounding marshy area of this remote sector of Austria, called **Seewinkel,** is a large natural wildlife sanctuary. It is dotted with windmills and reed thickets, and is a haven for birds, small animals, and some rare flora.

A newly opened spa and lodge, **St. Martins Therme Seewinkel,** is well integrated into this ecologically sensitive area. Burgenland's spas are famous in Austria due to the naturally warm water emanating from numerous springs throughout the area. The indoor and outdoor thermal pools at St. Martins allow guests to relax and recover in the invigorating waters. Day tickets are available for 20€, rooms in the adjoining lodge are also available (call ✆ **02172/20500** for further details).

Seewinkel is very different from Austria's celebrated Alps and their thick forests, and is little known to North Americans or even to most Europeans. In other words, it's a great place to get off the beaten track and add a little adventure to your travels.

WHERE TO STAY & DINE

Weingut-Weingasthof Rosenhof ★   A charming baroque hotel surrounded by greenery, and containing cozy, perfectly-maintained bedrooms and bathrooms. In an older section, you'll find a wine restaurant whose star attraction is the recent vintage produced by the Haider family's wine presses. The restaurant serves Hungarian and Burgenland dishes to visitors and locals. Dishes include wild boar cooked in a marinade thickened with local walnuts. Locally-caught fish, such as carp and the meaty *zander*, are in abundance. In autumn, the inn serves *traubensaft*—delectable juice made from freshly harvested grapes.

Florianigasse 1, A-7142 Illmitz. ✆ **02175/2232.** Fax 02175/22324. www.rosenhof.cc. 15 rooms. 94€–102€ double. Rates include half-board. MC, V. Closed mid Nov–Easter. **Amenities:** Restaurant; bar; sauna. *In room:* TV, hair dryer, free Wi-Fi.

FAST FACTS

Area Codes Country Code is 43; and 1 for Vienna. Within the country, dial 01 from any phone. In Vienna, 01 is necessary from a mobile phone. See "Staying Connected" for info, p. 60.

Business Hours **Banks** are open Monday to Friday from 8am to 3pm, and 5pm on Thursday; closed 12:30 to 1:30pm. **Government Offices** are generally open Monday to Friday from 8 or 9am to noon, 2pm or 3pm. **Other Offices** are open either 8am or 9am to 6pm, often closed noon or 12:30 for an hour. Regular **shopping** hours are Monday from 9 or 10am to 6pm, sometimes later at Christmas; and Saturday from 9am to 5pm. Some stores are open Sunday from noon to 5pm.

Cell phones (Mobile Phones) See "Staying Connected," p. 60.

Drinking & Drug Laws The minimum legal drinking age in Austria is 16 for wine and beer and 18 for hard liquor. For buying drinks that have less than 15% alcohol by volume, the minimum legal age is 16; for drinks with more than 15% alcohol by volume, the minimum legal age is 18. In both cases ID must be produced.

Possession of narcotics is a felony and depending on the amount, you may be arrested or even deported. For small violations (consumption, possession of small amounts) fines are usually the maximum penalty.

Driving Rules See "Getting There & Getting Around," p. 43.

Electricity As in most of Europe, Austria uses 220 volts AC (50 cycles), compared to 110–120 volts AC (60 cycles) in the United States and Canada. Many Austrian hotels stock adapter plugs but not power transformers. Bring a **connection kit** of the right power and phone adapters, a spare phone cord, and a spare Internet cable for your laptop—or find out whether your hotel supplies them to guests.

Embassies & Consulates The main building of the Embassy of the **United States** is at Boltzmanngasse 16, 1090 (✆ **01/313390;** http://austria.usembassy.gov). However, the consulate of the **United States** is at Parkring 12, 1010 (✆ **01/5125835**). Lost passports, tourist emergencies, and other matters are handled by the consular section. Both the embassy and the consulate are open Monday to Friday 8 to 11:30am. Emergency services 8:30am to 5pm.

The Embassy of **Canada,** Laurenzerberg 2 (✆ **01/531383000**), is open Monday to Friday 8:30am to 12:30pm and 1:30 to 3:30pm.

The Embassy of the **United Kingdom,** Jauresgasse 12, 1030 (✆ **01/716130;** http://ukinaustria.fco.gov.uk), is open Monday to Friday 9am to 1pm and 2 to 5pm.

The Embassy of **Australia,** Mattiellistrasse 2-4 (✆ **01/506740**), is open Monday to Friday 8:30am to 4:30pm.

The nearest Embassy of **New Zealand** is located in Berlin, Germany, Friedrichstrasse 60 (✆ **030/206210**), and is open Monday to Friday 9am to noon, however there is a consulate in Vienna at Salesianergasse 15/3, hours vary (✆ **01/3188505**).

The Embassy of **Ireland,** Rotenturmstrasse 16-18 (✆ **01/7154246**), is open Monday through Friday 8:30 to 11am and 1 to 4pm.

Emergencies For police assistance, an emergency doctor or an ambulance with paramedics, and for the fire department, call ✆ **112.**

Gasoline (Petrol) A gas (petrol) station is a *tankstelle,* in German. They sell super, normal, and diesel. Prices per liter range from .85€ to 1.50€, so it pays to shop around; generally the farther from the city the lower the price. Taxes are already included. One U.S. gallon equals 3.8 liters, and 1 imperial gallon equals 4.4 liters.

Holidays Bank holidays in Austria are: January 1, January 6 (Epiphany), Easter Monday, May 1, Ascension Day, Whitmonday, Corpus Christi Day, August 15, October 26 (Nationalfeiertag), November 1, December 8, and December 25 and 26. Check locally when you arrive in Austria. Some of these holidays fall on different days each year. Also see "Vienna Calendar of Events," in Chapter 3.

Hospitals Two hospitals with an emergency service are the **Allgemeines Krankenhaus Wien,** Währinger Gürtel 18-20 (✆ **01/404-00-0;** www.akhwien.at; U-Bahn: U6 Michaelbeuern/Allgemeines Krankenhaus),1090; and the **Krankenhaus der Barmherzigen Brüder,** Johannes von Gott Platz 1 (✆ **01/21121-1100;** www.barmherzige-brueder. at; U-Bahn: Nestroyplatz, Tram: 2 Karmeliterplatz), 1020. The Barmherzigen Brüder, the Merciful Brothers, is run by a Catholic order and will accept all emergency cases without insurance at no charge.

Insurance Most U.S. health plans (including Medicare and Medicaid) do not provide coverage for overseas travel, and the ones that do often require you to pay for services and reimburse you only after you return home. As a safety net, you may want to buy travel medical insurance.

Canadians should check with their provincial health plan offices or call **Health Canada** (✆ **866/225-0709;** www.hc-sc.gc.ca) to find out the extent of their coverage and what documentation and receipts they must take home if they are treated overseas.

Visitors from the U.K. and Ireland should carry their **European Health Insurance Card (EHIC)** as proof of entitlement to free/reduced cost medical treatment (✆ **0845/606-2030;** www.ehic.org.uk). Note that the EHIC covers only "necessary medical treatment." For information on insurance, trip cancellation insurance, and medical insurance, visit www.frommers.com/tips.

Internet Access Many hotels, coffeehouses, and other businesses offer Internet access, with Wi-Fi, online computers in the lobby, or with in-room connections. Internet cafes seem to be dying out.

Language Austrians speak German, but English is taught in schools from the early grades. Not everyone will speak English fluently, but almost anyone providing tourist services will, whether a hotel receptionist, waitperson, or someone working in a store in prime shopping areas. Cabdrivers might be another story, however. The Collins *German Phrasebook and Dictionary* should get you started.

Legal Aid The police are allowed to levy on-the-spot fines for traffic violations, but they are obliged to provide a receipt. Here the burden is on the state to prove a person's guilt beyond a reasonable doubt, and everyone has the right to remain silent, whether he or she is suspected of a crime or actually arrested. Once arrested, a person can ask the police to make a telephone call to a lawyer, or in the case of international visitors, your embassy or consulate. For help and assistance call Vienna Service Office (✆ **01/26026423**); Vienna City Hall Information, (✆**01/52550).** Or get in touch with your own embassy, which can often intercede for you in matters relating to your legal status. An EU site gives a good explanation of the options: http://ec.europa.eu/civiljustice/legal_aid/legal_aid_aus_en.htm.

Mail   Post offices *(das Postamt, die Post)* in Vienna are easy to spot with the yellow signs of "Post" or "PSK." The postal system in Austria is, for the most part, efficient and speedy. You can buy stamps at a post office or from the hundreds of news and tobacco kiosks, designated locally as *Tabac-Trafik.* Mailboxes are painted yellow. Newer ones usually have the golden trumpet of the Austrian Postal Service. At the Central Post office (Fleischmarkt 19, ☏ **0577/677-1010**) you can post letters and packages all weekend: Mon–Fri 7am–10pm, Sat, Sun, Holidays 9am–10pm. All over the city branches are open Mon–Fri 8am–6pm.

Newspapers & Magazines   See "Staying Connected," p. 60.

Passports   See "Embassies & Consulates," above, for whom to contact if you lose your passport while in Austria. For other information, contact the following agencies:

Residents of Australia   You can pick up an application from your local post office or any branch of Passports Australia, but you must schedule an interview at the passport office to present your application materials. Call the **Australian Passport Information Service** at ☏ **131-232,** or visit the government website at www.passports.gov.au.

Residents of Canada   Passport applications are available at travel agencies throughout Canada or from the **Passport Office,** Department of Foreign Affairs and International Trade, Ottawa, ON K1A 0G3 (☏ **800/567-6868;** www.ppt.gc.ca).

Residents of Ireland   You can apply for a 10-year passport at the **Passport Office,** Setanta Centre, Molesworth Street, Dublin 2 (☏ **01/671-1633;** www.irlgov.ie). Those under age 18 and over 65 must apply for a 12€ 3-year passport. You can also apply at 1A South Mall, Cork (☏ **021/494-4700**) or at most main post offices.

Residents of New Zealand   You can pick up a passport application at any New Zealand Passports Office or download it from the website. Contact the **Passport Office** (☏ **0800/225-050** in New Zealand or 04/474-8100; www.passports.govt.nz).

Residents of the United Kingdom   For an application for a standard 10-year passport (5-year passport for children under 16), visit your nearest major post office, passport office, or travel agency, or contact the **United Kingdom Passport Service** (☏ **0870/521-0410;** www.ukpa.gov.uk).

Residents of the United States   Whether you're applying in person or by mail, you can download passport applications from the U.S. State Department website at **http://travel.state.gov**. To find your regional passport office, either check the U.S. State Department website or call the **National Passport Information Center's** toll-free number (☏ **877/487-2778**) for automated information.

Police   Dial ☏ **133** anywhere in Austria.

Smoking   A smoking ban came into effect throughout Austria on January 1, 2009. Still, this being Austria, the ban has many exceptions. Bars and restaurants are allowed to divide the space. And bars and restaurants under 60 sq. meters (645 sq. ft.), can decide to be either smoking or non-smoking. In general Vienna is one of the last smoking havens in Europe, so don't be surprised that most bars and clubs are smoker-friendly. If being in a smoke-free establishment is important to you, be sure to call ahead and inquire.

Taxes   There's a value-added tax (MwSt) in Austria of 20% on hotel and restaurant bills (19% on alcohol), and 10% or 20% (depending on the product) on purchases. This tax is always included in the price. Visitors from outside the European Union can shop tax-free in Vienna. Stores that offer tax-free shopping advertise with an AUSTRIA TAX-FREE SHOPPING sign in the window. Refunds are available only when you spend more than 50€ in a participating store. You can arrange for a refund of VAT if you can prove that the goods on which you paid tax were carried out of Austria. To get the refund, you must fill out Form U-34, which is available at most stores (a sign will read TAX-FREE SHOPPING). Get one for the ÖAMTC (Austrian Automobile and Touring Club) quick refund if you plan to get your money at the border. Check whether the store gives refunds itself or uses a service. Sales personnel will help you fill out the form and will affix the store-identification stamp. You show the VAT *(MwSt)* as a separate item or state that the tax is part of the total price. Keep your U-34 forms handy when you leave the country, and have them validated by the Viennese Customs officer at your point of departure.

Know in advance that you'll have to show the articles for which you're claiming a VAT refund. Because of this, it's wise to keep your purchases in a suitcase or carry-on bag that's separate from the rest of your luggage, with all the original tags and tickets, and the original receipts nearby. Don't check the item within your luggage before you process the paperwork with the Customs agent. If your point of departure is not equipped to issue cash on the spot, you'll have to mail the validated U-34 form or forms back to the store where you bought the merchandise after you return home. It's wise to keep a copy of each form. Within a few weeks, the store will send you a check, bank draft, or international money order covering the amount of your VAT refund. Help is available from the ÖAMTC, which has instituted methods of speeding up the refund process. Before you go, call the Austrian National Tourist Office for the ÖAMTC brochure "Tax-Free Shopping in Austria."

Telephones   See "Staying Connected" for info, p. 60.

Time   Vienna is on Central European Time (CET), which is Coordinated Universal Time (UTC), or Greenwich Mean Time (GMT), plus 1 hour. Clocks are moved ahead 1 hour for daylight-saving Central European Summer Time (CEST) between the last Sunday in March and the last Sunday in October. For example, when it's 6pm in Vienna, it's 9am in Los Angeles (PST), 7am in Honolulu (HST), 10am in Denver (MST), 11am in Chicago (CST), noon in New York City (EST), 5pm in London (GMT), and 2am the next day in Sydney.

Tipping   A service charge of 10% to 15% is often included on hotel bills, but it's a good policy to leave something extra for waiters and 2€ per day for your hotel maid. Railroad station, airport, and hotel porters get 1.50€ per piece of luggage, plus a 1€ tip. Hairdressers should be tipped 10%, and the shampoo person will be thankful for a 1.50€ gratuity. When paying restaurant bills, Austrians usually round up by approximately 10% and to the nearest Euro.

Toilets   The most important thing to remember about public toilets in Vienna, apart from calling them *Toiletten* (twa-*lett*-en) or "WC" (*vay tsay*) and not restrooms, is not the usual male/female (*Herren/Damen*) distinction (important though that is), but to pay the person who sits at the entrance and keeps the facility clean. He or she has a saucer in which you're supposed to deposit your donation. It's tiresome, but toilets cost only about .40€, and the attendant keeps them clean. All airport and railway stations have toilets, rarely with attendants. Bars, nightclubs, restaurants, cafes, and hotels have facilities as well. You'll also find public toilets near many major sights.

Visas   Citizens of the U.S., Canada, the European Union, Australia, and New Zealand only need a valid passport if visiting Austria for under 90 days. In the case of visitors who reside in most other E.U. countries, a valid identity card from that country is sufficient. Citizens of other countries should be sure to check travel regulations before leaving. You can get these in English at **www.visahq.com**.

Water   Tap water in Vienna, piped in from mountain springs, is not only safe to drink, it also tastes good and is automatically served with coffee and red wine. Many people also drink bottled mineral water, generally called *Mineralwasser*.

Wi-Fi   See "Staying Connected," p. 60.

Index

See also Accommodations and Restaurant indexes, below.

General Index

A

AARP, 56–57
Abbey Heiligenkreuz (Abbey of the Holy Cross; Mayerling), 215–216
Abercrombie and Kent, 60
Access-Able Travel Source, 55
Accommodations, 72–97. See also Accommodations Index
  Alsergrund (9th District), 96–97
  Baden bei Wien, 219–220
  best, 3–4
  Dürnstein, 228–229
  Eisenstadt, 232–233
  family-friendly, 92
  finding a hotel, 72–73
  for honeymoons or anniversaries, 79
  Illmitz, 237
  Innere Stadt (Inner City), 73–86
  Josefstadt (8th District), 94–96
  Krems, 226–227
  Landstrasse (3rd District), 87–90
  Leopoldstadt (2nd District), 86–87
  Mariahilf (6th District), 91–93
  Mayerling, 216–217
  Melk, 230
  Neubau (7th District), 93–94
  Neusiedl am See, 233–234
  private homes and furnished apartments, 73
  Purbach am See, 235
  Rust, 236
  near Schönbrunn, 97
  seasonal hotels, 73
  Tulln, 237
  Westbahnhof (15th District), 97
  Wieden & Margareten (4th & 5th districts), 90–91
  Wiener Neustadt, 221
  Wienerwald (Vienna Woods), 213
A. E. Köchert, 189
AirAmbulanceCard.com, 55
Airport security measures, 44
Air travel, 43–45
Akademie der bildenden Künste (Academy of Fine Arts), 170
Akademietheater, 198
Albertina, 127–128, 163
Albin Denk, 191

Alfi's Goldener Spiegel, 204–205
Alsergrund (9th District), 65
  accommodations, 96–97
  restaurants, 123–124
Alter Steffl, 144
Altes Rathaus, 176
Altmann & Kühne, 187
American Airlines, 43
American Express, 52
American Express Travel, 60
American Foundation for the Blind (AFB), 55
Andau, 237
Antiques, 184–185
Apartment rentals, 73
Arcadia Opera Shop, 190
Architecture, 27–30
Area codes, 238
Art, 24–27
Art galleries, 185–186
Artis International, 207
Art museums
  Albertina, 127–128
  Barockmuseum (Museum of Baroque Art), 135
  Belvedere, 135, 138
  Ephesos-Museum (Museum of Ephesian Sculpture), 130–131
  Galerie des 19. und 20. Jahrhunderts (Gallery of 19th- and 20th-Century Art), 135, 138
  Gemäldegalerie der Akademie der Bildenden Künste, 138
  Kunsthalle Wien, 134
  Kunsthistorisches Museum, 139
  Leopold Museum, 134–135
  Liechtenstein Museum, 139–140
  MUMOK (Museum Moderner Kunst Stiftung Ludwig Wien), 135
  Museum Mittelalterlicher Kunst (Museum of Medieval Art), 135
  Österreichisches Museum für Angewandte Kunst (Museum of Applied Art), 148
  Secession, 140
Art Nouveau (Jugendstil), 29, 174
Askö-Sport-Centrum-Schmelz, 158–159
Askö Wien, 159
ATMs (automated-teller machines), 52
Augarten Porzellan, 191
Augustinerkirche (Church of the Augustinians), 128–129
Augustinian Herzogenburg Monastery, 225
Austrian Academy of Sciences, 180
Austrian Airlines, 43, 44
Aux Gazelles, 199–200

B

Bach Consort Wien, 196
Baden bei Wien, 217–220
Barfly's, 203
Bar Italia, 203
Barockmuseum (Museum of Baroque Art), 135
Bars, 203–205
Beer, 35, 36
Beethovenhaus (Baden bei Wien), 218
Beethoven Pasqualati House (Beethoven Pasqualatihaus), 155
Belmar (Havana Club), 200
Belvedere, 135, 138
Bergkirche (Church of the Calvary; Eisenstadt), 231
Bermuda Triangle, 203
Bicycle Rental Hochschaubahn, 156
Biking, 49–50, 156
Blue Danube Shipping Company, 47
BMI, 44
Boating, 157
Boat travel, 47–48
Boat trips and excursions, 47–48
Books, recommended, 30–31
Bookstores, 186–187
Botanischer Garten (Botanical Garden of the University of Vienna), 151
British Airways, 43, 44
British Airways Holidays, 59
The British Bookshop, 186
Bruckner, Anton, 34, 128
Brunnenmarkt, 189
Buchhandlung Walter König, 186
Burgenland, 210
Burggarten (Castle Garden), 151, 169–170
Burgkapelle (Home of the Vienna Boys' Choir), 129
Burg Kino, 207
Burgring, 132
Burgtheater (National Theater), 166, 198
Business hours, 238
Bus travel, 47, 49

C

Café Alt Wien, 207
Café Berg, 205
Café Leopold, 200
Café Savoy, 205
Calendar of events, 40–41
Camera Club, 201–202, 204
Canoeing, 60
Car rentals, 50
Carriage Museum (Wagenburg), 142
Car travel, 47, 50
Casino Baden (Baden bei Wien), 220
Cellphones, 61–62

Accommodations

Restaurants